TRIAL

Ordeal of the USS Enterprise

14 JANUARY, 1969

By

Michael Joe Carlin

Tuscarora Press

1993

Copyright © 1993
By Michael Joe Carlin
Post Office Box 98
West Grove, PA 19390

Library of Congress Catalog Card Number 93-091690

Printed in the United States of America
Mark One Printing
Philadelphia, Pennsylvania

TRIAL: ORDEAL OF THE USS ENTERPRISE, 14 JANUARY 1969, by Michael Joe Carlin. Reviewed by Admiral J. L. Holloway III, USN (Ret.), CO USS ENTERPRISE 1965-67, CNO 1974-78.

TRIAL is a remarkable book, virtually unique in its genre. It is a painstakingly detailed account of a major maritime disaster, factual and yet grimly gripping. Well it should be, as the author, Michael J. Carlin, was the Crew Leader of Crew 2 of the Purple Shirts in the flightdeck gang of the ENTERPRISE. On that fateful day he was in the thick of the conflagration, and his image can be seen in one of his book's photographs as a member of a hose team confronting a shattering explosion of fuel and ammunition on the ENTERPRISE's flight deck. Carlin has not identified himself in his book as one of the heroes of the story, and although he may lose some kudos by his modesty by writing the book in the third person, he has been able to attain a level of objectivity that truly transcends the limitations of a simple eyewitness account. Carlin writes well. His style is suited to the clear reporting of events, and he has an easy way of explaining the technical aspects of aviation equipment and flightdeck operations.

This is an important book about a epochal event in the history of modern nuclear carriers. Aside from showing that no matter how much training goes into the preparation of a carrier crew for combat operations (and the ENTERPRISE crew was solidly trained and well led), disaster can strike from the most unforeseen causes. But most importantly, the calamity demonstrated the toughness of the modern nuclear aircraft carrier. In spite of the fire in which more than half a dozen major caliber bombs exploded on the flight deck, the grim carnage was contained and the ship was not put out of action.

It is an unnerving story, but it tells what can happen when things go wrong when we are dealing with ammunition and fuel on a carrier flight deck. In spite of the graphic depictions of what it's really like in the inferno, the book ends on an upbeat note by showing that through the personal courage and sacrifice of dedicated sailors, the damage was limited and the ship was saved.

Carlin's book should be required reading for all prospective carrier CO's, XO's and Flight Deck Officers, and it should be on the reading list for the appropriate courses in the Naval Air Training Command and the Fleet Training Groups.

This is a book too, for the serious student of naval history, particularly those who have served aboard warships and operated from aircraft carriers. Michael J. Carlin has given us a story that is sobering, inspiring, and fascinating to read.

J. L. HOLLOWAY III
Admiral, U.S. Navy (Retired)

ACKNOWLEDGMENTS

My thanks for the considerable effort and patience of the following for their first hand accounts and other contributions:

Ned Baumer and Steve O'Brien who had the courage to stand exposed while taking rolls of spectacular pictures of the event and making a visual record of it.

Irwin Barnes, Steve Bell, Charles Brackin, Dennis Downs, Bob Foley, Larkin Garcia, Don George, Ray Gomes, Big John Guillot, Lash Hansborough, Billy Hawk, Jim Helton, The Sunflower—Nick Lasovich, Oliver Lee, Karl Mahumed, Henry Mendoza, Bill Martino, Bob McLaughlin, Bill McAllister, King Merendino, Steve Meyer, Frank Neumayer, John Plummer, Bill Proffit, Joe Rosa, Ron Ruland, Bill Shultz, Jim Smith, Mike Steussy, Twig Tordoff, Dennis Vaeth, Bob and Rich Weideman, Fred Whitehead Jr., and Steve White

Thanks also for the help and information supplied by the following:
    Paul Stillwell, Director of oral history, U.S. Naval Institute
    Stephen Millikin, Editor of *The Hook*,
        The Tailhook Association
    Michael Knapp, Ships Histories Branch,
        National Historical Center
    Gayle Garmise, Managing Editor of the *Veteran*,
        Viet Nam Veterans of America Newspaper
    Jan Jacobs, Editor of the F-4 Phantom 2 Society
    Don Bailey, Historian, RVAH-6
    Rene Francillon, Tonkin Gulf Yacht Club
    Edward C. Marks, AutoCad® illustrations

The average age of those in the Armed Forces of the United States during the Viet Nam War was nineteen years old. It was the youngest force America ever sent to war.

To those who possess the Virtue

INTRODUCTION

This account of the 1969 Enterprise fire is written in a tri-form text, so as not to mislead and confuse the reader a word of explanation is advised.

The first form of the text is established in the first chapter, The Legend, in which the metaphors used throughout the account are presented. These vehicles are introduced to enhance the main narrative and bring to light important facts of past catastrophes.

The second form is the main narrative, the nuts and bolts listing of the chronological order of cause and effect and damages. This is taken from logs, testimonies and over forty first hand accounts.

The third form is told from the point of view of another who was there. This is the personal odyssey through the terror of a V-4 Division crewleader. Although at times figurative, this account will take the reader to the very edge of the wall of flames. The reader will feel the pain of heat. He will be blasted from his feet by awesome detonations. He will come to know the Trial of Enterprise on 14 January, 1969.

TABLE OF CONTENTS

1. THE LEGEND 1
2. THE SHIP 11
3. THE TRIAL 39
4. THE FURY 69
5. THE TRUTH 99
6. THE STAND 129
7. THE PYRE 145
8. THE VIRTUE 187
9. JUDGMENT 213

APPENDIX

    Enterprise Carrier Air Wing 253

    Glossary 254

    Table of Rank 255

    References 256

1. THE LEGEND

Coast of Rhode Island

The heavy, humid silence of the darkness was shattered by the nearby bawling of a rooster. At his second call the woman rose from her bed and turned up the low flame of her oil lamp in the dark, second story bedroom. Her's had been a fitful sleep because of the discomfort of the August night.

The woman proceeded to the window and looked out at the darkened landscape below. The columns of cedar and pine, lining the edges of the sloping hill, only lent themselves to darker shadows. The night stayed hauntingly still. Farther out, the waters of South Cove and Lost River Bay were black and motionless. But high above and down to the horizon in all directions, the universe displayed its magnificence in shimmering starlight. The rooster crowed again, and then fell into silence.

The woman looked to the east. There hung the crescent moon and beyond, the brightest light in the sky, the morning star, in all its glimmering radiance. A faint band of light made the eastern horizon discernible, a slight separation between the dark waters of the sound and the starshot black velvet of the sky.

The rooster had not been wrong, she noted, and marveled again at this instinctive ability. The dawn was coming and bringing forth a new day on this 15th of August, 1698.

She held her gaze on the quickening light. Perhaps this would be the day. From the western darkness a shooting star suddenly rocketed across the universe with incredible velocity and disappeared into the east.

She beheld this fleeting journey in the blink of an eye, then it was gone forever. The arrow of the old weathervane atop the barn, barely visible, marked the direction of the meteors coming, It pointed west, the direction of the prevailing winds.

It would be another hot, uncomfortable day today, she thought. Perhaps there might be some relief from a westwind. The woman turned from the window. It was time to begin the new day. The first chore was to make her bed and in the long shadows of the neat, modest bedroom, she did this with a practiced familiarity. The bed coverings were only disturbed on the one side. The other, neat and long since cold. But as was her custom, she remade the bed and then, by the light of her lamp, she made her way down the stairs.

Outside, the rooster trumpeted his signal again. This time he kept on going. Soon the call was taken up by other birds, both near and far. As the light of day fell across the earth, the crowing of the birds was continuous.

The woman came out of the house with her lamp still glowing. She would need the lamps light in the barn. Halfway, she stopped and scanned the eastern horizon. It was still too difficult to see very far but from this vantage point, it would not be long. Her farm was on a finger of land standing out into Lost River Bay. This land, called Dark Neck Spur, made the distinction between the north and south coves.

A glare of sunlight now flared at the edge of the horizon and fired the waters of the sound. The light made the entire length of Dark Neck visible, and Black Point at lands end, two miles away, stood out clearly. She held her gaze to the east, searching the expanse of the sound. There was only water. The woman looked west, across the spur. The rays of the sun had not yet fallen upon the port of New Hope on the inner banks of North Cove. The upper spars and rigging of ships in harbor and rooftops and steeples of the town could just be seen above an obscuring low fog. The still salt air was warm and heavy.

The woman turned to her work. Her daughter and three

grandchildren would soon be ready and she had better get the milking done.

In the small fishing and whaling communities such as this one, all eyes watched the sea. The fortunes of entire towns depended on the harvests of these ships and the men and boys of these towns filled out the crews entirely. The sighting of a sail was an event of high occasion, anxiously awaited. Tall ships and sloops, returning from fishing and whaling grounds, traders bringing foodstuffs and manufactured goods were eagerly looked for.

The life of the maritime community was an uncertain one. Nearly every family could number at least one relative who did not return from the sea. Whaling was an especially dangerous enterprise requiring many long months in the cold northern seas. The whale ships did not bring back their dead. The woman came out from the barn and into the light of the full dawn. She surveyed again the eastern horizon, all but blinded by the brilliance of the rising sun. She could see nothing.

The woman carried her pail of milk into the house and saw that the three young grandchildren were up and milling about. The woman's twenty five year old daughter stood at the open kitchen window, the dawn light shining full on her face in luminous radiance. The daughter's hand was up to shield her eyes as she tried to see through the glare. The older woman knew her daughter's anxiety, day after day, searching the sound, hoping for her husband's return. She said something amiable to her daughter, trying to cheer her up, but the young woman's spirits were limp and hung as slack as the window curtains. It had been long months since he left and the tension and pain of separation was becoming daily more acute.

The mother knew her daughter's ache. Had she not gone through this same despair many times until finally her man never returned? Her beloved Ethan, she was told, was gone. Gone to join the Legion of the Dead of the Sea. For every woman and family, the terrible waiting was the same. Always the specter of the Legion was there for those whose lives were tied to the oceans.

The woman joined her daughter at the window, and both looked intently across the waters. As the sun rose it revealed the distant masts of a tall ship standing into the bay. They saw it together and were gripped with excitement. Could this be the ship?

Together they hurried outside and stood on the sward. They could see it now, a three master with canvas slack as bedsheets but she was riding in steadily on the incoming tide. And they saw she was being towed by one, no, two longboats. Two longboats in tandem they could see. And a sound, faint, but unmistakable came to them, carried clear and crisp across the waters. It was the rising, falling, sing-song challenge of the chanty. And it was answered directly by a lusty chorus of full throated hearts as the entire crew sang happily and the oarsmen pulled with a will.

The two women stood there, watching as the ship drew closer. Which ship?, they wondered, as the chant and chorus seemed to echo from the hills and vales all round about.

Presently, the sound of thudding hoofbeats brought them around. Old Ely Granger brought his galloping horse up hard by the road, scattering small stones and clumps of earth. Ely was the watchman at the Black Point Light at Lands End and with his long glass, acted as sentinel for the town. Ely knew the ship for which this family waited.

"It's her! It's the Spirit of the Wind!", he shouted.

Excitement and relief burst forth from the younger woman as she cried out in happiness. Old Ely held up a rough and scarred hand in warning, and the look on his face stopped the women cold. Then he called out to them again, a different timbre to his voice.

"She flies the Black Mantle!"

Wheeling the horse about and kicking it into a run, old Ely rode swiftly down towards the town. The two women, so long expectant, watched numb with shock as the whaler passed in full view below them, the sailors song still pealing across the waters. The joyous moment was shattered and cold fear seized and pierced them like the jaws of a great beast.

The BLACK MANTLE, the most feared harbinger of a ship returning from the sea. The Black Mantle warned of a tragedy upon the ship from which it flew and told anxious watchers ashore to prepare. The sea, always a force to be reckoned with, had claimed its tribute. Death had visited this ship.

The mother quickly moved to quell her daughter's rising hysteria. "You will frighten the children", she admonished, "Now collect yourself and let us get on with the morning's work and I will walk into town."

The woman wanted her daughter moving and busy as she herself wanted to be. The cold grip of panic were upon them. They went back into the house to get the children ready for the day. The daughter was overcome with foreboding. As the woman passed the table stand she stopped and rested her hands on the timeworn Bible which was always there from the time of her youth. She stopped and said a silent prayer that her family might be spared. In the name of Jesus, she fervently prayed.

The children were now gathered in the kitchen, hungry. The woman went and she and her daughter fussed and clucked about the children, making them a breakfast. Too young to understand, the young ones knew nothing of the Mantle.

The older woman busied herself and fought to suppress the rising tension. She had seen that terrible sign many times in her life and knew the anguish it would bring. Did it not announce the end of her own husband? Was it not the hated black flag that told that her beloved Ethan was no more? Her heart died that day. Her pain was so terrible she wished death might take her also. But soon she realized she had to be ever stronger for the sake of her young daughter, now fatherless.

Ethan had always insisted on putting things in proper financial and legal order before he left so that she would be prepared in the event of his not returning. He and the other sailors always referred to a man's death at sea as being, "Called to join the Legion." And they all knew of the uncertainty into which they would sail.

So Ethan would always say at their parting, "If I am called to join the Legion . . ." and would go on to list things that she should do and when. He would list also what provisions had been made. She understood the seriousness of the statement and also the superstition that the sailors clung to. To be out upon the vast and empty waters, when the ocean grew agitated at their presence and high winds moaned, heralding the tempest. And the seas grew dark in anger and would heave, and rise up, now great and towering. And the winds gave way to gale. Canvas snapped and torn to pieces as sailors fought a howling fury, the rigging, and their own hideous fears to keep the ship from foundering.

Mighty waves, hurled full weight against the wooden sides seeking to smash into splinters this impetuous man made thing which dared traverse. Howling gales blasting the crests of heaving seas into a blinding froth of driven rampage. A living thing, the ocean would come awake in moaning outrage over those who would trespass. Fury and fear unimaginable as Neptune demands his tribute, the battles lasting for hours or days on end.

And who could not understand that in the hour that a man loses his life on the lonely seas he is consoled by the fact that he will not be alone? The ghosts of all those who have gone before him will be there to gather him unto themselves, it being foreordained that until that day when the sea shall give up its dead, the Legion of the Dead of the Sea should collect all those who were taken upon the oceans. Then the Legion, consigned to the clouds that roam the seas, would keep its dead until the appointed time.

This then, was the superstition that sustained them. It was a legend told and retold from ages past. Perhaps there were those who did not believe in this, but Ethan did. He believed so strongly that it lent her assurance as he always said in their last embrace before he shipped out, "If anything happens to me, I'll be waiting for you in the clouds."

The woman told her daughter, "It would be best if I went into town." The daughter nodded gravely and watched as her mother walked out the door and started down the road. She had not gone far when a horseman trotted up and stopped to talk with her. The daughter could see that it was Ely come back from town. Then the horseman turned and galloped back the way he had come as the older woman's head bowed and her hands fell limp to her sides.

Seeing this, the daughter knew her worst fears had been realized. The hysteria she had been fighting so long to control rose up within her. She began to sob uncontrollably, her hands flung to her face in a last futile effort to hold it back. Seeing their mother contorted in sorrow and tears, the children ran to her, crying loudly at the sight of her distress.

The grandmother walked slowly back into the house. Never had she witnessed a scene of greater pain and anguish. Little ones clinging desperately wherever they could gain hold. Frightened young hearts, breaking in innocence at the sight of their mothers pain.

The grandmother walked in and joined the keening embrace. She held her daughter tight and said gently to the children, "Your mother is crying because your daddy is not coming back."

Great spasms of torment wracked the daughter as her mother held her, waiting for her to get through the worst of it. The children blinked wet eyes at their grandmother, uncomprehending. She gently told them, "Your father was lost at sea."

The wailing began again and the older woman did what she could to soothe and comfort. She waited while the young mother gained control of herself, the children calming down as she did. Then the grandmother told the children the legend of the Legion. She told how, in the hour of their fathers peril, grandfathers strong hands were there to gather him up. Now, she said, their father had taken his place in the Legion, and he would always be there, he and Ethan, in the low clouds that never come ashore.

The grandmother then told them that the townswomen would soon be here and that the ship's captain would be coming. They must be ready. Then she stood away, leaving the small family to heal. She walked slowly to the tablestand and seeking strength, laid her hands upon the old Bible. She did not know why this tragedy had to strike her family but she would not question it. Her belief in the Almighty was unshakable and she would accept this as part of His plan.

She opened the old book and began to turn the pages. They would be coming, she knew. They would be coming just as they had done before, to tell her about Ethan. She stopped turning pages at the Book of Revelations, sixth chapter. She knew what they would say, she thought, as her finger traced its way down the page. They would say that the sea had claimed him, just as they said it had claimed Ethan. But it was not the sea that had claimed them, she thought, as her tracing finger stopped. She was pointing at the 8th verse. No, the sea did not take them.

This one did.

And she read again the verse she already knew by heart. "And I looked, and behold, a Pale Horse, and his Rider's name was Death and hell followed with him."

The woman shuddered and closed the Book. The Destroyer had taken them. The Rider on the Pale Horse, maker of calamity.

The woman wavered, the impact of the tragedy descending upon her like a great crushing weight. She was weakening. She moved away from the others lest they see her crumbling. She went into the kitchen, to the open east window and leaned into it, hands supporting her weight on the sill. She would hide her face.

The brightness of day and clear blue sky cut through her like a knife. Surely, this was the only house of sorrow this day. She hung her head and closed her eyes as grief came upon her like nausea, the cry of the sea birds mocking her ordeal.

Her eyes welled up as she spent her last reserves of strength, trying to hold back the rising tide. Then the pain of anguish, loss and heartbreak crashed down on her like surf crashing against the rock. In this moment alone she buckled under the powerful and irresistible emotions surging through her and gave vent to the agony of the present and the long pent up past.

Hot tears blinded her. The ache of heartbreak was as if her entire body were being rent in two. She swooned. Desperately, she clung to consciousness, faint from the heat of effort. The sill was her rock and she held tenaciously to it as great sobs wracked her body and tears cascaded down her tortured face. Crushed and broken, sanity slipping away, she prayed for mercy.

Bent under the weight of the struggle, convulsed sobs shook her again. She fought mightily to hang on to something, to focus her mind in the heat of battle. Faintly, she became aware of a peculiar sound. She directed her entire being on this sound. It was a sound to cling to, the sound of peace.

Now, she understood this sound. It was the call of the sea birds which continued throughout her ordeal. But something was different. What had before sounded like laughing mockery, now seemed to be sorrowful cries of lament. The cries of the sea birds consoled her. They understood her pain and keened with her. The woman drew strength from their song.

A breath of wind blew upon her face. The wind slackened and then freshened into a breeze that stirred the curtains of the open window. Now the breeze held to a steady wind as it fell upon her, cool and salt clean. The old weathervane shrieked in rusty protest as it swung round under the influence of the wind. The arrow pointed out into the open sea.

Gratefully, she welcomed the freshening. The curtains in the window ruffled and then stood away as the wind continued strong and steady. The cool air sustained her. She inhaled long draughts of the ocean wind in measured breaths. She regained strength with every breath of the healing wind.

Her sobs were done, gone now. She again had control of herself. She held her glistening face into the welcome wind. Thankfully, she allowed it to caress her. The wind cooled and dried the hot tears even as they coursed down her face. She blinked the last of the blinding mist from her eyes and looked gratefully out to the open sea, whence came the wind. And they were there!

The low clouds that never come ashore.

2. THE SHIP

The twin 671 Gray Marine diesels throbbed easily as the MIKE boat hove to and slid away from the boat landing at the AMMO depot in West Loch. Once away, the diesels whined up as the coxswain increased power and maneuvered the boat to mid channel to clear Kekaa Point at 0620 A.M. on the 13th of January, 1969. It was dark, still fifty-three minutes to sunrise.

The coxswain positioned the boat to give himself room. The RPM's increased again and the boat vibrated under the power of the diesels as they bulldozed it through the dark waters. At the mouth of the West Loch channel, the boat swung north, around Waipio Point and into Pearl Harbor channel.

Lt. Robert A. McLaughlin of Patrol Squadron VP-17 was glad he had brought his flight jacket. The temperature, even in January, was 70°F but with the damp breeze the jacket was a good idea.

He rode along with other officers from differing squadrons and appointments, all chosen to be Operational Readiness Inspection, (ORI), observers for the next three days aboard an aircraft carrier due shortly off the coast of Viet Nam for combat operations against the enemy. The ORI team would observe and grade this carrier in all aspects of shipboard operations, both combat and routine. It was vital to identify problem areas, if any, and bring these areas to light. Bob McLaughlin's job would be to record the timing of launch and recovery evolutions from the ships Primary Flight Control. As a Naval Aviator, Lt. McLaughlin was looking forward to this.

The MIKE boat turned east at Hospital Point and traveled toward Pearl Harbor naval shipyard. From this distance he could easily see the carrier, even in the gloom. With her clean lines, broad shoulders and towering, space age island structure, this was a class of ship never built before and perhaps never would be again.

The boat plowed its way past the stern of the giant carrier. Bob

McLaughlin read the name boldly spelled out across her fantail in black letters against the ships gray paint. The name was a famous and proud name of the *US Navy, ENTERPRISE.*

They continued along, marveling at the size of this ship, the massive overhanging angle deck now above them. This ship projected an aura of speed and power and might. They approached the bow of the ship. There, the port anchor hung loosely from the hawse to just above the surface of the water. And what a mighty anchor it was. Thirty tons, and each link of the anchor chain, 360 pounds apiece.

The MIKE boat rounded the bow of the carrier and the throbbing of the diesels fell away to idle. The boat slowed noticeably as they coasted to the boat landing

On the pier, the rest of the COMFAIRHAWAII ORI team of observers were assembling, all one hundred and two of them. The aura of the coming dawn brought the dark mass of the Koolau Mountain range to the east into relief.

The ORI team began to file aboard the carrier, both officers and enlisted, on their respective brows. The imposing mass and geometry

---

Ship and Squadron Personnel Color Code

Blueshirt—Aircraft Handlers, Tractor drivers, Chock and chain crews. V1 and V-3 Divisions

Brownshirt—Squadron personnel responsible for overall care of individual Squadron aircraft.

Greenshirt—Catapult and Arresting Gear personnel, V-2 Division. Squadron maintenance crews.

Purpleshirt—Aviation Fuels crews, V-4 Division.

Redshirt—Ships Ordnancemen, G and GM Divisions, Crash/Salvage Rescue and firefighting crew, V-1 Division. Squadron Ordnancemen

Whiteshirt—Corpsmen, Medical Department. Squadron checkers and Liquid Oxygen crews.

Yellowshirt—Mark of authority for all Air, flight deck and Hangar Bay operations, V-1 and V-3 Divisions, Air Officer and Assistant Air Officer

Enterprise on 13 January, 1969, taken from the deck of the USS Rogers. Photo courtesy of Steve O'Brien.

of the most powerful warship in the world rode at her lines impatiently, waiting for these last to embark. The crew of the *USS Enterprise* had all been aboard long before this and the special sea and anchor detail had been set, enabling the ship to get underway.

As Lt. McLaughlin made his way up the officers brow, he marveled at this famous ship, the pride of the nation. This ship was the epitome of American technology, engineering and daring. This ship, largest warship in the world, was also powered by the world's largest nuclear complex, with eight reactors. And upon this magnificent ship was bestowed the name and legacy of one of the greatest ships of a great fighting Navy, *USS Enterprise*, proud name and tradition passed down by seven predecessors of the U.S. Navy.

Enterprise, it was the name given to a British sloop of war captured by American patriots in the Revolutionary War, when our Rebel Forefathers had no regular army, and no navy.

The capture was in itself a large and wondrous victory. The ship and crew soon won a naval engagement and word of the triumph was passed from city to town with the sound of bells ringing. The name, *USS Enterprise*, was born of fire and steel at the very dawn of American naval history.

The name and heritage was passed on to a second vessel, a 12 gun, 70 man schooner in the fledgling United States Navy. During the years, 1798 to 1800, America carried on a Naval war with France. The *USS Enterprise* captured a number of French Privateers. Her most spectacular capture was after a fight with a much heavier French vessel, the *Flambeau*, a brig of 14 guns and 100 men. The Frenchmen hauled her colors after half her crew were killed or wounded. *USS Enterprise* suffered 10 casualties, and added to the luster of her name and the honor of the United States Navy.

The Third in the line was built and christened, a 12 gun Brig, later fitted out to carry 16 guns. She fought in the War of 1812, outgunning and capturing the British 14 gun Brig, *Boxer* in a running fight after both Captains were shot down. The Commanding Officer of *Enterprise*, Lt. Burrows, refused to be carried below during the fight and lay on the bloody deck crying that the Colors must never be struck; *Enterprise* bore up and crossed the bow of the *Boxer* and raked her into submission. Lt. Burrows died after being handed the sword of his adversary. And it was in this War of 1812, that the tiny American Navy with six frigates and a handful of lesser vessels, dared to go to war against the most powerful navy in the world, which boasted 1,000 cruisers. The invincible Royal Navy held undisputed sway over the oceans of the world, having met and defeated every adversary for the previous 130 years. The Americans sailed forth to meet them. In God they Trusted, and in twelve ship-to-ship actions of comparable force, the U.S. Navy won outright in eight, and fought to a draw in two others. The young Navy proudly and jealously preserved the names and legacies of those victorious fighting ships and passed them on to successors: *Constitution, Constellation, United States, Essex, Hornet, Wasp, Enterprise.*

So it was that old CV-6 of World War II fame, was the seventh to bear the name. The original Big "E", was the most decorated ship in U.S. Naval history. It was the only ship to receive both the Presidential and Navy Unit Citations during four years of constant battle in the Pacific campaign and was upon occasion the only active United States Navy aircraft carrier left to oppose the Imperial Japanese Navy throughout a desperate series of slugging matches. And now this one. At 90,000 tons with a four and a half acre flight deck, she could accelerate faster and cruise at high speed longer than any capital warship heretofore ever imagined.

Lt. Robert A. McLaughlin saluted aboard and passed through the

Quarterdeck. To his right he noticed a glass display case with a folded American flag inside. He paused just briefly enough to read the legend inscribed, "Last National Ensign flown from *USS Enterprise, CV-6*"

Bob McLaughlin walked into the cavernous expanse of Hangar Bay One. This was the only carrier he had been aboard since flight school, and this ships size and dimensions were profound. The rest of the ORI team clambered aboard and were being directed to their berthing areas. Robert McLaughlin turned to go back to the Quarterdeck ladder and stopped. There, mounted outside the Quarterdeck hatch, were two massive bronze plaques. On each was the broadside profile of CV-6 and the proud name *USS Enterprise*. And listed below in chronological order was displayed the operational history of CVA(N)-65's namesake. Every raid, battle and major engagement was listed throughout the old Big "E" World War II years. And it took two-plaques to list them all!

As Lt. McLaughlin scanned down the long lists of battle, he understood more clearly the pride of the name, *USS Enterprise*, and the honor bestowed on this ship when it became the successor to bear the standard. And what ship, and what crew could fail to understand the responsibility to do honor to that legacy? The differences between CV-6 and CVA(N)-65 were great. The new *"Big E"* was faster, with over twice the horsepower. She was three hundred feet longer and 60,000 tons heavier. But the heart of old CV-6 was great, and the heart of a ship, which transformed a mass of steel to something approaching a living thing, was its crew. This ship and this crew had a lot to live up to.

Word was passed over the 1MC, "MAN THE RAIL", and Bob McLaughlin moved quickly to put his gear away and be ready to see some very important people. The ship was about to get underway.

At 0711, the Watch was shifted from the deckhouse to the bridge, and at 0738, all lines were clear. *Enterprise* gave a long blast on her ships whistle. She was underway.

On the portside of the flight deck, forward on the angle deck catwalk, a ladder led down to an open grate landing and passageway on the 03 level. There, standing in the hatchway, a V-4 Division flight deck fuels crewleader in dungarees watched, out of sight of the rail manning party in dress whites. To the crewleader, this landing was a special place where between the recoveries of aircraft he found precious few moments of tranquillity before the roaring began again.

Here, a clean smelling wind would almost dry some of his sweat soaked clothes before the waist cats began launching and Gas Control called out their recovery stations and the back breaking, mind numbing routine began again. Almost.

The great ship began to move forward and the crewleader gazed at the landmass in the middle of Pearl Harbor, only a stone's throw away. "It was here," he thought, as he looked across at Moku Umeume, Ford Island. It was here. Almost this same time of year, nearly this same time of day. Battleship Row, twenty seven years and thirty five days ago. What had it been like back then? *Oklahoma, California, Maryland, Tennessee, West Virginia, Nevada*, the fury, the fear, the bravery and the sacrifice. The test those men had to face. What was it like?

As the ship reached the end of Ford Island, and began a turn to port, word was passed on Main Communication, the 1MC, "ATTENTION TO PORT!" As one, the men manning the rail snapped to attention facing the portside. *USS Enterprise* was drawing abreast of the *Arizona Memorial*. "HAND . . . SALUTE!" All hands on deck snapped in unison and held the salute as *Enterprise* glided by.

The crewleader stood in his hatchway, arm raised in proud salute as his ship passed the battered tomb of the *Arizona* and the ghosts of the eleven hundred who rode her down.

"READY . . . TWO!" Salutes snapped away as the hulk of the *Arizona* fell astern. The crewleader tried again to imagine that day, not so long ago, when these men had met their time of trial.

The carrier had rounded Ford Island and now came down the west side where remnants of December 7th, 1941 were still visible. There lay the rusted wreck of the old battleship *Utah*, tomb of another score of Americans.

The crewleader could not help but wonder at the contrast in the nation between that time and now. That war had brought the country together with a singleness of purpose unmatched by any time before or since. It must have been a wonderful thing to have lived during that time, to have been a part of a common bond.

This war in Viet Nam, Southeast Asia, had brought forth divisiveness and turmoil heretofore unheard of. Contempt for government institutions, outright refusal to obey laws, rebellion on campuses, persons of stature and celebrity flagrantly aiding and abetting the enemy. They spoke out defiantly against their own, proclaiming those who served honorably in the Armed Forces of the

United States to be regarded as war criminals! These same persons touted the humanity of the North Vietnamese Communists while our prisoners-of-war were beaten, tortured, and starved daily, for years on end. A higher percentage of these died at the hands of their captors than any other war in our nations history. More than the Nazis. More than the Japanese. More than the North Korean Communists. Strife. Race Riot. Assassination. Cities burned and looted. And all the while a steady, daily stream of aluminum coffins bringing American sons back from a foreign land.

The crewleader was glad he was leaving again. America was experiencing a moral collapse that was painful to witness. What was once the proud stamp of every American, personal honor, was now loathed and reviled by the multitudes of shameless weaklings of the upper crust who found the weight of honor more than they could bear. These lashed out violently at the source of their shame, the uniformed Armed Forces of the United States. There was a division in the crewleaders generation as stark and bold as a swordpoint drawn through the sand. On one side, those who did their duty. On the other, those who opposed them, who knew no shame amidst the howling and gnashing of teeth.

The crewleader was glad he was leaving his country again. This would be his third WESTPAC tour and the last of his four year enlistment. He, like thousands of other veterans, could not understand the dissension and chaos at home while every day, young Americans were being killed and maimed in this place called Viet Nam.

The *USS Enterprise* slid down the narrow channel past Waipio Peninsula. The crewleader, still looking out to port, saw a number of young women and girls lining the banks and waving Aloha to the ship. It was a fine and friendly gesture. Thankfully, he waved back from the hatchway.

Lt. McLaughlin knew there would be some special people watching for him. He stood at the base of the ships massive island, behind the men in dress whites manning the rail. The ship was gliding down the channel past Navy housing at Iroquois point. As he scanned the crowded banks of waving people shouting goodbyes, he saw those he was looking for. There on the bank were his wife Diana, and their two young boys. Waving both hands, he drew her attention. She, in turn, pointed him out to the couples offspring. It was a fond and happy farewell.

And the people gathered there watched as *Enterprise* slid gracefully by and down the remainder of the channel and stood out to sea, following in the track of her three escorting destroyers, *Bainbridge, Rogers and Stoddart*. This ship was departing for her Operational Readiness Inspection, three days of intense drill and observation under simulated combat conditions. The ship would be observed and graded in all aspects of its routine and combat operations. This inspection would find and point out where the ship and its airwing were strong or deficient. After three days the ship would return to Pearl for one last night and the ORI team would leave the ship. Then the *USS Enterprise* would steam to the Tonkin Gulf, to a position known as YANKEE STATION, where she would relieve another great fighting ship with another great fighting name and tradition, *USS Constellation*, CVA-64. There, the *Big E* would begin her fourth WESTPAC combat tour of the Viet Nam war. For the skipper of the ship, Capt. Kent L. Lee, this would be his second consecutive tour in command of *USS Enterprise*.

To the watchers ashore, the *Enterprise* was fast becoming smaller. They could not guess her speed, nor could they see the boiling froth of her wake as Capt. Lee called for speed, first 15, then 20 knots. The four great five-bladed propellers, each 21 feet across and weighing 32 tons, clawed through the water under the influence of 70,000 shaft horsepower apiece. Capt. Lee called for 25 knots. Long bow waves of surf ranged far out from either side of *USS Enterprise* and her wake boiled and foamed. She raced out into her natural element, the open sea.

The crowd lining the banks at Iroquois point began to disperse but Diana McLaughlin and her boys stayed and watched as long as the ship was still visible. Finally, the distinct, square island structure of *Enterprise* disappeared over the horizon. She gathered her sons for the walk back to her home. "Three days," she told them, "Daddy will be back in three days and he will be looking for us at this very spot when he comes back." With that Diana McLaughlin and her boys walked away.

First Night

Sixteen hours later, Capt. Lee looked at his watch. The time showed 0015. He was anxious to get the remaining aircraft recovered and get this first days operations wrapped up. There were three aircraft still aloft, an F-4, the A-3 tanker and the helo. Even now, the Captain was aware of the unmistakable sound of a Phantom in the groove, the last stage of the landing approach. All eyes turned to the flight deck, a surreal specter in the low intensity diffusement of the red spotlights mounted high on the island structure. At first, a whisper, seemingly carried on the wind now gaining in volume and proximity. The pitch and howl of engines rising then falling away, now rising again as the aircraft maintained proper rate of descent through boosts of thrust and aerodynamics.

On the flight deck ABH2 Henry Mendoza stood just off the foul line in the Fly Two angle area waiting for the next trap. Beyond the dimly lit flight deck the sea was invisible in the absolute blackness. But all round about the starshot universe glimmered with a million glints of light, diamonds in the void. Henry Mendoza watched the stars above and behind the fantail and there he saw three geometric points of light dropping from the sky. This was the only sign that a hulking, 20 ton fighting machine was approaching at one hundred fifty miles an hour. The whine of engines, adding and cutting power, were nearly upon them. The lights descended rapidly, lower and faster, and suddenly, the Phantom dropped into the canopy of light a split second before it slammed onto the flight deck.

The great warbird caught #3 wire cleanly but the shock of landing bounced the starboard wing and main gear clear of the deck as the pilot threw both throttles to full power. The J-79 engines thundered and strained and the F-4 hauled the arresting gear cable out to its length. Henry Mendoza turned on his flashlights and they were immediately transformed into the eerie yellow wands that commanded and dictated all movement on deck at night. He gave the cut power signal as he moved into position in front of the still roaring Phantom. The pilot shut down and the thundering fell away to an obedient high pitched whine. Mendoza then gave the signal to raise and clear the tailhook. The arresting gear was retracted and with a boost of power, the F-4 quickly taxied clear of the landing area, following the beckoning golden wands with the steady up and down motion of Henry Mendoza. Then the left wand was held straight out at arms length as the right continued its cadenced beat. The F-4 quickly turned hard to the right, never stopping or slowing down as Henry Mendoza now swung both wands, one behind the other, pointing to the next director to take this bird, Little Joe Oates coming up from Fly Three. Joe's wands lit up and the Phantom pilot automatically tracked on the new leader.

Even as the deck was being cleared, the sound of the approaching A-3 Sky Warrior was growing louder and soon drowned out all other sounds on deck. This birds own distinctive engines alternately moaned and wailed as the pilot nursed the big jet down to slam onto the deck in the same shrieking trap. As the pilot cut power Henry Mendoza lit his wands to direct this bird forward to clear the angle for the helo recovery. The big Sky Warrior gunned the engines and rolled forward a few yards following the glowing yellow wands. Then the stop signal and the A-3's J-57 engines wound down to an ear shattering idle.

The aircraft, even before they were shut down, were immediately set upon by multitudes of color-clad personnel. Each armed with a flashlight, they swarmed over the birds as they taxied clear and then shut down. From Capt. Lee's view in the island, they looked like so many fireflies as their beams of light moved about and found their way among the dark silhouettes ranged on deck.

With the helo finally on deck and the recovery complete, Capt. Lee again looked at his watch. The time was 0038. This first days scheduled eight cycles of flying operations were now done, but it would still be an hour, or two, maybe three, until these support crews jobs were finished and they could secure. Kent Lee was anxious to get the crews rested. They would need what little rest they could gain from the remainder of this night, because tomorrows schedule called for ten cycles, fifteen hours of flying. That meant these same crews, not done yet, would be called to reveille only four hours from now.

Cyclic operations were to reflect the current Rolling Thunder air operations being flown in Southeast Asia. These operations were originally based upon the time it took for an airstrike to be launched, flown to target, strike, and return to be recovered aboard ship. The second strike would be launched just prior to and co-insiding with the recovery of the first launch. The time of this cycle, delivery and return, was one hour and thirty minutes from the point in the Tonkin Gulf known as YANKEE STATION. In the ninety minute intervals between launches, the recoveries would be spotted and refueled. Then re-spotted and armed. And then re-spotted for launch. All the while individual maintenance problems would require any number of aircraft to be moved into or out of the Hangar Bay.

It was found that ninety minutes was sufficient time to meet this schedule. But since that time the F-4 Phantoms, only carried aboard large deck carriers, had gone from a strictly fighter, to a fighter-bomber role with no additional time allotted for the increased demands placed upon the ship, aircraft and weapons handling systems. To meet these demands, the tempo had to be picked up to a hectic pace.

Capt. Lee, in command of *USS Enterprise* for the last eighteen months, with a combat tour on YANKEE STATION completed just seven months ago knew his ship and his crew could handle the pace. But he also knew the pace demanded rest. The ORI schedule for the second day was extreme.

Air, Weapons and Squadron personnel would be still working two hours after the last recovery. What was worse, because of requirements for the third day, tomorrows schedule moved the start of the days first launch up to 0645.

Capt. Lee did not agree with this schedule and voiced his opposition to it with FLEET TRAINING GROUP. He did not think it necessary to push things all the way to the breaking point. FLTRANGRU Staff advised Lee that all the other CVA's coming through the area had gone ahead with this schedule and none had complained. Capt. Lee maintained that just because they had not objected, that did not make this schedule right. He was advised to go along with the schedule and take it up with the Admiral later. This he would certainly do.

Capt. Lee looked down on the dimly lit flight deck. Groups of shadowy figures moved about the deck and aircraft. At his side was Capt. Robert A. Hoolhorst, senior observer, FLTRANGRU. Capt. Hoolhorst knew of Lee's concern over the next days schedule. To try and give him a little good news, he told Lee how *Enterprise* had done in this first days grading. "Your ship has been assigned a grade of 'GOOD', 85.0, for the overall mark today. A few low scores for some squadrons but OUTSTANDING grades in Damage Control and firefighting drills have given this ship high marks for the first day!" "This is impressive Captain! Most carriers do not grade out that high even after the third day when scores tend to go up."

Capt. Lee knew he would have some low scores with the Air Wing. The two VF squadrons had just transitioned from the F-4B to the F-4J. All three VA attack squadrons were newly commissioned or transitioned to new aircraft. The A-7 Corsair was new to Air Wing Nine. VAQ-132 was commissioned only two and a half months ago. Of the ships 9 air controllers, only 2 were experienced. Of twelve officers in Communications, only one had WESTPAC experience. But of the crew and squadrons, 70% were veterans of at least one WESTPAC deployment, some two and some three. And Capt. Lee, mindful of the FORRESTAL tragedy in June of '67, had managed to send over ninety percent of ships company and Airwing personnel, both officers and men, to advanced two and five day firefighting schools since the ships return from WESTPAC the previous summer. He knew he would have some low marks in some areas but he also knew that the effort put into firefighting and Damage Control drills over the last six months would pay dividends. "They will be even better tomorrow," he said as he walked off the bridge. "We will score higher tomorrow."

On the port side of the bow section of the flight deck, just forward of the angle, aviation fuels crew #2 was finishing up topping off the last four A-7s of the recovery from station #12. Each aircraft was fueled to a full internal load, 1,500 gallons of JP-5. With the station rolled back up, George Norsworthy climbed up on deck with the rest of the crew. He was still in the process of coiling up the cord of his sound powered phones as he said simply, "Two and six are late crews, we go to station #28."

With the last of the aircraft shut down, everyone on deck welcomed the peace. Wind over the deck had cleared the last smell of jet exhaust and now things were clean and cool and quiet. Men raised their goggles and took off their headsets. Only the sounds of tow tractors and chock and chain crews disturbed to silence. Any talking was done in low tones.

The flight deck Leading Petty Officer, Billy Hawk, had come up to Henry Mendoza. "We'll need you in Fly 3 tomorrow." Mendoza had been transferred from the *Hancock* to the *Enterprise* only two months ago to help alleviate a manpower shortage. His Fly experience on *Hancock* made him a trump card Billy Hawk could play anywhere on this deck.

"No problem," Mendoza answered easily. He himself had no problem fitting in with the V-1 Division gang. He made friends readily and already had something of a bond with one of the Divisions more colorful characters. Del Girty, one of the yellow shirts, had just married a woman of Mexican heritage the week before and loudly proclaimed his happiness. When Henry Mendoza informed Del Girty that he himself was married to an American Indian woman, Girty had erupted with a series of war whoops. "We will start a new nation, you and I. My father is full blood Cherokee, my mother, Irish!" They both laughed heartily at the prospect.

On the bridge, with the recovery aboard, the Officer of the Deck ordered 15° left rudder and steady up on course 090. Fuels crew #2 walked slowly aft, following the gang of aircraft handlers towing the tanker, side number 614. There was no hurry now and since they were late crew tonight, they would take their time.

The crewleader considered his crew to be one of the best of V-4 Division. With George Norsworthy and Jim Fitzgerald he had two veterans who could handle any situation. The new guy, Arrick, was a willing and eager hand and the rest of the crew were glad to have him. This cruise would be a long hard pull just like the other ones. But when you had a crew you could depend on, who counted on each other and worked as a team, it was a very proud and satisfying thing. The crewleader stopped his fellows half way down the angle and told them to look up into the night sky. "Look at this."

There above them the stars of heaven pulsed and glowed in shimmering majesty. A view such as this, the crewleader said, was beyond imagination. The constellations Ursa Major and Ursa Minor were easily identifiable with Polaris, the North Star, directly overhead. The Milky Way Galaxy, a broad band of light across the night sky with its center 30,000 light years from here. Swirls of stars, dust and gases clearly visible above and all around them. Farther out, a faint patch of light of what must be Andromeda Nebula. They stared upward.

Then as they watched, the entire universe began to slowly rotate as they stood in silent wonderment. It was as if the universe itself was passing in review, proudly displaying its dazzling beauty. Galactic and Solar cosmic rays, magnetic fields and solar winds, Pulsars, exploding Super Novae, Quasars and Black Holes. Who could comprehend such splendor as this, who could possibly comprehend it? They were humbled in their minuteness.

Crew #2 continued their trek to station #28, each of them alone with their thoughts after beholding the infinite grandeur and endlessness of the universe.

In the darkness of the Fly Three area, just aft of #4 elevator on the port side, a handling crew backed VF-96 F-4 #105 in beside F-4 #106. These birds were scheduled for the second launch tomorrow and they would stay in these positions until that launch. As the Phantom was backed up to the scupper, the aircraft director gave the tractor driver a signal for a hard turn so the tailpipes of the F-4 would not be blowing directly over the port Point Defense Missile Battery. As the tail of the bird cleared the battery, the director gave the chock and tie-down signal. With chocks in place, the tow bar was disconnected from the tow tractor and dropped to the deck. Tie-down chains were now rigged and tightened to the port and starboard main gear and the nose wheels, forward and aft of the aircraft and one tie-down chain forward towards the bow of the ship. In the long shadows cast by the tractor, young hands secured the two nosewheel chains and for the third chain, towards the bow, found the closest padeye under and between the split trails of the tow bar, which formed a right angle with the aircraft. Unseen by others, the young hands took up the slack and secured the nose wheel tie-downs. The tow bar was now locked in its position, blocking access for start-up.

On the forward side of F-4 #106, another handling crew backed the tanker, #614, into its resting place. This also was chocked and secured with the port main gear on #4 elevator and the starboard main gear on hard deck. Now chocked and secured, the handling crew moved back forward to help finish the re-spot.

Crew #2 arrived at a slow pace just as the handling crews pulled away. They surveyed their work at this station. This would take awhile. George Norsworthy had gone down into the catwalk and then down a short ladder to the hatchway of station 28. He immediately went to one of the three reels of black, heavy rubber 2½ inch hose. He grabbed the two handled Parker nozzle and pulled the hose across the deck and stood up on a bench and held the nozzle out a small bulkhead window. A hand reached down and took the nozzle and George stood back as the hose immediately began to pay out across deck and out the window, the reel spinning wildly until all the hose had been pulled free. Then he pulled another nozzle across the deck and held it out another window and stood back as the hose was pulled out to its length.

On deck Fitz and Arrick took the first hose towards the two Phantoms while the crewleader took the second to refuel the tanker. The VF-96 F-4 Phantoms were all configured with 370 gallon wing tanks in addition to a full internal load to about 2,600 gallons. The tanker had to be topped off to a 3,650 gallon load. The other crews would be securing about now, the crewleader thought. He was looking forward to piling into his own rack too. They were all very tired. Crew #6 was working aft along the starboard side with Nick

Lasovich in charge. Both crews would work aft on each side of the ship and then across the fantail. Then they would sweep the entire Hangar Bay and maybe even have to go back up forward on the flight deck. They could not secure until every aircraft not down for a maintenance problem was topped off and ready to go.

The fuels crews and other support gangs from a myriad of Departments and Divisions and Squadrons worked into the night as *USS Enterprise* steamed along in Hawaiian operational waters at 10 knots. At length, the long day was done and the late crews were told to secure. Wearily, the purpleshirts walked across the flight deck for the last time. They went into the starboard catwalk between some parked A-7s aft by the B&A crane. There they walked the passageway inboard to the V-4 Division berthing compartment at frame 215 on the 03 level.

The crews stepped single file through the hatch and silently made their way through the labyrinth to their own racks, aching for sleep. In this darkened compartment, just as it was all throughout the ship, the sound of deep, healing sleep was universal. There were no quiet conversations here. There was no late letter writing under low lights. There was no restless tossing and turning. Here, there were only the sonorous sounds of long measured breathing.

After quickly cleaning up, the crewleader gratefully climbed into his own rack. He stretched out to full length under the wool blanket and thought this was altogether luxurious. He looked at his watch. The luminous hands showed the time to be 2:45. Then he fell away into oblivion.

14 January, 1969

At 0400 the routine began again. Lights went on and men were roused from deep slumbers in all Air and Weapons departments and Squadron spaces. Only those designated as late crews would be left alone. These would be turned out shortly. Men emerged from racks still numb from the night before, mechanically progressing through the mornings regimen. Other departments had their own schedules but by and large the entire shipboard community was massed in support of flight quarters.

On the second deck aft, directly below Hangar Bay 2, the after galley was already in operation. These men had begun preparing for this breakfast an hour before. Now, grills hot and frying, tubs full and ready, coffee on, the cooks and messcooks stood at their stations waiting for the feeding to begin. At 0415 the line of messcooks at the serving bar heard the familiar sound. What began as a distant drumming grew in volume and proximity. The line of messcooks, eternally stung by the injustice of their predicaments, wore the universal expressions of indifference. They watched the hatchway directly to their front, starboard side, frame 215. There at once came a sound akin to a skier racing down a slope, interspersed with a pong-pong-pong in measured cadence. This was followed immediately by a resounding boom as a man landed full weight on both feet on the steel deck at the bottom of the ladder and bounded through the hatchway in one motion. In quick succession the swish-pong, swish pong-pong became continuous as men slid down the ladder rails, their full weight balanced on the heels of their hands. Men might actually touch feet with two or three steps of a ladder going from one deck down to the next, sometimes none at all. Never more than three. On big ships with big crews, you slid down ladders and bounded up them, taking rungs three at a time. There are no walks in the park on a carrier.

The first in the chow line this day, a noisy gang of brownshirts from VF-96, took stamped metal trays from racks and proceeded through the serving line. The messcooks each dispensed a different food and a man held his tray for that which he would have. The messcooks, with acute detachment, measured random portions and delivered these in apparently indiscriminate places in the diverse compartments of the tray. The men in line moved swiftly down the serving bar.

The gang of brownshirts of VF-96, plane captains, set their trays down at a far table. These men, all friends, had been exchanging an easy banter this morning although one of their number had been noticeably silent. Frank Neumayer thought he knew the reason. He was looking directly across the table at his friend, Pat Bullington.

"Had the dream again, Pat?"

Bullington sawed slowly at his food. Not looking up, he nodded in acknowledgment. The other four plane captains were at once silent. They knew of this dream and regarded it seriously. Many times in the past few months Frank Neumayer had found his cubicle mate awake in the middle of the night. He would be sitting up with his head in his hands, unable to sleep. It was the dream. When asked about it he would be unable to explain. In grim resignation he would only say, "It's the *Big E's* turn to burn."

The others knew what he meant. First the ORISKANY in '66, then the FORRESTAL in '67. With the massive amounts of fuel and ammunition handled amid the breakneck pace of carrier operations, the prospect of catastrophe was an ever present danger where they were going. Armando Limon gave Bullington an understanding punch on the shoulder. Randy Lorimor tried to lighten the atmosphere, "It's probably all this spam we've been eating."

Jim Ridenour, the big guy they called Rhino, felt called upon to address a wrong, "I like the spam! It's probably all those shots we got before we left Home Port in Alameda."

Pat Bullington shrugged and permitted a half smile. He appreciated the concern of his friends. This was something he could not explain, even to himself. It was beyond his understanding. He tried many, many times to just forget about it and go on but it was always there. He felt something.

The mess decks were rapidly filling up. Most of those eating wore the colored jerseys of the aircraft support groups. One of those, off by himself, also ate silently. AME3 Twig Tordoff, a greenshirt in VA-146, was disturbed about the nightmare he had last night. This was something new. He couldn't remember having anything like this since he was a little kid. This wasn't some dream about monsters and abstract things, this was about fire and terror and blood. Twig Tordoff was still shocked about it. He finished eating and walked away from the table, going forward on the starboard side. As he walked forward on the white linoleum tiles he tried to put the thing from his mind but it would not go away. He passed through the open armored door to the after bomb assembly area and saw that the ordnancemen were already busy with their work. Crates of green MK 82 500 lb. bombs and other crates of Snakeye high drag bombfins were already on deck, up from the after magazines. Weapons crews were busy breaking the crates down and joining the Snakeye fins to the 500 pounders. Completed bombs were already loaded, two to a skid, waiting to be sent up the after bomb elevators.

In the cool darkness of the flight deck, aircraft handling crews were preparing the deck for the first of ten scheduled launches. All aircraft were towed clear of the bow and go aircraft put into position for launch behind numbers one and two jet blast deflectors. The Fly two and Fly three areas were also rearranged. The same canopy of stars shimmered and pulsed as the carrier proceeded at a leisurely 8 knots, course 130°.

At 0530 Flight Quarters went into effect and the first weapons began arriving on the flight deck via the forward and aft bomb elevators. Loaded on skids, weapons appeared magically in the gloom. Rocket pods, both 2.75 inch LAU-68s and 5 inch LAU-10s, MK 82 bombs, cans of belted 20MM, Sparrow missiles and tubs of fuses came on deck. As the weapons were served up, Ordnancemen seized them and followed after various aircraft. Each man wrestled with his own load, balanced on the two-wheeled bomb skids. They would have to be man-handled to all points of the 4 acre flight deck looking for aircraft side numbers. The time progressed to 0625. The Officer of the Deck informed Primary that he intended to make a turn into the wind for the 0645 launch. Go Ahead. Watch your list. The Officer of the Deck ordered left standard rudder and the great ship began a slow turn that would take nearly ten minutes to complete.

The Exercise Strike Group for the first launch, fourteen aircraft, were in position. Lt. Robert A. McLaughlin stood behind the Air Boss and Assistant Air Boss seated in Primary. He watched beams of flashlights probing this way and that among the Go-birds spotted behind the bow and waist cats. It was his job as an ORI observer to watch and time launch and recovery sequences from this position. He was impressed with the industry he was witnessing on the deck below. The flight deck was a bee hive of endeavor, dark shapes in seemingly aimless wanderings and tow tractors growling with motions of purpose.

The brilliance of the universe began again its slow rotation about the activity on deck. The most distant stars of night were gone. The rotation continued until a low crescent moon stood squarely in the path of the carrier as she came about into the wind. Unseen, except by a few, a shooting star rocketed across the expanse of the heavens with incredible velocity and disappeared forever into the blackness above the crescent moon.

From somewhere on deck the low moan of a GTC-100 tractor mounted gas turbine huffer starting unit came to life. As RPMs increased, this unit quickly spooled up to a high pitched whine. Another unit fired up, then many. The start tractors made their ways to the Go-birds and hoses were attached and couplings were made.

The pitch of the start turbines rose higher still and held. From among the brooding, hulking shapes there arose a new sound. It was the sound of great engines as one after another, the warbirds were nursed into life. The sound became all pervasive, all encompassing. It was the sound of heat and power, serpentine and menacing. The flight deck was alive again.

Capt. Lee moved about the bridge monitoring operations. He allowed himself a largely invisible presence so that Fleet Training Group might observe and evaluate *USS Enterprise* Officers of the Deck who had instructions from Lee himself to conduct Flight Operations on schedule without necessarily consulting him. The Officer of the Deck ordered the helmsman, "Steady up on course three zero zero. All ahead standard, indicate turns for fifteen knots." The lee helmsman repeated the order and rang up standard on the engine order telegraph and adjusted the turns indicator on the propeller order telegraph.

Sixteen decks below, in the Enclosed Operating Spaces of the Reactor Control rooms above the four main power plants, the Throttlemen answered the "bells" by turning an indicator on the engine order and propeller order telegraphs to the same position as what was ordered thus indicating, "Order Received." Each of the four main power plants occupied the breadth of the hull with two reactors, A ahead of B, splitting the space longitudinally. On one side of the reactors was the steam side while the Reactor Auxiliary Room was on the other. The steam side was the engine room whose main components were the steam turbines, reduction gearing, ships service generators, feed pumps and the massive drive shaft running from the main reduction gear through various bulkheads to one of the ships four great propellers. In addition to driving one of the ships screws, each plant provided steam for aircraft catapults, two ships service generators and various auxiliary loads. The plants were numbered according to the propeller which they powered. With the two outboard shafts and propellers being splayed, those plants were placed farthest forward.

The propellers were numbered, from starboard to port, #1, #2, #3, #4. The plant layout was thus from forward to aft, #1 plant, #1 Auxiliary Machinery Room, #4 plant, #2 AMR, #2 plant and #3 plant farthest aft. Damage Control Central and Engineering Central Control nerve centers were located on the top level of #2 AMR.

Above the two reactor compartments in each plant stood the

very hot Cooling Turbine Generator flats. This level contained two turbine generators to provide electricity to the reactor coolant pumps, the reactor electronics and switchgear room and the Enclosed Operating Space or EOS. Inside the EOS, sealed off from the hum and whine of rotating machinery, the throttlemen turned a 30 inch hand wheel on the steam plant control panel. This wheel, the main engine throttle, opened a valve that increased steam flow into the main turbine. Beside each Throttleman were two Reactor Control Operators watching the two reactor control panels.

As the Throttleman increased the power to the steam plant, the reactor power output rose to match the new power requirement, The Reactor Control Operators monitored reactor parameters to insure the reactors were responding as designed and in a safe manner, occasionally moving the reactor control rods slightly to compensate for changing operating conditions. Behind the Throttleman and Reactor Control Operators, the Propulsion Plant Watch Officer (PPWO), monitored the entire operation by communicating with the rest of the propulsion plant and with Engineering Control Central.

On the flight deck, the knife edge orchestration of the launch, acted out thousands of times from this deck, was about to begin again. Aircraft taxied into position on the cats as the whine of engines spooled up and fell away. Catapult crews attached harnesses and the jet blast deflectors were raised. An F-4 on Cat 1 turned up to full power. Then, with a resounding crack, it went into afterburner. Two solid barrels of thrust driven flame drove into and blasted over the Jet Blast Deflector, bathing the rest of the deck in waves of heat and sounds of fury. The two J-79 engines strained under a continuous sonic thundering. The deck trembled underfoot. Then, the catapult shot the Phantom down the bow in flaming power and brilliance. The black sea flashed alight from the flare of blazing afterburners and the F-4 thundered and clawed and roared its way into the darkness, lighting its way with its power. It was an awesome spectacle. The launch was underway.

One after another, aircraft laden with fuel and weapons were hurled into flight by the two bow and two waist catapults. The first 16 of the days 130 scheduled strike missions against the bombing range at Kahoolawe Island were on their way. A faint aura of color far back in the ships wake heralded the first rays of a new dawn. The time was 0655.

Various night crews now began to secure from their duties with the certain knowledge that at least one General Quarters drill, maybe more, would interrupt their sleep.

The V-4 Division late crews were roused with the commencement of the first launch. The two crews had ample time. They had to be on deck for the first recovery. In a group they moved down to the after galley and joined the long chow line. A certain starched and pressed sailor in dungarees with the chevrons of an E-5 bold upon his creases stopped and surveyed the serving bar display with a deliberate eye while he carefully considered a breakfast. The chow line ground to a halt. The pressed sailor stood in front of the Grits-Man and regarded his fare critically. He kept his tray upturned against his chest. He sniffed. He declined the grits this day. He next moved to the Egg-Man and paused thoughtfully in wistful contemplation. No, he would not prefer to dine on eggs this morning.

The line of messcooks stared at this creature with openfaced contempt. The Cooks, unseeing, were busy at their trade. The chow line grew restive. The E-5 finally reckoned to try the chipped beef and toast. He smiled and held out his tray to the Toast-Man in his moment of decision. The Toast-Man resolutely gathered up two pieces of toast with his tongs and in the delivery to the tray managed to impale both pieces in a crushing grip. The Toast-Man, with great difficulty, could accomplish breaking the toast loose only with repeated bangings on the man's outstretched tray. The E-5 looked on in disbelief as the centers of both pieces were ripped out and crumbs spread over his entire tray. While he was gripped in shock over his toast, the Chipped-Beef-Man deftly placed a ladle load precisely from one end of his tray to the other.

"HEY!" The E-5 protested loudly, gaining the attention of the rest of the galley. The Lead Cook, a scowling E-6, with massive bare arms emblazoned with scenes of eagles and anchors, advanced upon the serving line and cleared for action.

"You're holding up my chow line!", declared the Cook.

"BUT HE . . ." and the wounded sailor held out his tray for inspection. Thereupon the Chipped-Beef-Man immediately strafed the tray with another load, this time splashing some on the cleaned and pressed shirt of the E-5. The man objected mightily and held the dripping tray away from the immaculateness of his person and the Toast-Man dutifully procured another serving of toast. The toast hung up on the tongs again, and the Toast-Man banged away in frustration till it broke free.

"MOVE THE LINE!!", the E-6 pronounced to one and all and shot a menacing glare at the offended sailor. The man sulked along but not before the Starboard Butter-Man dropped two pads of butter squarely in the midst of his breakfast.

The Lead Cook glared, the messcooks looked on in angelic innocence and the chow line began to move again. One of the many unspoken rules of shipboard etiquette had been resolved.

The first strike was well on its way when sunrise was observed at 0713. Ordnance for the second and third launches was already arriving on deck. The Hangar Deck throbbed with activity with A-7s scheduled for the third launch being armed with belts of 20MM rounds. MK-77 napalm bombs were filled and mixed in #1 and #3 elevator wells. The endless re-spotting of aircraft continued amidst the shoulder to shoulder stacking in both Bay 1 and Bay 2.

On the flight deck, 2nd launch re-spot activity was underway. The clean sea winds had swept the deck clear of jet engine exhaust and the light of a new day lent an invigorating air to the proceedings. To those who worked the flight deck, it was the only place to be. This was where the action was with the beauty and might of the sea and sky all around them. In heat and cold, in darkness and blazing sunlight, in rains and snows and howling winds they would work this deck and love it, regarding themselves as fortunate indeed. For who could consider the endless displays wrought by the Hand of the Creator and not be humbled by them? Placid and mirror-like one day, seas rising and swollen the next. Skies of bluest solitude with edifices of pristine and stately cumulus or disturbed and angry thunderheads affecting the waters with rampant agitation. Dawns and sunsets of dazzling panorama, and through it all their great ship cleaved the waters with resolute continuity, long waves of foaming surf casting out on either side. And who could not but marvel at such things as flying fish exploding from the sea like a covey of quail and skittering along the surface on marine wings? Or dolphins racing along in a game with the bow, hour after hour, jumping and diving, the laughter plain upon their faces? Or Leviathan, who spews a spout of address and raises great flukes in salutation? Is it a wonder seafarers forever long to return to the sea?

The carrier and her two escorts had turned back to face the

Eastern sun on a course of 090 and a speed of eleven knots. The following Westwind of nineteen knots was bringing with it a large bank of clouds, overhauling steadily from rearward. Few took note of the coming, so silently they came.

Throughout the crew it was understood that this day would be like the one before, and the one to come, only longer. These would be days of test and trial and gradings. Problems and drills of every sort would be imposed. They would be called to battle stations again today and again tomorrow just like they were yesterday. The call to General Quarters would be preceded by a small charge thrown into the water. This small explosion produced a thump vaguely felt throughout the ship signifying the emergence of a problem.

Only the Captain and members of Fleet Training Group knew the actual time of the General Quarters drill but from sources unknown, word was passed across chow tables, in passageways and work spaces to expect a GQ drill somewhere around 0830. No one knew who might have divined such information. The Starboard Butter-Man was chiefly suspect. No matter. Ships skinny in these areas was largely accurate and the crew would conduct themselves accordingly.

At a few minutes before 0800, the four to eight watches throughout the ship were being relieved by the eight to twelve watch. On the 011 level of the ships bridge, Ens. Karl Mahumed accepted responsibility for the Officer of the Deck watch from his predecessor who stood relieved, along with the rest of the bridge watch. The particulars of the hour were recorded:

Ships Heading: 090 Degrees
Ships Speed: 11 Knots
Relative Wind: 210 Degrees   9 Knots
True Wind: 280 Degrees   19 Knots
Anemometer Used: Port
State of the Sea: 3 second, 3 ft. swell

Swell: 310°, 10 sec. 8 ft.
Cloud Coverage: 8/10
Ceiling: 3,000 ft.
Temperature: 76.4
Sea Temperature: 76°
Visibility: 10 Miles

At approximately 0805 pilots for the second launch began emerging from the island in flight gear and carrying their helmets. The Captains and pilots elevators ran continuously bringing up aircrews to the 04 level. The *USS Enterprise* and her escorts were at this time 70 miles southwest of Pearl. Ahead of the carrier at 3,000 yards was the USS Rogers, (DD-876), in Anti-Submarine Warfare station. Five miles behind *Enterprise*, the *USS Benjamin Stoddart*, (DDG-22), followed. Due west at a range of 75 miles, *USS Bainbridge*, (DLGN-25), with the best radars, steamed in Anti-Aircraft Warfare picket station.

The night check personnel were mostly in their racks by now. They had put in a long night and were determined to get what sleep they could. Guys like Joe Rosa, AE2 of VF-92, already snoring in forward berthing on the 03 level. And King Merendino, airman apprentice, VF-96, the new guy sent to the ships laundry for three months. He was just climbing into his rack on the 3rd deck outboard of forward bomb assembly. Then there was airman Don George, AT shop, VA-145. His rack on the 03 level at frame 225 was right in the center of the landing area. Any aircraft that caught #1 wire slammed onto the deck right above him. He did not think that the flight deck was nearly thick enough. Every slam sounded like it would tear right on through. Then there was the shriek of the arresting gear being pulled out and retracted. He could even hear every dictum of the Air Boss over the bullhorn. Don George heard it all. The man strove earnestly for sleep. He needed it. He pleaded for it. The best he could do was to will himself into something of a trance. His subconscious was always acutely aware of sounds, waiting for that coming crash that would come right through the flight deck and into his rack. His survival instinct was strong. Don George heard it all. From the chimes of the ships bell marking every half hour to the continuous streams of messages coming over the 1MC. And every message, no matter how trivial, was preceded by some deranged Bosunmates virtuoso effort at piping. He heard all of it. He only had his eyes closed.

Fifteen frames aft, on the extreme port side, was compartment 03-240-6-L. This was VAQ-132 berthing. In the after inboard corner of this compartment, airman Steve Bell lay in his rack in a deep slumber. A bulkhead at his back separated this space from the next one inboard of it, a crews washroom called a head, compartment 03-240-4-L. Access hatches led into this head from the VAQ-132 space outboard and also inboard to the main portside Gallery deck passageway which ran from far forward to aft to frame 240 in a straight line. At this point there was a slight offset corner, then the passageway continued to its terminus at frame 255 where there was an outboard passageway to the port catwalk. The only compartments aft of this outboard passageway were #5 Radio transmitter room in the extreme port corner, and #5 Armory, the next compartment inboard of that. On the forward side of the outboard passageway was Repair Locker 7 ALPHA.

Steve Bell and the rest of the day sleepers were already down and out, all except AMS3 Jerome Yoakum. Yoakum was known to his mates in VAQ-132 to be meticulous and deliberate about things and he was still in the head at frame 240 taking his time showering. Then he would take a slow shave. Maybe he was just stalling waiting for GQ to be called.

The airman charged with cleaning the compartment knew better than to wait for Yoakum to finish up in the head and hit the rack. There was no telling how long it would take for him to do his thing. The airman had to swab down the decks of the two VAQ-132 spaces and the head at frame 240. He dragged his swabs and buckets of hot soapy water to near where Steve Bell slept and began to do this compartment first. He would go into the head when Yoakum was done. He didn't have all day. He had three decks to clean.

The Legion

At the urging of the Westwind a vast gathering of low, scudding strato-cumulus was forming, almost imperceptibly, above the sea into which the three warships proceeded.

The clouds themselves were individual, of differing dimension and volume, everchanging with the push of the incessant wind. Their dark undersides suggested a density beyond their sizes. The gathering clouds settled into a vast circular arrangement. The day grew somber.

Varying shades of white and gray lent distinction and contour to the cottony masses. The slowly curling silence of the sodden mists suggested a realm unique unto itself. But deeper look, deeper. Gently the wispy moisture rolled, revealing vaguely discernible shapes in the fog. In the slowly billowing interior of the swirling gray mists, the ghostly countenances of the Legion of the Dead of the Sea eddied and swayed in loose rank.

The Legion of the Dead wavered slowly in the drifting cloud, passively waiting. Their tattered uniforms bespoke of eras and ages past and present. There were fishermen and seafarers among the assembled but many entire groups were composed solely of sailors of war. There, the ghosts of the *Indianapolis*. There, *Bunker Hill's* nine hundred. There, the ghosts of the HMS *Prince of Wales* and *Repulse*. There, two thousand of the Imperial Japanese Navy from Midway.

Here, the dead of the *USS Juneau* and the dead of the *Houston* and *Yamato*. There, the ranks of old CV-6. And here, the two score of *Oriskany* and *Forrestal's* one hundred and thirty four. The dead of shipwreck and storm. The Legion, in their thousands waited. Composed of all those who died at sea, the Legion was marshaled by the wind to its assigned place and they waited. For one was coming. A Champion, against whose hand none could prevail.

At 0815 the start up of aircraft for the second launch began. The flight deck swarmed with men as final checks were made and arming completed. Lt. McLaughlin stood as observer behind the Air Boss in Primary and looked on with interest.

Five miles behind *Enterprise*, the *Stoddart* was detached from plane guard station so she could make some repairs. Down in the fireroom BM1 Jim Smith secured the fires in boiler 1A so they could fix a leaking check valve. Jim was having trouble with the young guys in his crew. There was lax discipline and other problems and most of his guys were young. He didn't think too much of them. He didn't think they could be counted on.

On the *Rogers*, in a screening position out ahead of *Enterprise*. The Officer of the Deck, Lt. Steve O'Brien, received the radio call to relieve *Stoddart* and ordered right standard rudder.

On the flight deck, ABH2 Henry Mendoza walked back towards the Fly-Three area. Walking with Henry was another yellowshirt, Jose Garcia.

Each Go Bird had any number of men working on it, checkers, ordnancemen, structural mechanics, plane captains, pilots, troubleshooters and handlers. Final fusing had not been completed. There was a problem with the arming wires. Someone had brought up the wrong lengths. Lt.(j.g.) Carl Berghult, VF-96 Weapons Officer, went personally and got the right size arming lengths. Then he personally delivered them to each of the four VF-96 Go Birds in Fly-Three. They were behind schedule because of this. The Air Boss, Comdr. Stollenwerck, called down to ABH1 Billy Hawk on his SRC-22 Mickey Mouse headset radio and wanted to know, "What's the hold up down there?"

"96 had the wrong arming wires and are in the process of stringing the new ones," said Hawk.

"Well they are holding up the launch, get them started!"

Anticipating the General Quarters drill soon to be called, several men throughout the ship walked unhurriedly to their GQ stations.

Down in Central Control watches were being changed as Reactor Officer, Comdr. Ned Kellogg, briefed his four station officers on the drills which were to be run on the GQ drill that morning. The four propulsion plant station officers were three Lieutenant Commanders and Lt. (j.g.) Lash Hansborough. Each had a mimeographed sheet listing the types of drills to be run and the times each was to start. Lash Hansborough looked at his sheet and noticed a training drill scheduled for one of his reactors in #4 plant.

Some of the Repair 7 Alpha men were already there too. Chief Arnold Douch was there and corpsman Clark and Seaman Long and the phone talker, Fireman Ray Friend. Outside the locker, in the hatchway to the catwalk, two men were busy chipping paint.

All of the pilots had manned their aircraft. The two Phantoms on the waist cats were turned up and idling. All of the Go A-7s on the starboard side behind #3 aircraft elevator were turned up. The A-7s were variously armed with 3 MARK 82s and LAU-10 or 68 rocket pods on each wing. At the end of the A-7 line, F-4 #103 was armed with 6 MK 82 bombs on the centerline station and a LAU-10 rocket pod on each wing. Outboard of the rocket pods were 370 gallon wing tanks. All 100 series VF-96 Go birds had this same configuration.

Across the fantail from starboard to port, #202 of VF-92 was a Go Bird armed only with Sparrow missiles. F-4 #114 was armed with Sparrows but was not going till the third launch. Not armed but Go was #214 and #113, VF-96 was Go and armed. Forward on the port side #105 and #106, both Go and armed, the tanker, #614 Was Go. A-7 #310 on #4 elevator was No Go and F-4 #112 behind the waist cats was a standby bird.

Plane Capt. Jim Ridenour had his pilots in #106 strapped in and started. Pat Bullington of #105 had caught the attention of a huffer driver and signaled that he needed a start. Frank Neumayer, all the way aft on #113, needed a start too but would have to wait till something became available from forward.

A huffer driver pulled up to #105 and tried to back up to the port side of the aircraft. He tried twice but couldn't get his tractor around the tow bar which had been pulled to the side and had a tie-down chain running up through it. If this F-4 were not started now, it would be dropped from the launch. The driver drove around to the other side and backed in under the starboard intake. He had to bend over in his seat to back in far enough so the hose would reach the hook-up. Pat Bullington took the hose and hurried to make the connection. Unknown to either man, the exhaust of the huffer turbine, which was already idling, was blowing directly onto the four five inch Zuni warheads and their gold brass fuses. They were level with the turbine and only eighteen inches away. The temperature of the turbine exhaust in the idle mode at this distance was 326 degrees Fahrenheit.

The Legion of the Dead looked down passively on the drama unfolding. It was given unto them of the gray reaches the knowledge of what was forthcoming. It was the appointed time. The hour glass was turned. As one they turned and looked to the western horizon, to the direction of the vaults which held the Westwind. There, at the farthest edge, an aura of light unseen by mortal eyes streaked across the waters, its course straight and true. It was the Champion.

Behold. The Horseman Cometh.

3. THE TRIAL

From out of the west a Rider on a Pale horse rode across the expanse with incredible speed. The Rider's face shone with such radiance as to make his countenance featureless save for the piercing gaze of cobalt eyes. His proportions were those of a mighty warrior and he wore only a short skirt girded at the waist. A broad belt about the skirt glowed with the writings of sacred things. His sandaled feet were laced to the knee. He was altogether beautiful. His terrible weapon, with the sacred mark on the pommel, was worn over his right shoulder, down across his broad back to his left hip. The scabbard strap ran over his shoulder and down his muscular chest carrying the weight of the great sword. An aura of light about him rendered all colorless except for the pounding stallion he rode. It was a Pale horse of terrific power and endurance whose long mane and tail flowed with the ride. The Pale horse was the color of death.

On Deck, Airman Apprentice Dave Reynolds of VF-96 was sent by his line chief to see if the pilots of #113 were going to accept that aircraft since it was missing part of the access ladder. He walked down the bustling flight deck towards the fantail to find them. On the 03 level, the crewleader and the V-4 late crews were just entering their crews' shelter where the other purpleshirts were gathered. As was customary, one of the new recruits was manning the phones. On the bridge Capt. Lee was doing paperwork in his sea cabin and Ens. Mahumed had just initiated left standard rudder to bring the ship into the wind for the 0830 launch. Henry Mendoza stood in the middle of the deck between Phantoms 105 and 106 waiting for the launch to begin. He was talking over the noise to another yellowshirt, Jose Garcia. Pat Bullington had made the huffer hose hook-up and signaled the driver to start. The driver turned the selector switch from idle to the bleed mode and the huffer turbine spooled up to 103 percent. The exhaust temperature on the Zuni warheads rose to 850°F.

On they thundered on soundless hooves, the high spirited charger untiring. They raced across the sea on an unerring course, leagues flying with each locomotive stride.

Dave Reynolds only got as far as 105. From there he could see that the pilots of 113 were already strapped in and the plane captain, Neumayer, was waving for any tractor drivers for a start. Dave Reynolds turned to go back to the line shack but just happened to look over at 105. He noticed something odd. The normally bright gold fuses on the warheads were rust colored. He also saw that the huffer exhaust was blowing directly on the rockets. Even as he watched, he saw the color go from rust to brown. Alarmed, he looked for someone in 96 to report to but everyone seemed to be busy stringing arming wires, Finally, pointing at 105 with exaggerated motions because the jet engine noise was so great, he managed to gain the attention of some of those on deck. AMS2 Henry Yates and

---

Navy Space and Compartment Locator Code

Locations on the aircraft carrier are identified by a four-variable locator code. All spaces and compartments on the ship have a locator code painted on the bulkheads. For instance, **locator code 03-240-4-L** tells the following:

"03" is the deck level. Decks above the Main Deck (also called the Hangar Deck) are listed in succession as 01, 02, 03 levels through to the highest level in the island, the 015 level. The Flight Deck is the 04 level. Decks below the Main Deck are listed as the 2nd deck, 3rd deck on down to the lowest level, 8th deck.

"240" is the frame number.

"4" is the space or compartment number outboard from the centerline of the ship. Odd numbers to the starboard and even numbers to the port. For example:

Centerline

Port   10-8-6-4-2- 0 -1-3-5-7-9   Starboard

"L" refers to how the space is used. "L" (LIVING) indicates crew's quarters. "M" (MAGAZINE) indicates weapons storage. "V" (VOID) indicates closed access storage.

AMS3 Jim Floyd were working under 105 and were unaware of what was going on but ABH1 James Martineau walked over and saw the problem. An argument ensued between himself and the huffer driver. Chief Ronald Hay saw the commotion and walked over. Lt. (j.g) Berghult went to see what was going on. Both engines of 105 were now running. Frank Neumayer finally got the attention of a huffer driver. It was later than any dared think.

Far ahead of horse and rider three specks were visible on the horizon, growing ever larger. With his right hand the Rider grasped the handle above his shoulder and with a rasping song of steel drew the great blade from its sheath. In a crushing grip of corded muscle, the steel held on high moaned in the rushing wind. The Pale horses eyes rolled in wild excitement and the steed lunged ahead, ever faster. Foam frothed his lips and nostrils and snorting breath came short and sharp. The specks ahead had become shapes easily distinguishable and the closest of these loomed up large and in a blur, fell away. Horse and Rider rode up the track of foaming aqua in a topaz blue sea of the largest ships wake. Even now, they could see, the big ship was beginning its turn. As the Rider on the Pale horse streaked across the after part of the flight deck, he brought his terrible swift sword crashing down.

The time was 0819:26.

Down in Engineering Central, Lash Hansborough and the other Propulsion Plant Station officers looked up from their briefing sheets. They all felt and heard the thump from above. This was a familiar sensation. It was the sound and feel of a very hard landing. All present assumed that this was what had indeed happened, even though they all knew no flight operations should have been in progress at this time.

"I don't like the sound of that one!" announced Comdr. Kellogg. Since it was not unusual for a fire party to be called away after a hard landing, Kellogg walked over to the Engineering Officer of the Watch, Lt. Comdr. Paulson, and said, "We'd better get more fire pumps on line."

On the 03 level Don George came out of his rack and landed

on his bare feet on the cold steel deck. His survival trip alarm had gone off and he stood there, instantly awake. Don George looked around wildly in all directions. No aircraft had come through the overhead and everyone else seemed to be sleeping soundly. Perhaps he had just imagined it, he thought, as he tried to slow down his racing heartbeat and heavy breathing. Maybe he was just overreacting. Then the 1MC came on and with no Bosun pipes or any other preamble, the squawk box blared.

"MAN ALL FOG FOAM INJECTION STATIONS!"

When the MK-188 nose fuses of the Zuni rockets reached the temperature of 358° the tetryl-lead azide primer reacted, lighting off the 15 pounds of Composition "B" in the warhead. This caused a sympathetic chain reaction of the four rocket warheads. The resultant detonation of 60 pounds of TNT caused horrific consequences.

A cone of high velocity shrapnel swept out laterally from the rocket launcher while the linear jet of the shaped charge warheads swept the deck to the front. To the right, the blast blew the forward end off the starboard wing tank and holed all four Phantoms across the fantail. As the level of fuel dropped in the wing tank flame raced in and erupted, blowing out the back end of the tank. The 370 gallons of JP-5 roared out of both ends of the tube. A napalm like effect rolled out forward and aft of 105, completely engulfing the aircraft and spilling into the catwalk, quickly burning electrical circuits and sound powered phone transmission lines.

To the left, blast and fragments cut the huffer driver in two, tore into 105's cockpit and holed 106, 614 and 310, wounding nearly everyone in the vicinity. The fuselage internal tanks and port wing tank of 105 were shattered. The lateral blast blew the centerline multiple ejection rack with three MK-82's forward and three aft, into the port Zuni rocket pod knocking its forward mounts off. The rocket pod came to rest on the port main mount tie down chain with the warheads on the deck pointing down and flaming fuel from the port wing tank pouring down directly on them. The centerline rack, with the six 500 pounders still attached, lay on the flaming deck.

Standing behind the Air Boss in Primary, Bob McLaughlin was momentarily blinded by the flash but was aware of fragments striking close by on the island structure. When his sight came back he saw havoc all over the after part of the flight deck and a fireball rolling out from under 105 to the middle of the deck. Most of the men appeared to be down. Many were now getting up and running. Some were dragging others. Some did not get up and the fireball rolled over them. Scores were streaming off deck to the two after port catwalk accesses. A stream of fugitives also went into the after starboard catwalks. Human torches, identified only by the presence of moving arms and legs, hurled, ran and staggered, completely aflame, out from the 105 area. The burning men were tackled, blocked and driven to the deck and rolled over till the flames were out. Rescuers were in turn set aflame with saturated fuel. Hands and arms, chests and faces, where there was initially one man burning, now there were two or three. None shrunk from the task while still others ran into the fray to save them.

In the V-4 shelter the crewleader led a charge out onto the deck. All of crew 2 and a few other individuals followed. As he ran up the ladder he saw a column of flame in the fantail area. The gang of purpleshirts raced down the deck. Two hoses were already being pulled out from the waist cats jet blast deflector area. Knowing there was a fire station much closer to the fire aft of #4 elevator, he yelled to the crew, "STATION TWENTY EIGHT!"

Yellowshirts Jerry McKenzie and Joe Oates were pulling those two hoses out to get them into action. As the lengths came on deck flight deck crews manned the hoses at intervals of a man every four or five feet. With the hoses being pulled out to the center of the deck, the two teams started moving them aft towards the fire.

Directly under and between the two Phantoms spotted on #3 and #4 waist catapults, Interior Communications Fireman Steve Meyer was at his post for the upcoming launch and recovery. His job was operating the PLAT deck edge video tape recorder. When he heard the Air Boss call for fog foam injection stations to be manned, Steve Meyer turned on the monitor to see what was going on. He recoiled in horror and fascination at what he was seeing on the screen. The recorder provided a video record of the ordeal and the automatic timer marked the times of the events precisely. The time at the startup was 0819:38.

On the *USS Rogers*, still over a thousand yards up front and coming down the starboard side of *USS Enterprise*, Lt. Steve O'Brien ran and got his camera and two rolls of film. It was already evident from *Rogers* bridge that a conflagration of considerable intensity was in progress. From the *Stoddart's* position aft, the carriers flight deck and upper works were already lost to view in smoke and flame. Jim Smith, still in the fireroom, received an order from the bridge to relight boiler 1A with all possible haste. The reason given was a fire on *Enterprise* and *Stoddart* would be going alongside to lend assistance.

A ball of fire rolled across the landing outside of Repair Seven, followed shortly by a stampede of screaming, bleeding men from the flight deck. The Repair Seven men were swept along with this tide as they tried to halt some of the wounded so the corpsman could attend to them. Ray Friend finally stopped two VF-96 brownshirts, one carrying the other in the passageway at frame 240. The brownshirt that was hurt was indeed badly wounded and the corpsman went to work on him. The brownshirt who was carrying him stepped into the head at frame 240, the same head where Jerome Yoakum was toweling off. Ray Friend pulled out the hose at the fire station at frame 240 seeking to back up Chief Douch who with the help of a couple of Ordnancemen, were running a hose from farther aft to the off deck access hatch.

The crewleader was first to reach the catwalk at station 28 and jumped down into it. The bulk of the tanker, A-3 #614 was above and just forward of the fuels crew as the leader handed up the firehose. The hose was equipped with an eight foot goose neck fog applicator. Two yellowshirts ran up and took the nozzle and they and the three purpleshirts pulled it out to its length. All of the men involved in this effort were liberally soaked with JP-5 pouring down from the wing and fuselage of 614.

The crewleader was determined to do his duty. He would be brave. In these years of fire and steel his entire generation was put to the test as had many generations come before. This was the eternal rite of passage of every young man in search of the TRUTH. Did he have COURAGE? The crewleader would accept the test. He would place himself in harms way.

Even as he turned the valve to charge the hose he was aware of the roaring of the fire building in volume unabated. It was louder than the shouted commands, louder than the screams and as he looked up to climb the ladder and take his place on the hose, he saw the price of the TRUTH.

There, scant yards away, overlooked in the excitement, a man was down on his hands and knees. The man was burned black with what looked to be hundreds of pink slits torn into his tortured skin. The man was in agony as could be seen by his limited movements.

He was rocking slowly from one side to the other, pain and determination evident on his twisted face. He was trying to get away. A Chief knelt beside him trying to help but afraid to touch him else the sagging, black skin would come away in slabs. The crewleader, eyes wide in horror, ran up the ladder and took his place on the hose team.

The Rider on the Pale horse pulled hard to the right on the reins. The stallion protested the restraint on his stride and threw his head to shake off the pull. The Rider held firm with his mighty left hand and turned his mount to a wide arching swing to the right. His first slashing attack had splashed his steel crimson and flecks of blood spotted both horse and Rider. His next attack would again come up the wake, this time through the billowing flame and columns of smoke which blotted out the sun.

Capt. Lee had by this time come onto the bridge. He took a quick look at the holocaust developing on the fantail. The four F-4's across the rounddown were lost in smoke and flame. Aircraft 105 was completely engulfed and fire was under 103 on the starboard side. Capt. Lee turned back to the helm. He could see the *Rogers* still ahead to starboard. He had to get some wind down the deck to blow the flames aft. He ordered, "Left standard rudder!"

On giving this order Ens. Mahumed announced, "The Captain has the Conn!"

Capt. Robert A. Hoolhorst, Commander, Fleet Training Group, had been observing from the after end of the bridge. When Lee had come on deck he quickly apprised him of the situation aft. Two weapons laden F-4's were already engulfed and two others of the same configuration were about to become involved. With the ship responding to the helm in a 3° list the burning fuel was flowing rapidly across deck and forward, threatening the A-7 line. He had no idea how it started or what had actually happened.

Lee knew the situation was desperate. Already directly involved were no less than thirty 500 pound bombs and at least forty 5 inch rockets aft and more of the same on the Go-birds stacked for launch behind the bow cats. The knowledge and lessons of the FORRESTAL tragedy were clear in his mind. In that fire scores of Air Wing personnel were trapped and killed in 03 and 02 level berthing compartments when General Quarters was called and they were locked in those spaces. Detonating weapons would doom the ship if she were not prepared. Capt. Lee looked at the time on the bridge clock and made his decision. It was nearly 08:20. The weight of Command hung heavy upon his shoulders. He gave the order, "Sound General Quarters!"

Henry Mendoza lay flat on his back. He was aware of a roaring in his ears. The last thing he remembered was a hot rushing wind. He looked to his right and there, just a few feet away lay Garcia, on fire from the waist up. Henry Mendoza tried mightily to get to Garcia but for some reason his right side would not respond. He looked down at himself and saw that his right leg was virtually severed above the knee. Henry saw the wall of flame and his leg and his blood and hung on the edge of shock. He tried again to get up but couldn't. He knew he was going to die.

Then, from out of the wall of fire a figure completely aflame walked slowly toward him. It was a pilot whose flaming clothing and flight suit was dropping in fiery tatters all about him. Portions of his helmet and face were falling away in flaming globs. The pilot was fighting for breath and his chest swelled as he sought air. The ghastly face opened its mouth to draw breath and a column of flame raced in to fill his lungs. The pilot teetered in his immolation, the last spark of life leaving him as he stopped over Henry Mendoza. Even as he toppled over, ABE2 Jacob Quintis of V-2 Division was running to him to put out the flame.

And the Rider whose name was Death burst through the wall of fire and in a blinding arc his sword sang again!

The time recorded was 08:19:46

Pilots were still scrambling to get clear and away from their aircraft and hoses were being pulled out on deck from the after starboard corner when the warheads of the port rocket pod of 105 erupted in three successive detonations. A hail of steel swept out again and the shaped charge warheads punched three 1 foot diameter holes through the 2½ inch armored deck. The first blew through into the head at frame 240. The second in the E-6 compartment just forward of the bulkhead separating these two spaces. The third outboard of these, into the VAQ-132 space, blowing directly down onto the 1MC squawk box that served the entire area.

Chief Big John Guillot had the watch in #3 Plant. He was in the process of turning the watch over to his relief for the forthcoming GQ drill when he felt the ship shudder for a second time. To him it felt like running over a log, a pronounced up and down motion. He knew something was definitely wrong. As he was bounding up the ladders to get to his GQ station he yelled to get all the fire pumps on line and man the 12JZ fire pump phone circuit. Then the stunning message blared over the 1MC.

"EXPLOSIONS ON THE FLIGHT DECK! THIS IS NO DRILL, THIS IS NO DRILL! MAN YOUR BATTLE STATIONS!"

The effect on the ship was electric! The running feet of 5,600 men drummed on ladders and vibrated in passageways.

"GENERAL QUARTERS, GENERAL QUARTERS!"

Don George had been right after all but he wished he wasn't! Shouted questions and bewilderment by men coming awake, "What Happened? Are We Being ATTACKED?"

"REPEAT! ALL HANDS MAN YOUR BATTLE STATIONS!"

Shouts of emergency and dire warning from those of the flight deck as they fled through the berthing compartments. "We're Being BOMBED! The RUSSIANS! CRASH ON DECK!"

"THIS IS NO DRILL, THIS IS NO DRILL! GENERAL QUARTERS, GENERAL QUARTERS! MAN YOUR BATTLE STATIONS!"

Beating feet and panic as the day sleepers and flight deck fugitives ran forward on both port and starboard main passageways. Many were clad only in underwear and shower shoes. Don George was determined to die with his boots AND pants on! He would not be fished from the water wearing only a pair of these ridiculous, billowing, white boot camp issue boxer shorts with his name, service number and basic training company number stenciled on them. He would take the time to dress.

Lt. Richard Martin, Dental Officer, was doing a general examination of a patient when GQ was sounded. Luckily the patient was only being examined when Lt. Martin left immediately and went to his GQ Station, Forward Battle Dressing Station in the forward bomb assembly.

Twig Tordoff had the first fire hose pulled out in Hangar Bay 2. He had it out even before GQ was called. It was in the Dream. Screams and shouts could be heard from the Flight Deck and above it all the Air Boss barking orders on the Bull Horn, "GET MORE HOSES ON DECK! WE'VE GOT TO ISOLATE AND CONTAIN. GET THOSE AIRCRAFT ON #4 ELEVATOR TOWED CLEAR!"

Chief Oliver Lee of VF-96 came out of the Airframes Shop just aft of the #4 elevator, Portside in Hangar Bay Two. The Airframes Shop was his GQ Station, but he told the other men there to stay while he went to see what was going on. He walked the few steps to #4 Elevator well and saw streams of raw JP-5 coming down through the aluminum slatting in many places. The wind was blowing the falling fuel into the Hangar Bay and onto the aircraft parked close by. Chief Lee ran back to the Airframes Shop and closed and dogged the hatch.

In Primary the Air Boss called down to Central Control and gave the Engineering Officer, Comdr. Bill Neel, a run down of what was going on. "We've got a large fuel fire going involving three or more aircraft in the Port Point Defense Missile Launcher Area. The Deck is stacked for launch and the aircraft are armed." Then he switched back to the bull horn. "GET THOSE TWIN AGENT UNITS IN ACTION!"

The Twin Agent Units were something new to the Fleet. *Enterprise* was allotted 5 units just before deployment, but so far only four had been mounted on available tractors. Of these, two units were in the hangar bay and two on the Flight Deck. The units themselves were two pressurized tanks and hose reels mounted on the back of a tow tractor. One tank held 80 gallons of liquid agent and the other, 120 lbs. of purple K powder. The hoses of the twin agents were incorporated into a single nozzle.

Airman Ernie Foster drove unit #20 back to the Port Side where a fog team was already in action. Airman Jim Lane drove unit #23 over to the Starboard side where the flames were now under Phantom #103, Hot Suitman Mike Piner took the nozzle of unit #23 while the other Hot Suitman, Donald Vaughn ran after unit #20.

On deck pilots were still shutting down and scrambling out of

From right to left, Purpleshirts manning gooseneck fog hose under intake of F-4 #106 right beside port twin agent unit which is about to go into action. Foreground, another fog gooseneck team coming out from port side. Hot Suitman Mike Piner runs to take over nozzle of starboard twin agent unit. Pilot of F-4 #202 runs out of the flames. Man down on deck behind twin agent unit. F-4 #103 already burning. Time approximately 0821. Official U.S. Navy photo, Osterbauer collection.

Men stand shoulder to shoulder on fog hose pulled across deck to cover a foam hose coming into action from the starboard side. Note canopy of spray from port twin agent unit near nose of 106. Official U.S. Navy photo, Osterbauer collection.

aircraft. The presence of jet exhaust hampered efforts to break out hoses in the Starboard cat walks and the foam hose farthest aft on that side was overtaken by the rapidly spreading fire. Pilots helped chase down and roll out burning men and strip off fuel-soaked clothes. The plane captain and Radar Intercept Officer of #202 were cut off from escape and had to jump from the Starboard corner, out as far as they could to get away from the roiling wake and fell 70 feet before they hit the water.

The pilot of #106, Air Force exchange pilot Major John Hefferman, credited with a MIG shoot-down flying from this deck the previous year, was wounded in the hand and arm in the second rocket detonation. As he got down from 106 his plane captain, Jim Ridenour, grabbed him and ran him across deck to the Island for shelter. As they got there corpsmen from Repair 7 Bravo were just arriving at this, their GQ Station. The corpsmen told the pilot to lay down while Ridenour ran back out on the Flight Deck. Major Hefferman complied with some difficulty. The deck was already covered with dead and dying and wounded.

Seventy-five miles west, in Radar picket station, *USS Bainbridge* (DLGN-25) received word of the *Enterprise* emergency at 0820:02. *Bainbridge* immediately rang up Flank Speed and came about to course zero nine zero and for the next two and a half hours slammed through rolling Pacific seas at 31 knots.

On the bridge Capt. Lee gave orders to activate the water wash down counter measures system. This was a series of flush deck nozzles evenly spaced throughout the Flight Deck to spray salt water in the event of a nuclear attack and rinse away contaminants. Not designed as a fire fighting device, the system might slow the spread of the fire and cool some of the weapons on deck. The various repair units at their GQ Stations were those responsible for opening the water washdown system valves in their areas. Word to activate the system was passed over the IMC and from Damage Control Central to all main repair parties. Capt. Lee watched the flaming deck, anxious to see the results of this order. Those F-4's lining the Portside with their weapons slung beneath them, were sitting squarely over banks of salt water nozzles of Group 12. He looked at his watch and noted the time. Nearly a minute had passed.

Burning fuel poured into both Port and Starboard cat walks and over the round down on the Fantail. Sheets of flame and smoke cascaded down to the surface of the water enveloping the Fantail and after Bay two area in heat and smoke. The fire in the catwalks destroyed communications lines and remote starting controls for high capacity Fog Foam Stations and lit off rows of rubber bags containing 12 man Life Rafts. The Flight Deck, Hangar and Hangar Bay CONFLAG Control Stations were all on the same circuit. When the circuitry was destroyed on the Flight Deck, communications and control were lost in the Hangar Bay.

The Legion of the Dead stood to rank in the mists, their vast arrays creating an amphitheater of formations. In the center, three figures stood forth. The foremost, wearing the Khaki of the American Navy, was flanked on one side by a senior officer of the Imperial Navy of Japan. On the other, a personage of ancient days, his raiment unidentifiable. The figure in Khaki held a closed book. This book would not be opened until the appointed time. There appeared before the officer with the book a new line of figures, facing him. At first there were five, then seven, then eight. The Legion of the Dead were not looking at the new souls. They were watching the Horseman. They saw him ride far out after the second attack and slow the charger into an easy loping turn. The Pale Horse threw his head and blew and snorted, foam and spittle flying. His mane and tail flowed and sawed like sea grass under the tides. The Rider let the winded steed slow to its own stride, all the while completing his long turn. He was coming back again.

The Legion of the Dead did not know the extent of the Horseman's ride nor did they know the count of the harvest. But in the few years since the appearance of these flat top ships, the Aircraft Carrier had swelled the ranks of the Legion of the Dead by many thousands. Would the next attack take hundreds at a single stroke as evidenced by the ranks of the *LISCOMB BAY*? There they stood, seven hundred strong, gathered up in an instant when their ship blew up and sank. Or would it be a day-long butchery like the slaughter on the carrier *Franklin*? There stood *Franklin's* men. No less than eight hundred thirty two, cut down by the Horseman's blade. The Legion of the Dead of the Sea, in languid serenity, watched and waited.

In the Hangar Bay the overhead sprinkling came on in both Bays 1 & 2 covering decks and aircraft with foam. The Hangar Deck Officer, Lt. Comdr. George Fisher came on deck to find his assistant officer, Lt. Thompson and the Hangar Deck Chief already organizing fire fighting efforts. Hose Teams were manned and fighting through the armored hatch on the Fantail and on the Port Side Jet Test Cell area and hoses were manned and ready in both bays.

Lt. Thompson assumed Hangar Deck Control and soon the loudspeakers blared throughout the cavernous hangar bays, "NOW ALL SQUADRON AND SHIPS ORDNANCEMEN ON THE HANGAR DECK REPORT TO HANGAR DECK CONTROL TO JETTISON WEAPONS!"

Lt. Comdr. Charles Brackin, the Ordnance Handling Officer, saw the initial detonation at 0819:26 on the flight deck monitor in Ordnance Control. He did not know what had gone off or what had possibly gone wrong but he knew the situation had to be stabilized fast or there would be hell to pay. He ran aft through the 03 level passageway. The passageway was filled with men running off in all directions in a high state of urgency, but it was fluid, without congestion. When he reached frame 159 he turned outboard and pounded up the ladder and emerged in the island at a dead run. Abruptly he stopped, to pick his way through the human wreckage already strewn about the deck. The sounds of suffering assailed him. The suppressed screams of the burned. The groans of the torn of body. The silence of shock of one who tried to halt the rush of intestines from pouring forth through his own fingers. Brackin high-stepped through the carnage and out through the starboard hatch onto the flight deck.

AO3 Billy Proffit was already there. Ships and squadron Ordnancemen immediately set about the task of getting weapons clear of the deck once they had seen the size of the fire back aft. Stacked behind the island for the third launch were four skids of MK-82's and four of LAU-10 rocket pods. In addition to these, several tubs of fuses and cans of 20MM were laying about. Billy Proffit started throwing the 20MM cans off #3 elevator while the others heaved up and staggered under the weight of the 500 pounders the few feet to the ordnance jettison chute just forward of #3 elevator. The first bomb rumbled down the chute. The second MK-82 promptly wedged itself sideways, jammed tight. Ordnancemen jumped down into the chute, kicking and prying. After herculean effort, they managed to break the bomb loose and with a shrieking protest of flying paint chips, it slid down and fell into the sea. Brackin had run up to help break the bottleneck. He had to shout to be heard above the din of the boiling flames back aft, "EVERYTHING OVER, SKIDS AND ALL! GET IT OFF! GET IT OFF!"

Big John Guillot, leader of Repair Five BRAVO near the starboard

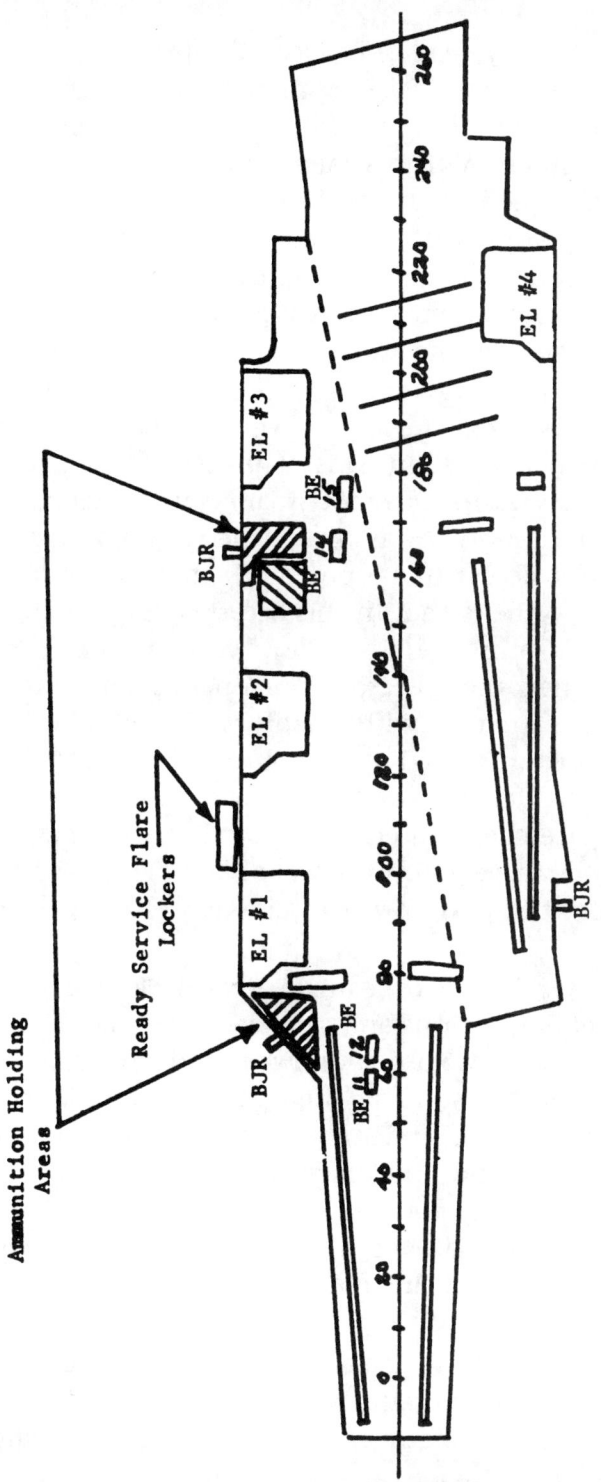

Ammunition Holding Areas and Ready Service Flare Lockers.

entrance to sick bay, had never seen his team muster so quickly for General Quarters. Five BRAVO's main area of responsibility was #2 and #3 enginerooms along with #2 auxiliary machinery room and aft on the mess decks. With his men returning from setting Condition ZEBRA, he got a head count and then got his OBA men ready. These were the men who wore the oxygen breathing apparatus. His fire teams were set and because the smell of smoke was getting heavy, he had all the others put their MK-5 gas masks on. No matter what was coming, these Repair teams would have to see it through.

The high capacity fog foam generator, #7, just off the main passageway was going full tilt. Five BRAVO men were constantly punching open five gallon cans of protein foam and feeding them into the hungry generator. Empty foam cans clattered about the deck. From where Five BRAVO was set up, the main passageway was joined by an off deck access to starboard which was the ladderway going straight up into the island. In this access passageway was the door to the pilots' elevator. John Guillot was still checking his men's equipment when the elevator door opened and out stepped three men carrying a stretcher with a badly wounded pilot in it. The pilots entire chest area was bleeding and burnt. Bits of smoldering, smoking flight suit were falling away along with a continuous dripping of blood. The stretcher bearers made what haste they could. Bloody shoes slid and staggered on the waxed tile deck. A gory red path was tracked across the passageway to sick bay. It was to be the first of many.

Henry Mendoza had begun to crawl. He was hit again by the second rocket detonations and as he lay there watched a hot suitman run up with a blast of purple K powder and extinguish both the pilot and Garcia. The hot suitman then gave the nozzle to someone else and grabbed the pilot under the arms and dragged him out. Other men had run forward and dragged out Garcia but Henry Mendoza was all alone. Nobody had come for him! He could feel Death's hand on his neck. The image of his own daughter flashed through his mind and he locked all his mental powers on this image. He had to live!

The flaming fuel was rapidly approaching when Henry Mendoza began to drag himself and his lifeless right leg forward. At the distance of an arms length, he could just keep pace ahead of it with all the speed and strength he had left in him. The intense heat was suffocating and burned his throat and lungs as he fought for breath from his exertions. Approaching the point of ignition, his clothes began to smoke.

The crewleader took his place on the hose. The two yellow shirts on the nozzle had given it over to the hot suitman and now they pressed ahead into the very jaws of Hell. They went under the direction of the Crash/Salvage Officer, W01 Jim Helton. Under the canopy of the fog applicator they advanced toward the inferno of #105. The hot suitman swung the applicator left and right, left and right, and the rest of the hose team felt a brief respite from the unimaginable heat from whatever direction the applicator moved. The flames were very nearly all around the fog team, the men wilting under heat which felt absolutely liquid. They clung to the cold hardness of the hose and tried to take what shelter they could from it. Wherever the fog spray went, the rest of the team whipsawed and undulated behind it, always seeking the shelter of the spray. The crewleader turned his head from the heat and hid behind the man on the hose in front of him. There he saw a pilot only a few yards away in a sitting position with his arms up and just beyond that, two red shirted ordnancemen down on the deck. In the time of that brief glimpse he saw the hideous sight of the fire race up and claim them. He saw them burn. The price of the TRUTH had risen.

"You gotta get up."

It was the sound of a voice coming from a distant place. Then it grew quiet again.

"You gotta get up!"

There it was again. Closer this time.

"GET UP!"

The tone and command of the voice made Frank Neumayer come awake with a start. He was aware, but he could not see. Something was pressing upon his eyes. And he had pain.

"GET UP! MOVE! YOU HAVE TO MOVE!"

He recognized the voice now. It was his own. He reached up to his face to alleviate the pressure on his eyes. The lens of his goggles was melted and pushing against his face. He pulled them away and blinked his eyes to focus. He was aware of the smell. The very air he breathed smelled burnt and spent. He was aware of burning sensations on his back and hand. He knew he was on fire and rolled to his back to smother it and beat his hand against his chest. His vision was coming back. He could see the blue sky and the outline of his aircraft, #113. The inside of his mouth and tongue were burned. He could hear a constant roaring behind him and knew it to be an immense inferno raging on the flight deck.

With the ship involved in a turn a small patch of deck remained on the port corner not covered by the flaming fuel. Frank Neumayer lay right in the center of this precarious sanctuary but he could see that it was growing smaller.

He could also see his condition. His hand was fully blistered. He had numerous wounds of the upper torso. He was paralyzed below the waist. The wreckage of his left leg was twisted around and bent back upon itself. His right leg was stiff and useless. He realized he was lying in a large spreading pool of his own blood. He knew from his condition that he was going to die. Why hadn't anyone helped him? He was all alone, The only way out would be to crawl over the fantail. Then he would only drown or be eaten by sharks. He could feel the life force draining from his body leaving him tired and peaceful. He made his peace with the Almighty. Dying wasn't so bad. He hoped his mom wouldn't take the news too hard. He wanted rest. He drifted.

"MANNED AND READY! MANNED AND READY! MANNED AND READY!"

The same report was repeated hundreds of times throughout the ship over a myriad of sound powered phone circuits. Each transmission was relayed to Damage Control Central in accordance with strict military discipline. Only space name, location and status were reported over the phones, keeping the lines clear and open for instructions. In Damage Control Central a grid board check-off list was marked as each Repair party and support unit called in, "MANNED AND READY!"

All Repair parties and units were on line except 7 ALPHA and support units 79 through 76. All these units covered the after third of the 03 Gallery deck level. The only communication that could be established was with unit 75 on the 03 level at frame 150. The phone talker of unit 75 reported in an excited voice, "Fire and heavy smoke aft in the 7 ALPHA area!"

Directly beneath the blazing inferno of F-4 #105, members of 7

ALPHA were trying to organize hose teams and tend and evacuate wounded coming down from the flight deck. Other members of 7 ALPHA and the after Repair units fought their way through streams of day sleeper evacuees in various stages of undress to get to their General Quarters stations, they were looking for others in helmets. Petty Officer 2nd, Jim Kemp, ran up the ladder to the 03 level, port main passageway, at frame 225. There, he had to step over two flight deckers down and bleeding with a corpsman over them trying to bind up some very bad wounds. Kemp ran aft to the fire plug at frame 235 where two hoses were being pulled out and men in action. Here he found Ray Friend, phone talker for 7 ALPHA, on the nozzle of a hose fighting fires in the head at frame 240. Burning fuel was pouring down into the space from holes in the overhead. Kemp took the nozzle of the second hose to back up Friend, Long and James as they stepped into the hatchway of the head. Other fire fighters were coming onto the scene as Marks and Holcomb of AIMD joined Kemp on the back up hose and Chief Douch dragged a wounded man out of the passageway. Then an incredible thing happened. The hoses went dead.

In the hangar bay, Lt. Comdr. Fisher tried to get the overhead foam sprinklers in Bay One stopped. The foam was already ankle deep and not really needed up there. With hangar crews trying to tighten up Bay One so that aircraft could be brought out of Bay Two, the foam on deck was more than just a nuisance. Tow tractors skidded, dual drive wheels spinning in the foam as aircraft were pushed and backed into every available space in Bay One, Hangar crews put their shoulders to the planes to assist the tractors on the slippery deck. Lt. Comdr. Fisher ran to #3 CONFLAG station to get the overhead sprinklers secured and the petty officer there said he had no control at all. Fisher noted that the control boxes were still safety wired shut. The CONFLAG watch also reported that they could not raise Damage Control on the 2JZ circuit to shut off the sprinklers.

Lt. Comdr. Fisher then ran back to order #4 elevator door closed because of fuel and smoke pouring in through the open well. The giant three section door, as high as the hangar bay, rumbled across its track sealing the elevator well and in the process, class Charlie fires erupted from the motors and circuitry from all the salt water pouring down on the door from overhead sprinklers. Fisher then ran back to Repair One ALPHA, fighting the fantail fire through the armored door and told them to get Damage Control to get the power off #4 elevator door because of the electrical fires that had started.

In Central Control, Comdr. Bill Neel ordered all available fire pumps brought on line. The gauges on the firemain showed that demand was exceeding supply. The ship had a total firemain capacity of 21,000 GPM with all 13 electric 1,000 GPM pumps and all four 2,000 GPM steam driven pumps on line. At the sounding of General Quarters, Condition ZEBRA was set segregating the firemain into six segments. The segments were, forward, midship and aft loops, both port and starboard. Total fire pump output was reduced to 17,000 GPM because #15 electric was disassembled with the impeller and upper casing on deck for a seal replacement. Ships instructions dictated that with both #15 and #14 electrics on the same suction line, both must be secured to provide double valve protection from the sea. These two pumps supplied water for the after port loop.

Comdr. Neel ordered valve 2-203-2 to remain open during the setting of ZEBRA to cross connect the after port with the midship port loop. Then he called up #2 plant about the status of #10 steam pump. This pump was down with a limiting governor malfunction and would take about an hour to put it all back together. Neel told them, "We don't have an hour! Get it back on!" Number 10 steam pump, along with number 7 electric, served the starboard midship loop.

All bilge pumping and flushing water was secured and cooling water to the Jet Blast Deflectors and Arresting Gear was shut down. While all available firemain assets were not yet on line, the demand of the fog foam and salt water hoses in action on the flight deck and 03 level exceeded 3,000 GPM. The hangar bay sprinkling groups depleted the supply by another 9,000 GPM.

The crewleader, like the others on the fog applicator team, hunched down and tried to shield his face behind his own shoulder. The tremendous heat from the towering billows of flame burned away exposed body hair and his very skin threatened to split apart. A twin agent unit to his immediate left had gone into action and the nozzleman, Ernie Foster, was making wide sweeps with the pressurized light water and had stopped the advance of the flames on that side. Donald Vaughn, the hot suitman on the gooseneck applicator had to forego the raging #105 and swing to the right because the flames had gone under the bombs and rockets of #106. The fog team watched in stunned horror as the fog spray hit the hot weapons and boiled away in steam.

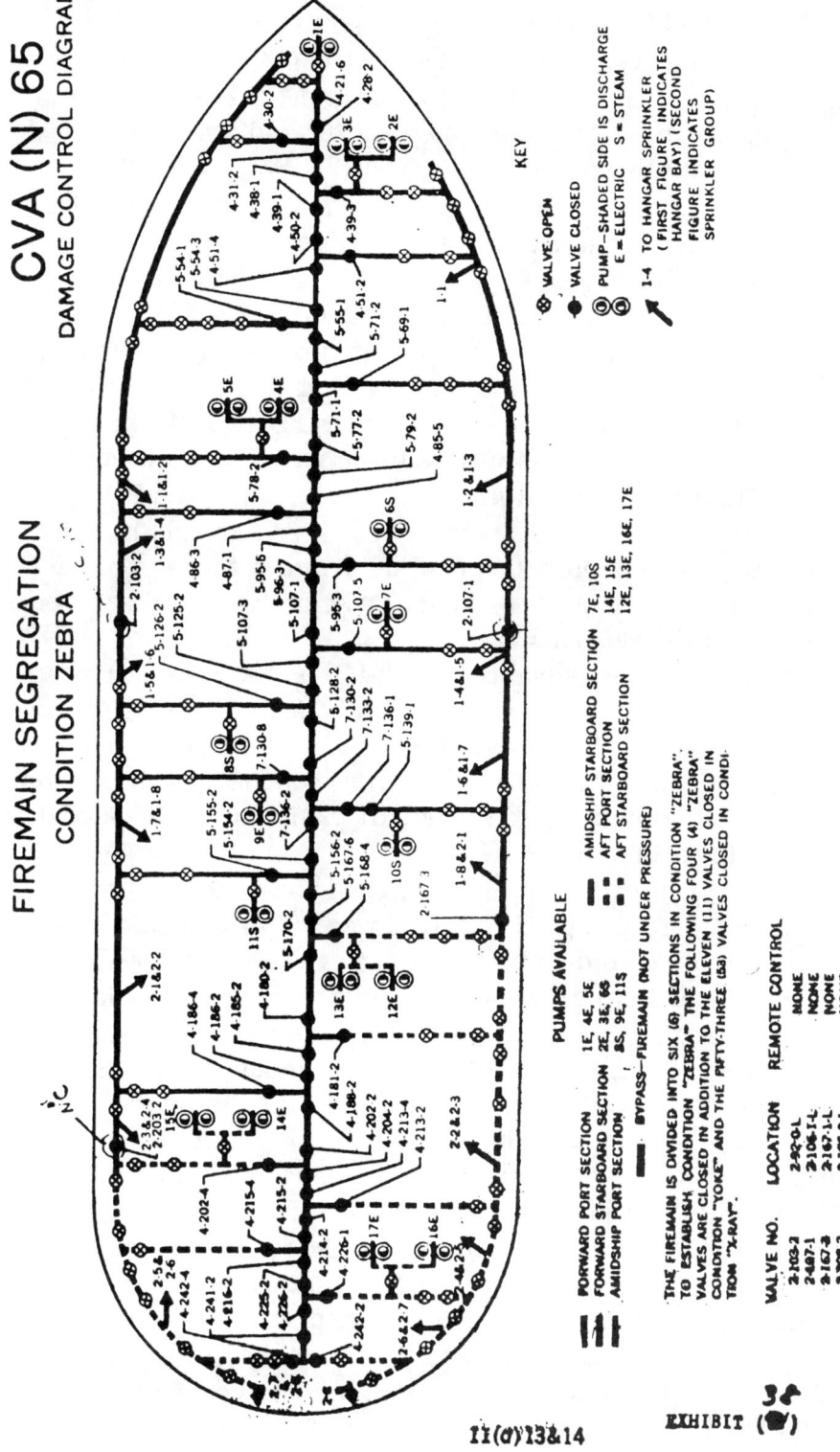

The spray of the fog canopy appeared to diminish and the team had to press in even closer to try and cool the weapons. Steam bubbled and hissed from the bombs under #106. The situation became all the more desperate when tractor and aircraft tires lost in the flames began to explode, "WHUMP! WHUMP! BOOMP!"

Sparks blew out from the wall of flame and rose overhead as liquid oxygen tanks and ejection seats started to go off, The fog team was fully committed to cooling the weapons under #106. Now, they could not even back out. They were trapped.

The crewleader was mesmerized watching the flames licking the weapons on 106 not ten yards away. The nozzleman swung the gooseneck from the bombs to the rockets and back to the bombs. The bright gold fuses of the bombs were turning darker. They were losing the race. They would need a miracle.

From the right, an advancing puddle of foam splashed its way down the deck and pushed and fluffed under the bombs of 106. Deliverance was at hand. It was Jerry McKenzie's foam hose, brought into action in the very nick of time.

McKenzie's hose advanced under the cover of a protective canopy of fog from a gooseneck team marching into battle with them. A blanket of foam was spread under 106 and stopped the advance of the fire there. The crewleader watched the hot suitman then swing his cooling fog to the left knocking down a bank of flame closing on his team.

From the bridge Capt. Lee weighed every option he had as Commanding Officer. Speed and wind were in his immediate control. He would use the wind to blow the flames aft. When the ship came about he would have 28 knots of wind confronting the flames. He could increase this to 50 or 60 knots of wind with a high speed run but this would hamper efforts to pull out aircraft as yet uninvolved and preclude any assistance he wished from the destroyers. He could put the ship over in a hard rudder turn, or a series of them and perhaps roll weapons and fuel overboard. Perhaps. But this would negate his wind advantage and make aircraft movement impossible.

Capt. Lee also knew he had men in the water and anything but a steady course would make finding and rescuing these men extremely precarious. Capt. Lee watched the firefighting teams pushing into the fire, responding to the exhortations of the Air Officer. A tractor was beginning to pull A-7 #310 off #4 elevator and another was backing in to #312 on the starboard side. The men were fighting, and fighting bravely. As Captain of the ship he had considered every option available and concluded that his only course lay with the crew. Indeed, they had trained for this. Now, it was up to them. Capt. Lee looked at his watch again. Nearly three minutes had passed.

Soon, he knew. It would begin very soon.

On the second deck, portside, frame 167, Yeoman 2nd Fred Whitehead Jr. put on his gear and assumed the duties of Repair 3 ALPHA phone talker. The Repair 3 locker adjoined the #4 aircraft elevator machinery room and was responsible for the 2nd deck and below, aft. No word of what was going on had reached the interior manned spaces of the ship. All hands did their duty with the absolute conviction that the Big "E" had been attacked!

"BY WHO? THE RUSSIANS, THE BASTARDS! THEY ARE ALWAYS TRAILING US WITH THOSE *&!!#@$ TRAWLERS! BUT HOW? MISSILE ATTACK! SUBMARINES!"

The Repair teams went about setting up and breaking out gear and all the while an ominous haze of smoke accumulated on the overhead. The smell of smoke was very heavy. A brief, urgent message flashed over the phone circuit, "Fire on the 03 level!" and the lines went deathly silent again. Then the lights went out and the soft beams of bulkhead mounted battle lanterns came on.

The now darkened passageways looked like lonely avenues lit at intervals by dim street lamps on a dark and foggy night. The wisps of smoke swirled and rolled about the lantern beams, absorbing the light.

In Forward Battle Dressing station Lt. Richard Martin had mustered in all hands. Assigned to this station were three corpsmen, one dental technician and eight stewards and all were present. Everyone could hear distant rumblings and feel strange vibrations and a grip of tense nervousness held them all. Lt. Martin addressed his men, "O.K. guys, this is what we were all trained for and this is what we had going through the period of refresher training and drills. Now we are going to have to put our cards on the table."

Lt. Richard Martin held the undivided attention of all his personnel. No sooner had he finished his speech, when he heard a rumble to his back and turned to see the bomb elevator doors roll open and out staggered three bloody flight deckers.

One of the great decisions of the day was to use the forward bomb elevators to facilitate the evacuation of wounded from the flight deck to the forward battle dressing station. The island itself was full to overflowing with wounded and as hatches slammed shut from the setting of condition ZEBRA, the dead and dying and stricken were soon heaped by scores all around the island.

A02 Dennis Downs was the only one left in Flight Deck Control. His job was Ordnance coordinator and had phone communication with the bridge, Damage Control, forward and after bomb assemblies and the bomb elevators. This was his battle station. Everyone else in the normally bustling Control room had gone out on deck. Downs had already contacted his men with the order to jettison everything on deck, now he phoned the bomb elevator operators with an order from the Weapons Officer to start sending wounded down the forward bomb elevators.

After giving the order to use the forward bomb elevators to get wounded off the flight deck Comdr. Reisinger, the Weapons Officer, called the Combat Information Center. He knew there was a live missile with warhead in the port point defense launcher and wanted it fired. There was no way to jettison from the system. The port launcher was already engulfed in flames and Reisinger wanted the missile fired before it exploded in the launcher. CIC gave the order, "FIRE!"

The gunner for the port defense missile launcher never heard the order to fire. He was fighting for breath, trying to keep from swallowing any more of the Pacific Ocean about a half mile behind the ship. The same fireball which roared into the port catwalk and lit off the port missile launcher had driven him to the edge and then over. It was jump or die.

Even as wounded were brought forward on the flight deck to the forward bomb elevators, weapons stacked there on skids for the third launch were being thrown over the side by ships and squadron Ordnancemen. Six 1,000 lb. bombs and eight 500 pounders fell into the sea just forward of #1 aircraft elevator.

Joe Rosa didn't have the time to put on socks when he was dragged from his rack at the sounding of "General Quarters." He only paused long enough to pull on his pants, with no belt, and jump into his boots. Now, shin deep in foam in Bay One, he slipped on unsteady footing to the #1 elevator well with a long belt of 20MM ammo draped around his neck and shoulders. His feet sloshed loosely in his boots and his foam soaked pants sagged and then dropped free from his hips. Joe hiked them up again with one hand and held them and made it to the well where the others were throwing belts of ammo into the sea. And all through this effort, aircraft were towed and wrestled, and foam was coming down and a continuous falling of bombs, some still strapped to skids, were slamming into the water just outside #1 elevator well.

Lash Hansborough hurried down the last ladder into #4 plant. He told Lt. (j.g.) Wanner to, "Get every pump we have on line!" He wanted a full pumpline on of three feed, three feed booster and three condensate pumps in addition to the steam driven sea water injection pump for the main engine condenser and both reactor auxiliary cooling water pumps.

The atmosphere in #4 plant was very tense. With hearing and feeling the only antennae to detect danger, those senses became very acute. There was no talking. Every man became a sensor unto himself. Faces beaded with sweat and the stamp of intense concentration turned upward to scan the overhead. Above them, somewhere, was a danger.

Lt. Comdr. Jack Parks, Flight Deck Officer, waved the tow tractor away from 614 and sent him to 310. Initially they wanted to bring 614 out but the tanker was holed and leaking and appeared ready to burst into flame. With McKenzie's foam and the other fog hose stretched across the path of the tractor, LPO Billy Hawk had some men lift the foam hose over the tractor driver's head as he brought out 310. McKenzie's team was still frenziedly blanketing the fires under 106's weapons, unmindful of what was going on behind them. They were suddenly pulled backward and the stream of foam began falling short of the fires. The men around the tractor lifted the hose higher to clear the nose of 310 and the McKenzie's team surged forward again to get the foam back under the weapons. The hose pulled taut under the intake of 310 and the tractor continued to pull. The hose bent then kinked, then split and blew apart in a blinding spray of foam. The tractor kept going, slowly enough so that the fog hose was successfully looped over the tractor and aircraft allowing them to pass.

The crewleader and those on his fog team were unaware of any of this. They were stunned by the hideous spectacle of a figure coming out of the wall of flame on his hands and knees. How could anyone still be alive in that fire? The hot suitman swung the fog applicator to the burning figure and put him out while several others ran forward to drag him away from the fire. All his clothes and fingers had been burned away. It was the pilot of 105.

"You have to WAKE UP AND MOVE!"

Frank Neumayer blinked open his eyes. It was that persistent voice again, the voice of warning. He was tired but he fought hard to focus his vision. Blurred at first, the images began to swim into alignment. There was a peculiar fizzling and popping sound very close at hand. He heard this audibly, above the roaring of the flames. He looked down and saw the spreading fire had met his pool of blood. The blood bubbled and cracked and boiled. The sole of his right shoe was on fire.

"So this was it," Frank Neumayer thought. "What a way to die!" He hoped it wouldn't hurt too much. Just one last look at what blue sky he could still see above his aircraft. His eyes widened. He saw movement.

Jim Ridenour had gone back on deck after taking his pilot over to the island. He ran back aft on the starboard side with a gang of others, running to man hoses, running to help wounded. Ridenour ran back to 103 looking to see if the crew had gotten out. The fire was almost completely across the deck and it was under 103. The pilots were already out so he ran around behind 103 to the catwalk and jumped down and found Randy Lorimor nursing a wounded arm and shoulder from the second rocket detonations. He got Lorimor on his feet and they started forward in the catwalk only to be stopped by flames spilling down from the flight deck. They backed off and went back up on deck between 103 and 202. Where they stood was now the only place on the starboard corner which was not burning. The way forward was blocked and the fire was burning under the line of F-4's across the fantail.

They ran and jumped from the starboard wing tank of 114 up onto the wing and scrambled over the fuselage and onto the port wing. In this way they hopped from 114 to 214 to 113.

Frank Neumayer saw the movement and recognized the figures as his friends Randy and Rhino. He saw what they were doing and knew where they would go. This was a chance he never expected. It was the only chance he would get.

Ridenour and Lorimor went over the fuselage of 113 and down onto the port wing. They didn't see their friend dragging himself towards the port catwalk with a strength born of desperation. They dropped to the deck and then into the catwalk at fueling station #30.

They got down into a crouch to shield themselves from the heat and moved quickly forward toward the ladder going down to the 03 level. They didn't see Frank Neumayer drag himself over the scupper just above that ladder. They moved with all speed for the safety which they thought lay just inside that hatchway at the bottom of the ladder. Only ten rungs to safety! Now six, now three!

Lorimor and Ridenour were knocked sprawling when the nearly lifeless body of Frank Neumayer crashed down on them at the bottom of the ladder.

The Rider on the Pale Horse rode up the ships wake and into the smoke and flame again. The charger tried to break free and run through the men on deck but the Rider restrained him. With a mighty hand the Rider gripped the reins and held the bucking stallion in check. He would wait for the opportune moment. Even now he could see a line of men nearly shoulder to shoulder across the entire deck. He would wait for the ranks to fill.

Jack Parks had another fog applicator coming into action on the port side. He had them add on extra lengths until the hose was long enough to cross the deck and give some cover to a foam hose coming into action from the starboard side at #1 wire. On the starboard side what wasn't in flames was covered in smoke so black and thick as to make visibility difficult. Henry Mendoza was still crawling for his life in the smoke just ahead of the racing flames but nobody saw him. With the ship still in its turn, the wind was blowing directly from port to starboard.

On the 03 level Steve Bell of VAQ-132 and the rest of the day sleepers were finally awakened by all the commotion of the hose teams fighting the fire in the head at frame 240. They jumped out of their racks and onto the soapy deck and slid and fell and grabbed what clothes they could. Friend and Kemp had backed out of the head and had sent Long over to the starboard side to see if there was any pressure over there.

At 0822:45 The *Stoddart* had boiler 1A re-lit and changed speed to 17 knots while she stationed the rescue detail. Jim Smith climbed the escape ladder to the main deck hatch to see what was going on. The *Rogers* had set the emergency assistance team and was abeam of *Enterprise* at 1000 yards. Steve O'Brien was on the ASROC deck taking pictures of the towering column of smoke which reached the height of the clouds and spread a vast black blanket under them cutting off the sunlight.

Lorimor and Ridenour were shocked and staggered at the condition of their friend. The severity of his wounds momentarily overwhelmed them until he managed a weak, "Help . . . me."

"We have to stop the bleeding!" Lorimor said, and immediately took off his belt and made a tourniquet on Neumayer's left leg. While he was doing this the flight deck rumbled and thumped and Ridenour ran into the 03 level to find something to carry him with. Lorimor stripped off Neumeyer's belt and made a tourniquet for the other leg, up at the thigh. Then Ridenour came running back with a blanket that he had ripped from the first rack he came to.

"We'll have to carry him in this! Let's go! We have to get out of here!" said Rhino, well aware of the weapons on those planes.

"Wait! Give me your belt!" It would only be a delay of a few seconds and with this Randy Lorimor tied the crushed and splintered left leg together with the right at the ankles.

Throughout the propulsion spaces watchstanders monitored firemain pressure gauge needles as they rose rapidly. For the aft port and midship loop the pressure rose, up from 75, past 100, through 125 towards the 150 PSI mark to be maintained in time of fire. The needles stopped abruptly at 135 PSI. There they held for a second, then wavered, then fell away down below 75 again.

When Lt. (j.g) Dave Fusco, scene leader for 7 BRAVO in the island got there, the area was already filled to capacity with wounded. Repair people were still arriving and men were trying to get equipment out and get organized. The first thing Fusco did was to clear out the many men who had brought and were still bringing in casualties from off deck. Fusco sent them out and gave his corpsmen and stretcher bearers room to maneuver. Hoses were rigged and two teams were manned and ready to fight on the 05 and 07 levels of the island. The 04 level became a staging area for sorting casualties and the Crash/Salvage locker was rapidly filled with dead and wounded as first aid was applied and Midship Battle Dressing station, just one deck below was breaking out gear and tables and getting set up.

The Rider held the Pale horse in check in the flames and permitted him to stomp and kick and finish off those down on deck underfoot. The Rider looked down from his mount with menace at those who would bar his way. Both horse and Rider were of gigantic proportions compared to the lowly mortals confronting them. The Rider held up his sword in a gesture of dedication and paused for the right moment.

The foam team advanced from starboard to mid deck under the fog canopy and unleashed a stream of foam towards 105. Both twin agent units were expending the last of their light water reserves. The fog team fighting 105 was holding its ground and another foam hose was advancing down the port side. Foam hoses were coming down the starboard side from forward and aft of the island. The A-7, #310, was towed clear of #4 elevator and the F-4 from #3 catapult was being towed updeck.

The last of the ships crew were reaching their General Quarters stations. On the 01 level, BM2 James Collins Snipes and two others raced up the ladder to the head at frame 240 on the 02 level. They had one ladder to go to get to their repair units. On the second deck Airman Apprentice King Merendino ran past Repair 3 ALPHA in the darkened passageway to the hatch leading down to the dry cleaning plant. He got through just as the hatch was being closed and dogged down.

Henry Mendoza was screaming for help but no one saw him. Then, a Zuni rocket motor roared into life from the flaming wing of 106. Sparks and flames of thrust shot out both ends of the tube and the men on hoses tried to make themselves smaller as they waited to die. Henry Mendoza looked over at the rocket blast and noticed Del Girty standing in the catwalk between 106 and 614 throwing another hose up on deck.

In the dark of Repair 3 ALPHA, a bleeding man was dragged by two others past the Repair team towards sick bay. A bloody track was seen marking their passage in the gloom. No one had as yet given any explanation as to what was happening because very few actually knew. Phone talker Fred Whitehead dared to break the suspense with a cryptic, haunting question to his friend, Joe Smith, somewhere on the sound powered net. The net had been tomb silent, in battle discipline. Then, the halting words, "Hey Joe . . . what's going on?"

The rocket motor had suddenly burned out, the propellant expended. The men on deck straighten up. It was anticlimax.

The bombs on the flaming deck under 105 reached reaction temperature. The terrible swift sword came crashing down. The time recorded was 0823:01

This photo taken after the first bomb detonation at 0823:01. Explosion not visually recorded by Osterbauer. Many men missing from original hose teams. Extreme right, Two men lead a wounded man away. Two yellowshirts on gooseneck nozzle at nose of 106. Flight Deck Officer walks from right to left. Starboard twin agent unit still in action. Official U.S. Navy photo, Osterbauer collection.

From right to left, 310 stopped, second line of defense forming across deck. Nose and cockpit of 106 covered in foam. Stream of foam being directed on the hulk of 105 from starboard foam hose now at mid deck. Gooseneck team covers fog team fighting 105. Men taking down chains of 312 with aircraft next in line in flames. Official U.S. Navy photo, Osterbauer collection.

4. THE FURY

The pressure of detonation broke up the 100 pound plate of the flight deck inside the ballistic shield and created a 8 foot x 7 foot hole from frame 243 to frame 240 where it sheared off at the bulkhead. The sides and aft end of the hole were petaled as if punched through its periphery with a can opener.

The blast and broken up flight deck plate blew down through the head on the 03 level, wrecking it and ventilation ducts and severing the salt water firemain. Communication lines and electrical cables were blown apart, power was lost and the debris ripped five separate holes through the 03 level deck and into the 02 level head below.

Bulkheads were sheared and ripped vertically. Blast and debris carried through the 02 level deck wrecking the entire space, and bursting through four holes into the Master-at-Arms shack on the 01 level where the inboard bulkhead was sheared and two pieces of flight deck plate cratered the deck but not penetrating. One piece did, however, tearing an 11 x 14 inch hole through the deck and stopping at the main deck below.

The heat of explosive burst the 03 level aflame and shortly burning JP-5 poured down through, draining from the flight deck and fired the 02 and 01 level compartments between frames 240 and 245 and began leaking down onto the main deck.

On the 03 level, Lorimor and Ridenour had just entered the main passageway and started forward carrying Neumayer in the blanket when the bulkhead of the outboard passageway bowed out suddenly from the explosion to within a few inches of the inboard one and flexed, just as quickly, back again. The three were blown into a heap with the certain knowledge that their delay had spared their lives.

Steve Bell and friends were also knocked down as they ran

Aircraft arrangement abreast and aft of the island at 0823:01. Aircraft #310 stopped with severed main gear.

forward in the port passageway. A rush of hot wind and things flying overtook them and laid them low. They regained their footing without a pause and never looked back, and ran even faster than before.

The two hose teams of Kemp and Friend were blown through the midship compartment to very nearly the starboard side of the ship by the blast of hot gasses. Laid out and stunned, they were disoriented for a time because all the lights had been knocked out. They made their way back to the port side and there, on deck, were two of their own down with wounds.

The explosion had blown out a main ventilation duct and a fireball had raced throughout the course of the ductwork. All the way down in darkened laundry on the 3rd deck, King Merendino and the thirty others assigned to this space felt the ship shaking from the tremendous blow. They grabbed for what handhold they could and looked at one another in wild astonishment. Then a rumble of rolling thunder and the space was lit up as a ball of fire roared out of the ventilation system.

As one man all thirty ran for the escape ladder to the 2nd deck. The topmost man seized the dogging wheel and spun it viciously as the stampede sought to escape the hellfire belching forth from the ventilation duct. They had to get out! Others, many others, pressed close on the ladder and many hands frantically turned the wheel. The dogging wheel spun, then tightened and came to a wrenching stop. Unbelievably, the wheel began turning back the other way.

Wild choruses of protest and damnation rang out from the laundry as the ladder was assaulted by as many as could gain purchase and all were turning mightily on the dogging wheel. Just above them, a nearly equal number of repair personnel fought to keep the hatch dogged closed. The repair men thought the ship had been torpedoed! Their responsibility was to keep the ship watertight and only Damage Control could authorize the opening of ZEBRA fittings. A series of urgent questioning's were shouted from above to be heard through the closed hatch, "IS THERE WATER COMING IN?!"

At once a howl of bedlam from below as all assumed to answer. A renewed mighty struggle on the dogging wheel and shoulders pounded against the hatch. Cursing and shouts of admonition from below, the melee of struggle. Blows were exchanged.

Finally a single coherent voice was heard shouting up through the hatch, "There is no water! Let us Out! There is FIRE! FIRE!".

With that the hatch was allowed to be opened and hose teams stood ready for what came from below. The laundrymen streamed out through the open hatch cursing and shaking fists and evacuated forward. The repair teams were thankful these men were permitted to get out, but they had to stay. The realization that those thirty laundrymen would have had to die beneath that closed hatch had there been water rushing in settled heavily on all those in the repair teams. Fred Whitehead heard over his phones the first reports and called them out to his team, "Fire in the Master-at-Arms shack! Fire 02-240-4-L! Fire main deck frame 240, port!"

The repair team stood to their posts in the smoky gloom. They stood ready in OBA's and helmets and gas masks with first aid gear and charged hoses. Those fire reports were the next three decks almost directly above them. The situation was tense. The repair teams knew that they would NOT be evacuated. They would fight it out here and win or die.

Chief Lee thought that with the fuel pouring down from the elevator, the hangar bay must have blown up. He looked at the dogged door which stood between them and the hangar bay and considered the possibility of all being aflame on the other side. There was an escape hatch on the deck leading down to the messdecks and he told his men to evacuate down there.

These men had the same trouble with the Marines on the other side of the hatch as the laundrymen had with the repair party. Finally, after much convincing, the hatch was allowed to open and down went Chief Lee's men to the second deck and filed quickly past the bakery where an irate baker shook an implement in his fist at them and threateningly accused, "You !&#$!! airedales are making my bread fall!"

The effect of the detonation on the densely packed hose teams on the flight deck was frightful. The hose teams were in so close, with distances ranging from 20 feet to the port hose teams to perhaps 50 feet to those on the starboard side, that the first and second ranks of firefighters and nearly everyone aft of the island, were cut down cleanly as a scythe stroke. Blast and flame and hails of metals ripped into and through flesh and bone with the most extreme violence.

The shock of the blow left everyone momentarily senseless. Some were down wounded, some down unconscious. Some were down in flames, some down forever. A terrific blast of sparks and flaming junk was blown in various trajectories. They whizzed and screeched across deck or shot upward, then fell from the sky. Men rose up from the rush of adrenalin and ran in retreat, some for a few steps only to fall again under the hail of flaming, falling wreckage. Ghostly specters rose alternately from the dead of the flaming moonscape and staggered in shock to their feet and numbly captured flopping hoses and resolutely took up the fight again.

In Primary everyone was stunned by the explosion and the shrapnel that hit all about the island. Lt. McLauglin saw the terrible carnage wrought on deck. Both twin agent units were knocked out. Hoses flopped about wildly, geysering spumes of foam and salt water. Men were on fire, the wounded moved feebly, the dead were still. Other men ran towards the fray and those down were mercifully dragged out. The A-7, #310, had been stopped cold with its port main gear severed. The tractor driver lay slumped across the wheel. The F-4 being towed up deck from #3 catapult was holed in the starboard wing and wing tank and the starboard tire was blown into shreds. The tractor continued to pull however, and the F-4 was dragged lurching over to the edge of #2 elevator where its leaking fuel streamed down through the slatting. The Air Boss was bellowing through the bullhorn at the men on deck to take up the fight.

The crewleader had stood in line on the fog hose looking into the wall of fire when the world flashed into a light of blinding purity. And the light was white heat, a heat much hotter than the wall of flames. They were blasted by a thermal charge of absolute energy as if they stood before the very Gates of Hell and those gates burst forth and vented Hell's furies upon them. They were blasted by the wave of searing heat and force and power while all round about talons ripped and claws slashed amid the rush of howling demons. All driven to incredible velocity by the sound of the detonation. Shocking in sudden completeness. Awesome in hollow finality. The sound was a single, terrible, Base Note.

They tumbled, blown by the force which contorted and crushed and sought to tear away all. The crewleader's brain pounded with the echoes of the cataclysm. The echoes reverberated on and on and he was carried along with their irresistible tide. The waves of the sound swept him, clear of the ship, clear of the sea. Along he tumbled, clear of the earth, the beautiful earth of blue and white and green as it spun gracefully, serenely upon its axis. Into the weightlessness of space where the sound would range forever as a succession of radio waves. Over and over, the sound hammered him and he was swept along, past the moon, past the planets, past the stars and on into deep space, into the farthest reaches of the galaxies. Through the cosmic winds and solar dusts and past the farthest Quasars and into the cold nothingness of the black void he tumbled, swept along helplessly by the pounding of the sound.

On the bridge Ens. Mahumed, as Officer of the Deck, was concerned with getting radio calls out and driving the ship. He stole an occasional look aft towards the fire but noted Capt. Lee calmly standing there and thought the situation must be under control. He resumed his lookout forward and watched the considerable activity on the deck below. Aircraft handling teams were moving planes up to the bow to make room for others to be towed up from Fly three. Even as they were doing this the bow water washdown system groups came on and drenched everyone with salt water. The jettisoning of ordnance continued through the soaking and everything appeared in good order. Then the deafening blast of the explosion and the heaving of the ship. The ballistic safety glass windows in the bridge flexed in and out from the concussion. Junk and burning debris flew past the windows, some impacting far forward amid the aircraft and men on the bow.

Ens. Mahumed took another look back. The fire had spread and the hose teams had been devastated. Many men were being dragged away. He thought of how high above the fire he was here on the 010 level. Then he looked down at the water. If he had to jump, it was 125 feet below.

Bill Proffit and the gang of ordnancemen were still throwing over weapons behind the island when 105's forward section blew. Metal and shrapnel tore into the island structure above and all around them. What did not penetrate fell smoking back to the deck. The Air Gunner ran up to Bill and thrust a key into his hand and told him to run forward and jettison the ready service flare lockers. Bill Proffit ran up to frame 105 in the starboard catwalk, between #1 and #2 elevators and unlocked the jettison handle. Then, and he had always wanted to do this, he gave the handle a yank and 178 MARK 24 paraflares, each of flaked magnesium and 2 million candle power, dropped into the blue Pacific.

Dennis Downs stayed at his post in Flight Deck Control. From his position he could see from the protruding windows both forward and aft. He answered the bank of phones on the bulkhead and most of the time never really knew who was on the other end. "What's going on up there?!!" Downs would give out as much as he knew, "The entire aft end is on fire! There are weapons on deck!!"

"Will there be any more explosions?!!" Downs took a look out the window. He knew it was inevitable, "Yes!!"

"YOU HAVE TO GET BACK IN THERE MEN, YOU HAVE GOT TO GET BACK IN THERE!!" Dennis Downs heard the Air Boss shouting direction over the bullhorn. He stole another quick look out the window. The most awful sights he had ever seen were piling up thick just outside the window and being dragged past. Another phone rang and he answered it, "Will there be any more wounded? Are there any more wounded coming down?!!"

Dennis Downs looked away from the window to his left to the open hatch and the passageway, and the Crash/Salvage locker facing him. He saw the streaks of blood on the bulkheads and the stacks of dead and dying in the locker. The voice on the phone was insistent, "Will there be any more wounded?!!" He looked again back out the window. "LET'S GET BACK AND FIGHT, MEN, WE'VE GOT TO FIGHT!! WE WILL LOSE THE SHIP, MEN!"

Downs saw that they were going back in again, re-manning the hoses. "Yes! More wounded!" he said, and shuddered as he did so, "Many wounded! MANY WOUNDED!!"

Someone was finally coming to get Henry Mendoza. With all the men down from the blast there were many coming back to drag them away and one was running for him. Henry recognized the man. It was the blueshirt, Bobby Ward. Henry held out his hand as Ward ran to him. He was saved. Then a terrific racket erupted in the starboard catwalk just across from them by the starboard missile launcher. Three lockers containing 125 sodium igniters went up like so many Roman candles with sparks and shooting fireballs flying everywhere.

Ward hunched down and waited for the explosion and Mendoza screamed at him and got his attention. With that Bobby Ward grabbed Henry Mendoza with his fists and lifted him as easily as a rag doll and ran up deck with him where they met a stretcher team coming back. Bobby Ward dumped Mendoza in the stretcher and the bearers took him at a run to the back of the island.

At Repair 5 BRAVO the pilots elevator was bringing the torn and burned down as fast as it could be cycled. John Guillot had his men keep the route to sick bay cleared to let them pass as evacuees from back aft were streaming forward. The 5 BRAVO men took whatever firefighting gear those coming forward were carrying. The deck was wet and streaked with foam, blood and JP-5. John Guillot had some men with swabs clean the deck after each passage to insure footing on the slippery deck. He also had three men with swabs and buckets whose sole duty was cleaning out the pilots elevator before it went back up. This was grim work with pools of coagulating blood and smells and bits of flesh and bone left behind.

In Forward Battle Dressing Station, the first three casualties had no sooner been patched up and moved out of the way than the bomb elevator doors rumbled open disclosing six badly wounded in stretchers. Bearers ran into the elevator and brought the wounded out to the waiting tables. There were severely burned, amputations, hemorrhage. Lt. Martin began a closed cardiac massage on one whose heart had stopped.

The Battle Dressing Station men were presented with agony and suffering far beyond what any training might have prepared them for. These pitiful beings in stretchers were nearly beyond help and suddenly put into their care. The men overcame shock and revulsion and pitched in without question and did their duty. Clothes were cut away, bleeding stopped, wounds cleaned, burn jelly and battle dressings applied, and all amid the most traumatic of conditions. Urine, Blood, Vomit, Brains, Feces, Bone, Bile, Intestines.

The buck stopped here and the men did not flinch. They couldn't. There was no time. The bomb elevator doors rumbled open again and another load of suffering was dragged out onto the red decks

At After Battle Dressing station, frame 220, 03 level portside, the men never had a chance to get set up before the explosion at 0823:01 wrecked the space, which was a squadron ready room. Filing cases and cabinets were knocked over and squadron gear littered the deck. The emergency water supply broke and water was draining into the mess.

Corpsmen were dragging men out from the terror back aft and were stacking them in the passageway. Head wounds, broken legs, smoke inhalation, they were loaded into stretchers with no time for splints and evacuated forward out of the increasing smoke and heat. Repair party men in OBA's swept through the area moving everyone out, evacuating forward. One of the corpsmen went back into the smoke and hot darkness aft on the portside and reappeared a short time later dragging two more wounded. These also were quickly moved out.

Frank Neumayer was vaguely aware of being dragged down the steps of a ladder in the blanket. Lorimor had no strength in his arm and shoulder and could only hold onto the corners. Rhino held the bottom corners and did the dragging while keeping Neumayer from spilling out. Frank Neumayer felt the scraping and banging of the ladder steps on his back but he didn't care. It didn't hurt. Nothing hurt. His friends were with him and they would get him out. He was safe. He drifted.

The crewleader had passed through the solar system and gone beyond, so far out there were not even stars any more. The pounding in his head had turned to an incessant high pitched shriek such as an escape of steam under pressure. The universe had become totally black and cold and there was . . . rain? HUH?! He could feel drops of water on his face. "HUH?" He realized he was staring into the blackness of the dense smoke overhead and then remembered that there was fire. FIRE!!

The crewleader staggered to his feet and got back on the fog hose. The two yellow shirts were still there on the nozzle but there were many others missing. The flames rose ever higher and tentacles of burning fuel sought to flank and envelope them.

In Central Control, watchstanders reported firemain pressure dangerously low and still falling in the port aft and midship loops. Comdr. Neel knew there must be a break in the main in the port frame 240 area due to the violence of the explosion and the fires reported down to the main deck there. He ordered valve 2-103-2 opened, cross connecting the forward port with the aft and midship port loops. The pressure gauge needles for these mains would rise only to 50 pounds per square inch as the desperately needed salt water was bled off through the bow groups of the water washdown system. They would fall again when the midship water washdown groups would shortly be activated.

From the Air Boss, from the 03 and 02 level repair units, from hangar bay hose teams there were urgent calls to Central for water. Starboard flight deck hoses would slow and then stop. Then they would sputter and pulse and then stop again. The hose teams would press forward as the streams fell short of their intended targes and entire teams stood exposed fighting with nothing but the merest piddling of water and foam coming out of the hoses.

Nick Lasovich was helping drag out another foam hose from forward on the angle deck. They played the hose out to its length and signaled frantically for someone to charge it. Men in the catwalk opened the valve in anticipation of what was to come, but nothing came. There was no water.

In the darkness and flame of the 03 level the remnants of 7 ALPHA gathered their wounded up and dragged them back towards the starboard side. Day sleepers were still spilling out of compartments and dispersed repair units were getting organized and evacuating everyone. The entire area was coal mine black with smoke and stalwart men pressed into the heat and uncertainty to come to grips with the danger, heedless of the situation just above their heads.

In the propulsion spaces #10 steam pump was put back on line with no limiting governor and a man was stationed with it to manually control the steam feed. A gang of men were working furiously to get #15 electric back together and strong backs heaved up the 150 lb. impeller by hand and set it back into the lower casing. Comdr. Neel ordered steam chest pressure raised from the normal 500 to the maximum allowable 550 lbs.

As the fires were reported in to Damage Control, the Bosun of the Watch passed the information throughout the ship over the 1MC. "Class ALPHA, BRAVO fires, Fantail, main deck! Fires, port side, frame 240 main deck, 01, 02, 03 levels, Class ALPHA, BRAVO. Class CHARLIE fires, Bay Two, #4 elevator door!"

AO3 Ron Ruland of GM Division had had enough! He was manning the missile shop, main deck, Hangar Bay Two, port side. He heard the fire alarms called out and knew they were just aft of the missile shop. He was locked in a very small space looking at 200 charged nitrogen bottles in racks and the way they cracked around after those explosions. Ron didn't know if they'd explode or not. He called Aviation Ordnance Control for permission to evacuate the space and the voice on the other end of the phones told him to wait for confirmation.

Twig Tordoff had been among the men frantically throwing belts of 20MM off #3 elevator well. There was some kind of commotion arising over the napalm that the Ordnancemen had been mixing in the well. The Hangar crews wanted to heave it over along with the mixing equipment. The Ordnancemen wanted to save what they could of their hardware. A heated argument ensued. The Hangar

Officer bounded over and commanded that they clear his deck of napalm, equipment and all! Over it went.

Ron Ruland was given the O.K. to clear out, which he hurriedly did and turned and dogged the hatch behind him. Twig Tordoff was watching the napalm go over, there to lend a hand if needed. That was when the next explosion rocked the ship at 0823:40. He felt the deck heave underfoot and heard the roar, then saw the entire tail section of a Phantom cartwheel, flaming, through the air outside #3 elevator well before he saw the fireball. Ruland spun to look over at #3 elevator when he heard the explosion. At first he saw smoke and sky. Then sheets of burning, raging JP-5 cascaded through the slatting overhead just before the elevator door rumbled across its track and sealed Hangar Bay Two.

The explosion that occurred at 0823:40 was a 500 lb. bomb lying on deck just under the afterburners of F-4 #103. It was probably one of 105's own forward section bombs blown across deck from the 105 blast. This was a contact explosion since there was no evidence of pocking found in the deck crater afterwards. That is, fragments of the bomb did not have time to separate and leave evidence of fragmentation. This explosion was termed as being a probable low order. That is, an incomplete burning of the explosive train. The blast was of sufficient violence however, to leave a crater 3 feet in diameter punched 3 inches deep into the armored deck and what is more, this explosion blew the tail and wing tanks off 103 and scattered its remaining bombs and rockets about the deck. Three of the bombs settled among the Phantoms enveloped in flame across the fantail.

On the 03 level Kemp and Friend were knocked off their feet again by this blast and the wounded man they were carrying moaned once and breathed his last. They picked him up again and struggled to the starboard passageway where they handed the dead man off to two others running by and told them to take him forward. Then they moved back to the port side.

In Primary there was no question that the ship was in a life or death struggle. Lt. McLaughlin was acutely aware of radio traffic from the flight deck and Damage Control which issued from bulkhead speakers. "NO WATER! THERE IS NO PRESSURE!" He looked over the junk strewn flight deck and saw there was little or no firefighting water on the port side and only two hoses with any real pressure on the starboard side. The men on hoses held their ground before the raging, thundering flames, anxiously looking rearward to see what was wrong. The foam hose farthest aft on the starboard side was again putting out a solid stream of foam cross deck onto the nose and cockpit of 106 and working the stream under the aircraft. From Primary the Air Boss was exhorting, "THAT'S IT!!, THAT'S IT!! GET THAT FOAM UNDER 106! WORK IT UNDER THERE!" The weapons on 106 were clearly visible in Primary.

The stream of foam splashed and fluffed and pushed the flames back. A solid blanket was steadily gaining, reclaiming the weapons from the fire. The bulkhead speakers in Primary announced a message from Central Control, "ALL AVAILABLE FIREMAIN ASSETS ON LINE!" The tension was rising in Primary as the situation looked redeemable. The Air Boss was cheer leading those on deck below, "WE'VE GOT TO MAKE A FIRE BREAK! WE'VE GOT TO GET 312 OUT!"

The group in Primary beheld the drama below with shouts and cheers of amazement. Even here the deck shook with the steady thundering of the flames. The hose teams still stood, great gaps torn through their ranks, but they still stood with little more than resolution. There, on the starboard side, a few heroic blueshirts had run in and were breaking down chocks and chains and were hooking 312 up to a tow tractor that had backed up to it and this despite 103 blowing up and 403 being aflame right beside it. These heroes closed to the very gates of hell and braved the most terrible of deaths. Bob McLaughlin and those in Primary cheered and applauded those trying to get 312 out. They saw the dual drive wheels of the tractor begin to spin in the foam and the tractor bucked and jumped under the restraining weight of 312. The driver laid into the accelerator and the drive wheels spun faster. The rear end of the tow tractor fishtailed, back and forth, and the wheels threw up foam and 312 sat there, obstinate and ominous with all those bombs and rockets slung beneath her wings. The witnesses in Primary fell into numb silence as the tractor slewed and bucked and the driver hunched low to escape the suffocating heat. The drive wheels continued to throw foam and the tractor bucked and lurched and staggered . . . And the nose of 312 began to move forward.

One of the group in Primary proclaimed, voice thick with emotion, "They're bringing her OUT!!"

Twig Tordoff had decided. If he were going to die, it was not going to be down here in the Hangar Bay. He ran to the offdeck hatch and started up the ladders to the island.

The crewleader stood behind the two yellowshirts at the nozzle

Detonation of Mark 82 on deck between 103 and 202 carrying sparks and debris high aloft. Man goes down under wing of 310 and another rises from the flames under nose of 403. Official U.S. Navy photo, Osterbauer collection.

Second explosion of 105 at 0823:48 blasts defenseless hose teams. From right to left, man wearing only trousers comes up on deck and is caught running across. Hot suitman Vaughn hit under nose of 106. Port fog team caught full on. Official U.S. Navy photo, Osterbauer collection.

and watched the pitiful spray working back and forth, trying to keep the raging flames at bay. They were not attacking the fire now, they were defending themselves from it with a noticeably reduced pressure. The crewleader wondered how he had gotten himself into this predicament. Then he remembered. He wanted to know the TRUTH.

The Rider had calmed the Pale horse and now the stallion understood and nervously pranced in the towering, boiling columns of smoke and flame waiting for the command to run again. But the Rider had no need to run now. His first two strokes from ambush were slashing attacks meant to bleed the prey. These were the killing blows and he had only to wait for the mortals to come up again. And they had! The Horseman raised his dripping blade on high!

Del Girty had been blown flat in the catwalk. He had fought hard to regain consciousness and he knew he was hurt bad and was weak. He saw flames spilling into the catwalk and the beckoning fires approaching. Death was reaching out its hand for him.

Del Girty painfully pulled himself erect in the flaming catwalk. Racks of burning 12 man rubber life rafts oozed their bubbling lava into the groping flames. He drew himself up and began to walk. With flames all around him he staggered, step by step, up the short ladder to the flight deck. On the 03 level, Dennis Marks had just stepped into the flaming head at frame 240 looking for wounded and on the flight deck, weapons laden 312 had been towed clear of the starboard A-7 line and the tractor driver had just turned updeck.

And then the sword of the Rider struck the deck like a lightning bolt!

The flash of the white heat again! The furies of Hell and the thunderous sound again! The crewleader fought with all his might to stop but the Radio waves were driving him out, away again! He was again leaving the Earth, propelled back among the planets and stars, swept along by the irresistible force of the waves. He groped and reached and tried to hold onto something but the waves of the sound carried him away and he disappeared into the void.

The mass of the low, scudding cloud layer had trapped the smoke of the fire beneath it and the smoke had spread under the clouds cutting off the light of day. The arena grew dark. The mists of the clouds themselves grew ever more dense and insulating. In the interior of the mists were differing shades of gray and silence. The new line of figures stood there, with the ghostly specters of the Legion of the Dead ranged by the thousands all about them. There was no sound here.

The new men stood in their places in the line and looked in wonder at the thousands, their torn and molding uniforms unfamiliar. Then they chanced at look at those in their own line and saw that all were looking about with the same interest. There was no talking here.

Several recognized familiar faces in the line and gave nods of greeting. There stood Tex and Little Joe and Ernie. Next to them was a pilot in flight gear and another officer in khaki and a red jersey. There was a squadron Chief from the flight deck along with some below deckers standing next to a man wearing only a towel and shower shoes. The rest were flight deckers. Their uniforms were all burnt and torn and somehow there was something strangely different about all of them. Their eyes. There was no light in their eyes. There were twelve in this new line. They also became aware of the figures facing them. There were three of them and even in the rags they wore it was apparent that they were Naval officers. The foremost of the officers wore the tattered khaki of the American Navy and he held in his hands a closed book. The new men understood. They were waiting. In the wafting mists and eerie silence they were all waiting. There was only patience here.

The detonation at 0823:48 was the after section of bombs from 105 lying on the deck. This produced a hole blown through the flight deck measuring 5 x 3 foot from frames 244 to 245 outboard of the ballistic shell. The flight deck was blown through and petaled back on the sides and forward end and sheared off at the bulkhead on the aft end. There were no signs of pocking, indicating a contact explosion.

The blast wrecked the VAQ-132 compartment on the 03 level, cratering the deck between frames 241 to 245 and blowing a 5 foot hole through the deck into the 02 level compartment and ripping apart the vertical stiffener. The branch lines for zone 12 of the water washdown system, which were charged but not activated, were blown apart, releasing precious water main pressure.

The 02 level suffered a shotgun effect with eleven separate holes, up to 3 feet in length, torn through bulkheads and deck and on into the 01 level compartments where six holes of up to 2 feet in length continued downward into the sea. All these areas were immediately set aflame and burning JP-5 poured down from above.

Kemp and Friend and the remnants of 7 ALPHA were again driven by blast to nearly the starboard side. With no firefighting water, no OBA gear and no communications, they evacuated their wounded from the choking smoke and heat and through the black labyrinth of compartments and passageways, made their way forward to find units 77 and 78.

On the 02 level dead and wounded were brought out by stretcher as hose teams coming up from the hangar bay fought their way up, containing and isolating compartment fires by cooling bulkheads and overheads with fog nozzles and then teams assaulted the raging compartments never knowing what was happening on the flight deck. They thought their ship must be under attack!

On the flight deck the explosion was another scythe stroke, cleanly cutting down everyone aft of the island. Flaming debris howled updeck or rained down as lava spewed from a volcano. Large pieces and small struck the deck and crashed among those who fled and parked aircraft and the sea was shot with splashes all round about.

The tractor driver towing 312 was blown completely out of his seat and 312 was holed and set aflame. The torn ranks of the hose teams were decimated again. Nearly all of the first teams in action were wiped out. F-4 #106 was now burning furiously, the foam blanket under the weapons blown away. The nose and cockpit of the tanker, #614 was alight and flames had enveloped 414 on the starboard side.

Lt. Comdr. Brackin and his two starboard side foam hoses had marched resolutely forward even with diminished and uncertain pressure. With this blast several men went down and one hose was completely severed while the other geysered several spumes from shrapnel. Without taking time to turn off the water his men bent back the hoses and sat on them, cutting off the flow so new hose lengths could be added. Those down were quickly dragged away. An officer ran up to Brackin and shouted in his ear, "WHAT CAN I DO

TO HELP?!" Brackin responded, "GET ME HOSE! I NEED MORE HOSE!"

On the port side Crash/Salvage Officer Jim Helton needed new hose too but he did not dare to take the time to change out torn lengths. 106 and 614 would surely go if what little water was being put on them were cut off. Rags, blankets, jackets, anything handy was wrapped around the rents to stem the escape of water to keep the hoses in action.

Henry Mendoza was lying in a stretcher with a score of others behind the island. The man lying next to him had been badly burned and his smoldering clothes had re-flashed and Mendoza was beating out the flames with his hand and screaming for help when the 105 aft explosion went off. The shock and violence skidded the stretchers and those able to cover their faces and heads to shield themselves were fortunate. Henry Mendoza watched a large flaming piece fly over the island with a ripping sound and was relieved when someone ran up with a PKP bottle and put his neighbor out. He would never forget the smell.

Casualties were piling up all around the island and some were being taken inside by corpsmen and Repair stretcher bearers. The two hot suitmen came staggering off deck. Mike Piner, his face smashed and streaming blood could not see. But he held up badly wounded Donald Vaughn who could. Vaughn gave Piner directions and the two managed to get themselves to the island. A couple of corpsmen whisked Henry Mendoza up and ran him around to the front of the island where the casualties would be more protected.

The crewleader brought himself back from deep space through sheer force of will. There was danger, somewhere . . . and he fought to focus his mind. But what? . . . He blinked away the last of the darkness and disregarded the ringing in his ears. He tried to concentrate. He was flat on his back on the wet deck and through intense effort, rose to his feet. The fog hose was lying on deck with the 8 foot applicator knocked out of it. There were no others still standing. In the narrow world of the original fog team, the crewleader was the last man. The wall of raging fire was completely across deck and surging forward by leaps and bounds up both sides. On unsteady legs he moved for the hose and picked up the fallen standard. He put the applicator back into the nozzle but it popped back out and clattered to the deck. He tried twice more before he finally locked it in correctly and stood there, seeking shelter behind the spray.

From right to left, a cluster of men helping wounded at extreme right. A purpleshirt takes over the gooseneck nozzle, Mike Piner still in action on starboard twin agent unit. Flight Deck Officer crosses from left to right. Men down on deck in flames. Tractor backs in to tow 312. Official U.S. Navy photo, Osterbauer collection.

312 still not pulled out. Foam hose attacks 614 as it begins to burn. Official U.S. Navy photo, Osterbauer collection.

Bill Proffit had come back to the island not really knowing what he would do next. He saw the terrible carnage stacked all around it and it shocked him. There was a certain stretcher with a hideous thing in it that was grinning insanely as Proffit went by. Then he saw that the poor man had been burned so badly that he had no ears or lips. And he was still alive, trying to get out of the stretcher.

Bill Proffit started to go back aft to get on a hose and was confronted with a scene from the Night of the Living Dead. Ragged, shuffling creatures with the look of Zombies moved slowly towards the island from all over the deck. They were torn and burned and bleeding and were the inevitable wreckage that washed up after every explosion. Proffit grabbed the closest one whose face was a mass of gore and pulled an arm across his shoulder in a fireman carry fashion and got him moving into the island. The hatch was open to the ladders leading down to sick bay and it was an easy path to follow with every step and every part of the handrails splashed and smeared with red blood and black clots all the way down.

Bill Proffit could feel the hot wetness soaking his jersey and sticking it to his shoulder and back as he walked the Face down the series of ladders. The Face moaned and Proffit assured him, "Don't worry Buddy, we're going to make it." With that he looked over his shoulder in compassion and saw that the Face was split wide open from the corner of the mouth to the ear. He saw the back teeth and tongue working to expel the choking blood which blew out upon Proffit's own neck. The blood bubbled and foamed, "Don't worry," he said, "We're almost there!"

After the last explosion, Dennis Downs heard the Air Boss trying to rally the men again, "YOU HAVE TO GET BACK IN THERE. WE WILL LOSE THE SHIP IF YOU DON'T GET BACK IN THERE!"

Dennis Downs looked out his window and saw the latest retreat had subsided. The Air Boss was keeping up a steady discourse, "WE NEED MORE HOSE BACK AFT!" The men surged back into the fray. Dennis Downs knew it was going to happen again. One of the phones on the bulkhead rang and Downs answered it while still looking out the window. He saw the aircraft which had been towed and stopped was now aflame. The gleaming gold fuses of the bombs and rockets made them very conspicuous. The voice on the phone said, "What's the situation up there?"

Dennis Downs was looking at the gold nose cones of the eight 5 inch rockets of 312 and the flames all around them. The rockets were pointing directly at the island. "It's very bad," Downs said, "and I think it's going to get worse!"

Twig Tordoff had been blown off his feet by the 105 aft blast just as he emerged from the island. He got back on his feet despite feeling like he had been run over by a truck and pushed two dislocated fingers back into their sockets. There were a knot of men forming a second line of defense on the port side. They were roughly from the centerline to port running on both sides of 310 and 112 and getting hoses up to make an advance on 614. The first line was practically chewed to pieces with only 2 of the original 7 hoses still in action. Twig Tordoff ran up and joined a group forming under the inboard wing of 310.

On the starboard side, another hose was being brought into action down the starboard foul line. This hose started at a plug by #2 elevator and lengths were added till it looped around aircraft stacked in front of the island and then went aft down the foul line.

Aboard the *USS Rogers*, the skipper, Comdr. George Hart, had called the crew to General Quarters and turned his 25 year old ship towards *USS Enterprise*. His crew were already pulling out hoses and dragging them to the upper works. Comdr. Hart knew the carrier had a loaded deck and he knew what he was getting his ship into. He was in Subic Bay, Philippine Islands, and saw the *Forrestal* after she came in from the beating she took in her 1967 fire. He saw the immense damage and had in mind what he would do if ever his ship were in position to deal with a carrier fire. That plan was now going into action. Men dragged a 2½ inch fire hose to the forward five inch gun turret and rigged it to the starboard barrel of the twin 5 inch mount. This way the hose could be trained by the gun director and kept in action no matter how hot it became. The Executive Officer, Lt. Comdr. Harris Sperling, took the Conn just as the first major detonation at 0823:01 filled the sky with flying debris. The shock of the explosion heaved the little destroyer upward as she closed to cross the track of the wake behind the still turning carrier. The wind blew the flame and smoke off the carriers lee side toward the approaching *Rogers*. The smoke rolled down the after half of *Enterprise* and a vast cloud of it hung on the surface of the sea.

The *Rogers* lookouts reported seeing a pilot go into the water and the *Enterprise* nearly obscured by smoke just before their own ship entered the bank at twenty knots. Harris Sperling kept his course which would cross the wake well behind the carrier even though she was lost to view. He had his radar to keep him apprised of distances. He ordered lookouts to keep the *Stoddart* in sight in case he needed room to maneuver. The report of another explosion was heard and felt throughout the destroyer as she ran blind through the acrid smoke. The bridge had become quiet as all hands strained to hear and the destroyer plowed through the oncoming seas. And then the report of a terrific detonation! Concussion rocked the ship and the *Rogers* seemed to lift out of the water. The sound of it was awesome and very close. Cries of alarm and Harris Sperling had the helm put hard over and the ship hauled out to port to get clear of the smoke.

Ron Ruland was helping to remove belts of 20MM from A-7's in Hangar Bay 1. He was told to be very careful with the cannon shells because they were very sensitive. The first belt he was handed clattered into a heap on the foamed over deck. Everyone near stopped and braced for what they thought was coming. But nothing happened. Then a general round of badmouthing and denunciation as tempers and fears were vented. Promises of great bodily harm if they ever got out of this alive were delivered. Challenges of contest were gratefully accepted. They all dearly wanted to have a go at each other. They came near to blows. The belt of 20MM high explosive incendiary was retrieved from the foam and thrown overboard.

"THE HOSE TEAMS IN BAY TWO NEED HELMETS! PERSONNEL ARE REQUESTED TO SEND HELMETS AFT TO BAY TWO!" This blared out over the hangar bullhorn. Ron Ruland ran forward and found a stack of helmets and ran them back to Bay Two. Hose teams were going into all off deck access hatchways and working upward on the ladders. Smoke was rolling out of several hatches on the port side and wounded were being brought out. A stretcher was carried past with a lifeless man in it with a very deep gash in his forehead. Ruland ran the helmets over to one of the port side hose teams and ran to find some more.

At 0824:13 another explosion rocked the ship. This was a 500 pound bomb lying on the deck between 103 and 202 at frame 246 on the starboard side. This was a contact explosion in that there were no signs of pocking. This event did not breach the deck because it occurred directly over the main longitudinal stiffener, a massive steel beam running forward and AFT. The force of the explosion crushed this beam and punched a crater six feet in diameter 7½ inches deep into the deck. The violence of the blast broke up the water washdown branch lines of group 11 on the 03 level.

Twig Tordoff was in the second line of defense forming cross deck. He was standing with several others under the wing of 310 when this latest explosion erupted. A storm of shock and heat swept them but he did not go down. The man standing next to him grabbed Tordoff by the shoulder and throat and was sagging to the deck. The man said, "Help me!" and Twig Tordoff pulled him back to his feet. The man was facing towards the bow and sagging again and becoming increasingly heavy and Tordoff wondered what was wrong with him because he did not look like he was hit. Then the man turned and looked at him and said again, "Help me!"

Twig Tordoff had learned long ago in Junior Ski Patrol training that when you went to someone's assistance you never let them know how bad they were because you had to keep them calm. He was prepared to use that training till the man looked at him and Twig Tordoff knew there was no misreading the horror on his own face. The man had a massive hole in the side of his head and his eyes stayed locked on Twig Tordoff as he sagged to the deck and died.

Big John Guillot had his men busy. Swabbing bloody decks and picking up the litter scattered around sick bay, helping out wherever there was a need. Streams of wounded were pouring down the ladder from the island and the pilots elevator was still going strong. Many of those coming down were under their own power and collapsing at the bottom of the ladder. Repair Five BRAVO men hustled these and others across the passageway to sick bay and picked up battle dressing wrappers and empty burn jelly cans and cartons. Number seven fog foam injection station was down to the last of its ready foam supply and Guillot had his men bring all of station eights supply over since it was not running. His men's hands were bleeding from handling so many of the five gallon cans and the injection station was filling with the empties. "Throw them out into the passageway!"

Five gallon cans flew out of the space and rumbled in the passageway to make way for full cans. A hatch to a berthing compartment the next deck down was opened and the cans were thrown down the ladder to clear all the refuse from the passageway. The empty cans banged and rumbled continuously down the ladder into the berthing compartment.

Dennis Vaeth was with unit 77 and moving hoses back to try and link up with 7 ALPHA. There were stretcher teams coming out of the darkness and smoke and many were succumbing to the smoke.

Dennis Vaeth and his unit 77 had on their OBA gear and pressed back to the fires of the 03 level. His job was an investigator and he went ahead like a scout for his team. He made his way back to the battle dressing station and waved anyone he saw forward. Battle lanterns were lit but the smoke was so thick the beams of light would not illuminate the deck. He saw fires in the passageway and moved back to report.

Henry Mendoza was still lying in a stretcher in front of the island when the water washdown system came on. The shock of the salt water spraying into his wound brought him abruptly out of his momentary calm. A gang of corpsmen began moving the wounded into the island and grabbed Bill Proffit just as he came back up from sick bay. Proffit took the head of Mendoza's stretcher while the corpsmen took the other end and went through the island hatch and to the ladder going down to the battle dressing station. There was not enough space on the ladder for anyone beside the stretcher so the corpsman who was holding Mendoza's tourniquet yelled for someone below to hold it. The stretcher bearers continued down. "Somebody get the tourniquet!" the corpsman yelled from above, "Get the tourniquet!" But those below were momentarily stunned.

Henry Mendoza raised himself up in the stretcher and yelled at one of the frozen men below, "GET THE TOURNIQUET YOU SON OF A BITCH!!" The man immediately came forward and took and twisted the tourniquet. The pain drove Henry Mendoza flat. They took him off to the side and the ship reeled under another heavy blow. Both corpsmen looked to the overhead waiting for something to come through. They laid Mendoza down and did a few things to him and the taller corpsman kept looking at the overhead. The other corpsman was asking excitedly, "Was it like this on the *Forrestal*?!" "Is this what it was like?!"

The tall corpsman looked back at the overhead, beads of sweat standing out on his face. The ship rumbled and shook again. "It was just like this," he said, not looking down, "It was JUST LIKE THIS!"

On deck the effort continued as more hose was found and backup teams were formed to plug the gaps between the first and second lines. The Air Boss kept up his exhortations and the men on deck found themselves in four basic categories. The men on hose teams were to the fore. Those dragging away casualties were the next tier. Gangs moving aircraft and throwing weapons over were the third and fourth of the basic groups. There were others doing sundry things, whatever might be needed to be done, such as finding new hose and such, but the mass of men on deck of necessity fell into one of the four groups.

As those in the first and second ranks fell they were dragged away and others ran up and took their places. The hose teams now were not as densely manned as before and the spacing was wider. There was no direction to do this but it was more of a common sense realization of those survivors still on their feet. When there was a need, whether to man a hose or to carry off wounded or anything, those standing back would come running in. Stark and terrible lessons had been learned about standing shoulder to shoulder across the deck!

The crewleader still thought he was alone on the gooseneck hose but behind him George Norsworthy and two other flight deckers took their stand. Then, at 0824:27, an explosion and fireball burst up from the flames just off the centerline to left. This did not have nearly the force of the other explosions and was most likely fuel tanks going up. Warily, the hose teams held their ground.

Henry Mendoza lay in his stretcher in the battle dressing station. He thought he would feel safe here. There were others lying about, some were obviously dead and the doctors and corpsmen were busy putting people up on tables and working on them and then placing them off to the side such as where they had placed him. Henry Mendoza watched as the catholic chaplain came and prayed at the side of the dead. He had the purple sash of the Death Sacrament across his shoulders. Henry watched as he finished with one, then another, and then he came looking at him. The priest knelt next to him and Henry said, "It's O.K. Father, I'm not going to die."

The priest put his hands together and in the ancient language, began his prayer, "Per istam sanctam Unctionem." Henry Mendoza's eyes grew wide at the thought that the priest knew something that he didn't. He tried to protest, "LOOK, I'm alright, O.K.? I'm alright." The priest never missed a beat, "Gratia sancti Spiritus, et ne nos inducas in tentationem," It was like the priest was sealing his doom. "I said I'm alright, take care of someone else!" The priest held the side of his hand inches above Mendoza's forehead and began to make the sign of the cross. "In nomini Patri . . ."

Henry Mendoza reached up and grabbed the lapels of the chaplains coat, "I'M NOT GOING TO DIE!" And the hand came down, "ET Filii . . ." Henry Mendoza was shaking him now, "YOU

SON OF A BITCH, I'M NOT GOING TO DIE!!" "Et Spiritus Sancti", and the hand of the priest completed the sign.

The priest gently took the hands of Henry Mendoza and placed them back on his own chest. Then he rose and moved on. There was much to be done this day for the chaplain.

On deck the F-4 Condition Bird, #201, parked beside the island forward of #3 elevator was broken down and hitched to a tractor. Then it was towed out and taken as far away as they could take it, to the very edge of the angle deck.

Lt. (j.g.) Ned Baumer was standing mid deck just forward of the island with some other aircrews who had gathered there. They all expressed tremendous concern for their squadron mates back aft. They could see the dead and wounded being dragged away almost continuously. Ned Baumer had been ready to launch from #3 catapult when the fire started and just happened to have a camera loaded with film with him this day. He stood there taking pictures of the awesome spectacle and many times was tempted to run and take cover. But with the camera he knew he was recording something extraordinary, so he stayed, fascinated by what was happening. Men down, dead or wounded, others on fire and running away. Still others running towards it. The first launch was flying, circling the ship, watching the show. Ned Baumer stayed on deck with his camera and took some of the most spectacular pictures of the day. The thought that the ship might sink was uppermost in his mind. All the while he was taking his pictures he heard the Air Boss shouting out direction. He would see the men on deck respond to the direction and move back in. A blast would go and wreck the effort and cause terrible suffering. The Air Boss would rally them and in they would go till another explosion cut them down.

Ned Baumer watched it all and recorded what he could with his camera. He watched them time and again go back in and stand up to it. Then they would be cut down and others would go forward to take their places and it would happen again. The Air Boss would rally them and they would gather and surge and in they would go . . . again. And again. It was a humbling experience. It was a day none here could ever forget.

Ray Gomes was a new guy. He had only been aboard for two and a half months and was in Reactor Training Division completing the qualifications required to become a Reactor Operator. His General Quarters station was #3 engine room, Control Equipment Area.

In the short time he had been aboard he really learned a lot about the reactor operations. He was also given intense instruction on the social stratum of the various engine rooms. He was told, for instance that those of lesser capacities were generally sent to the forward engine rooms, particularly those loudmouth buffoons of #1 plant who were always boasting, "We have the longest shaft in the Navy!" It was common knowledge that all loose cannon's of the Reactor Department were dumped into #1 plant.

And the whole gang from #2 plant was suspect. This plant was known as the "White Elephant" because everything was painted white and all exposed pipe and rails were chromed! This plant was used as a showpiece for tours by Navy V.I.P.'s. How could anyone be normal in a place like that? Watch out for them! A very stuffy crowd up there, nothing but Hollywood types.

The gang from #3 plant had their own distinction. Being the rearmost engine room, all propeller shafts passed through their plant. They had their backs to the wall and protested loudly, "We get the shaft from everyone!"

Ray Gomes liked the easy camaraderie of the engine room. He had never been on a ship before and this was his first ORI. The older hands told him what to expect. There would be drills, emergencies and simulated attacks throughout the three days. Ray Gomes had taken heed of what to expect but with the way the ship was shaking he was really concerned, and said so to one of the veterans, "They are going way overboard with the realism bit."

The veteran was uneasy too. None down here knew what was really happening to their ship, but there was one thing known for a certainty and he spelled it out for Ray Gomes, "Whenever we go to GQ, they never say, 'THIS IS NOT A DRILL.' There is something serious going on!"

On the bridge of the *USS Stoddart*, the Skipper, Comdr. Edmund Taylor was slowly closing the distance to *USS Enterprise* at the ships best speed. To those on the bridge it was incredible that the carrier was still steaming along. There was general agreement that the *Enterprise* was doomed. CIC Officer, Ens. Mike Stuessy thought so too and he knew something about history. He knew this was the very situation which devastated the Japanese carriers at MIDWAY, attacked with their flight decks and hangar bays full of armed and fueled aircraft. He was witnessing what he was sure was the destruction of his countries mightiest ship and it was an awesome spectacle. Fireball after fireball roared skyward and the sound of the detonations were heavy and shock waves swept across the sea and was felt here on the *Stoddart*. They could see the red flames rolling high up in the column of thick black smoke which rose thousands of feet into the air.

In Damage Control Central, Condition ZEBRA was reported set by all repair parties with the exception of 7 ALPHA. Repairs 4 and 5 and 7 FOX reported energizing the water washdown countermeasures systems in their areas of responsibility. Sporadic reports of fires in 7 ALPHA were received by the unit 73 phone talker but no direct communications as yet from 7 ALPHA.

On the Hangar deck #3 elevator door had to be opened again because there was still another skid of napalm left out in the well. As the door rumbled open Joe Rosa and a gang ran out to the skid and heaved up the napalm tank and threw it over the side. The tank hit the water with a splash but stayed on the surface close aboard as it moved quickly aft in the wake toward the heat and flame. Joe Rosa and the others cleared the well hoping the tank would not explode till #3 door was closed again.

The tank did not explode. It bobbed and wallowed in the wake and passed right under the blazing #7 sponson and rolled in the screws roiling turbulence with sheets of flaming fuel pouring down from catwalks and the fantail round down. The tank passed out of danger and was soon far behind. It was just another of an increasing number of objects which would dot the seas, marking the ships track, but hampering search and rescue efforts.

Across deck sponson #8 was blazing and the fire had gotten into the jet test cell area. Hoses were played on these fires through hatches but with the source of fire continuously pouring down, not much progress could be made. Sponson #6 on the port side was also on fire from sheets of flames pouring down and #4 elevator well, on the other side of the closed door, was burning. Reels of spare arresting gear cables and yellow gear stowed there were blazing away.

Ron Ruland came running back with a load of helmets for one of the port hose teams fighting on #6 sponson. There was a haze of smoke up to the overhead in Bay 2 but those hatches the fire fighting teams were disappearing into were very dark with black smoke rolling out of them. The men on the teams passed the helmets up to the forward elements. Ron Ruland thought he had better find himself a life jacket so he went back to Bay 1. There were still a lot of frantic yelling and cries of, "Throw anything over that can explode!"

He found a life jacket locker and took an armload back to the Bay 2 hose teams. He thought the jackets might afford some protection from the flying shrapnel. He could distinctly hear screams and shouted orders from the flight deck just before #1 and #2 elevator doors rolled shut. There was still no explanation of what was happening. Anyone who looked like he might be from the flight deck was immediately confronted. Answers were demanded. "PLANE CRASHED! WE'RE BEING BOMBED! EVERYTHING IS BLOWING UP!"

Ron Ruland had his life jacket. He was already a pretty good swimmer. He knew the Hawaiian Islands were in the area and not too far distant. The possibility of having to go into the water and swim for it was in his mind.

In Central Control the Reactor Officer was there with the Chief Engineer and the Damage Control Assistant. For Reactor safety reasons, the Reactor Officer was considered senior. He was responsible for all propulsion plant operations but the Engineering Officer looked after everything else. Central Control was in constant contact with the captain on the J-dial telephone and the Air Boss on the 21MC. The upper decks kept calling for more water and Engineering was putting out all they had without shutting down the SPS 32 and 33 cooling water exchangers. If they did this they would gain another 1000 GPM of water pressure but would knock the radars out of commission.

Comdr. Kellogg noticed the mid starboard loop pressure steadily falling and told the Engineer and Damage Control Assistant, "You are way too low over here!"

It was decided to keep the SPS cooling water exchangers on and save their 1000 GPM as a last trump card. Then, the order went out over the phones, "Raise steam chest pressure on all steam pumps to 600 PSI and maintain a continuous watch on them!"

Bill McAllister was at his General Quarters station. He was the #1 man on the #1 hose of Unit 22. That meant he was the nozzleman on the attack hose and the #2 man would move up if he went down. The #2 hose was to back up and protect the #1 hose from heat.

Unit 22 had on all their gear, OBA's, helmets, gloves. So far, they had seen no action but their hoses were out, manned and ready up here, forward of the mess decks behind the armored watertight door on the 2nd deck. Unit 22 was secured into its GQ station with the only communications being the sound powered phones and the 1MC. The phone talker would relay what information he heard to the rest of the team but it wasn't much and often conflicted with reports of fires and locations passed over the 1MC. The men of the team were very quiet. They could feel the ship shaking violently. They could hear the reports of fires back aft. They knew only one thing, this was NO DRILL!

Bill McAllister stayed at his manned hose near the armored door. He heard the Bosun call out the fire locations and one of them, the Master-at-Arms shack, was just forward of his own working space, the Education and Training office. He, like most of the men below, mentally tracked the course of the fires whenever they were called out. They had made repeated checks of their spaces looking for fire, smoke, water, any signs of trouble. They had found no evidence of damage. While they regrouped, Bill McAllister leaned back against the armored watertight door sealing off these spaces from the mess decks. He faintly heard the banging of the bomb elevator doors and muffled shouts from the other side. He moved over to look through the Plexiglas port hole of the armored door to see what was going on. He was stunned by what he saw.

There was Forward Battle Dressing station in all its agony. Bearers were bringing stretchers filled with the most terrible suffering out of the elevator to the portside of the space where five tables were set up and working. It was a ghastly scene. Wounded were placed on the tables and set upon by any number of attendants. If a table were not open the casualties were stacked in the center of the deck until they could be taken. Orders of priorities were established for the waiting. Those on the tables were immediately set upon and a constant rain of clothes, boxes and wrappers fell to the deck. As quickly as could be, those on the tables were moved away, some this way, some that. There was constant, red motion.

Bill McAllister recognized two Dental Officers as the ones directing the first aid efforts. These and the attendants had on green scrub suits with some of the others dressed in dungarees and they all moved rapidly among the tables. The attire of everyone was liberally saturated with splashes of blood. Those who were not cutting away clothing were sewing. At times, it appeared that everyone was sewing. All but one man. This man had a wringer water bucket on wheels and some mops. The man swabbed under the tables at a frantic pace and Bill McAllister could see that he could not keep up with the job. The blood ran off the tables so fast and in so many places that no matter how fast the man worked, the deck was becoming one vast red smear, growing continually darker.

Bill McAllister called for the others to come and look and soon the entire unit were taking turns looking through the port hole. There were tears streaming as men of the unit begged permission from their officer to let them go and help. The officer could give no permission. Their battle station was here, in this space, and here they must stay until relieved. Bill McAllister looked out the window again. Just below him and off to the right he saw several stretchers stacked along the bulkhead for as far as he could see. Those in the stretchers lay still, covered over with gray wool blankets. Bill McAllister would never forget the sight. The grim tables, the silent blankets, the jellied elevator deck and the thousands of red footprints going to and from these places on the white tile deck.

5. THE TRUTH

Lt. Robert A. McLaughlin saw and heard it all from his vantage point in Primary. There were the continual pleadings from those on the flight deck for water. He heard the exchanges from the Captain, from Central, from Sick Bay and the Hangar Bay, all coming clearly over the Primary communications speakers. Central was putting out all they had, there must be breaks in the firemains. There was grave concern about the fire getting into the Hangar Bay. Reports from there said all aircraft that could be moved from Bay 2 into Bay 1 were in progress and that the athwartship doors, separating the Bays, would then be closed. No fires were as yet in Bay 2 but flames were pouring off the flight deck from #3 elevator on the starboard side all the way around to #4 elevator on the port side. Three sponsons were aflame as was the jet test cell on the main deck. Fires were being fought on the 03, 02 and 01 levels on the port side. They were fighting with everything they had. The situation was critical. If the fires got into the Hangar Bay, Capt. Lee felt they would lose the ship.

Bob McLaughlin had seen some excitement before. He had forty combat missions flying P-3's out of Cam Rhan Bay. He had been mortared and rocketed on base. He had been chased by MIGS around Haiphong and Hainan Island off China. He routinely took ground fire over Nha Trang as he circled to land during Tet of '68. Red tracers arcing up to and past his aircraft on his deliberate and predictable night approaches. He had seen some excitement, but nothing compared to this. This was like watching a volcanic eruption from the rim of the volcano. The debris flying through the air was continual. He saw several empty ejection seats rocket out from the flames and arc over the side. He saw one hose team after another decimated. The fire was advancing by leaps and bounds. Aircraft were still stacked tightly on #3 elevator all around the island to #2 elevator. Soon the flames would get to them and the entire island would go.

With the Air Boss coaching and cheering them on, the starboard teams held their hoses high enough to let a tow tractor back in under them to hook up to A-7 #300, which had to come out first to unlock the pack on #3 elevator. The teams went back to fighting the raging flames advancing up the A-7 line and the furiously burning 312. The situation looked hopeless. Streams of salt water played back and forth across the blazing hulks only to disappear into the ferociously billowing bright orange flames. The water was having no apparent effect. The foam blanket laid down under 313 and 414 could not stop those aircraft from blazing away and pouring their own thousands of gallons of fuel onto the deck.

To Bob McLaughlin and the others in Primary it looked like there would be no stopping the wall of flame. They had to make a fire break. The crew was still breaking down chocks and chains on #300 when F-4 #202 exploded and a sparrow missile rocketed out of the fireball and streaked upward and dangerously close to the island. Lt. McLaughlin watched the burning missile go by, spewing flame and leaving a white smoke trail and reaching about two hundred feet before it began to tumble and then fell back into the sea.

The crewleader could not move. He was frozen to the deck still holding the gooseneck nozzle and hiding behind the small cloud of fog spray. The flames tried desperately to get around and through this small protective curtain and soon they would find a way. The crewleader was numb. He could not make his legs move, they felt like wood. He could not think. He commanded himself to think but he was overwhelmed. He had dared to learn the TRUTH and now the weight of the TRUTH was crushing him.

Over and over a struggle was going on in his mind and it left him immobile. The lessons of his life passed through his brain. There were the stories of relatives who fought in wars and were told in revered tones. HE flew his bomber back from Germany with two engines shot out. HIS tank was blown up under him and he lost his toes and part of a foot. HE was behind the lines on a mission and was grenaded and wounded in the face. HE bailed out over the water and became tangled in his shroud lines and drowned.

They were brave. The crewleader tried to be brave but his mind was telling him to run.

Do your duty.

RUN!

Be brave.

GET AWAY!

Honor.

YOU WILL DIE!

Never tell a lie.

A chorus of cheers erupted in Primary as A-7 #300 began moving out. Flight deck LPO Billy Hawk had a gang of men pushing on the aircraft to assist the tow tractor as it slid and skidded in the foam. The starboard teams made way for the aircraft and tractor as they cleared the elevator and made their way up deck. It was a very small triumph. Bob McLaughlin watched the A-7 go by and saw it stuffed into the pack just forward of the island. It was pulled in behind the F-4 with the shattered gear and wing tank, the one that was leaking fuel all over #2 elevator. There were men with buckets trying to catch the fuel as it flowed out of the ruptured tank. If the fire got up to these aircraft, the entire flight deck was doomed.

The Rider on the Pale Horse prepared for his next attack. He saw the aircraft being towed out but could not strike. With a mighty hand he restrained the nervous charger until he was ready. There was a pathetic mortal standing there in his way and this ones name was not written down in the BOOK. And the Rider whose name was Death dare not take anyone whose name was not written in the BOOK.

The crewleader wavered. He could not feel his legs. And then a Voice blazed through his mind. The clarity and power of the Voice shocked and stunned him. Above the thundering flames, above the constant cracking, above the conflict in his own mind the Voice was clear and powerful. And the Voice said, "IF YOU STAY HERE, YOU WILL DIE!"

The crewleader dropped the nozzle. He was stunned by the Voice. It was more awesome than the fire or explosions or anything of this earth. The Voice was Cosmic and the crewleader knew absolutely that it was not his own. He turned on his wooden legs and began to run. The knowledge that he had failed his test filled him with shame. The TRUTH was a terrible thing to know.

The crewleader had gone only a few steps when a terrific blast went off behind him. The force of the explosion drove him up the deck but he did not fall. He felt the searing wave of heat and the sting of many small things driven into him. He heard the furies of hell unleashed and the rip and tear of talons and claws all around him. He heard the howls and shrieks of the demons and then in an instant, they were gone.

The crewleader stumbled along fighting to keep his sanity. He consoled himself that the danger from the explosion was passed. For the first time he saw the deck in this direction and it was littered with junk and wreckage and death. The A-7, #310, that was stopped in front of #4 elevator had a large hole ripped in the fuselage and fuel poured from it covering the deck. The crewleader realized he would have burned to death if he did not leave. As he ran past the A-7 he saw a purpleshirt down on deck with a gaping head wound. He told himself again that he was out of the danger. Then an F-4 main gear and tire assembly fell out of the sky and hit the deck just in front of him. The wreckage bounced mightily back into the air and over the port side. The crewleader was stunned. The falling main gear had very nearly killed him. Shocked by this new danger, he looked up. The sky over head was filled with all manner of smoking, flaming junk an it was all coming back down. He covered his head with his arms and ran past the dead as the hail of wreckage struck the deck all around him. The terror of the nightmare had taken his measure. What madness. Momma.

The crewleader ran straight for the catwalk and dove into it just as another blast went off and he heard metal striking and flying off in all directions.

The blast that went off at 0825:32 was the bombs of aircraft 113. This produced a 13 x 16 foot deeply petaled hole on the flight deck and wrecked #5 armory and #5 radio transmitter room below it on the 03 level and blowing that deck wide open. Broken up pieces of the flight deck and shrapnel and one unexploded, superheated 500 pound bomb took out the entire 03 level deck between frames 256 and 260 and continued downward. All the surrounding bulkheads were deflected and torn loose from their welds. The storm of blast and metal next crashed onto the fantail dishing in the deck in three places and denting the capstan and tearing four holes through the deck of approximately 1 foot square wounding several of the firefighters and depositing the headless body of a man who was in #5 armory at the feet of the Repair officer. The 500 lb. bomb went through the deck sideways and sheared a neat hole. The friction from ripping through the metal deck made the bomb even hotter. The capstan machinery room was the next space down and the pieces of plating tore a 1 ft. hole in the deck and deflected off a vertical stiffener and ripped a 2 x 1 foot hole out through the transom. The bomb tore a 2 x 4 foot hole through the deck and smashed its way into an Air Department storeroom where it hit the vertical stiffener crushing it and tearing it loose and then deflected, cherry red by now, ripping a 5 x 3 foot hole through the transom a scant 3 feet above the waterline and slammed into the ships wake. The bomb continued downward in the 76° blue Pacific, boiling the water as it went. Through the turbulence created by the ships four great screws it descended, past the great rudders, down and down it went carrying its 198 pounds of high explosives. The water of the depths grew ever colder and the weapon fell away to the bottom of the sea. There is no explicable reason why the bomb did not explode.

    E-4 Rob Weideman was manning the phones all the way down in #2 shaft alley. He never heard GQ sounded but knew it was supposed to go and figured that he just did not hear it. He didn't know why, but the lights had gone off some time ago and it was dark and warm down here. He listened in to the voice traffic over the phones and the reports of fires here and there. He thought it was just a drill. He had no idea what those loud noises were or what was making the ship shake so much. He just manned his space like he was supposed to, all the way down here, well below the waterline. He was alone in this space. All he had for company was the continually turning, rumbling shaft and the blue sparks from the contacts of the torque measuring units that snapped at each rotation of the shaft. The blue sparks were especially bright in the dark.

    The explosion at 0825:32 of 113 also skidded another of its bombs up the deck where it came to a brief halt squarely between 415, 313 and 312 where it stopped on a welded seam of the deck. At 0825:36 this hot bomb exploded lighting off 313 and 415, laid most of the starboard teams to the deck and blew open the welded seam 6 feet wide and 15 feet long. Burning fuel poured down into this hole and also drained down into the holes blown open by 113 all the way down to the 3rd deck.

    The crewleader was pressed as close as possible under the slight overhang of the flight deck in the catwalk. When this latest blast and the flying junk had subsided he relaxed a little and looked around. He was astonished to see two of his crew, Fitzgerald and Arrick, pressed against the bulkhead on either side of him. They were equally astonished to see him. There was a general round of back slapping and relief and expressed wonder that any of them were still alive. Happiness for a friends safety beamed like sunshine from grinning faces. They all felt that it was a miraculous thing that they had made it back from the hose. The crewleader asked a quick question, "Where's George?"

The others didn't know and they all raised themselves up to peer over the scupper and scan the flaming deck. Incredibly, there was George Norsworthy. He was staggering, tottering up the deck trying to get away right in front of them. The three purpleshirts jumped up onto the flight deck as one man and ran out and grabbed their crew member. He collapsed at their touch but never hit the deck as they gathered him up and ran back to the safety of the catwalk. Gently they passed him down and then proceeded at their best speed, ducking the entire way, to get him back to their crews shelter.

George Norsworthy closed his eyes and gave himself over to his friends. Jim Fitzgerald had him by the legs and Arrick had him by his belt. The crewleader supported his upper torso, with one hand under his back and the other under the back of his neck. They could see that he was hurt in several places. His dungarees were bloody and his jersey was bloody. He had a gaping hole and a large chunk of meat missing from his inner forearm. They ran him all the way forward and down the ladder and inboard to their crew shelter. When they carried him in they had no idea what to do with him but there were several other purpleshirts there and they laid him down. A.R. Theide took over from there, his face ashen, and yelled for someone to get a stretcher while he tried to stop the bleeding. The crewleader was grateful that someone knew what to do for Norsworthy. He looked down at his hand, the one that supported Norsworthy's neck. It was wet and sticky and red with blood. Someone said, "Kreisler is paralyzed back in the catwalk!"

The crewleader looked at his men, "Let's go get him." With that the three took off at a run.

Central Control ordered all Damage Control units to sweep their areas after the latest explosions and wanted an update on the situation of #15 fire pump. The report was that the upper casing, 250 lbs. of dead weight, had been manhandled back on and was being bolted down. The coupling and other piping would take some more time to make up. This was just what Commander Neel was waiting to hear. "O.K.", he said, "Clear #14 of tags and line it up for start!"

There was still no direct contact with the 7 ALPHA locker and specific firemain ruptures had not yet been pinpointed. Repair 1 ALPHA reported fire on the fantail and Unit 35 of Repair 3 reported fire in the capstan machinery room at frame 2-258-4-Q. Unit 35 moved to surround and isolate the blazing compartment and rigged hoses to cool bulkheads while two hoses fought through the compartment hatch. Investigators went out and soon another report was sent to Central, "Fire, class Alpha, Bravo, aviation storeroom, 3-258-4-Q!"

When the investigator swiftly made checks of his spaces after the explosions of 0825:32 and 0825:36 in the Unit 35 area, he had his OBA gear on because of the darkness and smoke in this section of the ship. After several other dogged hatches were opened and inspected and dogged again, the investigator came to the dogged hatch of the capstan machinery room. The sounds most prominent to the investigator with his OBA mask on were the continual, mechanical inhale and exhale of his own breathing and the very audible double beat of his own heart. The investigator never knew what might be waiting on the other side of these dogged hatches but his duty required him to find out.

He came to the vertical armored hatch of the capstan machinery room and with his gloved hands he took the dogging wheel and broke it free to the left, releasing the dogs. And as soon as they were clear the door burst outward, knocking the man down and flames of rage roared out and sought to devour. The flames rolled and flexed and filled the overhead and the investigator regained his feet and drove his shoulder into the door, driving it back. With all his might he forced the door and re-dogged it, containing the flames. Then he went forward to report.

Unit 35 dragged their hoses through the passageways to deploy in front of the capstan machinery room door. Other teams of 35 maneuvered to surround the space and discover the extent of the damage. Hand signals were given, and understood. Fog teams set up in front of the door and opened their sprays to cool the bulkhead and door while the 1½ inch attack hose was brought into position.

With salt water beading and streaking the OBA masks of everyone from the fog sprays the Repair Officer hand signaled the attack hose. "READY!" The men on the #1 hose nodded in unison. The Repair Officer turned and pointed at the man, soaked by the fog spray, standing ready to open the hatch. The man grabbed the dogging wheel in both hands and nodded to the officer. The Repair

Officer raised his right hand and the #1 hose opened a solid stream directed just to the right of the door. The hand was dropped and the wheel turned and hell burst the door open and flames roared out into the passageway and fought with demon fury to get through the wall of fog spray and lay waste to the hose teams.

The wall of spray began to take effect. After the first and second surge the flames from the capstan machinery room did not seem to come out as far. The hose teams never faltered and held their ground and the 1½ inch solid stream was directed straight through the door. Gooseneck applicators were thrust from either side into the open hatchway and in this way the teams forced the fires backward, reclaiming their ship, attacking the flames from every point.

On the 03 level it was different, Unit 77 investigator Dennis Vaeth scouted deep into the coal mine blackness, groping his way. The smoke was so thick it was difficult to see his hand in front of his face. He and his backup each carried a pillow case full of OBA canisters along with them as they slowly felt their way through the passageway. They could feel the temperature rising the farther back they went. Then they could see a faint light through the smoke and could hear and feel a constant rumbling. They moved closer. The faint light was now bright and flashing, FIRE!

Flaming fuel poured down into the starboard passageway from the breach made by the bomb lying on the deck at frame 205 and this was the fire that Dennis Vaeth saw. They made their way back to report the location of the fire to their unit which was dragging hoses and setting up de-smoking gear.

On the port side of the 03 level Unit 77 with remnants of 7 ALPHA pressed straight back through the passageway with their hoses. The situation on the port side was even worse than on the starboard side. The smoke was more extensive and it was even hotter. These men had been working back towards 7 ALPHA and had been close enough to see the flames ahead until the thick pall of smoke and darkness obscured it. As it was, they were all the way back to frame 230 when they were stopped by virtual blindness. Runners were sent forward to bring up de-smoking gear and OBA men and spare canisters, all they could carry. The heat was stifling. Sweeps were made through compartments while the hose teams were stalled and anyone not in a repair unit was evacuated. This was Damage Control work.

These Repair units had already taken a considerable knocking around and had to find and rig hoses from secondary sources for water, but they moved in to attack. The heat and exertion from dragging hoses and gear and the pounding of adrenalin caused the thirty minute OBA canisters to run out in half the time. Fresh OBA men were sent to relieve the hose men one or two at a time and pillow cases were stripped from racks and filled with spare canisters and dragged along with the teams. They fought their way back, cooling bulkheads with fog spray and directing solid streams ahead of them into the black smoke. The flash of flame could be dimly seen through the smoke and tremendous heat radiated from it.

The pressure in the hoses was unsteady. Streams of water would pulse and waver and sometimes stop altogether. Without the protective shield of fog spray the heat would quickly engulf them and the teams would wilt and bend low and move laboriously backward, giving ground.

Steve Bell had come up on deck and was helping download weapons from the A-7's stacked behind the bow cats. The water washdown nozzles in the flight deck were going strong up here, spewing water twenty feet into the air where there were no aircraft parked and where the streams hit wings and fuselages the water blew out in all directions. Everyone was soaked by it. The salt water would spray into eyes, temporarily blinding the men, but the effort went on.

Steve Bell found himself working as a team with a chief. They would come up under a bomb still loaded on the wing racks and hold their arms out, whereupon an Ordnanceman would release the bomb. The weight of it would nearly take them down to the deck. Through herculean effort they staggered under the load to the port side of the angle. The bomb slipped from their grasp and hit the deck with a heavy metallic thud. They both thought they were dealing with 250 lb. bombs and couldn't believe how heavy they were. They heaved and dragged and cursed the weapon over to the angle where they finally threw it over. The tremendous physical effort left Steve Bell and the chief light headed and seeing spots before their eyes. And even above the roaring flames back aft they heard a periodic crack of something of high velocity zing past or whang from the deck and go off into the distance. Steve Bell and the chief went back for what they thought was another 250 lb. bomb. There were only 500 pounders on the aircraft that day.

Billy Hawk was soaked with salt water from the washdown system too but he was glad of it and it felt good after bringing 300 out. He noticed the wind was beginning to carry the spray towards the aft starboard corner. The ship was coming into the wind.

On the bridge Capt. Lee was anxiously waiting for his ship to complete its turn. He would employ the wind as his weapon. A wall of wind to throw against a wall of fire. He had Main Communications contact CINCPACFLT with a report of the ships situation and a request for helo MEDEVAC and that the ship would possibly need medical teams and blood sent out by helo.

Capt. Lee stole a quick look forward at the sea. The waves were coming on in long, parallel ranks bearing on the port bow even as the bow of the carrier swung majestically into them, to take the ranks head on. "Another 15 or 20 seconds," he thought, "And I'll have the wind."

Casualties were dragged from the deck and brought inboard from many flight deck access points on the 03 level where Repair units took them and rendered first aid and moved them out to Battle Dressing Stations or to Sick Bay. The flow from the flight deck and 03 level was continuous. Just as the flaming fuel poured downward through every hole and open door, so too were the stretchers, seemingly under the laws of gravity, endless streams of them, all flowing downward.

The island evacuation route bore the heaviest burden of traffic with stretchers and walking wounded clattering continuously down the ladders towards Sick Bay and Midship Battle Dressing Station. The steps and handrails were slippery with blood and moving an unconscious man down in a stretcher was very hard. The man at the bottom of the stretcher bore most of the weight and many times the casualty simply spilled out. Stretchers were sometimes placed athwart the handrails and skidded down but some inevitably got loose. Volunteers took up positions where they could at the base and outboard of the rails of the ladders to help pass the wounded down. The sight of an already terribly suffering man crashing down the ladder steps was painfully sorrowful. The grisly procession was kept moving, always moving, downward.

The three purpleshirts ran back in the port catwalk to get Kreisler. They ran low, past those seeking cover, past others attending or dragging away wounded, with a steady zing and buzz of things flying just overhead. They ran all the way back to #4 elevator, just past the tail section of F-4 #112 parked overhead. There, flat out in the catwalk and unable to use his legs, lay "Chunky Charlie Kreisler," at 6'-4" and 240 lbs., he was the biggest man on the flight deck.

They saw that he was unconscious but he was alive. He moaned incoherently. They could not see any blood on him and didn't know what was wrong but heaved his vast bulk up, the same way they had carried Norsworthy. This was no place to tarry. They hauled him up and proceeded to run, keeping low. With such a weight suspended between them, whose arms and legs flopped lifelessly, it was a very difficult thing. They grunted from the exertion and banged along for all they were worth with the mass of Kreisler continually moaning and slipping from their grasp. They grew very weak from the strain. They had made it only halfway back to the V-4 crews shelter when the hulking weight of Chunky Charlie Kreisler slipped away and bore them all down and the four of them fell into a headlong heap in the catwalk.

At first they all lay there breathing very hard and being very weak. The trip with Norsworthy must have taken a lot out of them. They had all been running on pure adrenalin for some time and now that they were down they felt the rush of tension subsiding. They just lay there, drained. They took long measured breaths to satisfy their bodies demands for oxygen. They realized they were spent. The crewleader slowly sat up and leaned back against the bulkhead, breathing hard. He lolled back his head and watched Fitzgerald and Arrick fight off exhaustion and come into a sitting position beside him. The three sat there, leaning back, breathing like steam engines. They were beat.

At their feet Chunky Charlie moaned and groped about with his arms, hands and fingers reaching. His eyes were still tightly closed. The three regarded him with exasperation, knowing they would have to carry him again and they did not possess the strength.

"GET THE *#+$$@*% UP KREISLER!!" The demand brought forth a twittering of reckless laughter from the three. Chunky Charlie, for all his impressive size, was notoriously faint hearted and it was something marveled at by all who knew him. They still could see no mark on him, "KREISLER, YOU PUSSY, GET UP!!" The laughter erupted again, this time bordering on wild hysteria.

They reluctantly began to move to take up their painful task again when one thoughtfully pointed out, "This is like trying to carry a 250 pound water balloon!"

That was what did it. The reckless twittering exploded into hilarious, uproarious, hysterical laughter. The sheer abandon of the wave upon wave of laughing rendered them incapable of anything. Never in their lives, before or hereafter, would they ever laugh like this. It was wild and pure and flowed like the surge of waters from a dam break. They laughed loud and long and were delirious and helpless, wracked from the outpour of guffaws. The tension and the terror and all the pent up fears found release through the sheer joy of laughing.

They couldn't stop it. Surely others heard the hilarity and looked with amazement into the catwalk. There was little doubt that these three were the only ones laughing on such a terrible day as this. They tried to stop it but the hysteria flowed. Their sides ached with the pain of it. They fell over and tried to draw away from one another. On and on they laughed.

The last of it finally subsided and left them heaving and drained. They all fought with conviction to suppress the rest of it out of respect of the pain of others. They felt shame. They had to get on with their mission. Kreisler groaned through closed eyes and weakly waved his arms, "OH SHUT UP!"

A re-flash of hilarity laid the weak men low. They groveled. And then the deck and catwalk shuddered and brought them up, quick, out of their stupor.

At 0826:19 aircraft #214 exploded, punching a 9 x 3 foot crater 2 inches deep into the flight deck. A sparrow missile shot straight up, out of the fireball followed one second later by another one. Both missiles left visible white smoke trails shooting up into the vast, towering column of black smoke.

On the flight deck #4 jet blast deflector had been raised to protect the F-4 on #4 catapult from the flaming, flying metal. Two foam hoses were forming under its cover. Jerry McKenzie had jumped down into the catwalk adjacent to the jet blast deflector to shut off water pressure to one hose which had blown apart when it was dragged across some razor sharp shards of jagged metal. When a new length was added in, Jerry McKenzie opened the valve. As soon as the pressure filled the hose an officer had the two teams move out from behind the jet blast deflector and advance down the deck to get back into the fight and bring their foam and water hoses to bear on the blazing tanker on #4 elevator. Jerry McKenzie stayed in the catwalk making sure all the foam and salt water fireplug valves were fully open.

As the teams drew closer to #4 elevator, Twig Tordoff distinctly heard the high pitched zing of what he was sure was the rivets popping off the airframe of the tanker. He thought of the fuel boiling and expanding the fuselage and wing tanks causing the rivets to pop loose. He grabbed the officer by the arm and shouted to be heard above the roaring flames, "ITS GOING TO GO! THE RIVETS ARE POPPING! THE TANKERS GOING TO GO!"

The officer shook loose and addressed a denunciation and the teams pressed on, splashing foam on the deck as they went. Twig Tordoff had been right about the fuel boiling in the tanks of 614 but something far worse was about to happen.

The Rider on the Pale Horse held back to let these two hose teams expose themselves. He would let the Pale Horse trample those underfoot after his blow. He waited as they funneled between 310 and 112, which were not yet on fire. At 0826:25 he sprung the trap and struck with all his fury.

F-4 #106, which was lost in the flames behind 614, still had all her bombs on her racks and at this time they blew and exploded the pressure cooker of the tanker right next to it. The detonation of the bombs and the simultaneous eruption of 6000 gallons of JP-5 caused a cataclysmic explosion. The blast from 106 blew 614 into a hurricane of liquid fire and metals which swept forward with such fury that 310 and 112 were blown several feet forward and holed by hails of metals and both burst into flames.

The teams were caught full on and blasted from their feet and clawed and ripped by flying metal. The fury of the dragons of hell breathed their flaming breath on the teams and ravaged and scathed them. Flames rolled updeck and splashed into the catwalk. Jerry McKenzie was still there turning valves when the blast of pure fire roared right up the catwalk and set him afire. He reacted with all he had. Knowing he was completely aflame, he got up and ran up onto the flight deck and kept on running towards the bow. The wind was blowing his own flames away from his face and he ran into it so he could breathe. Someone ran up and tackled him and then another came and they rolled him over and over. The man who tackled him was beating out his own flames. Others came and helped till the flames were out.

Fuel tanks erupt in starboard corner. Osterbauer collection.

F-4 106's store of 500 pound bombs explodes blowing the pressure cooker of 614 into a million points of light. An entire group of firefighters goes down between the three air craft seen here. This explosion lights off both 112 and 310. Official U.S. Navy photo, Osterbauer collection.

Jerry McKenzie knew he was burned. He got up and immediately went into the island and joined the procession heading down the ladders to Sick Bay. By the time he emerged from the hatch at the bottom where John Guillot's men were assisting those going into Sick Bay, he was trying very hard to stifle his own screaming. All he remembered was someone shouting, "Here comes another one!" And then two corpsmen ran up to him and they each blasted him with a shot of morphine. Before he went out, he saw them both dig into their bags and bring out two more needles. Then they both blasted him again.

Twig Tordoff got up off the deck. He was unhurt but there was a terrible carnage wrought among the others. Those that could, ran in to bring those down out of the flames. He found himself on the end of a stretcher, taking one of them into the island.

The 106 blast caused a 22 x 18 foot, deeply petaled hole in the flight deck outboard of the ballistic shell. The hole sheared off at the frame 235 bulkhead but overlapped and blew down through the frame 230 bulkhead. What was left of the edges of the hole was deeply pocked, indicating that it was a non-contact explosion, in that the fragments had time to form. The aft and side bulkheads were blown outward and deflected and ripped loose from their welds and the frame 230 bulkhead was rent and blown to pieces. The salt water and foam firemains were blown through. The 03 level deck was holed cleanly from frame 230 to 235 and cratered and buckled as far forward as frame 225. Broken up pieces of flight deck plating blew down and outward in all directions, ripping through the passageway where unit 77 was fighting and blasting through the compartment next to them. The high velocity blast and metals blew out and wrecked the 02 and 01 level spaces as far forward as frame 225 where they tore their way out of the ship and drove into the sea. Pieces passed through the 02 and 01 levels and strafed #6 sponson. Flaming fuel poured down through all.

A storm of hot gases and flying metal blasted the firefighters in the next three levels down. Unit 77 was just about abreast of the area, fighting aft, when the terrific explosion sent great pieces of metal tearing through decks and bulkheads all around them and knocked them all to the deck and took out the firemains.

On the bridge Karl Mahumed was watching the action when the 106/614 explosion went off. The blast sent storms of fragments all over the deck, with many hitting into the island structure. Flaming wreckage was crashing into the aircraft parked forward. He saw a man far up on the bow collapse. He was thinking about how far he would have to jump again when Lt. Comdr. Joe Lybrand came up and relieved him so he could go to his battle station.

Lash Hansborough was in the Enclosed Operating Space of #4 plant when the 106 blast went. They had all been watching the fluctuating firemain pressure gauges with absorbing interest while hearing the constant demand for more water from the flight deck. When 106 went off it was so violent that it knocked a coffee cup off the desk all the way down in #4 plant. Lash Hansborough watched it skid across the deck plating. He looked out the round window and saw the dust cascading down into the plant again. It was incredible the way the ship shook. They saw the needles of the pressure gauges fall dramatically. Within seconds there were the inevitable calls from the flight deck for more water. The propulsion plants were putting out all they had. Nerves were on edge and the tension was thick. Someone exploded into verbal castigation, "Don't those *#%$$#* deck Apes know that if they want more %##!! water we can't give it to them by just opening more (*&#$!!) VALVES!!"

The four purpleshirts were knocked down by the blast. The mass of JP-5 from the 106/614 explosion napalmed its way in a rolling fireball up the deck and port catwalk, horribly scourging all in its way. The waves of flame roared all the way to the jet blast deflectors, just a few yards short of the purpleshirts. The searing heat of the fireball continued on and scathed them and they quickly picked up their charge and pressed on, expending all reserves of strength to get to the cover of their crews shelter.

The #4 jet blast deflector, raised to protect the F-4 on #4 cat, did just that. A 500 lb. bomb hurtled out of the 106/614 explosion, blasting through anything and anyone in its way, and crashed into the backside of the deflector shearing away two of the massive steel lifting arms. There, it stopped, smoking behind the deflector.

Capt. Lee saw the terrible explosion of 106. He saw the flames leap from aft of #4 elevator to well forward of it. He saw fully one third of his ship totally engulfed in flames. But now, he had the wind. He could see the flames and the smoke blown backward by it, coming straight down the deck. At last, he had the wind, 28 knots of it and more if he went to speed. He watched the flames give back under the force of the wind.

The Rider on the Pale Horse saw the fires brought to bay under the influence of the wind. He marshaled his powers and raised them up, yea raised them ever higher. The flames gorged and devoured. They roared back, violently shooting skyward, carrying high all manner of flaming debris. Aye, the wind! Like a bellows to the forge, the flames fed on the wind, consuming all and roared ever higher again. Insatiable, the flames grew hotter and soared in rolling thunderheads and burned with a brilliance of a white heat.

And the Rider whose name was Death saw the works of his hands had lain many low. All those who dared oppose the Horseman lay broken on this side of the ship. Not a hose was still in action here. He wheeled the Pale Horse back into the cover of the flames. He would prepare an ambush for those on the other side.

Bob McLaughlin and everyone else in Primary had recovered from the terrific 106/614 detonation. The scene on deck was one of utter devastation. All port side hose teams were wiped out, there wasn't one left in action. The deck was thickly strewn with wounded. There were still three hoses fighting on the starboard side and the Air Boss was dictating, "GET A HOSE TEAM OVER TO 310! AND GET THAT PHANTOM CLEAR OF #4 CATAPULT!"

And those who came forward to re-fill the ranks did so with the fearful knowledge that they were feeding themselves into the meat grinder. They were not ordered into the fray by anyone, but were rather compelled from within themselves. They were responding to the force of a simple virtue. The virtue was a common bond shared by all those who answered their country's call to war and accepted the hardships and sacrifices as their duty. They were the average American.

At 0826:41 a bomb lying on deck under aircraft #214 blew the F-4 into a shooting fireball, punching a 3 foot diameter crater and inch deep into the deck in heavy plating.

Lt. Comdr. Charles Brackin had his two teams engaged in desperately trying to hold the flames back from the island and the aircraft parked on #3 elevator. The other hose was moving over to center deck under the direction of the Air Boss. Brackin's teams had no more hose and could advance no farther. More than once the teams had marched in to get their faltering streams more directly into the blaze and stretched the hoses till they ripped out of the brass couplings. There was no more hose to be had on the flight deck.

Commander. Al Bureau had run up to confer with Brackin, trying to be of whatever assistance he could. Brackin's need was the same as before, "HOSE AL, ALL YOU CAN FIND!"

Ens. Karl Mahumed took the Captains elevator for the trip down to his General Quarters station. This would be a much faster way to travel down to the 03 level. The elevator itself was rather small and Mahumed stood facing the door feeling himself rapidly descending. The elevator stopped at the 03 level and the door opened and Ens. Mahumed stepped out into the passageway and started across to take up his duties as Repair Officer of Unit 75 on the port side. At his back the elevator door closed and the car started back up to the 010 level.

Steve Meyer and the other Interior Communications men were now trapped in their space. The access hatch from the catwalk next to the Fresnel lens was totally involved in flames. They all watched the monitor and the spectacle of the flight deck violence was unbelievable. They heard the Air Boss coaxing and presently a hose team came into line of sight, directly in the cross hairs of the screen. The hose team marched in lock step, heading towards the blazing 310 and then a brilliant flash of white light blinded the monitor, and the ship heaved and shuddered. When the monitor screen cleared they saw a jumble of bodies where the hose team had been and a nozzleless hose flopping insanely about them.

The Horseman had come up through the flames and at 0827:08 brought his great sword cleaving into the blazing 312, blowing its weapons. Blast and shards of hot metal swept the deck in all directions.

Brackin was still standing by the island with Al Bureau when the A-7 exploded and metals stormed into the island and one particular howling thing passed just over their heads with the sounds of great sheets of rending canvas and smashed into and through the island. The piece, which turned out to be a strong back mounting bar from a 500 pound bomb, tore through the island bulkhead and blew apart the 8 inch firemain riser which served the entire island structure, the ONLY firefighting water in the island. The strong back deflected downward slightly and crashed through the Captains elevator door and smashed through the back of the elevator car on its way back up to the 010 level. The car stopped cold and the strong back punched in the bulkhead, but did not pass through it into Flight

Deck Control.

When the strong back blew the riser apart it knocked everyone in 7 BRAVO off their feet and wounded many with the flying metal. The release of the pressurized salt water showered all over the 7 BRAVO space in a deluge. There were many wounded and terribly burned lying on the deck and the salt water poured all over them, quickly filling the deck to the level of the ladder coaming. The water poured down the ladders, all over the many casualties and men carrying them down. It poured and washed the ladders all the way down to the 2nd deck. The Repair Officer himself ran down to the riser valve on the 03 level and shut off the flow of water to the island. Such was the emergency to relieve the suffering of the wounded, many of whom were in grave danger of drowning.

When the flaming wreckage was blown forward from the 312 blast, it was not immediately set upon by the two remaining teams, so great was the urgency to hold back the wall of flame. Someone realized in horror that there were burning bombs among the junk and got the teams turned around. Brackin called out for the EOD while he took two weapons alternately under spray, The bombs were holed by shrapnel and flames issued forth from the holes. The spray of water would put out the flames from one bomb and then sweep to put out the other, whereupon the first would re-flash again.

Billy Hawk had the nozzle of the other hose and was directing a weak spray back and forth across the broken open bomb at a distance of six feet. The green explosive filler burned with stubborn obstinacy. It would not be put out. Billy Hawk kept his spray on the weapon and with clenched teeth, waited for the blast that would blow him to pieces. The hose became very heavy and he grew increasingly tired. He felt his strength draining away. The weapon continued to burn and Billy Hawk turned to get the next man to take over the nozzle. The next man and the rest of the team were thirty feet away and still backing up. He was alone on the nozzle.

Brackin's men were going to pick up and throw the flaming weapons over under cover of the spray. The EOD ran up and stopped them and told them to cool the weapons where they lay. The destruction caused by detonation would be far worse at or below the waterline than here. It took all the courage they had to stand in place and play the water back and forth between the weapons and watch as the EOD knelt down in front of each and carefully unscrewed the fuses.

The drama was too much for a certain greenshirt. Recognizing the imminent destruction of all if the bombs were not thrown over, the man ran forward and thrust his hands out to grasp one. Brackin saw him coming and pushed the nozzle over to direct the stream of salt water squarely into the man's chest, just as he bent down. The blast of water knocked him off his feet and the stream rolled him over and over.

The greenshirt was stunned, but rose up and came back again with the singular intention of grabbing the bomb. Brackin shouted the order, "BLAST HIM!"

Three times this scene repeated itself until the greenshirt finally understood. Brackin appreciated the bravery of the man and saluted his gesture of self sacrifice in this critical hour. But this was also a time that demanded the coolest of thinking and rock steady nerve.

Capt. Lee had seen and felt the latest blow from the bridge. The word was passed that all firefighting water for the island was knocked out. There were burning live weapons scattered about the parked aircraft on #3 elevator and one bomb was perilously close to the island. The port mains were wrecked in a number of places and not enough pressure could be brought to bear to charge even one hose over there. The only hose teams still in action were turned away from the fires to cool weapons near the island. The hose blown apart in the center of the deck was not yet repaired and the wounded were still being dragged away. There was now nothing holding back the wall of fire.

Capt. Lee looked forward. He received a report from Central that pressure was falling again. They could not keep up with the demand with fires being fought in so many places and the other parasitic loads bleeding off pressure. He took a hard look at the many spouts of salt water springing from the deck among the tightly packed aircraft abreast and forward of the island. This curtain of spray had kept the flaming debris from igniting these aircraft. The water washdown system, and two foam hoses blanketing the deck forward, were the only things keeping the flames from claiming the entire flight deck. The life of *Enterprise* hung in the balance. He made a command decision, "De-activate the water washdown system and all fog foam stations forward of the island!"

The three purpleshirts staggered through the hatch, into the V-4 crew shelter where they lay the mammoth Kreisler down at the nearest place. A.R. Theide had something of a first aid station set up and was directing what to do with the wounded brought in off deck. The remainder of crew #2 stood gasping for breath, trying to regain themselves. They all heard the word passed over the 1MC for blood donors to report to Sick Bay.

The V-4 phone talker received a message and barked it out to the assemblage, "They want someone to go back and de-fuel 112!"

A tirade of anger and protests erupted and fists shook in the air and great stores of tension and wrath were vented, all directed at the hapless person of the phone talker. Bitter lamentation was pronounced about the eternal disregard and stupidity of those in authority. Some of the younger men were shocked at this display of mutinous blasphemy, and began to back out of the room to go do that which was ordered. The crewleader stopped them, "112 is already on fire, we just came back from there. All the blood in this room couldn't help it now."

The men began to calm down, the younger of them grew somber. The lesson taught by the veterans was clear. Fools rush in where angels fear to tread. A recollection struck the crewleader like a thunderbolt and he asked of everyone the question, "Who is that laying on the deck back on #3 cat?"

"Asbury," someone said, "I saw him get hit!"

The crewleader had forgotten about the purpleshirt down with the great head wound. With 310 aflame, the fire would be very, very close. Crew #2 was about ready again, it was now or never. "Let's Go!"

Jim Fitzgerald had already gone out and found a rigid wire stretcher from the passageway and now the three pounded back out and up the ladder to the catwalk, then up another to the flight deck. There was no time now for advancing under cover.

They took off at a sprint, down the deck, back to where 310 blazed away and their mate lay in a pool of his own blood at the edge of the spreading liquid fire. Into the very jaws of the Dragon they ran. Fires raged from 112 to 310, straight across deck. Their fear was very great, and the crewleader prayed as he ran.

"Eternal Father strong to save"

And the wind howled down the deck with the sound of a great rushing. It moaned a steady song of sorrow as it was drawn into the raging furnace. The sound of it was the wail of the Angels of Heaven in mourning.

"Whose Arm doth hold the distant wave"

And the furnace hurled its heat and flame skyward with great violence, carrying high all manner of debris. And the ship and her decks quaked and shuddered under the volcanic thundering of the firestorm as if the very seas trembled and shook in awe of the Fury.

"Oh hear us when we cry to Thee"

And they stopped at him struck down and placed him into the stretcher and they were seared and suffocating from the heat. The crack and roar of exploding things was continuous as molten metals flowed and bubbled in the conflagration.

"For those in peril upon the sea!"

And they raised up their dead and ran with the burden as fast as their wills and bodies would take them. And the terror was very great. Straight across to the island, across the very face of the maelstrom they ran, anticipating at every step the stroke that would cut them down. The Horseman let them pass.

They reached the protective mass of the island on the forward side of it where they slowed to a stop, nearly dead from the effort. This was even worse than before! Their lungs ached for want of air. Miraculously, they were unhurt.

No great feat of sport, no touchdown ever scored could match the breathless desperation of that run. Winded, they staggered through the hatchway into the island with their dead, looking to give him over to some corpsmen. The passageway was ankle deep in bloody water. The deck of the Crash/Salvage locker was covered with bodies half submerged in the red wash. The crewleader looked into Flight Deck Control and there, ashen faced and looking at them, were a chief and a second class petty officer wearing purple jerseys. The crewleader wondered, "What were they doing in here?"

A voice said, "DOWN HERE!" They looked and saw the Marines were passing wounded down the ladders. The Marines stood aside and let them proceed down with the dead man.

In Central Control, Comdr. Neel saw the pressure falling away on the Midship starboard loop from the effects of the ruptured firemain in the island. He immediately ordered valve 2-103-2 opened, cross connecting the starboard Forward with the starboard Midship loops.

In #4 Plant EOS, Lt. Hansborough and the others watched in amazement as the pressure for the starboard mains steadily free-failed all the way down to 15 PSI where it weakly stabilized. They were hearing repeated urgent requests over the Main Communications speakers to get the flight deck water washdown system secured forward. Then the engine room watch called up to report that the steam pump put on with no governor was cavitating badly. It was inevitable. Going flat out with everything they had on line and down to 15 or 20 PSI the steam pump was running away. The impeller was going wild and the engine room watch was told to leave it on line but to stand clear in case it let go and exploded the casing.

Lash Hansborough was absolutely sure that there were explosions going off above and somewhere aft of them. Although no word of any explanation had been passed, his best guess was that Hangar Bay 2 was blowing up. The general feeling down below was that the firemain pressure was low from overuse, with all the systems they had on line going. That is why Hansborough told the engine room watch to leave the steamer on line. If they needed it up there that bad, keep it running!

He shot a quick glance at the door to the escape hatch and wondered if they would have to use it. This same feeling was an unspoken fear shared by everyone in the lower spaces. Those whose duty kept them in places below the water line were ever cognizant of the chances of their being trapped below. They all looked with suspicion at the escape hatches. Down here, there was no way of knowing what might be waiting for them on the other side.

Frank Newmayer was unconscious when they hoisted his torn body onto a table in Sick Bay. There was hectic activity here, with wounded on every table and bunk and lining the bulkheads on the deck. The flow of incoming was so great that all wards were opened and those stabilized were quickly shuttled back out where they were put under observation on the messdecks. Newmayer's clothes were cut away and his burns and wounds were quickly addressed by several corpsmen and doctors. Plasma and I.V. solutions were started in his arms and a corpsman monitoring his vital signs told all that the patients pulse rate was going up, way up! His blood pressure was checked and it was found there was no pressure at all! Like the steam pump running wild because of burst mains, the man's heart was racing for want of blood to pump.

The heart of Frank Newmayer raced out of control and then just stopped and he died under the hands of the Medical team. "HE'S GOING OUT! HE'S GOING OUT!"

Shouts erupted and directions were given with the greatest urgency as those working on him refused to let him go. They squeezed and banged on him like a New York City mugging. They coaxed and pleaded with him. They challenged and dared him while they pounded and massaged. Like an old farm tractor, they kick started the heart of Frank Neumayer back into sputtering life. A corpsman found a pulse and cried out, "HE'S COMING BACK!"

Those attending expressed the elation of having dodged a bullet. Many had already been dodged, and there were many more to come. This was only one of a great many grim triumphs achieved by the professionalism and dedication of the entire Medical Department.

Billy Hawk had sagged to his knees under the weight of the hose, still directing the stream onto the 500 pounder. He couldn't blame the others for backing away. There were not that many still on deck and those left had taken a fearful beating. If the bomb blows, why should everyone have to die?

Just when the faltering flight deck teams needed it most, relief came in the form of the ships Marine Detachment. A gang of them charged out of the island and ran up and took over Billy Hawks hose and bolstered the other teams fighting and reforming. Billy Hawk and the others were glad to see them. With the fires closing on the island, they had to hold the line here or it was all over. The Marines, they knew, would not retreat.

The *USS Rogers* had cut across the *Enterprise* wake and come up to within 100 yards astern and to port of the exploding carrier. Lt. Comdr. Harris Sperling had his best man take the helm while he called out orders from the open wing of the bridge. Blast and flaming fuel had sprayed out ahead of them and burned on the surface for a time. The carrier was virtually lost in a wall of smoke and flame from astern and Sperling hauled off to port to get clear of it while the *Rogers* closed the distance. The flames shot skyward and billowed and rolled in their ferocity. The shock of concussion was very sharp and heaved the little ship upward. Shrapnel zinged and clanged from their decks and splashed the waters all around as they maneuvered to get closer.

At 0827:26 a bomb on deck exploded on the portside in the 106 area, just as the F-4 on #4 cat was being towed clear. The Air Boss continued to cheer lead and now he said, "ALL RIGHT, THAT LOOKS LIKE THE LAST OF IT! THAT'S ALL OF THE ORDNANCE! LET'S HANG ON AND SAVE THE SHIP!"

The ragged teams reformed. Port side survivors dragged dead hoses back and saved what they could of them and plugged into bow stations forward of the angle. Where new lengths could be found they were added on and new lines of battle were arrayed. They hauled the hoses as far toward the flames as they would reach, even though there was no pressure in them. Then they stood there, waiting for the pressure to come back.

The decimated hose on the centerline was re-manned and the severed length taken out. This team tried to respond to the direction of the Air Boss when at 0827:42 a rocket pod from 312 which had been blown to the right of the centerline, just adjacent to #4 elevator, blew. This punched a crater 2 feet in diameter, 2 inches into the deck in heavy plating. Blast and shards of hot metal swept the deck.

Twig Tordoff had just stepped back onto the flight deck with his stretcher when a Marine Officer ran up and told him to bring it to #3 elevator. The bombs which were blown there were being thrown over. The first was removed by screwing a hernia bar, a section of pipe used to lift the bombs up to wing racks, into the bomb and manhandling it over the edge of the elevator. It was very difficult to carry a MARK-82 in this way. The bomb was dropped, bar and all, into and through the safety netting of the elevator. Twig Tordoff had a stretcher that was a sheet of canvas slung between two poles. He laid it down and a gang rolled the weapon into it whereupon eight men picked up the stretcher and lurched their way to the edge of the elevator. The weight of the bomb drew the poles together and the eight men strained to stay apart. Since Tordoff was the first man on the left side, the momentum of the eight carried him over the edge of the flight deck and he dropped into the safety netting which was ripped through from the first bomb.

The Marine Officer had come forward from behind and grabbed the collar of Tordoff's jersey just as he was on his way through the netting and into the blue Pacific 70 feet below. He clung desperately to the stretcher and his own weight was pulling the next two men in line over the edge. The stretcher nearly touched the deck and

Flames now rage from 112 to 310 straight across deck, no hoses left on port side. Hoses in view coming back from bow stations. Official U.S. Navy photo, Osterbauer collection.

F-4 is towed clear of #4 catapult, making a firebreak. Thunderous explosion erupted just after this picture was taken in the 106 area. Official U.S. Navy photo, Osterbauer collection.

threatened to spill its load onto Tordoff's own head as everyone strained with all their strength to pull back. Tordoff dangled for an eternity and then the Marine hauled him back up through the netting to land, pale and shaken, back on the flight deck. The rest of the bearers were spent. They lay the stretcher down and rolled the bomb over the side.

The team then went back and gathered up the last bomb in the stretcher. They hauled and staggered under the load to the elevator again. This time, they threw stretcher and all through the netting. The entire time, everyone was aware of a continuous cracking heard even above the roar of the flames and they all waited for the blast which would cut them all down.

The blown apart 8 inch firemain riser in the island initiated a flood of water which deluged the 04 level and rose above the coaming and cascaded down the open ladders, all the way down to the 2nd deck. At each level in between, an accumulation of bloody water about the ladder coamings made the passage of stretchers increasingly more difficult because of the slippery conditions.

Lt. (j.g) Dave Fusco, Repair 7 BRAVO, had electrical circuits secured in the island, averting imminent Class Charlie fires and called for the Emergency Repair Crew to plug and patch the broken firemain. Hence, all electrical power, excepting emergency systems, were shut down in the island. Strike Operations were evacuated from their spaces. Nick Lasovich was helping out on the starboard side when he heard someone yelling for men to push out the RA-5C VIGILANTE parked up against the island. Nick ran over and joined the twenty five or thirty men who were straining for all they were worth on the aircraft. It would not budge. They put their backs and shoulders to it with cords of muscle and veins standing out from the effort. The gang in Primary saw the drama below and the Air Boss barked out direction, "GET SOME HELP ON THAT VIGILANTE! WE HAVE TO GET THESE BIRDS CLEAR OF THE ISLAND!"

Another eight or ten men ran up and threw their backs into it and the 37 ton aircraft began to move. Feeling the aircraft yield, they all fought with renewed exertion to overcome inertia and gain momentum to get the monster rolling, but the weight of it was so great that despite their mightiest effort, the machine progressed only slowly updeck. The Air Boss and the whole gang in Primary cheered them on, "COME ON! PUSH THAT MOTHER! LAY INTO IT BOYS, LEAN INTO IT! THAT'S IT! MOVE IT OUT! MOVE IT OUT!"

Big John Guillot's 5 BRAVO men were still going strong. He had men bringing up cans of foam from wherever it could be found and breaking into storage areas looking for more. He had men assisting casualties into Sick Bay and others keeping the decks and passageways clear of all manner of debris. John Guillot had a good idea of what was happening to the ship. Wherever he went his phone talker was there, tagging along, relaying every message he heard passed over the Damage Control and Engineering circuits. He also had direct communication with the Medical Department and also whatever could be picked up from those bringing casualties down from the flight deck.

There were a number of volunteers who came up continually to 5 BRAVO and asked if they could help. John Guillot looked at these men and smiled. They were the ones who stayed in their air conditioned offices when the Repair parties sweated through their innumerable drills wearing helmets and masks and full Damage Control gear. It was nice to know that these men were there to be counted when there was real work to be done. "Sure," he said, "we have plenty of work for you to do!"

FIVE BRAVO had their hands full finding new sources of foam and keeping the fog foam injection station fed and running. They had men out securing the water washdown system valves in their areas and helping with the wounded. John Guillot also had to keep two fire teams intact and ready to fight. Sure, glad to have you! The volunteers were put to task doing the sundry things and relieved the Damage Control men. They helped carry away the empty foam cans and bring up new ones. A gang of them were sent into Sick Bay where they were used to monitor individual patients while the Medical Staff proceeded with their assembly line pace.

All this hectic activity with the constant and steady flow of the torn and maimed coming down the ladders. Each sufferer and wound was shocking in its own right and bore grim witness to the savagery of the fight from above. Bodies cleaved through flesh and bone as if from axe or sword stroke, or crushed and mangled as if chewed in the slavering jaws of wild beasts. Pathetic things torn asunder as if rent by the stroke of great talons. The ghastly red parade marched by.

Presently, three purpleshirts carrying a fourth in a wire stretcher stepped through the hatch and stumbled their way towards Sick Bay. The sight in the stretcher was terribly obscene, giving hint to what may lie in store for all. The men of 5 BRAVO watched the purpleshirts go by in silent respect and steeled themselves for the time when they would be called forth to go and face the Fury.

The purpleshirts crossed the passageway and went through the door into Sick Bay. As soon as they stepped in the stretcher was snatched away from them and they were left to eddy and swirl in the sudden calm at journeys end. It was the crewleader's idea to join the blood donors line. It was a shameful act of doing something, anything, to keep from joining the hose teams again. The crewleader had dared to know the TRUTH and was left naked and humbled by the knowledge of it. He would never seek to know the TRUTH again.

The three purpleshirts stood in the blood donor line and looked about them. They were the only ones here wearing the colored jerseys, the mark of the flight decker. They were objects of stares and unspoken questioning's from all the others. The V-4 men bore the marks of battle. They were wet with foam and water. Their cuts bled freely from about their bodies and mixed with the large dark stains of the blood of others. No one spoke to them but the looks said it all, "What was happening?!" The purpleshirts had no answers for them. How could they explain the madness?

The deck suddenly heaved and shuddered under the force of another heavy blow. The blood donor line was rocked and shaken and looked wildly about waiting for the overhead to come crashing in. The shock of it had brought the crewleader back to his sense of duty. He looked at his men and said, "Let's Go!" Crew two bolted for the door and ran up the portside ladders to regain the flight deck. At every armored hatch they had to stop and wait for the Damage Control parties to request clearance over the sound powered phones to break ZEBRA and let the flight deckers get back up on deck. By the time Crew two emerged into the thundering catwalk outside their crews shelter, they were nearly suffocating from the claustrophobic feeling of being trapped below. It was with relief that the crewleader ran out of the hatch and up onto the deck to face the cauldron. It was with relief! Having seen the alternative, he would take his stand here and face the foe, yea, and would not turn from it again. For he had seen the trap laid by the Horseman. The fog of His presence was everywhere below. It wafted through the hatches and passageways, and clung to the overheads in all' compartments and spaces. It was the pall of death which silently spread and accumulated, its smoky tendrils reaching out to touch all those below and gently, sensuously, stroke them with deaths own hand. The crewleader shuddered at the thought of what fate might lie in store for those unfortunates whose duty kept them below. As for him, staring death in the face was far preferable to waiting for it unknowing.

6. THE STAND

The phone talker for Repair 6 ALPHA, which was the magazine washdown system of After Bomb Assembly, received a call from DC Central and promptly relayed the message to the Repair Officer, Ens. Mike Clark. They were instructed to remove the MARK-24 paraflares from deep stowage magazine 5-167-4-M. Just after the message was received, the EOD came down and also told Clark that the flares had to be removed and ejected from the ship.

Mike Clark had only been aboard the ship for less than a month. He was originally to have been the 1st Division Junior Officer and had since been assigned Weapons Division Coordinator. He had only been down in the magazine washdown for three drills and was not yet totally familiar with everything. He had a copy of where all the magazines were and how to flood them and also what was contained in the magazines. The paraflare locker in question held 455 MARK-24 flares. These, he knew, were the munitions which had killed so many on the ORISKANY in '66. They were very dangerous to handle and if one were lit below decks, as in ORISKANY'S trial, there was virtually no way to put them out.

Ens. Clark wanted to flood the magazine but DC Central did not have the water to spare and told 6 ALPHA again to get the flares out. With fires up to frame 190 on both port and starboard sides above and down to the 3rd deck behind them, there was no time to lose.

Mike Clark did not like the idea. He had been on the bridge when the initial rocket burst had set everything aflame on the flight deck and knew what weapons were on deck. He had immediately rushed down to his Repair party and since then they all could feel the terrific beating the ship was taking. He did not know precisely the extent of the fires but knew they had to be close because DC Central wanted the flares out. He sent some men of the After Bomb Assembly crew to the magazine with the instructions, "If you can get

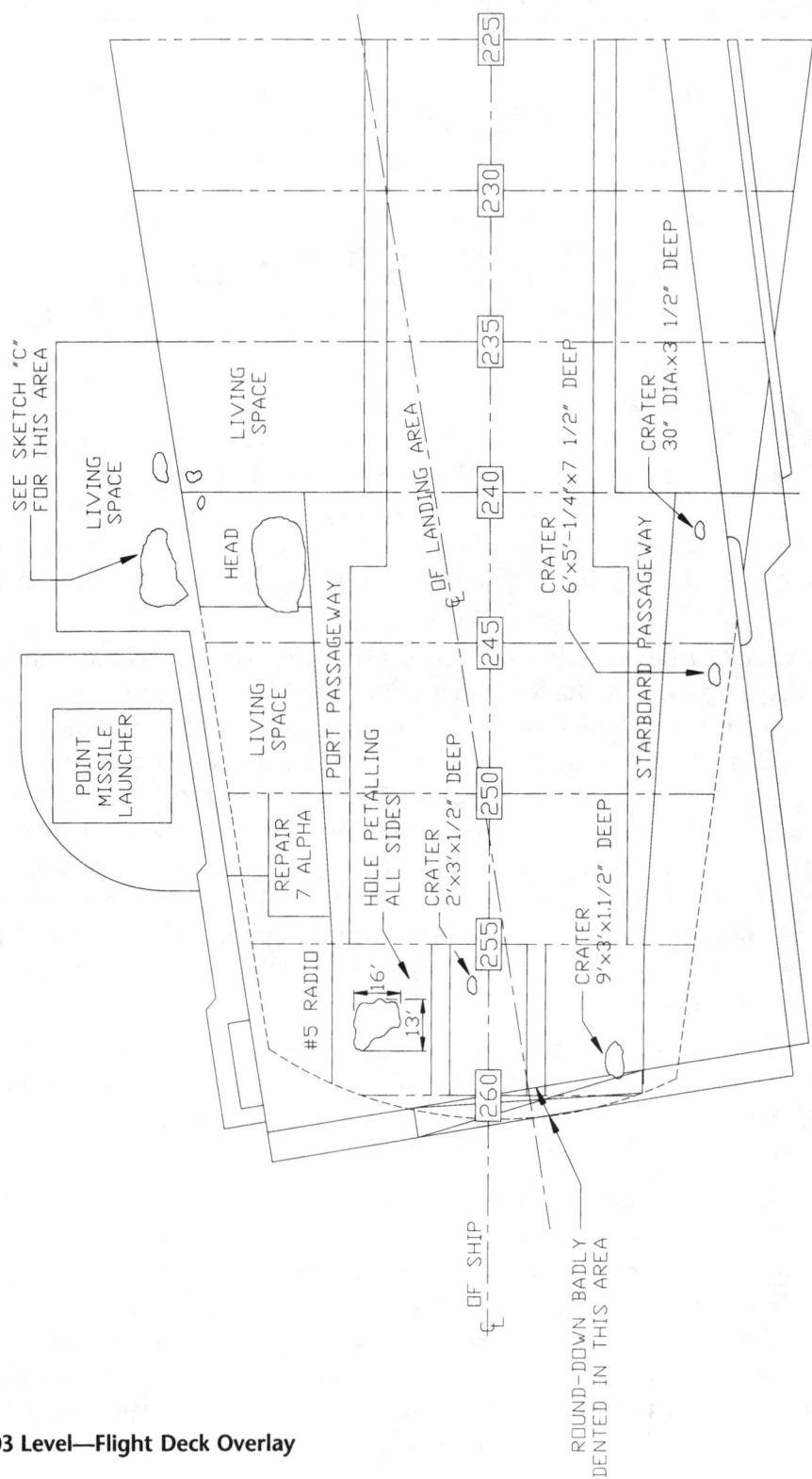

03 Level—Flight Deck Overlay

in and remove them, do it! If not, come back and we will flood it!"

Repair 3 was also removing MARK-24 flares from another magazine only 25 frames from areas afire. Down in magazine 6-225-2-M men were carrying out flares two at a time. DC Central had also ordered these munitions ejected rather than flooded. All hands knew the danger that these flares presented and the removals proceeded quickly, but with the utmost respect.

Unit 76, on the 03 level at frame 181 was busy sending OBA men and hose back to Units 77 and 78 and rigging smoke eductors to clear the passageways and spaces. With fires being fought only ten frames back on both sides of the 03 level. The Repair Officer for Unit 76 had to make his own decision. There was a magazine at frame 180 and he did not know what it contained. For the officer, whose responsibility was the entire area and all the men in it, this was a lonely decision that only the man in command on the spot could make. He ordered the magazine to be flooded. This placed a further parasitic load on the already overtaxed firemain system and directed water desperately needed on the flight deck into the magazine at frame 180. The magazine contained only harmless gun pods.

With the flames poised to take the island and virtually nothing left to stop them, the Air Boss requested Hangar Deck Control to send up their two twin agent units and all the extra hose they could spare. Hangar Deck Control tried to comply but with power secured to #3 and #4 in flames the only way to get them up was the forward elevators, and they had been so tightly packed with aircraft towed forward, with wings overhanging, that those elevators could not be lowered.

Several V-3 Division Airmen climbed up the #3 elevator well to the 02 level mezzanine and dragged 2½ inch charged hoses up after them. They had no direct communications with anyone on the flight deck but through repeated shouts and wavings, hoped to gain the attention of someone on deck who might then drop a line to pull up the desperately needed firefighting hoses. This did not happen. The turmoil on the flight deck was to great for anyone to notice the valiant efforts of those only a few feet below them.

Lt. Comdr. Fisher, Hangar Deck Officer, had problems of his own. Hose teams attacking fires on #6 sponson reported sheets of flaming JP-5 pouring down from #4 elevator and the catwalks forward and aft of it. Spare reels of arresting gear cables and equipment stowed in #4 well were blazing away profusely. Since power was secured to the closed #4 elevator door, Lt. Comdr. Fisher ordered a Crash forklift brought back to tow open the door.

Aircraft had been moved away from the proximity of the door and Repair 1 teams, bolstered by V-3 personnel, set up hoses to fight the fires when the door was opened. The Crash forklift backed in, parallel to the massive door and a tie down chain was secured to each. The forklift driver put the machine in low gear and it lurched forward, snapping the slack out of the chain. First one drive wheel, then the other, alternately broke free and spun on the salt water covered non-skid deck. The tires spun and were scored and heated from the friction and then they began to dig in. The forklift strained at the taut chain, skidding both left and right, bucking and swerving and finally, the door broke free.

Under the power of the forklift, the giant door rumbled backwards and the hot gale of the inferno swept in from the opening. Walls of fog spray were blasted at the breech and the hot wind and flames rolled over and under, reaching into the Hangar Bay with tentacles of flame, seeking to devour. They roared in ferocity and might as banks of fog and solid streams checked every advance by maneuver and the flames howled and raged in fury at those who would hold them at bay.

Twig Tordoff was back on stretchers taking wounded down to Sick Bay. Helping him was Russell Tyler, Airman, VA-145. The two of them skidded their charge down the red ladder hand rails in the steady procession going down. They were too tired, and it was too dangerous to try and carry a man in a stretcher down the slippery ladders. As it was, skidding a man down the hand rails was an absolutely white knuckle trip and they fell more than once. The man in the stretcher was in very bad shape, but it was the best that they could do.

They stumbled into Sick Bay with hands and arms and shoulders aching and a corpsman told them to lay the man down on the bench in the passageway where the blood donors line was formed. They would get to the man as soon as possible, such was the influx of casualties. The corpsman then turned and forcefully told a black man who was getting up from the bench to sit back down. The black man protested. He said he had to go back to the flight deck and help. Twig Tordoff recognized the black man as one who was carrying another in his arms that they had passed on the way down the ladders on their first trip. The black man started to get up again and the corpsman protested loudly and ran over and forcefully restrained him.

Twig Tordoff wondered why they wouldn't leave the guy alone. He noticed something peculiar about him and did not realize what it was at first. Then he saw that the black skin was cracked and parted away from all his joints and bone white tendons could be seen working through the openings. Blood seeped from the corners of his mouth and eyes and all his joints. The man had been burned totally black. The corpsman continued to explain why the man had to stay there. And then a shadow of resignation swept across the eyes, glittering with pain, and he slumped back against the bulkhead.

The peculiar smell, and the full reality of the situation stunned Twig Tordoff, and it was then that the black white man turned and looked at him. The black white man was the very apparition of Death itself, already laying claim to the body. Those eyes locked on to Tordoff's own with the horror of the sure knowledge of what was shortly to come. And the eyes beseeched, and the apparition said, "Please . . . Pray for me!"

Shaken as they were, the two bearers were unable to move until the apparition was joined by the other, who rose up as if journeyed back from the dead and croaked, "Me . . . too . . . Pray for me."

Units 77 and 78 battled and groped in the hot, choking blackness of the 03 level. Where one fire would be put out in one place, another seemed to flash into life behind them. Individual acts of bravery and industry kept the teams fighting. The hoses would repeatedly lose pressure. Investigators ranged through the black passageways and compartments looking always for flames and sources of water. Hoses even had to be rigged and hauled up from the next deck down. To those on the 03 level, thinking fast and moving fast were the only defense when the hoses went dead.

For Dennis Vaeth, it was the Pearl Harbor attack all over again. He did not know who or why or how, but he was sure the *Enterprise* was being attacked. He thought of the tomb of the ARIZONA, silently rusting beneath the waters of Pearl Harbor. He thought of the ordeal of those ships and men in that fight, 27 years ago. So this is what it was like, he thought. It must have been just like this!

At 0828 Central received a request from Repair 2 to log open the watertight door at frame 2-72-3 to throw weapons overboard. Immediately afterward, the first good news of the day was relayed from Repair 1 ALPHA. They reported a firemain break at 1-240-2-L and they were at work by-passing and isolating the break. This was the news everyone in Central was waiting for. Find the breaks, then seal them off. Then they would be able to put everything they had on the fires.

At 0830 Central Control commenced sending extra personnel and equipment from the propulsion spaces to the 7 ALPHA and 1 ALPHA areas. Those who went carried their own gear and also spare OBA canisters, C02 and PKP bottles and cans of foam.

On the *USS Rogers*, firefighters stood ready on exposed decks as the destroyer drew abreast of the exploding carrier at 85 yards distance and closing. Gunners Mate, 3rd, Steve White and Gunners Mate, 3rd, John Plummer, both ASROC Gunners, stood with some others manning a 2½ inch hose on the ASROC deck behind #1 stack with the launcher right behind them. It was with the greatest trepidation that they and the others of the *Rogers* stood their ground as Harris Sperling maneuvered the little ship in close to bring her hoses to bear.

A continuous rain of burning embers and lesser junk fell all about them as they drew closer to the holocaust. Steve White knew what they were getting into when he saw a figure drop from the blazing flight deck fantail, through the dense smoke, and splash into the carriers wake. The figure was completely engulfed in flames and were it not for the flailing arms and legs, it could not have been identified as human. At such a harrowing sight, Steve White was thankful the burning man had hit the water, even though he knew that the man would surely drown. And there were always the sharks.

The smoke and flames were rolling down the fantail and port side of the Big "E" with large palls of smoke trapped low on the water. Steve White looked back, 500 yards astern of them the *USS Stoddart* was coming up through the smoke. There was virtually no way they would see the man in the water. Then, about 30 seconds after the burning man dropped into the water, another fell from the fantail into the wake. This man was not on fire and his red jersey could be seen clearly until he went under. The man hit the water with a splash and was quickly left behind in the smoke.

Lt. Steve O'Brien had climbed up on the top of the Gun Director to take some pictures. The flaming fuel pouring down from the fantail and coming down in sheets along the portside was flowing so freely he thought it was being pumped over the side. Besides the roaring of the flames, a continuous crackling could be heard and tracerlike objects were shooting outward, over and in front of the destroyers path. The Gun Director began to turn as 51 mount was trained outboard to bring the lashed 2½ inch hose into action. Steve O'Brien looked down and saw that the Gun Director Officer had closed the hatch down to a mere slit. Then he heard a thump and twang and looked around to the director antenna, against which he was leaning, and saw that several holes had been shot through it. He decided to get down from there.

On the bridge of the *Rogers*, the level of excitement became greater with every yard of closure. Sheets of flame poured down at intervals at what looked like one half of the carriers length. Burning hulks of aircraft hung precariously over the catwalks just above them as they closed to 50 yards. Showers of sparks cascaded down on them and the ping and twang of high velocity objects hitting into their ship increased as they brought their hoses to bear.

Harris Sperling quieted the anxious shouts of warning and steadied nerves by talking quietly, in a normal tone of voice and walking the bridge slowly. He did not yell instructions but walked over to whomever he wanted to address and looked them in the eye and said, "Request *Stoddart* to stand clear as we are making emergency maneuvers."

On the bridge of *Enterprise*, Capt. Lee could not see the *Rogers* because of the smoke and he wanted to clear the port side for her so he ordered a course change to 310°, which would put the wind slightly to port of the centerline.

Billy Hawk directed one of the few remaining tow tractors to back up to the tow bar on the KA-3 tanker on #3 elevator. Most of the rest of the tractors were either burning aft or disabled with blown out tires from flying fragments or jagged metal on deck. As it was, the left rear dual drive wheels outboard tire of this tractor was holed and flattened. With the hook-up, the chocks and chains were broken down and the flames only yards away and the driver put the machine in low gear and the KA-3 began to move off the elevator.

Brackin's two hoses were hotly engaged with sputtering pressure on the head of the A-7 line trying to hold back the flames from the tanker and the E2-A early warning Radar aircraft still parked on #3 elevator. The hoses could not be withdrawn. The tow tractor driver tried to drive over these hoses but when the front wheels hit them, the back drive wheels broke traction in the slippery foam and spun ineffectively.

Billy Hawk and about twenty others threw their backs into it and heaved with all they had on both the tractor and the aircraft to get the tractor over the hoses. Then at 0831:05 aircraft 112 exploded punching a trough 9½ feet long and 1½ feet wide an inch deep into the deck. The blast clawed those on deck and took the driver out of the seat with storms of high velocity fragments. Metals struck into the aircraft and island and clattered smoking to the deck all about. Billy Hawk jumped into the vacant seat and put the tractor into reverse. He backed the tanker up till its main gear stopped at the deck edge scupper. He snapped the gear selector into low/forward and stood on the accelerator. The diesel roared into high RPMs and surged forward, with the drive wheels spinning in the foam. The flattened outer rear tire slapped the deck at each revolution and Hawk fought the inertial resistance of the 40 ton tanker to build up speed. The steering wheels of the tractor hit the hoses and the whole show skidded to a stop. Undaunted, Hawk went into reverse again. The racing engine howled and the tractor fishtailed under the restraining weight as it pushed the tanker back to the scupper again. Lt. Comdr. Jack Parks, the Flight Deck Officer, was cheerleading Hawk over the SRC-22 Mickey Mouse head set radio they were both wearing while he was trying to get more water and foam onto the flaming A7's on the starboard side. The deck was being raked and strafed by exploding 20MM ammo from these aircraft, and they held 400 rounds apiece. Even more ominous, the starboard main gear of 414 had just burned through and collapsed and the blazing hulk lurched over to the side exposing a fully loaded rocket pod mounted on the port wing.

Lt. O'Brien had climbed down from the Director and gone into the Signal shack on the Signal bridge to change the film in his camera. A chief was in there trying to keep communications with the bridge open. When the 112 blast went off at 0831:05, a pressure wave of shock swept the *Rogers* and knocked most of the exposed hose teams off their feet. The concussion blew the safety glass windows of the Signal shack, which were hinged at the top, loose from their fastenings and they swung inward with great force to slam into the overhead. The two men would have been decapitated had they been standing any closer.

Junk of all sizes rained down on *Rogers* and a piece of wing the size of a car hood crashed onto the main deck where it was quickly seized and thrown overboard. There was a very great danger to all hands from the exploding ordnance of the carrier. The forward

MARK-32 tubes, behind the 5 inch turret, were loaded with three torpedoes and the ASROC launcher held a full load of eight missiles in their thin aluminum boxes. Piercing through the terrific racket that raged beside and above them, all hands on the *Rogers* heard with relief an authoritive voice bellow "ALL RIGHT! THAT'S THE LAST OF IT! THAT'S ALL THE ORDNANCE! LET'S GET IN THERE AND GET THOSE FIRES OUT!!"

The Legion of the Dead of the Sea patiently held to rank in the silence of the wafting fogs. The numbers of the new ones had grown to two ranks of ten and still more to come. Those of the multitudes gazed down and beheld the drama. They could see the fierce Rider on the Pale Horse and his flashing sword and the terrible work he had done. They could see the little destroyer pitching close aboard the blazing carrier and watched with passive interest to see what the Horseman would do. Had not the Legion seen this same attack before? Had they not witnessed this very same trap laid for a ship to come alongside to give aid to a burning aircraft carrier? AYE! Yea, and there they stood, in the places of honor in the foremost ranks of the Dead! They were the hollow-eyed of the carrier *Princeton* and those who came to their aid stood arrayed next to them. Their mouldering rags bore the shoulder patch of the cruiser *USS Birmingham*. Here they stood in tattered silence, the scene below nearly the same as when the Horseman claimed them, 25 years ago. The *Princeton* hangar bay blew up with the *USS Birmingham* close aboard to help fight the fires. Storms of tearing metal and blast swept *Birmingham's* exposed firefighters and at a single swordstroke, 600 were cut down. Of that number, 250 *USS Birmingham* men were delivered unto the *LEGION* that day. And they all stood now and bore witness.

Billy Hawk had backed the tanker as far as it would go. He had to do it THIS time. He HAD to do it THIS time. He would be careful not to break traction on the slippery deck but it would be a very close thing. He needed to get up enough speed to carry him across the hoses.

He pulled the gear shift into low and fed in enough power to get the aircraft moving. With every inch he traveled he fed in as much power as he dared for fear of losing his traction. He steered the tractor slightly updeck so the wheels would hit the hoses one at a time. The diesel was howling wildly at full power now and Hawk could feel the drive wheels beginning to slip in the foam. The front wheels of the tractor hit the first hose and slowed slightly till the rolling 40 tons of the tanker slammed into it and pushed it over the hose. Hawk was standing on the accelerator now, trying with all his might to push it straight through the floorboards. The drive wheels threw up foam and water and bounced over the hoses on deck and bit into the non-skid surface and kept the 40 tons rolling at speed. Both tractor and aircraft bounced over the hoses on deck and Hawk turned towards the bow with rivulets of sweat pouring into his eyes, nearly blinding him. Throughout it all he heard the repeated shouting's in his earphones from both the Air Boss and the Flight Deck Officer, "PULL THAT MOTHER!! PULL IT!! THE ROCKETS ARE GONNA GO!! MOVE IT! MOVE! MOVE! MOVE! MOVE! MOOOOOOVE!!"

Twig Tordoff and Russell Tyler had come back out on deck and moved toward the centerline hose team when they had to get out of the way of the wild man towing the tanker off #3 elevator. The tail of it had just cleared the track when a flash erupted from the wing of 414 and a rocket roared from it, then another, and then a third rocket fired from the pod and roared, belly high, across the flight deck.

Twig Tordoff was enveloped in, and blinded by the flare of the rocket thrust. After the third one passed, he heard the high wailing of a thin scream trailing away. Shaken by the nearness of the thing, he looked himself over and in disbelief, found he was whole and unhurt. He was also alone. Where two had stood, now there was only one. The time was 0834:56.

Those on the bridge of the *Rogers* and Steve O'Brien in the Signal shack looked on in horror as two rockets shot past, and then a third fishtailing wildly. They fired across the *Rogers*, 30 feet in front and bridge high. The greenish yellow flaming thrust left sparks and smoke trailing after them. The first two slammed into the sea 200 yards out and the third hit in at half that distance. The acrid smoke and fumes settled on the bridge and the crew grew increasingly agitated. Everyone thought *Enterprise* was jettisoning her port point defense missile battery and there were shouts of incredulous indignation, "Don't those *#!!$!! know we are HERE?!!"

Harris Sperling had other things to worry about. With his ship only 20 yards away from the carrier and her upper works nearly touching the overhanging deck, he had to anticipate the Venturi effect he knew was coming. The wind and water funneled between the two ships at a faster rate than it did outside of them. This resulted in uneven forces being played upon the destroyer, with high pressures forward as the forces were compressed, and low pressure aft as they were released. This lower pressure caused a suction effect with the stern of the destroyer drawn towards the already dangerously close carrier. The excitement on the bridge was reaching fever pitch when Harris Sperling walked over and laid a hand on the shoulder of the Lee Helmsman. He looked him square in the eye and calmly said, "Tell Engineering I need all back emergency on the port engine!"

Billy Hawk was still screaming updeck with the tanker and its dangerous load of 24,000 lbs. of JP-5. Who knew what was coming next? It could be more rockets or bombs or 20MM fired into the aircraft could explode it. He had to get the tanker as far away from the flames as fast as possible. The only place to take it was all the forward on the angle where the Phantom from #4 cat and the Vigilante pushed from #3 elevator were already parked. The tanker rumbled along obediently, its starboard wing catching in the folded rotor blades of a helicopter which was dragged along, all the way forward.

The Rider on the Pale Horse held his great sword on high, poised to strike. He had seen the tanker coming out, gorged with fuel, and an opportunity to wreak a terrible havoc. But the sands had passed through the hourglass. The attack of the Horseman was done. In fifteen and a half minutes his great blade had been splashed and washed in the blood of three hundred and seventy one. It was the blood of youth, pure and sparkling and the brightest red. The chargers nostrils were flared with the smell of it, and his eyes rolled and he made guttural noises and pranced with impatient excitement. The Rider held him in check and with fierce eyes fixed those on deck with a malevolent stare. They were coming back again.

With his dripping steel held high, the Rider pulled the Pale Horse hard over and kicked him into a run back into the flames. He looked over his shoulder with a fierce gaze at his foemen. It had been a battle worthy of a Champion, and his raised sword was a gesture of magnanimity from a Champion's hand. Then the Horseman sped into the flames and was gone.

The Legion of the Dead watched in ghostly silence as the Angel whose name was Death streaked across the surface of the waters with his back to the Westwind. Very soon, his aura of light had gone over the southeastern horizon and disappeared. The Legion held to their places. The attack was done but the drama was not yet over. It would be only a short time until the ranks were filled and time here meant nothing. They were waiting for the roll to be called.

At 0835:07 an explosion went off in the starboard A-7 line back aft and Capt. Lee ordered the ship slowed to 5 knots to give the destroyers a better chance to bring their fire hoses in to action. He also saw that the ranks of those on deck had been severely thinned and called over the 1MC, "YOU MEN ON THE HANGAR DECK, WE NEED YOU UP HERE BADLY! THIS FIRE IS STILL NOT UNDER CONTROL AND YOU ARE NEEDED ON THE FLIGHT DECK!"

Joe Rosa joined a gang of men pounding up the ladders to the flight deck. He had no idea what he would find when he got there. The talk he heard on the Hangar Deck was that there were hundreds killed and half the flight deck was gone and the fires were working their way forward. He never really knew how bad things were till he stepped out of the island. He was not prepared for what he walked into. It was far, far worse than anything he had previously imagined. He looked around and there, lying on deck very close to him, was a red helmet. He picked it up and slapped it hard onto his head, aware of the presence of whines and zings all around him. The helmet, he knew, had once belonged to another. He shuddered at the thought and took his place on one of the starboard teams.

In Midships Battle Dressing Station, directly below the island, Comdr. Noel Wilke, Assistant Dental Officer, needed more space to handle the many casualties coming into his area. He had his four stretcher bearers break into the adjacent chiefs quarters to use it as a hospital ward. Clothes, shoes, footlockers, everything was cleared out except the racks, mattresses and blankets. The flow of wounded were quickly directed to fill this new area.

There were all manner of problems to deal with, burns, amputations, sucking chest wounds, broken and crushed limbs and a vast array of missile wounds. Communications were constant with Medical over the ships telephone and Comdr. Wilke kept up a running appraisal of the conditions of his patients. The Battle Dressing Station phone talker relayed the situation reports over the sound powered phones to Central Control. Morphine and other strong pain relievers were brought to the station without asking for it.

In Central, word was finally received from 7 ALPHA from the

Unit 76 phone talker to report a hole in the overhead at frame 232, portside, size and compartment unknown due to fire and smoke. Then Unit 77 called in to report a hole in the overhead on the starboard side, frame 03-195-5-L, with flaming JP-5 pouring into the space. Repair 1 BRAVO called to report they had a number of stretchers ready to send wherever they were needed. A report was also received that a pump room aft and the diesel switch gear and diesel rooms were taking heavy smoke. The men manning those spaces were told to stay low and to wet their shirts to cover their faces if the smoke grew too heavy. They had to have these men monitoring the fire pumps to keep them running and it might be necessary to put the emergency diesel generator on line.

The men stayed in their spaces. They did so with the full knowledge that they might have to die there. The specter of asphyxiation rolled languidly into the compartments with groping tendrils. It clouded the overheads and the thickening mass claimed more and more of the entirety of the spaces, searching them out. And the watchstanders remained.

Damage Control reported pressure on all mains had been brought back up to 150 lbs. and holding. Sprinkling groups in Bay 1 had been shut down and bow groups of the water washdown system had been secured. Individual Repair party officers reported groups of men still coming down from above and up from below. Repair teams made sweeps through these areas and moved these people out and sent them forward. Then they re-checked and secured all ZEBRA hatches and fittings to make sure there was no open path for the fire to get through.

At 0837 Central directed Repair 3 to send men to #4 emergency diesel generator with OBA gear and spare canisters for those manning the spaces and directed Repair 1 FOX to send C02 and PKP bottles to 1 BRAVO in Hangar Bay 2. They received a report from Repair 3 that the fire in compartment 2-258-4-Q was under control and the Air Boss reported that all ordnance was now clear of the flight deck and the fire was now under control.

The flames were still raging furiously on the flight deck. If the Air Boss thought the flames were under control, he was the only one who dared to say so.

On the *Rogers*, even as close as 20 yards, the three forward hose streams could not reach the catwalks of the overhanging flight deck before the nearly 30 knot wind blasted them into spray and swept them aft. These were the hoses from 51 mount, the torpedo deck and the flying bridge. On the ASROC deck, the curtain of salt spray swept back from the forward hoses was a blessing. Two 2½ inch hoses were set up and fighting here, which was just abreast of #4 elevator of *Enterprise*. Sheets of solid flame were pouring with a heat so intense, one hose had to be turned on to the ASROC launcher to cool it and keep the weapons from exploding.

The water between the two ships was very rough and the footing on the destroyer was slippery and uncertain. Steve White felt they were so close, he could reach out and touch the carrier. His hose was training on the burning sponson forward of the elevator, and it was very hard to control the stream from the tossing decks of the *Rogers*. He could dimly see dark figures through the sheets of flame and knew them to be firefighters in the hangar bay. The smoke was very heavy and at times obscured all vision along with the gales of salt water from forward. Without that curtain of water on them, survival from the heat at such close quarters would be extremely uncertain.

John Plummer was one of the gang hosing down the ASROC launcher. He swore he saw some men go over the side of the carrier. He saw that debris had rained down everywhere on the *Rogers* decks and several pieces close at hand were identifiable as canopy Plexiglass. He saw several racks of twelve man rubber life rafts dropped from the carriers forward catwalks, they were automatically inflating even as they went by and he saw them, through the smoke trailing far astern in the wake. He also saw the blazing hulks of an A-3 and an F-4 on either side of the elevator and the wreckage of their tail sections looked likely to come crashing down. And the *Rogers* was too close to avoid them.

At 0839, Unit 77 reported fires and firemain breaks in compartment 03-230-2-L and Repair 4 reported the Education and Training office was taking water from above. Repair 3 flooded the after inflammable liquid storerooms with CO_2 and secured power in compartment 3-186-0-L.

Capt. Lee had another radio call issued for medical assistance and word was passed over the 1MC for blood donors with green cards, groups 1 through 5, and those with blue cards, groups 1 through 5 to report to Sick Bay immediately.

Billy Hawk had run the tractor back to pull out the E2-A, the last aircraft on #3 elevator. As flames roared right next to it, heroic blueshirts went under the aircraft to break down chains and pull chocks. Hawk fed in power and the tractor lurched forward, this much lighter load rolling fast enough that he cleared the hoses on the first try. The wall of flame was so close to the E2-A that it was not realized until it rolled off the elevator that its folded port wing was completely ablaze.

The crewleader stood as #3 man on a saltwater hose moving aft to take on the blazing A-7, #310. When the tow tractor turned updeck, the burning E2-A was rolling right up to his team. The nozzleman swung the stream and poured a solid blast directly onto the flaming wing. They were shortly joined by another portside saltwater hose brought into action with high and steady pressure. The two streams hit the wing and blasted out in all directions, playing back and forth along the length of it with telling effect while the E2-A continued to roll by. Everyone involved was amazed when the sprays of saltwater snuffed out the flaming wing in less than a minute!

This was the first time since the beginning of the fire that the flight deck was served with full and constant firemain pressure.

The crewleader watched, stunned at the easy victory over the burning E2-A. The contrast was so sharp between this and the terrible beatings the hose teams had suffered earlier, he could hardly believe it was out! There was no hot wave of blast to scythe everyone to the deck. There was no hurricane of steel rending great gaps in the ranks. There was no raging ball of flame rushing up to claim them and lay waste to another large portion of the deck. The E2-A had been subdued. They had struck a blow.

Like a fighter in the ring, whose opponent, at will, delivers a series of knockout punches, and yet they kept getting up. Time after time, driven to the canvas with the terrible punishments they were dealt, and yet they had managed, somehow, at the very count of ten, to stagger back onto their feet. The terrific mauling the nearly defenseless hose teams had suffered had left them numb with shock.

With the E2-A out, the port teams moved in the mechanical lock-step of men advancing battering rams. Their solid streams playing the deck ahead of them, they moved in to fight the raging flames of 310 and 112. They marched forward, crouched down behind a shoulder as if advancing into a gale. But it was a storm of steel they would shelter from.

On the starboard side, it had been a terrific slugging match with the teams taking a tremendous battering. They would be driven back, through losses of personnel, hoses, water pressure, but they would regroup and attack again. Overall, the fire had fought its way updeck by leaps and bounds and in its fury had wrecked every defense put up against it except a ragged band of bleeding stalwarts who made a stand at #3 elevator. The efforts to disarm and jettison the three burning 500 lb. bombs blown among the parked aircraft near the island on #3 elevator, and the timely and heroic removal of those five aircraft from on and around #3 elevator, and the two F-4's from the waist catapults created a firebreak. It was a line drawn in the sand by swordpoint. Here, the maelstrom crested at high tide. Here, it surged and howled and blazed in all its might and fury, clawing and reaching out for the defenseless mass of the island structure. And here, it broke against the stand.

7. THE PYRE

Nick Lasovich was one of the men on the starboard hose teams. So was Bill Proffit and Joe Rosa, with the red helmet tight on his head and his beltless pants falling down. Like everyone else on deck, Nick Lasovich was sure he was going to die. He saw men go down, horribly mutilated after nearly every blast. The slaughter was indiscriminate, as if an invisible hand selected those to cut down. He was sure the next one would lay claim to him. He, like the great majority of the crew that day, called fervently upon the Creator of the Heavens and the Earth to spare him the horror being meted out to others. He made promises of great personal sacrifice. He would change his ways. He would walk the path of righteousness with renewed conviction, if only he would be spared. He was earnest.

In his shame, Nick Lasovich recalled his pleas for protection. He knew if he made it out alive his promises would turn out to be empty, and forgotten. So now, in this hour of Reckoning, he asked only for that quality that all the others had humbly asked for. "Please Father, Give me the courage to stand and not falter. Please help me to endure and do my duty, and see it through to the end. So help me, JESUS."

Nick Lasovich, #3 man behind the nozzleman, steeled himself as the teams marched into another assault on the line of burning A-7's on the starboard side. He chanced a look of longing at the beautiful blue Pacific Ocean and her cool refreshing waters. He wanted to jump for it but was no swimmer. A thought came to his mind of the hockey goalie equipment he had just bought on his last leave when he was home. He now doubted that he would ever get the chance to use it. He looked down at the water again. Death down there or death up here. There was not very much to choose from.

A blast of foam from another hose moving up from behind swept the team and momentarily blinded them. They were all covered with foam and Rosa's already sagging pants were threatening to let go. He had to hold them up with one hand. The crack and racket of exploding 20MM shells and the angry buzz and zing of flying things sounded like they were walking into a hornets nest.

The teams slowed and Lt. Comdr. Brackin was there, coaxing, pushing, and leading them into the flames, "COME ON! IT'S JUST FIREWORKS! THEY WON'T HURT YOU! LET'S GO!"

In Primary, it began to look like they had indeed stopped the relentless advance of the wall of flames. Hose teams were moving against the fire all across the deck. The counter attack was at hand. Then a burst of glass erupted and showered in on everyone. Lt. McLaughlin happened to be sheltered from it by a Captain from Fleet Training Group who took the brunt of the shards. They all looked to see what had happened. There, one of the after facing impact resistant safety windows had two basketball sized spider web impact fracturings. The inner laminated pane of Plexiglass had burst inward into a thousand pieces and there, lodged in the center of the spider webs, were two 20MM projectiles.

The heat radiated by the inferno compounded in intensity with every step taken forward. The flames billowed and hurled smoke and great rolling fireballs high into the air. The fires cracked and thundered like the sounds of thrust from great rocket engines. The crewleader watched the heavy saltwater stream from the 2½ inch hose reaching for the now fully aflame 310 as they pressed the attack. A vast burning lake of JP-5 was under 310 and 112 and all the way across deck, from port to starboard.

They dragged the heavy hose closer and closer to bring the stream to bear. Forward they marched, till the incredible heat threatened to burst them aflame. The heavy stream of salt water drove in through the orange flames and struck the canopy of 310. The water then spewed out in all directions, becoming an eye in the center of the hurricane. Wherever the stream played, it revealed that section of the aircraft, and it was remarkable where once all was aflame, the blast of saltwater showed the aircraft was not yet consumed. Back and forth the nozzleman played the stream, from the top of the flaming aircraft, working his way down. The crewleader was mesmerized, watching the blast of the stream. Beneath it could clearly be seen the numbers, 310.

The stream of saltwater was all powerful. It swept the flames from the fuselage wherever it went. The flames would return after each sweep but were progressively weaker. The crewleader fought to keep from hoping for too much. Could this be? They were gaining on the flaming 310 and beating the flames into submission. To the right he saw the *USS Rogers*, very close alongside, and she was pitching and rolling violently! Men could be seen on her upper decks directing four or five hoses towards the burning #4 elevator. The crewleader felt humbled at this display of bravery as he watched the little ship sail into harms way to help the stricken carrier. He felt proud to be part of the Armed Forces of the United States of America, where from the greatest to the least, a common bond of professionalism and dedication to duty was everywhere prevalent.

He watched the stream slowly play back to the tail of the A-7, then move back to the nose. The side of the aircraft facing the team was virtually swept clear of flames except for the brilliantly blazing tire and magnesium wheel. The nozzleman moved the stream from the nose of the aircraft in a quick motion to put out the last of it. The crewleader watched the stream move back towards the wheel and arc through the air to strike directly onto the blazing magnesium. A flash of blinding light and the team was assailed by a storm of absolute energy and were blasted from their feet by the violence and thunder of the exploding magnesium. Pyrotechnics rocketed in every direction as the stream of saltwater hit the burning magnesium dead on. The force of the explosion punched a 10 x 1½ foot trough 2 inches deep into the deck. The time recorded was 0841:00.

The hose team sagged into insensibility from the terrific blow, momentarily stunned. To a man they held a death grip on the powerful 2½ inch fire hose even as they went down and were for a short time, senseless. They all knew, even in their last conscious thought, what a wildly flailing, killing thing this hose would become if they dared to let go of it.

The firefighters on the 03 level were also rocked by the explosion, which occurred just inboard of the main port passageway where many of the Repair units were moving up hose and equipment for the firefighters farther aft. Repair 7 ALPHA asked Central to keep them informed of the situation on the flight deck and Central repeated that all ordnance was clear. Central directed 7 FOX to send additional men back to 7 ALPHA. The main trouble areas within the ship were fully confronted. 7 ALPHA, with its support units were holding the line keeping the fires from moving forward on the 03 level. Repair 1, with the Hangar Deck forces and its support units were keeping the fires out of the Hangar Bay and confined to the off deck and sponson areas. They were fighting these fires and also fighting upward through the 01 and 02 levels to link up with 7 ALPHA. Repair 3 had the lower deck fires confined to the Capstan Machinery room on the 2nd deck and the aviation storeroom on the 3rd deck.

The crewleader and the others on deck were still trying to blink away the last of the shock while they held their ground. The nozzleman continued to sweep from side to side, perhaps unaware of what had just exploded in everyone's faces. Mechanically, he made his sweeps, wherever the flames remained under the wreck of 310. The team moved in to get the stream onto the brilliant flames still blazing on the other side of the aircraft. It was the other tire and magnesium wheel, and the nozzleman, without hesitation, laid the stream full onto it. The result was the same. A stunning detonation which punched an 11 foot x 2 foot x 2 inch deep trough into the deck and blew the engine right out of the hulk of 310. Pyrotechnics rocketed skyward and debris was carried high aloft in an awesome display and shock swept both *Enterprise* and *Roger's* decks. The time was 0842.

The second magnesium explosion rocked the firefighters on the 03 level, punching in the overhead just outboard of the main passageway. Both occurred between frames 200 and 205.

The *USS Stoddart* had gotten steam up and went to 25 knots, straight up the track of the carrier. When the *Rogers* requested that she stand clear for emergency maneuvers, the *Stoddart* stood out to port as she closed up. Those on the bridge of the *Stoddart* marveled and cheered at the seamanship displayed by the *Rogers*. They all knew that only the steadiest ship handler could Conn a ship that close and not collide. The Officer of the Deck had to know what would happen every second as the ships position changed and anticipate the influences being exerted upon his ship by forces unseen. He had to know this and tell his men what to do and when to do it just seconds before it had to be done.

With the massive *USS Enterprise* cleaving the seas, 45,000 tons of water was displaced and pushed out to either side in a constant, underwater tidal wave. The *Rogers* present position, which she held to bring her hoses to bear on the fires, put her squarely on top of the big ships pressure wave. This wave was only visible on the surface, but vast forces of displaced water were in effect far down below.

As the pressure wave hit the tapered bow of the destroyer, the

The PYRE. Upper works of ROGERS seen above smoke to right. Nearly all combustibles in the fire have by now been consumed. 310 will shortly be engulfed entirely. Official U.S. Navy photo, Osterbauer collection.

Scene shows a solitary hose team pressing back to take on 112 and 310 while another team comes back from the bow. ROGERS still in action. Raised #4 jet blast deflector which stopped a burning 500 pound bomb from crashing into the F-4 on the catapult. Official U.S. Navy photo, Osterbauer collection.

bow was forced up, out of the water, and also pushed over into an outboard roll. The pressure wave forced the bow of the destroyer outward, taking more of the wave broadside and the little ship had to be held in place by compensating with rudder turning it in toward the carrier. As the bow rose up, released from the pressure wave, the ship rolled back towards the carrier and the bow plunged back down into the sea. Tons of blue water swept over her forecastle and held her down until the underwater pressure wave and her own buoyancy threw her over into another outward roll while the bow exploded clear of the churning sea. Tons of seawater swept down her main deck, threatening to wash overboard anything not lashed down. She had to hold her position precisely, because if she did not keep the pressure wave on her bow, she would follow her rudder and turn into the carrier.

USS *Stoddart* turned to starboard to take station on the starboard quarter of *Enterprise*. She was crossing astern in the wake, lost in the smoke when the two magnesium explosions blew at 0841 and 0842. The shock of the detonations was felt by all hands as the *Stoddart's* decks rose up from it and she groped about blindly in the acrid, choking smoke trying to take her station.

At 0845 Central reported to Conn that Repair 1 had the fantail fire under control and white smoke was reported by Repair 3 on the 2nd deck at frame 186. Repair 7 FOX reported smoke in compartment 03-87-6-A. 7 BRAVO was directed to send all available gear back to Unit 77. Electrical power was lost on the bridge and a report came that men were trapped in the Chief Master-at-Arms compartment at 1-225-4-Q just off the hangar bay. The doors were jammed closed from buckled decks from the detonations on the flight deck. Repairs 1 ALPHA and 1 BRAVO requested investigators and hose teams with OBA's sent to Hangar Bay 2.

At 0850 Central reported to Conn that the fantail fire on the main deck was again out of control. Repair 3 reported the class ALPHA fire in compartment 2-258-4-Q was out with re-flash watches set. Two five foot holes in the deck and overhead were observed. The after gyro was out of commission.

Ens. Karl Mahumed had taken over as Repair Officer of Unit 75 on the port side. The locker was manned and ready when he got there and when Damage Control requested that his team supply the Repair teams aft with OBA's and all the canisters they could spare, his men moved out immediately. Unit 75 also had to take over the several wounded coming through the catwalk access passageways. Stretcher bearers and corpsmen of the Unit moved these people inboard and down, according to the evacuation routes Damage Control had laid out. Officers state rooms were broken into and blankets were stripped from racks to throw over the wounded, Nearly all of whom carried the heavy smell of JP-5. Some were being carried and some were walking, but the passageways were kept clear. They kept them moving, moving, always moving, down to the Battle Dressing Stations and Sick Bay.

The Air Boss had been right, Where before the entire after one third of the flight deck had been one vast thundering cauldron of rocketing orange flames, now the interior of it was mostly black smoke. The fires that still raged were along the starboard A-7 line and around 310 and 112 and #4 elevator. Although nothing could be seen of the rest of the deck for the smoke, neither could towering flames be seen through it. The fire had burned with so great an intensity that it had consumed nearly all the combustibles on deck. The flight deck fight was waning.

While the fires were being fought on board, the HC-1 Seasprite helicopter of *Enterprise* was combing her wake for survivors. Four times the HC-1 lowered her crewman into the sea to make rescues while the skies overhead were blackened from the smoke which rose up from the carrier miles away.

At 0854 the *Stoddart* rode out to starboard to get clear of the blinding, suffocating smoke which the wind was blowing off the starboard quarter of *Enterprise*. *Stoddart* was initially ordered to try and close the fantail and play water on those fires. The smoke was so black there was zero visibility and the stern of the carrier could not even be seen. Then they were ordered to try to assist on the starboard quarter but the smoke was just as bad there and with no visibility a collision would have been unavoidable. So the *Stoddart* hauled clear of the smoke.

Jim Smith was still topside, standing in the portside escape hatch. He had been watching the drama off and on for the entire time between runs back down to the fire room. As his ship cleared the smoke on the starboard side he thought he saw a figure fall through the smoke and splash into the water. He saw blue clothing and flailing arms. Jim Smith had doubts whether the *USS Enterprise* would make it through its trial, so severe were some of the explosions. He could see the firefighters on deck standing into the fires and he thought they were very brave. He felt if the *Enterprise* did not make it and went down, most of those fighting the fires would go down with the ship. Watching the crew of the Big "E" renewed his faith in American youth. He knew the crews of both ships were largely the same in age. They were mostly just a bunch of young guys from street corners. Jim Smith knew from watching the firefighters aggressiveness that many of them had surely been hurt and killed. He changed his attitude with regard to his own crew. Jim Smith was proud.

A radio message was sent out by the *USS Bainbridge* and word of the *Enterprise* disaster was received in Pearl Harbor and a Coast Guard MEDEVAC helicopter was scrambled, followed minutes later by four Air Force H-3's from Hickam field and Navy and Marine choppers from Barbers Point.

At 0855 Repair 1 BRAVO reported live ordnance on the fantail and the EOD was immediately sent down to dispose of it. Ron Ruland was one of the guys manning a back-up hose in the smoky gloom of Bay 2 when the EOD ran up and said he needed volunteers to go back to the burning hell of the fantail to empty flare lockers. There was a great deal of fear about the possibility of the fire getting down into the magazines. If that happened, the ship and the crew were doomed. Ruland watched as a half a dozen heroes charged back into the smoke with the EOD and then he decided he had better go to the forward bomb assembly to get the magazine key in case the magazines were to be emptied. The forward magazines held most of the explosives.

He ran to take the ladders down to the second deck but the stretcher traffic was too heavy so he decided to go up forward. Before he left he noticed a man curled into a fetal position off to the side of the passageway and the man was mumbling. Ron Ruland knew this guy and went over to get him up. The man was obviously in some kind of shock and kept mumbling to himself, "His head is gone! His head is gone!"

Ruland pulled the man to his feet and led him through the foam to the forward end of Hangar Bay 1 to the ladder down to the mess decks. He took the man down the ladder and walked squarely into the agony of Forward Battle Dressing Station. The sights and sounds and smells were so many and so horrible that he was stunned by it. Corpsmen and others were working on the most pitiful suffering imaginable. One of them came up and led the shock case away without ever saying anything. He watched them go, adding another score to the thousands of bloody footprints tracking to and from all points on the white deck, Ron Ruland went back up the ladder and was recognized as being in GM Division. He was presently enlisted to operate the bomb elevator bringing casualties down from the flight deck.

At 0856 Central directed Repairs 4 and 5 to send two additional hose teams to Hangar Bay 2 and Conn passed the word to Central that magnesium fires were burning on the flight deck on the starboard side aft of #3 elevator and #3 arresting gear. These fires burned especially hot and it was feared that they might burn through the flight deck onto some 03 level firefighters before they could be put out on deck.

Watchstanders in the after liquid oxygen plant reported smoke in the spaces but no direct approach of fires. It was decided not to jettison liquid oxygen because of the danger involved unless the storage space became directly threatened.

Orders were sent to Repair 3 specifying breakers on the 2nd deck load centers to be opened to cut electrical power and the possibility of hazard to areas where fires were being fought.

With power out on the bridge, the ship went to battery powered 3-digit phones. At 0900, eighty miles away, the phone rang on the desk of Commander Paul Jula of the Navy Administrative Unit at Tripler Army Hospital, Pearl Harbor. The call was routed from Commander, Western Sea Frontier, informing him of fires and heavy explosions on *USS Enterprise* southwest of Pearl, MEDEVAC assets were on the way to the stricken ship and casualties would be brought to Tripler.

Commander Jula then dialed the office of Army Major General Conn Milburn and explained, "There has been a fire on *USS Enterprise* about 75 miles off Oahu, and it looks bad!" With that, the one thousand bed hospital went into its Mass Casualty Alert. This was precisely the type of disaster that the staff at Tripler trained and practiced for with exercises carried out several times a year. Everything except absolutely necessary surgical appointments were canceled. All clinics in the hospital were closed. Nurses ran down the lists of their patients, selecting which ones could be sent home if beds were needed. The emergency ward was set up for receiving disaster victims and 27 stations in the center were set up for processing blood donors and Queens Medical Center in Honolulu also set up blood donor stations. Patients helped orderlies in moving beds and tables to set up for the disaster victims and 8 man Army evacuation teams moved in to take station at the Tripler Helicopter pad. Staff members of facilities at nearby Schofield Barracks sped to the hospital.

Honolulu Mayor Frank Fasi was alerted to the disaster and a directive was immediately issued to all department heads to permit city and county employees to take compensatory leave to give blood for as long as the crisis lasted. A radio appeal for blood went out over local Television and Radio stations.

In the Repair 1 ALPHA locker, portside aft in Bay 2, things looked like they were beginning to stabilize. The fantail fire was confined and all other fires were being held back from the Hangar Bay to the off deck compartments. There was a growing unease, however, about the increasingly heavy smell of JP-5 permeating the after part of Bay 2 and Jet test cell area. It was widely known that fuel vapors had caused a number of carrier explosions in past years and everyone was greatly concerned about the fumes and where they might be coming from. Then, as if a valve had been opened from somewhere above, a heavy flow of raw JP-5 came splashing down the ladder and spilling into the locker and adjoining passageway. A foam hose was turned onto these spaces and a blanket of foam was laid down and Repair 1 had to evacuate its locker and set up in Bay 2.

Fuel Control was called to ensure that all JP-5 risers had been drained back and Fuel Control reported that all JP-5 lines were indeed drained back to below the 3rd deck. Wild rumors began to circulate about where the fuel was coming from. It was widely believed that flight deck fueling station #30, which was overhead and blazing away, had broken risers and the fuel had to be continuously pumped out to keep the flames from going down the pipes and getting into the tanks. The fuel was, in fact, coming from the destroyed aircraft on the flight deck. This fuel, which totaled 35,000 gallons, poured flaming into the many holes blown through the flight deck, down as far as the 3rd deck where firefighters were engaged in cooling and extinguishing the flames. Walls of fog spray and streams of saltwater and foam knocked out the flames and dissipated the fuel in the various levels and compartments. The fuel, being lighter than water, reformed and floated on top of the accumulations of firefighting water and was the first agent to spill over the entrapment of coamings and splash its way down to the lower decks.

Repair 1 ALPHA was directed to establish communications with Central via the X40JZ. This circuit had been burned through however, and 1 ALPHA maintained communications through 1 BRAVO and by means of runners reporting to the Hangar Deck CONFLAG stations.

At 0901, Repair 3 reported raw JP-5 coming down from the hangar deck and flooding #11 fog foam injection station on the 2nd deck. Foam was laid down and the station was secured and evacuated.

At 0903, Unit 77 reported ruptured JP-5 and steam lines in compartment 03-205-1-L and fire boundaries had been set up around it. Unit 78 reported class Bravo, Charlie fires in compartment 03-191-10-L. The Damage Control Assistant directed the 7 BRAVO officer to tour the 03 level to get an overall status of the situation from 7 ALPHA personnel. His report was that all fires appeared under control with fire boundaries set but that Unit 78 was having difficulty with fire and smoke in the 03-230-2-L area, and needed additional de-smoking gear. Central reported the situation to Conn that the 03 level fires were under control and all fires were being fought by Repair parties.

On the flight deck the fires still blazed but the hose teams pressed them closely. Slowly, small sections of the deck were reclaimed as clouds of fog spray followed by blankets of foam pushed the walls of flame back. Blackened, twisted junk and smoking, charred pieces of grotesque things were revealed. Vapors of steam rose from the near boiling water on the re-conquered areas, so hot was the flight deck where the flames had been driven back.

The crewleader watched his team pressing closer to the stubborn fires of 112 and behind 310. He did not believe, nor did his team believe that the fight was out of this fire. There had to be more. Then, a roar and a flash of sparks and light from over on the starboard side and a Zuni rocket howled out of the flaming wreckage of the A-7 line. The thrust of the rocket flashed out of the tail pipe and also from the burned through side of the motor section. The rocket roared to the center of the flight deck at a height of 15 feet where it nosed down and did a spark and flame spewing somersault. All hands stood mesmerized as three times the rocket turned down to drive its warhead into the flight deck and three times the side spewing thrust turned it back up again, only inches from contact.

It was a wildly cartwheeling, deadly display of fireworks. The hose teams watched in stunned resignation as the rocket spun and flashed right across their front. They all waited for the warhead, packed with 15 pounds of TNT, to hit the deck and sweep them with blast and shrapnel. No one bothered to duck.

After the third complete somersault, the rocket cleared the deck and dropped dramatically before turning another tumble just over the forecastle of the *USS Rogers*. The rocket spun a few more times before driving into the sea, out of harms way. The crewleader watched the harrowing knife-edge drama of the rocket flight till it roared clear of the destroyer and then turned back to the business at hand. The rocket was now just another thing of the past.

In Repair 5 BRAVO, Big John Guillot was nearly out of five gallon cans of foam for the injection station. Repair teams had scoured the area and cleaned out all available sources. They were down to about a five minute supply. Guillot called down to #2 and #3 engine rooms and requested the ready supply in those spaces be sent up. Those down below protested that if the fires got down into the propulsion spaces, or if a fire started from overworked motors or something they would have nothing left to fight with except a couple of C02 bottles.

John Guillot responded that if they didn't get things under control on the upper decks soon, they wouldn't have to worry about the engine rooms. Central Control, which was monitoring all phone traffic, broke in to direct all extra personnel out of the propulsion spaces to join up with Repair 1, and to take all foam, OBA's and extra canisters with them to the Repair 4 and 5 areas to constitute a reserve.

To Ray Gomes and the rest of the men left manning the engine rooms and reactor spaces, the specter of being trapped was never more ominous. They watched all their firefighting gear being hauled up the ladders leaving only one OBA and canister per man. They all considered the very real possibility of mass suffocation.

Frank Neumayer came to from a long, long way back. The incessant chatter of the corpsman brought him around. At first he could not understand what the corpsman was talking about but now he realized he was being asked a battery of questions. Trying to concentrate on the corpsman brought the world back into focus. He saw that he was in a stretcher up against a bulkhead and he was covered with bandages. Tubes were sticking into both arms draining blood and I.V. solutions into him. Frank Neumayer looked around. Randy Lorimor was sitting against the bulkhead next to him and smiling. Randy's arm and shoulder were heavily bandaged. There were wounded lining the bulkheads and on every table. All the doctors and corpsmen were busy working on wounded. There was a cluster of silent stretchers with blankets thrown over them off to one side. No one had to tell him about those.

Frank Neumayer needed some water bad. He felt his tongue swollen inside his mouth and he tried to say, "Water!" The best he could do was a kind of croak but the corpsman knew what he needed and was ready with some gauze he had soaking in water. "Here," he said, "just suck on this." Neumayer opened up and the corpsman put the gauze into his tortured mouth and the cool liquid felt so good on his tongue he hesitated to pass it down his parched throat.

"Go ahead and swallow," the corpsman said, "I'm staying right here with you." So Frank Neumayer pressed the cool water from the gauze and swallowed it down and the corpsman would insert another and take out the old whenever he opened his mouth. In this way, Neumayer began to come back from the edge. He wondered where Rhino was and mumbled to Lorimor but could not make himself understood. A vague thought came to him as he took stock of his battered condition. Pat Bullington had been right.

On the other side of the room, away from Neumayer and Lorimor, a desperate battle was being waged on one of the surgical tables. A badly wounded man was clinging to life by a thread and the medical teams were doing everything possible to bring him back. They had blood pouring into him and it was draining away almost as fast. This man was one of the most critical of those not already dead. If he could be stabilized, like some of the others, he would be put on the first chopper going to the beach. There was no telling how many more wounded would be coming into Sick Bay. There was no way of knowing when this horror would end. The medical teams could not concern themselves with what was going on elsewhere, they and the facilities aboard were being pushed to the limit and there was no time for concern about anything else.

The word given was that helicopter MEDEVAC units would be arriving in about an hour and this man, if he could hold on, would go out on the first. A chart was prepared listing extent and severity of wounds and what medicants had been given. All information needed by those ashore to continue the work was written down by a corpsman taking dictation from the doctors. The corpsman scribbled in all he had been given and then went back to the first line of identification which he had passed over. The corpsman reached out and lifted the dog tags hung around the man's neck. He read it twice to be sure he got it right, then he wrote in block letters, "LIMON, ARMANDO (NMN) B71 28 40 VF-96."

Don George was on one of the hose teams organized in Bay 2. He had survived so far but thought it unlikely that he would make it through the day. He and those with him still had no idea of what was happening or why. All they knew was that there had been a series of terrific explosions and that the flight deck and most of the after part of the ship except for the hangar bay was in flames. Don George could see flaming fuel coming down in sheets through the open #4 elevator door. Those in charge were constantly yelling for everyone on the hose teams to keep watching the bulkheads and overhead for blistering or other signs of overheating or fire. It looked to Don George as if all the inner surfaces were about to erupt into flames. He was looking very hard.

Then came a shout from someone at the head of his hose, "O.K., LET'S GO!!" The team banged into motion, dragging the heavy weight of the hose. They marched through an aft portside hatch and worked their way up the ladder into the heat and smoke. All compartments and dead storage spaces they came to were opened and wet down to keep them from getting so hot they would catch fire. This was on the 01 level. The fires of the 02 and 03 levels were still raging directly above them.

At 0906 *Enterprise* received a radio message from *Rogers* reporting a large hole through the stern of the carrier from which JP-5 was draining into the sea. This was not visible earlier with the large volumes of smoke swirling about the fantail. Since the *Stoddart* was unable to take station on the starboard quarter of *Enterprise*, she was directed to look for five men known to have gone over the side. The *Stoddart* then hauled off to starboard and dropped 500 yards astern to search in the wake.

On the flight deck the starboard teams moved aft reclaiming the deck a foot at a time with banks of fog spray protecting solid stream hoses that told more and more heavily on the diminishing fires of the A-7 line. A tide of foam moved along with the assault sealing the deck from re-flash. The accumulation of JP-5 floated on the saltwater on deck and flowed to the lowest point, which was the weld split in the flight deck in front of the hulk of aircraft 313. The JP-5 poured into the space and added to the conflagration Unit 77 was fighting on the 03 level between frames 195 and 215. Unit 77 was attacking from two sides of the compartment with another team cooling the inboard bulkheads. Teams drove through hatches with clouds of fog sweeping ahead of them. Solid streams played back and forth across blazing bunks and mattresses barely discernible in the intense smoke and heat. The flames at the hatchways were knocked down but no gain could be made in the raging interior.

As the spaces filled with fire fighting water from Unit 77 and from water and JP-5 draining from the flight deck, the JP-5 reformed and floated over the coamings to flow in its raw state down the three levels of the ladderway to come splashing into Hangar Bay 2 at frame 205 on the starboard side. Elements of Repair 1 BRAVO turned and laid a hasty blanket of foam in the ladderway and then secured the hatch. Raw fuel was now pouring down to the main deck on both port and starboard sides and down to the 2nd and 3rd decks on the fantail. Fires were still being fought in the open #4 elevator well with its blazing reels of arresting gear cables and other equipment and aft on the fantail. With the added menace of the fuel pouring down, all electrical power was secured in Bay 2.

The starboard teams knocked out the last of the flames from the wreck of 415 and took 313 and 414 under attack. Lt. Comdr. Brackin again passed over a much contested section of the battlefield and a thing he had been stumbling over in the knee deep foam with every assault and retreat. A raking blast of fog spray had cleared a way enough of the foam to reveal what the obstacle had been. The charred and blackened meat, the white splintered bone and the ooze of grisly fluids confirmed what Brackin had feared. The obstacle on deck was one cut down and consumed where he lay. It was grim knowledge indeed. The ebb and flow of battle had trampled this one underfoot and now the white splintered bone protruded from the mass and pointed the way back, into the pyre. Come, the Dead beckoned. Come, and see what has been prepared.

At 0910 investigators from Repair 3 found a water washdown system valve ruptured from the shock of explosions and bleeding off firemain pressure on the 2nd deck at frame 255. The rupture was secured and isolated. Further forward, fire boundaries were set up on the 2nd, 3rd and fourth decks between frames 178 and 215 in case the fires from the flight deck and 03 level followed the JP-5 down to the 2nd deck.

As more flames were swept clear in front of what was left of 414, several bomb casings were found, hot and smoking. One casing was split wide open with the last of the explosive filler still burning. The hose teams turned on these potential hazards as soon as they were recognized and kept water on them while the EOD was sent for. Conn was notified and passed the word to Central about the hot bombs with particular concern regarding the 03 level fire parties fighting directly under them.

At 0916, Unit 78 reported an inability to secure firemain cutout valve 02-240-4-L and isolate a break in the main because of heavy smoke and zero visibility. De-smoking gear with seal beam lights and battle lanterns were requested. Repair 1 ALPHA reported personnel removing flares from the 01 level at frame 245.

To the crewleader and everyone else on deck it was as if the white flag of surrender had been raised. There, unmistakably, vast clouds of gray and white steam were rising from the port side in nearly equal proportions to the smoke. Here and there stubborn magnesium fires still blazed intensely, but it was evident that the Fury had been subdued. Having learned the hard way, the hose teams only directed fog spray on the magnesium fires to cool them to the point of killing them. The smoke and steam obscured the bulk of the flight deck and the fires on #4 elevator and the hulks of the A-7 line would be beaten down and re-flash angrily back into life but it could not be long now. New teams from forward were coming back and there was very little left to burn. The Flight Deck Officer saw the starboard missile battery through the smoke and noted that the battery was charred but whole and asked for information about the contents of the battery. Aviation Ordnance Control Center was contacted and it was found the battery was loaded with five missiles with inert warheads. The teams took the battery under solid streams to cool it down. There was still the danger of the missile propellant exploding.

Repair 3 reported the accumulation of heavy smoke in their area and requested additional portable blowers and ducting. All available blowers were already in use and Repair 3 was directed to start 2nd deck ventilation fans which had not been de-energized and open selected 2nd deck main passageway hatches to facilitate de-smoking.

Bob Foley was the throttle watch down in #2 engine room and had the sound powered phones on. Although nobody knew exactly what was going on, Bob Foley had passed 5 BRAVO on the mess decks on his way to his GQ station after the first wounded had come down the pilots elevator. The sight of the blood sloshing up against the bulkhead and the endless track of red footprints were still vivid in his mind. Whatever was going on, it was deadly serious. There were excited reports over the phones of wiped out areas. There were somber rumors of the deaths of friends in the repair parties. The violence from above announced it. Feeling this mighty ship staggering under the blows confirmed it. The rumors were taken for fact.

And now smoke began to roll and belch in clouds through the ventilation system, accumulating a gray haze on the overhead. Those below were caught in the grip of a cold fear. If they had to get out, it would be like going from the basement to the roof of an eight story burning building where every floor was likely to be aflame. There was also another rumor. It was passed along in low tones from one to another. The Marines were said to be stationed at all escape hatches with orders to shoot if those coming out were not led by an officer.

On the hangar deck, hose teams were still fighting in #4 elevator well. The reels of arresting gear cables were out but would re-flash from sparks and flame coming down from the elevator. A magnesium fire on the elevator itself blazed away violently as it melted down through the aluminum slatting and structure. Large glowing meteors of molten aluminum fell from above and exploded into the heaving seas between the carrier and the destroyer. The crash fork lift was brought back to the well to push the cable reels over the side. The safety wire stanchions at the edge of the well could not be lowered, so the fork lift driver bulldozed the reels of cable through the wires. V-3 and Repair personnel threw other flammable equipment over while sponson #6, just forward, still blazed away. On the after end of the well, flames roared upward out of the elevator cable trunk as JP-5 drained off deck into it and re-ignited as it flowed downward.

On the Main deck fantail, firefighters were trying to fight flames on the deck and above on the transom while white phosphorus blazed and popped on the 01 level. The EOD and his volunteers waited till the flames were driven back from the pyrotechnics lockers on the 01 and 02 levels of the fantail, and then ran in to throw over 470 white phosphorus igniters, 1132 signal flares and 540 smoke grenades.

Dennis Vaeth had been helping to carry de-smoking gear back to elements of his team fighting on the starboard side. He was standing in the passageway that led out to the flight deck at frame 205 and decided to risk a look to try and find out what was happening. He stepped through the hatch to the landing below the catwalk and pulled off his OBA mask and saw that everything was black and melted from heat with foam and JP-5 everywhere. He went up the ladder to the catwalk and was stunned at the scene of devastation that was far beyond anything he expected. Nothing but smoking junk littered the flight deck and hulks that were once proud fighting aircraft were unrecognizable. Hose teams were in action right above him and some were directing their streams on bombs lying on the deck. The bombs were precisely over the heads of some Unit 77 firefighters just below.

If a picture could tell a thousand words, this scene told a million. He could see the mast of a destroyer on the port side, very close aboard. He also saw that what had once been aircraft on that side had been obliterated, bearing mute testimony to what those tremendous explosions had done.

Dennis Vaeth had been holding down his fears while he did his job for the past hour. He, like all the others, did his duty without regard to personal risk. As he stood now, seeing the unbelievable destruction on deck and what had happened just above him, he began to tremble violently.

At 0918 Repair 3 reported white smoke in #4 elevator machinery room on the 3rd deck. De-smoking gear was rigged as the space became intensely hot and paint blistered and popped. Although there was no fire in the machinery room, it was clear that fire was blazing in the trunk the next several decks above. Much needed OBA's and canisters were brought back by Repair 4 and 5 personnel. Repair 3 reported 4 feet of fire fighting water in compartment 3-255-4-A.

Henry Mendoza was hyperventilating. For some reason he began breathing rapidly and sweating freely. He had been faring fairly well for the past half hour or so, lying in his stretcher. Perhaps he was too involved, listening for what was happening on deck and around him, to have noticed before. Now that things had quieted down up above, something was happening to him and he grew afraid.

Henry Mendoza called to a corpsman going by on some errand, "Hey! What are the symptoms of shock?" The harried corpsman stopped and looked at him and then continued on his way. Mendoza lay still, sweating profusely, trying to stay calm. Another corpsman came by and this time he reached out and grabbed him by the pant leg. "HEY!!", he demanded, "What are the symptoms of shock?" The corpsman looked down at him and his eyes were wild. He was the one from the *USS Forrestal*. The corpsman pulled free and said, "I will get the doctor."

Ron Ruland ran the bomb elevator down and helped carry the wounded off. There were so many stacked around in Forward Battle

Dressing Station that this load of casualties had to be taken directly back to Sick Bay. The man in the stretcher Ruland was carrying was badly burned and smelled heavily of burned meat and fuel. The four stretcher bearers made all haste to get him to his destination. As they neared Sick Bay, several stretchers with casualties were stacked along the bulkhead of the passageway. The man carrying the forward corner of the stretcher in front of Ruland chose this time to begin throwing up into his white hat. From his position at the back of the stretcher, Ron Ruland did not have time to avoid one of the stretchers lying there and his ankle bumped into it. A man was lying therein, burned black, and as Ruland looked down, the man's blackened and bubbled scalp slid from his head with a sucking sound and fell to the deck.

At 0924 Conn advised Central that the hot bomb on deck, starboard aft, had been de-fused. Capt. Lee ordered *Rogers* to trace the wake for survivors and she hauled out to port. Central directed Repair 1 FOX to send additional personnel to the Hangar Bay to assist in fighting the fires on #4 elevator and also to send three OBA men to #4 elevator machinery room. Repair 7 FOX reported a salt water valve rupture in compartment 03-76-1-L and requested seal beam lamps and battle lanterns to be sent to Unit 73 along with as much hose as possible to the frame 200 area. Repair 1 BRAVO requested 2½ inch fire hose nozzles sent to the locker as soon as possible. Unit 75 reported the class ALPHA fire in compartment 03-200-8-V out with men standing by, guarding against a re-flash.

The crewleader trudged ahead with his team. They were moving in to the last flame still visible, the flame shooting up through the aluminum slatting of #4 elevator. The starboard teams were still hosing down smoking wreckage but the ordeal looked like it was nearly over. It was almost too much to hope for. Then the voice of the Air Boss blared out over the bullhorn, "EVERYONE STAND WHERE YOU ARE!! THERE IS LIVE HIGH EXPLOSIVE ON DECK! I REPEAT, THERE IS LIVE H.E. ALL OVER THE DECK! DO NOT MOVE IF THE DECK IS NOT CLEAR!"

The hose teams looked around. The deck was certainly not clear. Smoking junk and pieces great and small littered every square foot of it. They all held in place where they were, the water nearly boiling on the hot flight deck. The crewleader's hopes of salvation were dashed. Now they were standing in the middle of a mine field. The nozzlemen turned their hoses and blew away all litter at the feet of their teams. Then they blasted pathways through the rubble. Other hoses coming from up forward swept the decks as they came. The crewleader was watching the progress when an officer came up from behind and gave him a push on the shoulder, "YOU, YOU, YOU AND YOU! GO UP FORWARD AND BREAK OUT PIPE RACKS FOR STRETCHERS!"

The officer had selected every other man on the hose team for this duty and the crewleader took off at a run with the others. Delirious with joy at the thought that he had actually been ordered to leave the team, he ran to the forward berthing areas and gratefully joined a gang taking down pipe racks. He had been saved from the Fury.

Nick Lasovich stood with his stalled team on the starboard side in the middle of the wrecked A-7 line. It was his luck to be standing next to a burned and blackened body. A stretcher team came up and laid their stretcher down next to the dead and then did the gruesome and unnerving task of placing the hideous thing onto the stretcher. The team then picked up the stretcher and with hands slippery with gore, promptly dropped it back to the deck. The dead spilled out and had to be put back in the stretcher. The bearers were reaching the limits of sanity. The hose team backed away as far as they could to get clear of the dreadful scene.

The bearers heaved up the stretcher and again they dropped it with a wet thud, spilling its contents. The hose team erupted in blasts of ridicule and denunciation at the carelessness of those on the stretcher. The bearers bellowed back explicatives and with hands balled into fists announced the certain gleeful destruction of any and all who dared to step forward. The hose team roared back at the challenge. They would by all means settle this when the danger was done, and it would be a pleasurable experience at that. The stretcher team gathered up the dead and staggered away delivering continual verbal assaults rife with violence on the hose team. Both sides vented themselves on each other, the bellowed wrath releasing great stores of pent up tension. The hose team turned back to the tasks at hand with determination, having seen what other chores had to be done. No one envied the duty of the stretcher bearers.

Comdr. Noel Wilke had been getting ready to begin evacuating his worst casualties down to Sick Bay and Henry Mendoza was his worst case. Wilke was given a route by Central Control, what ZEBRA fittings to break and what hatches to go through and ladders to go down. Mendoza was getting intravenous feedings and saline solutions and also had a tourniquet which was preventing the major bleeding of his leg. This would require a man on each side of the stretcher as it was carried around corners and down ladders. Comdr. Wilke checked out the other route to the pilots elevator and there were men there who said, "This elevator is for you people to use, this way!"

So Henry Mendoza was carried into the elevator for the ride down to Sick Bay on the 2nd deck. He was still sweating and having trouble breathing till they laid him down next to another V-1 Division man from Crash/Salvage. This man had a large piece of metal protruding from his thigh. Seeing this and talking to the man had a calming effect on Mendoza. Henry asked the man who got hurt. "A lot of guys," said the man, "Little Joe, Tex, Ernie, a lot of them."

At 0930 Repair 1 ALPHA reported that the class A fire on #4 elevator was out and that there appeared to be no further danger from JP-5 in and around the locker. Attempts were being made to pump it out. Unit 78 requested all steam be secured on the 03 level aft of frame 180. Repair 3 reported an 8 foot hole three feet from the deck in compartment 3-255-1-A and compartment 8-200-6-V was flooded solid with water and fuel.

Henry Mendoza was carried from the pilots elevator and placed against the bulkhead in the passageway while some corpsmen went into Sick Bay to see what to do with him. He lay there a few minutes till they came back and then carried him in. They passed through several spaces and finally put him onto a table in the corner of a compartment. Henry looked around. The guy next to him was badly burned. His ears were gone and he was bleeding from there and his eyes, nose and mouth. The man was also shaking violently. The others on the tables around him were silent, covered over with gray wool blankets. The only ones here were the dead and the dying and Henry Mendoza lay in the midst of them.

The man next to him shuddered violently again and Mendoza stared at him. A great spasm drew the burned man into a contortion and then he stopped. His breath released in a long exhale that bore the rattle of death. The man's life had passed from his body an arms length away and Henry Mendoza watched as the gray blanket was spread over the now silent form. He looked from one to the others and it was evident that he was the only one still alive here. He was also in great pain.

At 0945, 7 BRAVO reported the firemain in the island was 50%

patched. Fires still burned on the 03 level and Hangar Deck Control reported a re-flash on #8 sponson. Repair 1 ALPHA reported that the fantail fire was still out of control. Unit 77 requested more OBA's and canisters to the scene and a man in #4 emergency diesel room was overcome by smoke. Capt. Lee changed course to 032° and brought up speed to 10 knots to take a more direct course to Pearl.

At Navy Housing on Iroquois Point, Diana McLaughlin was having coffee and small talk with a woman friend she had known from Whidby Island. The woman's husband was a Bombardier/Navigator in VA-145 aboard *Enterprise* and the two were to be companions for a few days. They were sitting at the kitchen table when the phone rang.

Diana McLaughlin answered it and was startled to hear the news of the *Enterprise* disaster from the Commanding Officer of Patrol Squadron-17. He went on to explain that if Bob was where he should be, he was out of the danger. She thanked him for the news and hung up and the two women turned on both the television and the radio for further information. Diana McLaughlin disregarded the Captain's explanation of where her husband should have been. He had taken his camera along and intended to bring back some pictures.

Billy Hawk was leading hose teams spraying water and foam into the jumble of engines and crumpled wing sections where 614 had been and the hole in #4 elevator. There was another column of smoke boiling up just aft of this and Hawk turned a team onto it. It took awhile for the realization to set in that the smoke was not coming from wreckage on deck but from fires in the compartments below. It was at this point that the men on deck understood that great holes had been blown through the flight deck and fires from below were still burning from them. Foam teams were brought up to pour streams down into the holes and recognizing this new hazard, everyone stepped lightly, and then only on cleared sections of the deck.

Bob McLaughlin knew it was finally over. There was no other mood in Primary than that of quiet and humble thanksgiving, They had come perilously close to losing the ship. The fantail area was still smoking and spewing steam from fires below but long hose teams were snaked back from forward stations all the way to the end of the deck, blasting debris clear and advancing a blanket of foam as they went clear across deck.

The deck itself was a blasted and cratered battlefield with an acrid stink rising from the pyre. The evidence of the fury of the fire and the power of the explosions were plain to see. Only the cockpit, starboard wing and front half of the fuselage were left of 310. The aircraft with the tow tractor still attached were blown sideways from blasts and the magnesium explosions had blown the A-7 engine 15 feet from the aircraft. The remains of 112 were nothing but a gutted shell with everything facing aft burned and melted away.

All that was left of 312 was the nose section of the fuselage with the tow tractor still attached. The nose section lay on its side at #3 wire and its engine was blown back to #1 wire. Everything else of the aircraft was gone. The tractor itself was a charred and blackened hulk, knocked sideways from the detonation.

Of the A-7 line, all were burned and melted away except for engines and wing sections. These had become welded to the deck. Of the Phantoms in the starboard corner to across the fantail, 103, 202, 114 and 214, all were burned and blown away down to the blackened remains of their engines.

On the port side, smoking craters marked the places where 113, 105 and 106 had been parked. Except for an F-4 nose and nose wheel section sheared off at the intakes and lying upside down towards the center of the deck at #1 wire, nothing at all remained of these aircraft. They had been completely obliterated. The tanker, 614, had been reduced to nothing but two engines and the port wing lying on the deck and perched atop the gaping hole burned through #4 elevator.

No less than ten tow tractors could be seen scattered around in the rubble of the after flight deck, black and squatting low with their tires burned away. Two of these were those heroic efforts to tow 310 and 312 clear when their drivers and tires were shot out. Two others were tractors brought back to try for other rescues only to be holed and abandoned. The smoking hulk of the port twin agent unit sat there, with a story all its own.

Bob McLaughlin decided to step out of the confines of Primary to the open deck outside the door which faced the fire. There, he looked up at the holes and wreckage and dangling wires of the island's upper works. And there also, was another thing that he saw. Just above the door to Primary, embedded into the Quad radar to the depth of a foot, a snakeye high drag bomb fin had been pressed flat side in, much as a footprint into soft mud.

Twig Tordoff was on a stretcher detail, removing a smoking 500 lb. bomb found under some junk forward of #4 elevator. Being on the front end of an eight man stretcher team, he did not have a lot to say about what direction was taken. The team banged and staggered through a windrow of blackened bodies as they made their way through the junk. Twig Tordoff accidentally stepped on one of the dead and nearly went down trying to avoid it. Some fool loudly protested. "Hey! Don't You Have Any Respect For The Dead?!" Tordoff bellowed back, "IF THIS THING GOES OFF IT WON'T MATTER MUCH WILL IT, YOU *%##@* CLOWN!!!"

Nerves were frayed to the breaking point and maintaining composure was difficult.

On the bow section of the flight deck aircraft were moved to re-spot and clear the bow to land aboard the MEDEVAC units which were clawing their way across a heavy cross wind to get to the ship. The Air Boss passed word to the Flight Deck Officer to expect the first at 1000. The wind would be on the port side so all aircraft on the bow were stacked along the starboard side to leave a landing area open. Casualties would be brought up on deck by means of the forward bomb elevators.

At 0940 Hangar Deck Control reported the fire on #8 sponson was out and Repair 1 ALPHA reported entering bomb stowage room 1-179-1-A to investigate. #4 emergency steering was evacuated to steering gear room #4 due to heavy volumes of smoke and Repair 1 BRAVO requested extra OBA's and canisters sent to Bay 2. Central directed Repair 4 to send hose teams back to relieve Repair 3 and Repair 5 was directed to send ten men to 7 BRAVO in the island. Central reported to Conn, eight men dead, no names given.

At 0953 fires continued to burn on the 03 level and fantail. Central advised Conn to take a smoother course due to JP-5 sloshing around on lower decks. Capt. Lee ordered the ship to come to course 310° as Coast Guard helicopter #1408 came into view on the horizon.

Nick Lasovich was still manning his hose on the starboard side when someone came up with an armload of snow shovels. "We need some guys on these shovels!" the man said. Nick Lasovich told him what he could do with his snow shovels! He had stayed on this hose all through the worst of it and he wasn't about to leave now and go shovel #%*$&# snow! Joe Rosa took one though, Even though he had to hold up his trousers with one hand he was eager to help out. "We have to clear the deck," the man told Rosa, "watch out for H.E. and parts!" Joe Rosa still had his red helmet pressed tight onto his head and was ready but somewhat bewildered. "What parts do you mean?"

The flight deck was quickly re-claimed when the last ordnance had exploded. Virtually all the fuel had been consumed by then also. Official U.S. Navy photo, Osterbauer collection.

Foam team attacks the last of the Fury through the massive hole blown through the flight deck by the 113 explosion. Official U.S. Navy photo, Osterbauer collection.

he asked. The man with the shovels walked on and said over his shoulder, "You will know it when you see it!"

King Merendino had nothing to do since the laundry had been evacuated. He had been hanging around up on the forward mess decks trying to be of some help. The dead were being lined up along a bulkhead up there and he decided to go back and volunteer his services at Sick Bay. There was plenty to do there and he was put to work as a stretcher bearer carrying those waiting in the passageway into Sick Bay and carrying others out who were able to be moved and lining them up on the mess decks. The sights he saw were horrific with the burn cases being the most pathetic.

After a time, a corpsman came up and asked him if he would go around and try to get the names and service numbers of the wounded. He did this but found it difficult and painful to ask those suffering for information. There was a certain pilot whose face was burned and blistered and still struggled to tell Merendino what he had to know.

King Merendino wished he could do something to ease the suffering and then a thought came to him. He went up to a doctor and asked if it would be alright to go to the galley and see if he could get something for the casualties. "Go ahead," he was told, "Good idea!". With that he went out the door and ran up the passageway to the forward galley.

At 1000 the Coast Guard SH-3 helo drew up to a hover along the port side of the bow. The pilot had to match the ships speed of ten knots against the seventeen knot headwind while holding an altitude of about twenty feet above the flight deck. Responding to directions from a yellowshirt on the bow, the pilot slid the machine over the deck and then expertly set the helo down. Blueshirts ran in and attached tie-down chains to each main mount and the Coast Guard pilot looked over and saw his flashing rotor blades were only a few feet from the parked aircraft along the starboard side of the bow.

Bill Proffit had gotten the job of running one of the two forward bomb elevators from the flight deck. As soon as the helo was on deck, word was passed to Sick Bay and the first two MEDEVAC cases were brought out and carried forward with four stretcher bearers and a corpsman on each side holding up plasma and I.V. bottles. They then entered the bomb elevator and the stretcher was laid to the deck with only the corpsmen and the casualty remaining. They were then elevated to the flight deck and when they came to a stop Bill Proffit said, "O.K.!" and six men went on and picked up the stretcher and hastily made way across deck to the waiting helicopter.

The crewleader chanced a glance at the wounded man from his position at the back end of the stretcher as the team ducked under the beating rotor blades. The man was bound and bandaged and unrecognizable to anyone. The crewleader hoped this anonymous sufferer was not anyone he knew, and then he felt a sharp pang of shame at this thought. This man could be anyone!

The group stopped at the open cargo door of the helicopter and a Coast Guard crewman reached out and took the bottles and plasma from the corpsmen. Then the corpsmen climbed in and finally, the stretcher containing Armando Limon was carefully hoisted aboard and skidded across the bay to make way for another stretcher.

Before Bill Proffit sent the bomb elevator back down, a load of pipe racks were thrown on for use as stretchers for those in need below.

At 1005 Central reported all fires out but presently re-flashes occurred in compartments 03-205-2-L, 01-225-3-Q and 03-235-6-L. Fire boundary teams were in place surrounding these trouble areas and were cooling containment bulkheads and overheads. Heavy smoke still rolled out of the fantail and #4 elevator well.

At 1010 Combat Information Center reported Coast Guard C-130 Hercules #1351 on the scene as acting Search and Rescue Commander. A helicopter dropped a flare in the water far astern to mark the position of a floating body and the *USS Stoddart* steamed towards it. Capt. Lee brought the ship to 340° and increased speed to 15 knots. All donors with A Negative blood were to report to Sick Bay immediately.

Commissary Chief Irwin Barnes was in charge of the forward galley. He kept his men busy and out of the way of the Damage Control and stretcher teams going up and down the passageways. He had some hot soup already going and a phone talker from one of the Repair parties told him that the after galley was out of commission. Irwin Barnes did not question the man. He started putting on everything that was in the galley and had his men bring whatever they could out of the reefers without breaking ZEBRA fittings. Some from the DC teams went to help and presently armloads of breads and canned meats were coming back into the galley.

All hands were impressed to making and boxing sandwiches and soups with coffee and fruit juice in containers. Forward galley was ready when word was passed that Damage Control teams would be fed in relays as they were relieved. A sailor standing in the passageway shouted to Irwin Barnes, "HEY CHIEF! DO YOU HAVE ANYTHING I CAN GIVE TO THE WOUNDED?!" Irwin Barnes thought a second and then went to see what was at hand. He picked up a big box and slid it over to the sailor. It was a case of frozen papaya cups.

Three Air Force H-3 helicopters came into view with another miles away and radioed the carrier for instructions. They were told to make an approach pattern from behind and up the port side of the ship to the bow, once Coast Guard helo #1408 was clear.

The Air Force pilots expressed some reservations about landing conditions and the limited amount of deck space with aircraft stacked along the bow. Smoke and steam was still rising from #4 elevator well and pouring out of the fantail, obscuring the after part of the ship. Although the Coast Guard crews had experience landing on moving ships at sea, this was something new to these Air Force pilots. They would have to set down on a moving ship with a heavy crosswind to contend with. "Don't worry!", they were told, "Just watch the yellow shirted aircraft director and he will bring you in!"

The Air Force pilots slowed and went into the pattern aft of the ship, waiting for Coast Guard #1408 to get clear. As they drew closer they saw that there had been enough room cleared where #1408 was sitting that it might not be too bad. Then they received a message from *Enterprise* advising them to stand clear because the ship intended to change course to 000° once the Coast Guard helo had cleared.

At 1022 the two casualties were aboard and the accompanying corpsmen had scrambled on and Coast Guard helo #1408 gently lifted from the deck and banked away to the left to beat its way clear of the ship. Capt. Lee ordered a course change to 000° and increased speed to 20 knots. Repair 1 BRAVO reported a re-flash in #4 elevator well and #3 CONFLAG station reported 5 inches of water on the deck.

Miles astern of the smoking carrier, the *USS Stoddart* maneuvered through what seemed to be hundreds of 12 men inflatable life rafts, half submerged and under inflated. They had been jettisoned from the catwalk racks of *Enterprise* and dropped by the Coast Guard Search and Rescue C-130. They and the *Rogers* would spend the rest of the daylight hours searching these rafts for survivors but would find no one. The flare dropped from the SAR helo marked the only body that would be recovered. The flotsam in the carriers wake stretched for miles.

A swimmer from the *Stoddart* pushed the body through rolling seas till it was in reach of outstretched hands. Jim Smith was one of those on deck who helped hoist the body aboard. The dead man showed the signs of blast and heat with all his clothes blown away except the waistband of his underwear. Jim Smith inspected the waistband looking for some identification. He did not know it, but the man was from his own home town of Muskogee, Oklahoma. The identification he was seeking was there, but reduced to a single stenciled word and barely legible. Jim Smith read it carefully to make sure he got it right. The word spelled, . . . G.I.R.T.Y.

At 1030, power went out in Mid-ship Battle Dressing station and battle lanterns were turned on and emergency lighting was on in the operating lights. Water was pouring into the station from the portside firefighting and it was ankle deep. Steady evacuation's to Sick Bay were continued, using the pilots elevator.

With the ship headed due north at 20 knots, the Air Boss told the Air Force pilots to come aboard. This would be a tricky situation, especially when he said he intended to land three helo's on the very limited space of the bow.

Air Force helicopter # 12574 crept alongside, matching the 20 knots of the carrier and taking the 17 knot wind on its port quarter. The pilot kept the nose of the helo slightly to port to face the wind and brought the machine to a hover over the water on the port side of the bow 15 feet above the flight deck.

As the pilot held the hover abreast the bow he looked down to his right where the yellow shirt was standing at the very edge of the bow, motioning for the helo to come in to its right. The pilot glanced at the row of aircraft parked at his right and noticed the tapered bow of the ship. If there was enough room to set down here, there was only JUST enough.

The Air Force pilot eased off of the cyclic control, reducing slightly the pitch of the rotor disk. With the force of the wind the machine began to slide in while keeping pace with the carrier. The pilot watched the steady motioning of the yellow shirt and gently brought the H-3 over the bow. When the landing gear was clear of the port scupper the yellow shirt gave the stop signal and the H-3, hanging 15 feet above the deck, began to vibrate in the disturbed air. The yellow shirt now carefully made the down signal and the pilot of #12574 knew without being told, that he had to square up his machine as he set down to keep his tail rotor clear of those parked aircraft. He added slight right pedal to square up the helo and then eased up on the collective control, reducing rotor blade pitch to begin his descent. As the torque lessened on the H-3, careful pedal adjustments had to be made.

The pilot had to have absolute confidence in the Navy yellow shirt on deck. The Captain, Air Boss and entire crew of *Enterprise* had to have absolute confidence in the ability and competence of the Air Force to even try such a precision maneuver.

The pilot of the #12574 felt his wheels touch down on the deck of *Enterprise* and he settled his weight down on the ship. He and his co-pilot had been holding their breath for the last 20 seconds to touch-down. They both watched the yellowshirt and acknowledged his thumbs up with one of their own as he ran under the rotor to land Air Force #12575 directly astern. The pilots and crew of #12574 breathed a sigh of relief as their door rumbled open. They all looked to the line of aircraft parked there and the flashing rotor blades which seemed to be within inches of them. In truth the blades were missing those planes by the distance of an arm's length. There had been absolutely NO margin for error.

In Forward Battle Dressing Station, things began to slow down a little. Lt. Richard Martin was able to get back to some of those who were put aside after stopping the bleeding. As the day wore on many volunteers had come forward stating they had nothing to do and wanted to help. Lt. Richard Martin used them to monitor patients and to evacuate the worst to sick bay. One section of the Battle Dressing Station was set aside as a morgue, and before the morning was over, there would be thirteen silent stretchers stacked along the bulkhead.

At 1030, *Bainbridge* signaled she had *Enterprise* in sight at 14 miles range. She then reduced speed to 20 knots and changed course to 042° to take station 3000 yards ahead of *Enterprise*. The *USS Moctobi* also was sighted, reporting for duty. Repair 1 BRAVO reported fires still being fought in #4 elevator well were under control. Estimated time of arrival at Pearl Harbor was 1330, bearing 033° true, range 67 miles.

At 1038 Air Force helicopter #12575 landed second in line on deck with her flashing rotor blades a few feet from the tail rotor of #12574. All power in Hangar Bay 2 was secured and class A fires re-ignited in the radio shack at 03-255-5-Q, fueling station #28 aft of #4 elevator and fire on the main deck in the cable trunk at 1-233-1-Q.

Central requested all wire stretchers to be sent to Sick Bay. Conn reported to Central that fire main ruptures on both the port and starboard sides of the 03 level had been isolated. Repair 1 ALPHA reported men fighting fires in the cable trunk at 1-233-1-Q and requested OBA men to the scene. Unit 78 was still evacuating casualties down the pilots elevator. The ships radar was down.

At 1046 Navy helo Benzene 22 landed third in line on the bow bringing help in the persons of 4 doctors and 2 Medical corpsmen with supplies of blood plasma. Central directed Repairs 4 and 5 to send available fire fighting teams to Bay 2. CONFLAG station #4 reported heavy fuel smell coming through the ventilation system. Unit 75 asked for and was given permission to throw 20MM shells over the side. Conn reported to Central that the two fire stations farthest aft on both the port and starboard sides of the flight deck were ruptured.

Air Force helo #12574 was loaded up and ready to go. The pilot got the lift off signal from the yellowshirt and nodded his head in recognition. He quickly scanned his gauges for a check. He moved the cyclic forward and left, anticipating the wind that would push him into the parked aircraft to his right. He then pulled up on the collective, changing the rotor blade angle. As he felt the machine lighten and to begin to vibrate from the torque he had to add pedal to compensate for the torque and to keep the tail rotor from skidding around and chewing up the parked aircraft. With a quick scan of the engine and rotor RPM gauges and torque indicator to see that the needles were within the limits and the machine therefore not overloaded, he lifted off deck and pitched to the left to get clear of the ship and into undisturbed air over the sea.

Don George and his team dragged and hauled the heavy hoses up to the smoke filled darkness of the 02 level. Every space they came to was taken under spray to cool them down and keep combustibles from flashing. The bulkheads and overheads groaned and popped from the stress of heat expansion and hissed sharply under the sprays of water. It was plain to the hose team where the heat was still intense and these areas were kept under spray. As the fires and heat were cooled the tortured steel groaned again in contraction and compression, and it seemed like it all would just fall on them and swallow them up.

Men on the flight deck were quickly carrying stretchers from the bomb elevators to the waiting helicopters. Those who carried the stretchers were flight deckers, mess cooks, corpsmen, and others evacuated from spaces below who came up to help. Teams of six bearers with one or two corpsmen would snatch a stretcher off the bomb elevator and move it to the side so the elevator could go back down for another run. There they would squat on deck around the casualty, waiting for the signal from the helicopter crews. Then the corpsmen would say, "LET'S GO!", and they would rise as a team and quickly run the casualty to the open cargo door and wait for the corpsmen to hand up the plasma and I.V. bottles. Then the stretcher would be slid across the helo's deck and the team would run back and take their place for another rotation.

At 1050, five minutes after Air Force #12574 lifted off, BENZENE 22 departed with a load of casualties. Two minutes afterwards, Air Force helo #12571 settled into the spot BENZENE 22 had just vacated. Four minutes after that, Air Force #12575 departed. And it would go like this, with three Marine helicopters shortly to join in, landing as many as four at a time on the smoking deck of the speeding carrier.

Coast Guard #1408 would make three MEDEVAC's. The Air Force helo's made a total of six. Marine helo's EW-3, EW-2 and #148118 made seven. Navy MEDEVAC helo's made four for a total of 20, carrying two or three casualties at a time.

At 1052 in the Hangar Bay, Repair 1 ALPHA and BRAVO, with elements of Repairs 4, 5 and 2 and support from V-3 Division and other volunteers, had teams advancing up to the 02 level at two points on the port side of Bay 2 and one on the starboard side advancing up the ladder at frame 215. Fires were still being fought on #8 sponson, the cable trunk and compartments at frame 230 on the port side from the main deck to the 03 level, compartment 03-195-5-L on the starboard side and intermittent re-flashes from these areas back to the fantail.

Central directed Repair 1 ALPHA to send personnel casualties to Forward Battle Dressing station to relieve the pressure on Sick Bay. Repair 5 requested, and was given permission to set condition YOKE on the 2nd deck main passageways from frame 138 aft to draw all smoke out. With the ships radar down, low visibility lookouts were posted.

At Navy housing on Iroquois Point, Diana McLaughlin and her friend stayed glued to the television and radio for details of the disaster. The situation was reported to be grave with an unknown number of dead and wounded. MEDEVAC units were even now flying to and from the stricken carrier and Tripler Army Hospital had gone to Mass Casualty Alert to receive the victims, blood donors were asked to proceed to Tripler and Queens Medical Center in Honolulu.

There was as yet no concrete information given and the two women were riveted in place because they knew they would be contacted here by phone or messenger when any details could be had. They were both discussing this aspect when the sound of footfalls on the walk outside brought them up short. They both turned to see the khaki clad legs and shined black shoes of a man in uniform striding up to the house. They both shuddered when the man stopped at the door, fearful of what news this harbinger might bring. They held their breaths in suspense, waiting for the knock. It never came. The postman turned and went on to his next delivery.

On the television, news cameras panned the bulk of Tripler Army Hospital and grim reporters announced that the staff had been standing by and ready since 0945. Three ambulances and their crews waited at the helicopter pad for the five minute drive to the hospital. In the emergency unit, a staff of 7 doctors, 2 interns, 4 nurses and 15 corpsmen were waiting.

Frank Neumayer was only vaguely aware of being trundled out of Sick Bay and through the passageway to the forward bomb elevators. He was very weak and very, very tired and the banging trip did not bother him at all. The corpsman at his side talked incessantly and Frank Neumayer understood only a few words of what he was saying. He drifted off, losing consciousness, and began to fall away,,,, spiraling,,,, down and down,,,, into a vast, dark, emptiness.

Frank Neumayer distinctly felt the rush of a cold cosmic wind here in deep space. The wind was constant and strong and invigorating. The wind carried with it the salt clean smell of the vast and beautiful blue sea. Frank Neumayer stopped his free-fall into the void. The cool brisk wind and the smell of the ocean made him think of the color blue. There was a light shining far away and he felt himself drawn to it, coming back from the darkness with great speed. The sound of his return from the abyss was the rushing of the wind in his ears. The light was getting larger and brighter.

There was another sound, vague. It was a sound not of the wind and the sea. It was a sharp and raucous sound and it grated his solitude. Frank Neumayer opened his eyes to the beauty of white clouds across a blue sky. It was a breathtaking vision. But the noise was still hammering at him. He turned his eyes and focused on the face of the bellowing, pounding corpsman.

Frank Neumayer could not understand what the man was saying. The face and expression of him told of a great urgency. There were others about him and Neumayer felt himself being carried with haste towards another noise. He saw above him the flashing rotor blades of a helicopter and felt himself being lifted up and passed into it. There were others there and they shouted to be heard above the noise. There was no blue or white beauty here, all was drab green. There was no cool, clean wind here, only noise. Frank Neumayer felt the machine begin to vibrate. Then he drifted.

By 1115, the stubborn fires at 03-195-5-L on the starboard side, and those from the main deck to the 03 level at frame 230 on the port side would be put out to re-flash again from the spontaneous combustion of hot metals. Repair 7 BRAVO reported all power had been restored to the island structure. All blood donors having orange cards were to report to Sick Bay immediately. Three Marine helicopters were reported inbound from Pearl with medical assistance teams. Central reported 13 dead.

On the flight deck, green rubber body bags were handed out to those not engaged with snow shovels or fire hoses. Lines of men carefully sifted through the stinking junk to recover the inevitable. These remains had been blasted, burned and blown apart. The things recovered from the pyre were gruesome beyond imagination and never whole. It was a ghastly duty to have to perform after enduring the trauma of the battle. Snow shovels carefully scraped things from the deck and loaded them into the waiting green bags. It was terrible to see how a human could be burned away to a very small thing by the flames.

The work went on, sifting and probing through every part of the wreckage claimed by the fire. A helmeted Marine came by with a lump covered with a blanket and wanted to know from anyone, "I've got someone's foot here, what should I do with it?" Parts and pieces were picked from the rubble, sometimes by smell. Twig Tordoff had a green bag. Most of the things he found were so blackened, he had to poke at them to discover whether it was flesh or metal. At one point he found some things that were easily recognizable. They were fingers.

Joe Rosa was shoveling through the rubble throwing what he

could over the side. The wrecks and remains of the aircraft were to be pushed over and paths had to be cleared of the sharp metals, live high explosives and those other things. On the fouled deck a glint of reflected sunlight flashed from something close to Joe Rosa's feet. He shoveled around until he found it, a thing of gold in the blackened mass. He reached down and picked it up and cleaned it off on his own shirt. The thing was bent but unmistakable. It was a wedding ring.

The fires would flash into life again in the dark, gaseous confines of those various compartments and spaces where the metals radiated with a fierce heat. The flames would roar in defiance and quickly blaze out of control until they were brought to bay again. The hose teams maneuvered throughout the maze of passageways and compartments, always attacking, flanking and surrounding the fires.

Like the serpent seeking to throw its coils about its prey, the slow constriction of the hose teams gradually trapped and choked the life out of the fury. Sprays of salt water and foam wrenched it from its last bastions. The heat seethed in hatred and the metals hissed and snapped in contorted agony as it was slowly exorcised from them with the cooling sprays. The fury died hard but die it did as the last of it was driven down at 1138. It would rise again no more. The trial was over. The ordeal of *USS Enterprise* was done.

Henry Mendoza heard a discussion going on between a doctor and one of the corpsmen not far from his table. The doctor said, "No, we will keep HIM here and assign one of the Barbers Point men to him." Hearing this, Mendoza was relieved. He did not want to be moved again. Presently, two corpsmen came over to his table and one told the other, "This one needs someone to keep an eye on him."

The corpsman who stayed was from the Medical Assistance Team flown in from Barbers Point and he looked down at Mendoza and said, "I am going to stay with you." Henry Mendoza looked up at the corpsman and was struck by the color of his soft, blue Angel eyes. He was about to say something when the Catholic Chaplain entered the room. The priest looked around at the many blanket covered mounds atop the tables and began a general administration of the Death Sacrament. Henry Mendoza began jabbering to one and all, reassuring everyone that he was alright and in no need of the

Blessing. The priest proceeded anyway and strafed the entire room. For the second time, Mendoza felt himself sentenced.

When the priest had finished, Mendoza fell silent. He was very tired and in much pain. The corpsman with the Angel eyes knew what he was feeling and told him that he needed to tighten up the tourniquet. He also said, "This is going to hurt."

"Go ahead!," Mendoza told him, "It hurts already anyway!" And then a wave of pain crashed down on him like the surf pounding upon the shore. Henry Mendoza remembered the pain lasted for a long time and Angel eyes stayed right with him, applying pressure. Finally, a doctor came to the table and looked down at Mendoza and said, "We're going to put you out now."

Henry Mendoza bit down on clenched teeth. He was beginning to sweat again. The pain was nearly overpowering. He nodded in acknowledgment to the doctor. After that, there was nothing.

The vast host of the Legion of the Dead of the Sea stood mute in the slowly swirling gray fastnesses. They stood arrayed about the new men who had been gathered into three short ranks to take their place in the Legion. All here were looking down at the drama of the MEDEVAC effort with the comings and goings of the helicopters like so many honey bees busily working their hive.

The hollow-eyed officer in mouldering khaki was presently joined on either side by the figure in the tattered dress of the Imperial Japanese Navy and the ancient one from times remote. These three faced the ranks of the new men who stood patiently, silent in the wavering mists. There was no time here, no sentiment, only silence.

The figure holding the book then opened it and he of the Imperial Japanese Navy then addressed the lines of new men. It was a communication, neither spoken nor heard, but understood by all in this realm of mute softness.

"We will now call the roll . . . State your place and years."

There followed a moment of drifting silence, then:

"AKERS, Paul, 3rd Division."

"Here, sir. Tacoma Washington, 18 years old."

"ASBURY, David, V-4 Division."

"Here. Middleton Ohio, 21 sir."

"BERGHULT, Carl, Lieutenant Junior Grade, VF-96."

"Sir! Chicago, Illinois. 26 years old Sir."

"BERRY, James, Lieutenant Junior Grade, VF-96."

The mists slowly purled and eddied about them as they waited. There was no answer.

"Lieutenant Junior Grade James BERRY?!" The communication was expectant. There was only silence.

The three figures looked to the line of new men and then all three looked into the open book. A shadow of concern passed between them. The men standing in line sensed something was wrong and began to look themselves over. After a pause,

"We will continue."
"BOVAIRD, Richard, VA-215."
"Here Sir, Brockway, Pennsylvania, 22."
"BULLINGTON, Patrick, VF-96."
"Here, Pheonix, Arizona Sir, 24 years old."
"FLOYD, James, VF-96."
"Here, Sommerville, Georgia Sir, 22."
"FOSTER, Ernest, V-1 Division."
"Here, Sir. Eugene, Oregon, 22 years old."
"GIRTY, Delbert, V-1 Division."
"SIR!, Muskogee, Oklahoma Sir, 24 years old!"

The drama below was not yet over. Five MEDEVAC units were in the air, beating through the heavy crosswind, making their best speed towards Tripler Hospital. They were spread out over 60 miles of ocean when a crisis occurred simultaneously on two of them. The hearts of two of the casualties had stopped beating and they were immediately set upon by the attending corpsmen. Frantic efforts were made to revive the two during the remainder of the flights. Through an absolute miracle, one man was brought back from death.

"HAY, Ronald VF-96."
"SIR! Tannerville, Pennsylvania, Sir. 30 years old."
"HOLBROOK, Roger, A.I.M.D."
"Here Sir, Paintsville, Kentucky. 21 Sir."
"HUNT, Dale, VF-92."
"Here, Yuma, Arizona, 21."
"LACEY, Donald, VF-96."
"Here, Bend, Oregon, 20 years old Sir."
"LIMON, Armando, VF-96."

Ghostly silence pervaded throughout the scene as puzzlement again passed over the countenances of the three.

"LIMON??"

The men in ranks stirred and looked up and down their lines. The roll would continue.

"MARKS, Dennis, A.I.M.D."
"Here, Milwaukee, Wisconsin, 22, Sir."
"MARTINEAU, James, VF-96."
"Here, Providence, Rhode Island. 27, Sir."
"MASON, Joe Carroll, VF-92."
"Here, Houston, Mississippi, 19 years old, Sir."
"MILBURN, Dennis, VF-92."

Silence.
The three figures turned to one another and again regarded the open book. What passed between them was not understood by those in the assembly. They would proceed.

"NEUMAYER, Frank VF-96."

Silence.
The three figures drew into conference. Presently the officer of the Imperial Japanese Navy turned and walked off into the deep mists, disappearing. The officer with the book continued,

"OATES, Joseph, V-1 Division."
"Here Sir. Butler, Alabama. 21."
"PYEATT, Buddy, Lieutenant Junior Grade, VF-96."
"SIR!, Jal, New Mexico, Sir. 25."
"QUINTIS, Jacob, V-2 Division."
"Here. Shoemaker, California. 21,"
"SNIPES, James, 3rd Division."
"SIR!, Person County, North Carolina Sir. 28."
"TYLER, Russell, VA-145."
"Here sir, Elkhart, Indiana. 23."
"VON FELDT, La Verne, V-1 Division."

"Here. Great Bend, Kansas. 20."
"WARD, Robert, V-1 Division."
"Here. New Matamoris, Ohio. 20."
"WEBSTER, John, V-1 Division."
"Norwalk, California sir, 22 years old."
"YATES, Henry, VF-96."
"Here, Honolulu, Hawaii, 32."
"YOAKUM, Jerome, VAQ-132."
"Here. Duluth, Minnesota. 22."

The questioner looked up and closed the book. He regarded the three ranks before him. They all stood patiently, at ease. There was no need of hurry here. From the depths of the fogs the tattered one of the Imperial Japanese Navy re-emerged and resumed his place among the three. Then he quietly announced, "Another is coming."

The endless rank on rank of the Legion of the Dead of the Sea held formation in the ghostly wisps of vapors curling about. They waited.

A figure came slowly through the fogs and moved towards the line of new men. All here looked upon him as he stepped forward to take his place in line. From the first rank, the ghostly countenance of Pat Bullington turned and nodded to the new man in recognition. The new man nodded back.

After a pause, the figure with the book asked, "You are?"
The answer was, "LIMON, Armando, VF-96."
"Your place and years?"
"El Paso, Texas, 26 years old sir,"
The roll had been called. The officer closed the book and passed it to the ancient one. Then he announced, "Twenty six present for duty, three missing."

Coast Guard helo #1408 touched down at the Tripler helo pad with the first two MEDEVAC casualties. Newsmen and reporters tried to get some information about what was going on out at sea but the first patient was quickly passed from the helicopter bay into the waiting ambulance with two doctors climbing in after him. They then sped to the hospital. The second casualty was sleeping the eternal sleep, and put off to the side. The newsmen felt frustration, there would be no information from these.

Officials of the Honolulu police force had contacted Major General Milburn to offer whatever assistance was needed in handling traffic between Pearl and Tripler. They notified him that a squadron of motorcycle police officers from the Honolulu Police Department would be waiting outside the Nimitz Gate at Pearl to escort a fleet of 20 ambulances and three buses from the ship to Tripler when she came in.

The flight deck clean up continued with everything destroyed being thrown or pushed over the side. The mobile crane was employed for this purpose and promptly broke down. The Crash Fork lifts were brought up from the Hangar Bay and the hulks were pushed over, all except some engine and airframe sections along the A-7 line which had been welded to the deck from the molten metals. These could not be broken loose.

A morgue was set up in the forward port corner of Hangar Bay 1. Canvas barricade screens were put up in place and the dead in their body bags were brought up the bomb elevators and carried over and stacked in rows on the deck. Ron Ruland was still running the elevator and helping to carry the bodies.

All the hose teams stayed in place and boxes of sandwiches began to appear throughout the ship. For all those who craved something cool for their parched throats, an abundance of frozen papaya cups were handed around. The crew were impressed with the propriety of the gesture.

By 1208, all compartments throughout the ship were reported to be de-smoked. Repair parties probed warily in the darkness, inspecting the black and twisted wreckage of the 03 level. Beams of light played through the gloom of the ruined spaces looking for the last vestiges of the fires. Here and there, small columns of white smoke rose lazily and hoses were opened upon them.

The glare of bright sunlight shone down through the holes blasted from above and Damage Control teams stepped carefully around these places, mindful of the shorn and buckled deck plates. There was a halo of light beaming down into the drifting smoke of the head at frame 240. The light illuminated a ghastly graveyard which spoke volumes about the violence of the explosions from above. Repair personnel retrieved what was left, numb to the horror of it. Stretchers were brought forth and loaded with things and then hauled away to be added to the count. The teams then probed into the last extremities of the blasted port side, looking for the last of the dead. Two more were found in the passageway outside of the 7 ALPHA locker. Perhaps one was dragging the other to safety. Perhaps they spent their last ounces of strength to reach this place. They were both flight deckers.

By 1230, eighteen casualties had been delivered by helo to the Tripler pad. As fast as one chopper unloaded and lifted clear, another would set down. Army medics rushed for the open doors and carried the stretchers at a gallop beneath the beating rotor blades. The three ambulances could not keep up with the pace and the overflow of stretcher cases began to stack up on the lawn. Reporters pressed in to try and get information from the wounded. Most were silent. The smell of burned, dead flesh permeated. There was a certain heavily bandaged man in a stretcher whose eyes were seen to be open between the wraps of white covering most of his face. A reporter knelt down next to him and thrust a microphone close to the man's face. "What Happened out there?" he asked urgently. The eyes closed tight and a tear tracked down from the corner of the eye to vanish into the white cloth. The eyes slowly opened again and they looked skyward, searching. A pained and halting voice struggled beneath the bandages, "I . . . don't . . . know . ."

"GET AWAY FROM THOSE STRETCHERS!!", a command thundered. It came from a mammoth Army Sergeant bearing down on the newsmen with mighty strides. The Sergeant had balled his hands into fists with the intention of doing battle. He raised one to point an accusing finger at the reporters with all the menace of leveling a rifle barrel, "STAND CLEAR!!"

The newsmen scattered from the path of the Sergeant like dust before the wind. Empty cartons of medical supplies and loose jetsam flew and spun about in the swirling rotorblast.

On the *USS Enterprise*, damage reports and assessments came to Capt. Lee from the various Divisions and Squadrons even as the Crash fork lifts tumbled wreckage over the sides and fantail and Repair units probed through the dark, ruined spaces below. Fifteen aircraft had been totally destroyed with a number of others suffering lesser shrapnel and blast damage. Elevator #4, and #4 jet blast deflector were out of commission.

The LSO platform with the 19 MC hot line to Primary along with the Fresnel Lenses and controls were destroyed. Both port and starboard Point Defense Missile Systems were out of commission. All electrical and sound power circuits aft of #3 elevator on the flight deck and 03 level were destroyed. All catwalks aft of #3 elevator were sagged and buckled from heat. All fog foam and salt water firefighting stations aft of #3 elevator were destroyed. Flight deck fueling stations #26 through #30 were destroyed with many tanks in the JP-5 system contaminated with salt water, foam and other foreign matter. All deck edge electrical service in the area were destroyed. Combat Readiness Stations 11 through 16 were destroyed or zero grounded.

All arresting gear and barricade control stations were destroyed. All boom interlock switches and cables on the B and A crane were destroyed and the control station was zero grounded. Seven holes of up to 20 feet in diameter were found blown through the flight deck, with dents and heat damage causing many more obstructions. Two 5 x 10 foot holes were burned completely down through #4 elevator to the sea.

Transmitter room #5 was obliterated and #4 and #7 Radio's on the 015 level had severed transmission lines. Three Whip antennae were holed and nicked by flying fragments. The SPS-32 and 33 long range and computer tracker radars had been shot through with 30 holes up to 6 inches in diameter. The AN/SPS-GC medium range antenna was holed twice and the control cables severed. One dipole of the 8200 system had a bomb fin embedded into it. Three corner reflectors, one starboard aft, two port aft, had been carried away. Various control and transmission lines were ruptured and shattered by flying fragments and high velocity impacts. Central reported 25 dead were recovered.

Detonation in starboard corner throws sparks and debris high aloft. Photo courtesy of the Tailhook Association, Baumer collection.

Explosion on the port side sends a fireball roaring skyward, a thing of terrible beauty. Glowing drops of burning fuel and red hot metals cascade downward. Photo courtesy of the Tailhook Association, Baumer collection.

Detonation in starboard corner. White smoke trail of Sparrow missile is seen coming out of it. Photo courtesy of the Tailhook Association. Baumer collection.

Cataclysmic 106/614 detonation. A terrible mauling for the defenseless fire fighters. Photo courtesy of the Tailhook Association, Baumer collection.

Hoses being pieced together and brought back from forward stations. Foam blanket spread under parked A-7 Corsairs. Situation critical. Photo courtesy of the Tailhook Association, Baumer collection.

Rogers closing on *Enterprise* port side as hoses are brought into action from forward stations. Photo courtesy of the Tailhook Association, Baumer collection.

On the ASROC deck of the *Rogers* fire fighters brave intense heat as the distance between ships closes to twenty yards. Photo courtesy of Steve O'Brien.

Rogers closes on the flaming carrier. The spray of the 2½ inch fire hose lashed to the starboard gun barrel of 51 mount is driven backward by the wind. Photo courtesy of Steve O'Brien.

Starboard A-7 line where most of the remaining junk had become welded to the deck. Men with snow shovels probe through the wreckage and a greenshirt at center right wrestles with a body bag. Note helmeted Marines. Photo courtesy of the Tailhook Association, Baumer collection.

The gutted shell of 112 and 310 blasted into a twisted wreck. Photo courtesy of the Tailhook Association, Baumer collection.

Aircraft are stacked forward on the angle to make a fire break. Official U.S. Navy photo.

The Crash fork lift bulldozes wreckage towards the fantail. Photo courtesy of the Tailhook Association, Baumer collection.

8. THE VIRTUE

At Tripler Hospital the response to requests for blood donors was overwhelming. By 1300, a line had formed from the various receiving stations in the hospital itself, out the doors and far down the road. Jarrett Whit road, the only access to Tripler, was clogged and stalled with scores of vehicles as volunteers continued to arrive. The outpouring of support was humbling. No less than eleven hundred Americans stood in line to bleed for the *Enterprise* crew. Eleven Hundred!

Tripler Hospital called Queens Medical Center in Honolulu and asked them to take the overflow of blood donors. Queens Medical responded that they were unable to keep up with what donors they already had! There were four hundred standing in line there. In these dark days of turmoil, when it was fashionable on campuses and intellectual circles throughout the country to deride and scorn the Armed Forces, the Cream of a Nation rose to the top. The volunteers had to be turned away, there were so many. They had to be turned away.

Frank Neumayer remembered when he landed at the Tripler pad because he was dropped in his stretcher as he was being loaded into an ambulance. He remembered being carried briskly into the hospital and quickly passing through a number of doors before stopping. He remembered a lot of people wearing white, cutting away his bloody bandages and going to work on him. Most of all he remembered looking up into the eyes of a nurse and her cool reassuring hand on his forehead. It was at this time that he began to think that he just might make it. Frank Neumayer had been teetering on the edge for four hours. Now, under the hands of the Mass Casualty staff at Tripler, his heart stopped beating, for the third time.

On *Enterprise*, at 1339 all personnel, with the exception of Repair parties and necessary flight deck crews, were secured from General Quarters. Thereafter, individual Divisions and Squadrons were called to muster at different places throughout the ship. Word was passed for the V-4 flight deck crews to muster back in the crew shelter.

They all came back together and an accounting was made by each of the six crews. The mood in the shelter was grave. Very little was said. No one felt like talking and only the briefest of information was given. Asbury was dead. Kreisler, Norsworthy, Bemisdarfer and Thompson had been carried off deck. Poole and Hill had walked off but all were in Sick Bay or worse.

The crewleader of crew #2 went to a small locker and pulled out a clean, dry purple jersey to replace the fouled one he was wearing. As he took off the old one someone from behind said, "Hey, your back is bleeding." The crewleader dismissed the news and pulled on the clean jersey. Nearly every man on deck had cuts and welts from flying shards of metal. He would certainly not seek attention for such a trivial thing, not after the horrific Red Badges of Courage suffered by others.

Someone there made a pronouncement of something he knew for a fact. He said it in a low tone, addressing everyone, or no one in particular, "V-1 got beat up bad."

All heard these words. No one there said anything. There was nothing to say. They all had seen the nearly endless flow of horrors being dragged back from the hose teams. No one could make any sense out of what had happened. No one knew what DID happen. It was simply a furious, hideous, bloodbath of a nightmare that left everyone shaken. None here would ever be the same again. Of the 22 men of the V-4 crews, 7 were down.

The crewleader had to get out of the shelter and Lasovich, Fitzgerald and Arrick felt the same way. They all wanted to go back and see the holes in the deck now that the deck had been cleaned off. The flight deck was now a place where all hands would come to survey the battlefield. Men walked about in silent groups of two or three and pointed out the scars and holes of things which had been driven into and through the island structure. They paused and considered the tremendous heat which had reduced the starboard A-7 line to pools of molten metals. They saw the sagging catwalks and the melted Point Defense Missile launchers. And they stopped and gaped in awe at the yawning craters punched through the deck on the port side, and the charred and blasted compartments below. They tried to imagine it. They tried to visualize what fantastic power had done these things. They spoke in low, reverent tones. What bloodshed was surely wrought by such violence!

The crewleader thought about it too. He stood by the holes where 105 used to be. He looked at the maw of the hole where 113 had been parked. He looked back a short distance to the place where his hose team had been annihilated. The four purpleshirts all felt the same thing. It was all too incredible! It was so incredible that it could not even be talked about. Not this day, not tomorrow. Not for a very, very, long time.

The crewleader had to get away. The stink of burned wreckage and that certain sickly sweet smell still hung like a pall over the deck. He wanted to go where it was clean.

Diana McLaughlin and her friend were watching the newscast from Tripler hospital. The scene showed a long line of blood donors and then panned to the helicopter pad and the considerable activity there. The loud beatings of rotor blades from the continuous comings and goings of the MEDEVAC helo's could be clearly heard outside the house.

Presently, two officers came to the door with news. One was the Commanding Officer of Patrol Squadron-17 and he told the women that all O.R.I. staff and all VA-145 officers on *Enterprise* had been accounted for and the names of their husbands were not on the casualty lists.

In the cavernous hangar bays of *USS Enterprise*, the green body bags were still being brought up from below and carried over to be placed behind the screens with the armed Marine standing guard. They would be stacked in rows on the deck and there would be many more than the twenty five men listed as dead. Many of the bags contained only remnants and pieces.

Musters were being held even while this activity was going on. The work of cleaning aircraft cockpits and other sensitive areas of foam and salt water in Bays #1 and #2 was begun while the shin deep foam on deck was just beginning to dissipate. The enclosed hangar bay stunk with the smell of it.

All hands went about their duties, ever mindful of those screens and the growing rows of silent green rubber bags being placed there. Suddenly, there was a rumble. The rumble was heavy and prolonged and all hands looked wildly about, thinking that it was beginning again. Then a flash of golden sunlight burst into Bay 1 as both #1 and #2 elevator doors rumbled across their tracks in unison. A steady gust of clean sea wind swept through the Bay and cleansed it. The vast blue sea and the foaming white surf of the bow wake could be seen without. The endless majesty of the blue sky was bright, with a low cloud mass moving away, far to the east. The sun poured down its healing rays in generous profusion and the beauty of the sea and sky and sun were as though nothing had ever happened. The cool breath of the sea wind told all, "What was before is done!"

From the different muster lists being held, a clear accounting of the human cost came to light. The heaviest toll was naturally taken in the Air Department and Squadron personnel on the flight deck, and in V-1 Division and VF-96 in particular. V-1 Division was responsible for the entire flight deck and was the primary fire response organization. VF-96 suffered the highest loss of aircraft, six, and bore a heavy brunt of the initial casualties. The casualty lists reflected these, and other areas of responsibility, utterly.

The muster lists would initially show a total of seventeen missing. All but two of these would later be found among the as yet unidentified dead.

The four purpleshirts walked forward on the flight deck, keeping clear of the helicopter landing areas. Fire hoses were still out on deck and deployed to some of the various holes on the after port side and fantail, but they were not even charged. These hoses would stay on deck, even when the ship was tied to the pier. A number of men stood and manned these hoses, but they were not the ones from early on. The purpleshirts, like the other survivors of the fighting hose teams, had all drifted away. They had all gone to someplace quiet and serene. They went off to themselves. They had all gone someplace to bleed and heal.

The four purpleshirts continued towards the bow, where the giant number 65 was painted. They walked silently, slowly passing around and between the parked aircraft along the starboard side. From across deck, other purpleshirts had seen and followed the pilgrimage. They kept going until they were at the very forward most part of the bow, ahead of the first aircraft on the starboard side. Here, looking forward, only the rolling blue Pacific and the somber expanse of the now cloudless sky could be seen. The warming rays of the life-giving sun fell full upon them. The welcome strength of the sea wind renewed them and swept away the past. The purpleshirts sat on the non-skid surface of the flight deck, facing the far horizon. All was blue.

The fire of adrenalin was rapidly draining from them. They were very tired. None had spoken even a single word. None wanted to hear. There was only the sound of the welcome sea wind, and the steady crash of surf as the great bow of *USS Enterprise* cleaved the waters below.

Others, now, were coming forward. They came in small groups, by two's and three's. Gatherings of men in blue jerseys, or green or brown or red. Every color of jersey and the khaki and chambray shirts of below deckers. They all sought the peace of the wind. All sought the solitude. All came to rest and heal.

As *Enterprise* plowed north at 20 knots, she left behind her three escorting destroyers who were joined by two Fleet tugs and another small auxiliary vessel to search for survivors. Overhead, Coast Guard C-130 and Navy P-3 patrol aircraft flew as the miles of debris left in the track of the carrier was systematically screened. The major problem was the hundreds of semi-inflated life rafts strewn from one horizon to another. Each one had to be searched.

At first, attempts were made to haul the rafts aboard. This proved difficult because they were extremely cumbersome and unwieldy. The process was time consuming and costly. A man on the *Stoddart* had his hand crushed under a pelican hook while trying to bring a raft aboard. Motor whaleboats were then maneuvered alongside and men punctured the rafts with knives in order to sink them. The life rafts which appeared so reluctant to float proved virtually impossible to sink! Firearms had to be passed out to riddle the rafts to pieces after each was searched. Only then would they stubbornly slip beneath the waves.

On the flight deck of *Enterprise*, men reclined and rested, each lost in his own thoughts. The Trial of the ship had been the Trial of every man and all hands reflected upon themselves as to how they had stood up to the test. The Trial had been the Judgment. Each man had been exposed by the Terror. Each man had been laid bare upon the dock, his most intimate, inner self weighed upon the scales for all to see. Each man had come to know himself. Each had come to know the TRUTH and the knowledge of that revelation was a heavy burden of humility.

Throughout the ship it was quiet. There were no announcements made over the 1MC. There were no instructions or directions passed over the bullhorn by the Air Boss. The helicopters would continue to evacuate wounded, but all those not engaged in this activity were permitted to rest. All throughout the ship the pace had trailed off and everyone had time to think. All hands were thankful for the peace.

On the bow, Nick Lasovich sat Indian fashion watching ahead to the far horizon for the first glimpse of land. His friends around him reclined with closed eyes but he knew they were not sleeping. Far ahead, where the sea lightened to meet the sky and the sky darkened to meet the sea and the horizon was an indistinct blur, the mists of a cloud could be seen. Nick Lasovich watched this for some time. There was not another cloud in the sky now, only this one, far down on the horizon. The cloud was forming and slowly grew in stature as the ship made straight for it. Nick Lasovich waited until he was sure. He waited until he could clearly see the dark peaks thrust up through the cloud. It was the most beautiful and welcome sight of any mariner. It was land. He said, "There it is!"

The others rose up and looked. They would behold this spectacle as it was beheld by all sailors throughout the millennium. No glittering jewel or fine thing of gold, nothing else of this earth could match the majesty of this sight. The deep, shimmering Pacific blue gave way to a radiant halo of turquoise waters and out of this halo great mountains rose sheer and towering from the sea. Verdant spines and crags marched like soldiers into the distance. The dark green of the mountains grew ever darker towards the heights and the clefts of them were black. The mighty hills were girded in their glory by mists of white and a stunning carpet of glittering beige lay at their feet. The very blue of the sky itself paled in the presence of such beauty.

Down in Sick Bay, Henry Mendoza was beginning to come out of it. He blinked his eyes and struggled with a peculiar heavy sensation. He looked up and Angel Eyes was still there. When Henry finally got his eyes focused, the corpsman told him there were some of his friends there to see him. Henry looked over and there stood a gang from V-1 looking at him. They looked very sad and disheveled. They were wet and dirty and fouled with ashes and blood. They looked like they had been crying. Billy Hawk was there, and next to him stood Warrant Officer Jim Helton with blood pooling on the deck below his right pant leg. Henry asked them about Little Joe and they all sadly shook their heads. Then he asked about Tex and Girty and they shook their heads again. Billy Hawk handed Henry a guitar and Mendoza recognized it as the one he was going to buy from

Bobby Ward. Henry Mendoza knew what it meant. He closed his eyes as the wave of sorrow crashed down on him. He heard one of the group openly crying and it was having an effect on everyone. It was very hard, but Henry Mendoza managed to say the words, "He . . . saved . . . my life . . ."

By 3 o'clock 40 men had been evacuated by helicopter to Tripler Hospital. All eight operating rooms were in use and going full tilt. A total of 46 men would be landed at the Tripler helicopter pad. At Pearl Harbor, preparations were under way to receive the carrier. Ambulances and buses were lined up at the pier where *Enterprise* would be berthed. Yard construction and repair officials were there with senior Navy brass to go aboard as soon as possible to survey the damage. Twelve Red Cross volunteers set up a canteen and concerned people were arriving by the hundreds. The ship was due in one hour.

Vast crowds lined the shores from Ewa Beach and Fort Kamehameha inland on either side of the narrow Pearl stream. All looked south, watching the paths of the bustling helicopters. Where once the far horizon fell away into empty distance, now the white square mass of the island structure of *USS Enterprise* hove into view. There it is! Word quickly spread and onlookers stood on tiptoe with hands shielding out the bright sunlight from their vision to range a faraway sighting. Eyes strained into the distance. The wide flight deck could be seen, riding high and proud above the sea. The unmistakable lines and beauty of the Big "E", the only ship of her class could now be clearly seen and recognized. With every seconds passing the carriers immense dimensions grew in stature. She was coming very fast.

All Damage Control and Repair Party personnel remained at their stations even though the rest of the ship was winding down. The danger of re-flash and the loss of watertight integrity from the gaping holes blown down through the ship made the continued presence of Damage Control teams essential. The special sea and anchor detail was set.

Ens. Karl Mahumed, Repair Officer for Unit 75, was relieved at the scene. This was done so that he could assume the duties of Officer of the Deck when the ship was tied up alongside the pier at Pearl Harbor. Ens. Mahumed left his repair team and went down to his stateroom where he quickly changed into dress whites. He would have to be on watch in 30 minutes.

All Battle Dressing Stations had by this time transferred their stretcher cases to Main Sick Bay. Those that were able, were patched up and sent back to their units to clear the congestion in the medical spaces. In Sick Bay itself, preparations were made to transfer the remaining serious cases by ambulance to Tripler as soon as the ship tied up. Patients were loaded back into stretchers with corpsmen standing by for the word to begin the evacuation to the Quarterdeck.

On the flight deck everyone was still sitting or reclining, watching the approach to the crowded shores. This was the first time that any could remember that this ship would sail into port without the call, "MAN THE RAIL!" There would be no pageant of sailors in dress whites standing in position at intervals all about the edges of the flight deck and upper works of the ship. There would be very few clean sets of dress whites or any uniforms whatsoever for a vast number of the crew.

One of the purpleshirts on the bow told his brothers, "Look who is coming." They all turned and looked aft. There could be seen one gang of loungers after another getting to their feet and manning the rail in their dungarees and the various colors of flight deck jerseys. Many were still ragged and wet and bore the signs of battle. There was a singular presence striding along, ordering everyone to their feet. It was a Chief in a purple jersey.

The V-4 Division Chief came up to the bow and the last of those still not standing on this starboard side. They were about a dozen of his own men, all wearing purple. "GET UP!" he said with his accustomed glare of disdain on his face, "STAND UP AND ACT LIKE MEN!"

The purpleshirts slowly got to their feet while the Chief glowered at them. The crewleader of crew #2 stood very close to the Chief, facing him. The Chief turned his scowl upon the crewleader and the two stood there, locked in a fierce stare. These two had briefly looked into one another's eyes once before on this day. This was the Chief who found duty in the island when the bloodletting flowed on deck. This was the Chief frozen into shock at the sight on the stretcher that crew #2 carried through the island hatch. This was a man to whom the TRUTH had been revealed and now he stood facing another who KNEW.

The expression of the hard eyed Chief never changed as he sought to back the other man down. The other dared to take the stand of the accuser and knew himself to be right. A muscle twitched in the set jaw of the Chief, then nervously twitched again. The Chief turned on his heel and bounded across to the port side where he noisily continued his quest. The purpleshirts watched him go. All down the portside he ordered the men to their feet and it was because of him that every manjack was standing when the ship sailed past the crowds.

The men on deck stood and looked down as the ship slowed and entered the narrow waterway leading into Pearl Harbor. The hundreds lining either bank jostled and hummed in speculative commotion as the stately ship approached them. They could see no mark from here, surely the news was worse than what had actually happened. But then the ship drew closer and dangling lines and cables could be seen hanging from the ships highest works. The blackened and paint blistered sides of the ship, down to the waterline, came into view. And as surely as the ship left a wake in its passing, so to did she leave a hush in the vast crowds as she drew abreast. All fell silent as the great ship glided by. Burned and skeletal hulks and blackened and sagging metal told of the heat. The shot scarred and riddled island structure told of the density and velocity of flying things. And the gaping blown through transom with wreckage hanging from it and the blasted fantail with the holes torn through the stern just above the waterline told of the fury.

The crowd was silent. There were no wavings or hellos, only the shock at the evidence at hand. The sailors looking down were silent. All fought to suppress the rising lumps in their throats as the horror became clear on those faces below. The only sound was the gentle lapping of the waters as the ship slid past and the metallic slapping of the dangling cables in the wind. A certain woman broke the stillness of the crowd when she let out a cry and ran for the nearest telephone booth. She had binoculars in her hands. She had seen the one she feared for.

Big John Guillot was still at his station at Repair 5 Bravo when the wounded were brought back out of Sick Bay. He and his team had seen the horrors flow past in a steady parade all morning. Now, they were coming back out again, no less pitiful for all their white bandages. The pilots elevator was used to take the wounded up to the Hangar Deck where they were taken to the Officers brow being rigged on the Quarterdeck. Way had to be made for the jumble of attendants with each stretcher. They carefully held the life giving bottles and bags aloft to keep the flows moving. John Guillot and his men stood back and sadly and silently watched the procession coming out of

Sick Bay. Many of them only had one leg now. Or one hand.

As soon as the Officers brow was in place, Officer of the Deck Mahumed ordered the waiting wounded to be carried off. The Navy ambulances and buses stood in line to receive the stretchers coming down the gangway. The Senior Navy brass and shipyard officials fought their way up the brow past the stretcher teams coming down. They must have thought their own missions to be the most important. Officer of the Deck Mahumed thought otherwise. It was his deck and these wounded would be carried off first thing. He placed his imposing 6'5" and 240 pound frame at the head of the brow and bellowed, "GET OFF MY QUARTERDECK!" Then he pointed a finger like a harpoon and commanded, "CLEAR THAT GANGWAY!!" The shipyard officials and Navy brass, with all their gold braid, turned and retreated back down the brow.

Henry Mendoza was the last casualty carried off. He felt strangely giddy and saw that the Officer of the Deck bore an expression of consternation. Henry Mendoza saluted as he was being carried by and said, "Request permission to go ashore, Sir!" Karl Mahumed returned the salute and said, "Permission granted, Sailor!"

He was carried down the brow past the impatiently waiting officials, then slid into the back of an ambulance and hurriedly driven away. As the ambulance approached NIMITZ Gate, four motorcycle officers of the Honolulu Police Department fired up their mounts and sped out and flanked the ambulance, two in front and two in back, to escort it through rush hour traffic. Spectators lined the streets watching the many ambulances and escorts speeding past. The pavements and sidewalks throbbed under the pounding thunder of escorting Harley-Davidsons and sirens warned all to stand clear.

Henry Mendoza was lying quietly in his stretcher with two corpsmen attending him when the ambulance swerved hard and he skidded across and slammed into the side, knocking the corpsmen down. "HEY,", they yelled, "watch what you are doing!" The driver yelled back in exasperation, "It's all these crazy people! They won't stay out of the way!" Then he addressed Henry in a more conciliatory tone. "Don't worry Buddy, I'll get you there if I have to run somebody down to do it!"

The irony of the statement was not lost on Henry Mendoza. He was still giddy and high on pain killing drugs. For the first and only time of the day, he smiled.

At Tripler, the medical staff still had 16 patients awaiting surgery when the ambulances began to arrive bringing 19 more. This was the biggest emergency ever to hit the 1000 bed hospital, eclipsing even the TET Offensive of '68.

Out at sea, the search continued the remainder of the day and throughout the long night sweeping back and forth over the area of the *Enterprise* fire. One sailor from the carrier was known to have gone over and possibly a second man. On and on searchlights played across shimmering black waters and lookouts strained their eyes into the darkness. The endless Pacific waves had claimed their due. The search ships would find nothing.

Hours later and 12,000 miles to the east, a solitary soldier stood in a lonely place with his bayoneted M-14 at right shoulder arms. The soldier was the sentinel at the Tomb of the Unknowns in Arlington National Cemetery, and he stood within a halo of stark light at the north end of a carpeted track. It was well past the midnight hour, into the deepest time of quiet. The clear, starshot night was absolutely still and very cold and the soldiers breath steamed from his nostrils at every exhalation. The soldier stood perfectly still. He was mentally counting off the seconds, facing south.

The soldier wore white gloves and a heavy overcoat over his impeccable dress uniform because of the 9°F temperature. The soldier was a new man from Tennessee and it was given to the new men to walk the Guard at the Tomb of the Unknowns on the night rotations until they had perfected their walks and learned the history of Arlington. Only then would they be prepared to be a day sentinel, under the greatest of scrutiny. The soldier from Tennessee was a new man to this post, but beneath his heavy overcoat two rows of medals blazed upon his chest for service to his country in that place called Viet Nam. Chief among the medals he wore were the Purple Heart and Silver Star.

The new man from Tennessee held his position until the exact time and then stepped forth and began his walk. The walk of the sentry was precise and deliberate, each step, 21 inches in length. The steam of his breath swirled back over his shoulders with his passing. The sounds of the sentries steps were sharp and audible, as measured and pronounced as the workings of a great clock. The sounds of his walk were stark and alien in this place of silence.

The new man from Tennessee counted off his steps. The silent, sacred mass of the sarcophagus bearing the Unknown from World War I, and the crypts of the Unknown soldiers of World War II and Korea to either side of it, were to his left. The words etched into the stone sarcophagus he knew by heart, "Here Rests in Honored Glory An American Soldier Known but to God."

The soldier from Tennessee continued his walk in exact cadence, carefully counting off the steps. On the twenty first step, he stopped at attention, mentally marking the time as he stood facing south.

The soldier from Tennessee was troubled with the unrest in his country. He was outraged by the mindless assassinations and saddened by the riots and racial tensions sweeping major cities. Worst of all, the soldier from Tennessee felt betrayed.

South, he knew, into the darkness beyond his halo of light, stood the 13 foot tall, white marble, Argonne Cross. In this vast tomb of the good and the great that was Arlington, the Argonne Cross commemorated the sacrifice of an earlier generation of Americans in the war of their time. Two thousand of that wars one hundred thousand dead lay in ranks beneath simple white headstones with the Argonne Cross in their midst. South was also the resting place of the Apollo 1 astronauts who died on the launching pad. Generals and Admirals, scientists and common soldiers from the nations 200 year history rested there. South also was the place of the U.S.S. LIBERTY Memorial where fourteen of the ships thirty four dead from Israeli attack in 1967 lay. The soldier remembered.

The soldier from Tennessee reached the end of his count. On the twenty first second, he executed a slow, mechanical, left face to the east, towards the Tombs of the Unknowns. The soldier from Tennessee had seen the 11PM news with the latest reports of the fighting in Viet Nam. The newsman briefly read off casualty figures and body counts with much distaste and then reported on the *USS Enterprise* fire. On the television screen the ship was seen filmed from above on her way back to Pearl. The newsman told of the dead and wounded and the damage to the ship, the great holes in her flight deck speaking volumes. He then went on to recite estimated costs to repair the ship and replace destroyed aircraft. The newsman leveled a look of disgust straight into the camera and paused for effect. He then went on to announce, "In other news . . ." and gave acute coverage of anti-war protests wherever they might be. Persons of these movements were solicited for their views. No anti-American diatribe was too unsavory to air to a national audience.

The soldier from Tennessee had felt shame. There were the routine scenes of American youth of means desecrating the flag. They shouted bold denunciation against the country and vented hatred. Spittle blew from raging lips. They were seized with a courage borne of righteousness. Only those of wealth and higher learning could understand that serving your country at war was a despicable thing. They laid claim to a much higher moral fiber. They had too much to lose.

The soldier from Tennessee wondered about the *Enterprise* dead. He remembered the *Forrestal* tragedy of '67 and knew that eighteen of her dead lay in a common grave in the fields just behind him. Would those of the *Enterprise* be buried here? The soldier knew that on the average there were 35 burials a day on these grounds and most of them were returning in aluminum coffins from Viet Nam. These fields, which now held 150,000, were the tombs of servicemen from all of the nations wars. In these confines were written the history of America.

At the count of twenty one the sentry executed another left face and then in mechanical precision, moved his M-14 from right to left shoulder arms. Flashes of reflected light shone hotly from the blade of the chromed bayonet. The soldier from Tennessee was facing north. In the western fields, he knew, were the Spanish-American war Memorial, the Battle of the Bulge Memorial and the Confederate Memorial with over 400 soldiers of the Confederacy buried around it. Also to the west was the mast of the U.S.S. MAINE and 150 of her dead.

The soldier from Tennessee recited the arrangement and memorized this history of his country. He felt that he was on hallowed ground. He had been told by his fellows that this indeed was a special place, one of haunting serenity. They also told of their own night walks when all was still and quiet. They said that they felt they were not alone. The sentry could feel it now. In these cold and silent fields of the Dead, the stillness of the night hinted of whispers. He could feel,,, a presence.

The soldier from Tennessee stepped out on his next walk, The sounds of his footfalls echoed sharply from the massive stone edifice of the Memorial Amphitheater looming to his left and above him. Inscribed into the stone of the Amphitheater, the words of Abraham

Lincoln, spoken after the sacrifice of Gettysburg, commemorated the duty rendered by those interred on these grounds. The soldier recited those words, "We Here Highly Resolve That These Dead Shall Not Have Died In Vain."

The soldier from Tennessee was bitter. He knew that the blood being poured out in Viet Nam was wasted. He knew that the Dead of his generation were indeed dying in vain. The soldier stopped his walk on the twenty first step and counted the seconds, facing north.

To the north lay the Korean War Memorial, the Iwo Jima Memorial, the graves of fourteen Unknowns from the War of 1812 and the graves of eleven veterans of the Revolutionary War. A vault also lay to the north. It was the Tomb of the Unknowns of the Civil War, containing the bones of 2,111 soldiers, both of the North and of the South. These fields also contained the Eternal Flame, and the grave of the young President. The soldier remembered the words of the young President which challenged his generation, "Ask Not What Your Country Can Do For You. Ask, What You Can Do For Your Country!"

The soldier from Tennessee counted off the last of the seconds and executed a precise right face. He was looking east. Out there, he knew, vast ranks of headstones ranged in formation all across the rolling hills of Arlington. Etched into the stones were the names and dates of life of those who rested beneath. Nearly all sleeping here had answered the call of their country and had worn the uniform of her Armed Forces. To the soldier from Tennessee, these vast hinterlands of stone were a sacred place. Of each one could be said, "Here lies an American Hero."

The soldier from Tennessee felt a common bond with those resting in this land. He felt he shared something that once was singular in the American character that was sadly lacking in some today. The soldier from Tennessee was at a loss to explain it. He executed another right face and precisely and mechanically shifted his M-14 from left to right shoulder arms. A flash of light shone from the blade of his bayonet. And just beyond the soldiers illuminating halo of light, gathered all round amidst the silent stones and leafless trees, the ghosts of 150,000 had come to watch the soldier. Their uniforms hung in rags and tatters as they stood in endless ranks, drawn to this single beating heart. In the silence of the Tomb, they whispered.

The ghosts of the Brotherhood of the Dead had come to watch

the soldier. The sounds of his steps were sharp and measured as he began his next walk. The vapors of his breath steamed and swirled. The Brotherhood of the Dead counted off the steps. This one had earned entry into the ranks and when his time came, he would be one of them. The soldier from Tennessee possessed the one requirement that would gain him admission into the ranks. He was a holder of the VIRTUE. The VIRTUE was at once a simple thing and yet shameful to those who had turned away from it. The Brotherhood of the Dead knew what the soldier was thinking. The answer to his thoughts was over there, beyond the halo of light, standing mute and commanding in the darkness. Over there was a monument bearing a stark inscription, etched deeply into the stone. The inscription was a testament to those who were holders of the VIRTUE. And the inscription damned those who were not.

The inscription had been deemed worthy by a grateful nation whose freedom had been gained and sustained throughout its history by those of its citizens who had stepped forward to defend it. The inscription told of a VIRTUE more powerful and more sublime than courage. The inscription was a tribute.

And there, upon the rock
in the frosted cold,

Glared a stark pronouncement,
carved deep and bold

An epitaph to them,
to be forever told

Is but a single word

HONOR

On the 15th of January, 1969, having found nothing among the wreckage at sea, the names of Joe Carroll Mason, AOAN, VF-92, and Henry Strickland Yates, AMS2, VF-96 were added to the toll of the *USS Enterprise* dead. These last men were listed as MISSING—ASSUMED DEAD—REMAINS NOT RECOVERED:

On the 19th of January, 1969, Lt. (j.g.) James H. Berry, VF-96 and Dennis Ray Milburn, AMH2, VF-92 died of wounds.

The toll of the dead of *USS Enterprise* was twenty eight.

Frank Neumayer survived.

9. JUDGMENT

On 16 January, 1969, a formal Board of Investigation assembled on board *USS Enterprise* at 0800 and proceeded to review the preliminary investigation conducted by Rear Admiral Cagle.

The Board convened at 0935 on 20 January, 1969.

Present:

Rear Admiral Frederic A. Bardshar, U.S. Navy, Senior Member
Captain John E. Parks, U.S. Navy
Captain Martin G. O'Neill, U.S. Navy
Commander Lawrence F. Hicks, U.S. Navy
Lieutenant Robert E. Smith, U.S. Navy
Lieutenant Commander Thomas E. Flynn, JAGC, U.S. Navy,

COUNSEL FOR THE BOARD

All matters preliminary to the inquiry having been determined, the Board was opened.

WHAT FOLLOWS ARE SELECTED TESTIMONIES SUBMITTED IN THE INTEREST OF THE READER. CAUSE AND EFFECT HAVING BEEN DETERMINED AND PRESENTED FAITHFULLY IN THIS BOOK, TAKEN FROM TESTIMONIES FROM THIS INVESTIGATION, QUARTERMASTERS, DAMAGE CONTROL AND SHIP'S LOGS AND PLAT FILMS AND STILL PHOTOGRAPHS. LET THE READER UNDERSTAND THAT THESE TESTIMONIES WERE SUBMITTED WITHOUT THE BENEFIT OF A CAREFULLY RECONSTRUCTED SCENARIO.

Kenneth R. LOVELL, Naval Architect, Ship's Naval Engineering Center, Washington, D.C., was called as a witness, was sworn and testified as follows:

Questions by Counsel for the Board:

Q. Would you state your name and present position for the record, sir?
A. Kenneth R. Lovell, Naval Architect, Ship's Naval Engineering Center, which is actually the Ship Protection Section.

Q. Mr. Lovell, what is your professional area of specialization?
A. Ship Protection.

Q. Would you give a brief outline of your educational qualifications and your area of specialization?
A. Education is, college degree in Mechanical Engineering, Bachelor of Science; and other special courses in mathematics and so forth. As far as specialization, I've been primarily experienced in testing and observing of tests, writing up conclusions, and also a good bit of war damage, casualties of a nature involved here.

Q. And approximately how long have you worked in this field?
A. Twenty-eight years.

Q. Would you describe the purpose of your visit to *USS Enterprise*?
A. To observe the damage, look at it, collect data, as much as I can, with the prime idea of going back and analyzing it and seeing if we could indicate changes in ship protection and criteria.

Q. And how long have you been here, sir, for this visit?
A. Four days, since Saturday morning.

Q. And during the period of this time, have you had an opportunity to examine the ship protection systems aboard the *USS Enterprise*?
A. I have.

Questions by Commander Hicks:

Q. Mr. Lovell, would you please describe the damage to the flight deck and probable cause of that damage? Identify the damaged areas by size and approximate location. The record can show that the Board holds a copy of the plan to which Mr. Lovell is going to refer. (Exhibit 9)

Counsel for the Board: Excuse me, Admiral, do we intend to introduce this as an exhibit before the Board?

Senior Member: Yes, let's do that.

Witness: I haven't really planned to work from those because I was considering the flight deck. I do have a blueprint here (Exhibit 10) where I have some notes.

Senior Member: We can introduce them both.

Witness: There are a number of holes and dents indicated here (referring to Exhibit 10), starting with the holes because I think they are the most important. On the port side, at frame—just after frame 230 and outboard, in material that is less than the plate of the flight deck, there is a very large hole. We measured it as 21 feet long and 14 feet across. This is petaled back, and the petals you can see, are very badly pocked, obviously with fragments from the bomb casings which indicate that they did have time to form. It indicates that it was above the deck. The bombs were up off the deck. The size and violence of this indicates clearly a high order explosion and several—more than one. It's difficult to tell exactly how many, but at a guess, three or more at one time. Possibly more, two more. So this is essentially a non-contact, high order, multi-bomb explosion. There is a smaller hole directly, almost directly after that, right in the corner here. This is a different pattern, in that.

Senior Member: Would you identify the frame number?

A. Yes. It is just forward of frame 245 and just outboard of the shell. This, too, is in light plating. The pattern here is different, in that it is petaled, but the petals are not pockmarked, indicating that the explosion was from a weapon that was lying on the deck. The hole is about the size you would expect from a 500 pound bomb in this

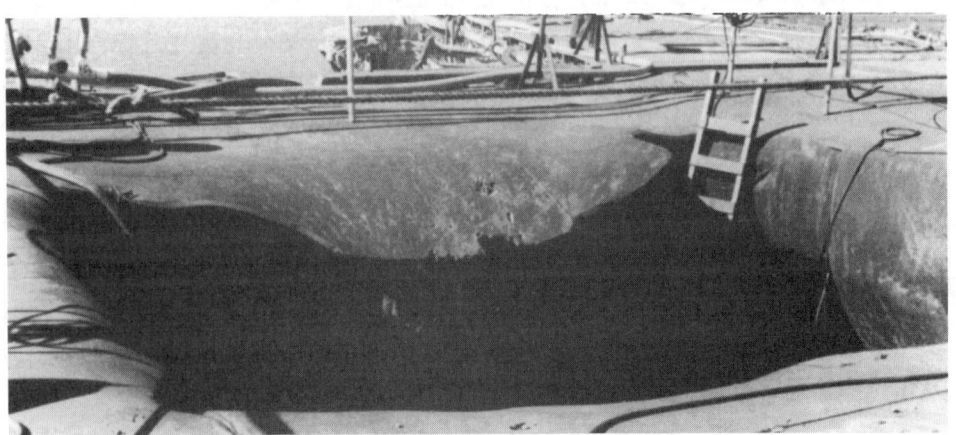

Massive hole where F-4 106 disintegrated from multiple Mark-82 detonations at frames 230 to 235 port side. Note evidence of pocking, indicating a non-contact explosion. U.S. Navy photo, Gates collection.

Shows backside of #4 jet blast deflector where unexploded bomb smashed into it shearing two lifting arm mechanisms away, U.S. Navy photo, Gates collection.

type of plating. It is 8 feet by 6 and one half feet. With this kind of an explosion one of the things that is characteristic is that you get a break-up of the flight deck itself. Pieces of the plating which, because of very high pressures that are involved, will bend down. Essentially secondary fragments. That is, pieces of the flight deck plating itself. It will take off with quite high velocity, it will be quite heavy, and consequently will have a great deal of penetrating power.

And, as we follow through, as indicated on the other sketches, we find holes quite large that go considerably down into the ship. Considerable distance down into the ship. The next one is in the flight deck plating proper. It is just aft of frame 240. Again there are no pocking of the petals. It is petaled down, but there is no pocking. This indicates again contact, high order because of it's size, 11 feet by 7 feet, and the heavy plating. It will indicate there was probably more than one bomb there. One bomb is not supposed to do this. It is possible, that lying there on it's side, it could. The heavy plate was originally chosen with the idea that if it is hit in the normal fashion with a bomb, it would not penetrate the heavy plate, 500 pound bomb specifically. But if it is lying on it's side, the pressure is greater and it could possibly do this. But I don't think so.

Questions by Senior Member:

Q. A multiple, first order, high order could?
A. Yes, sir. Next large hole is back on the fantail. Again this is on lighter plate. And there are petaling's. As a matter of fact, this is a classic case of petaling, all directions, like a flower which you get from a contact explosion. There are other evidences of it. For instance, a very large hole, extremely bad fragments in the fantail down below, and going on down out through the stern of the ship.

Another indication that it is a contact explosion is the explosion damage to the compartment below the transom, the longitudinals on both sides of the ship. These were burst which were outward from the center of the explosion, which actually pulled up part of the deck below the edge and bowed it. It actually split the deck below. That again is a fairly large hole. It is 16 by 13 feet, and it's entered at frame 258. Anyway, it would be a contact of high order. It could be a single but it was probably more than one.

The other large hole is on the starboard side, in the first strake of the heavy STS, (Armored steel), just aft of frame 205. This is almost

Mockup places aircraft over holes blown through deck from bombs of the original 105. U.S. Navy photo, Gates collection.

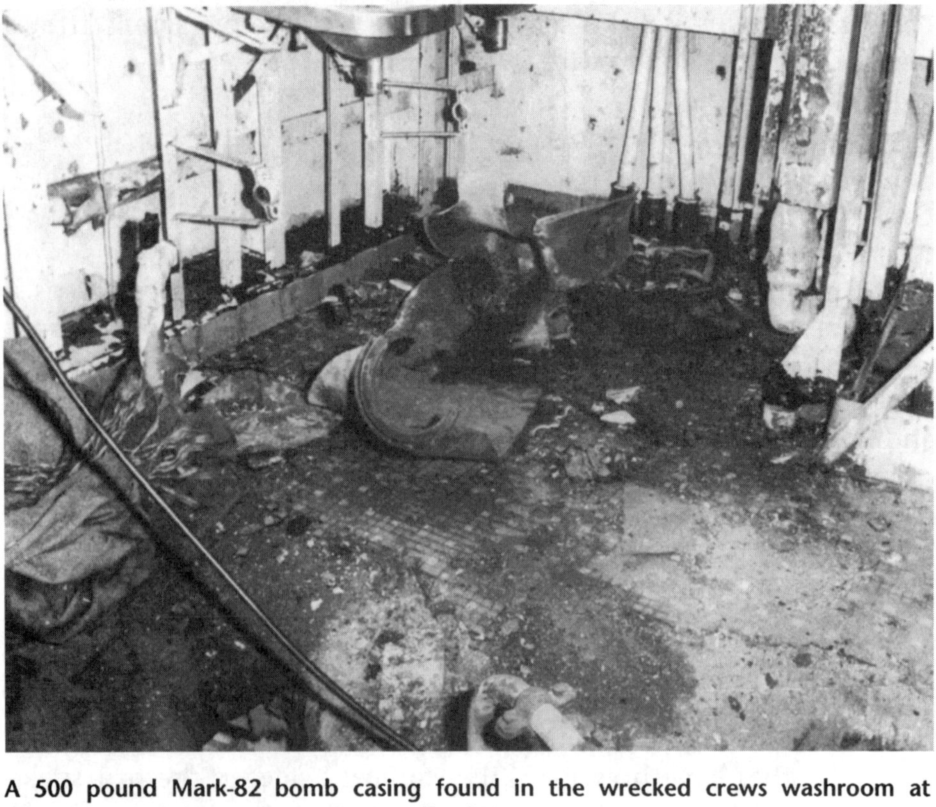

A 500 pound Mark-82 bomb casing found in the wrecked crews washroom at 03-240-4-L. U.S. Navy photo, Gates collection.

Hole blown through deck from frames 256 to 260. This was where 113 was obliterated. Lack of pocking indicates a contact explosion. U.S. Navy photo, Gates collection.

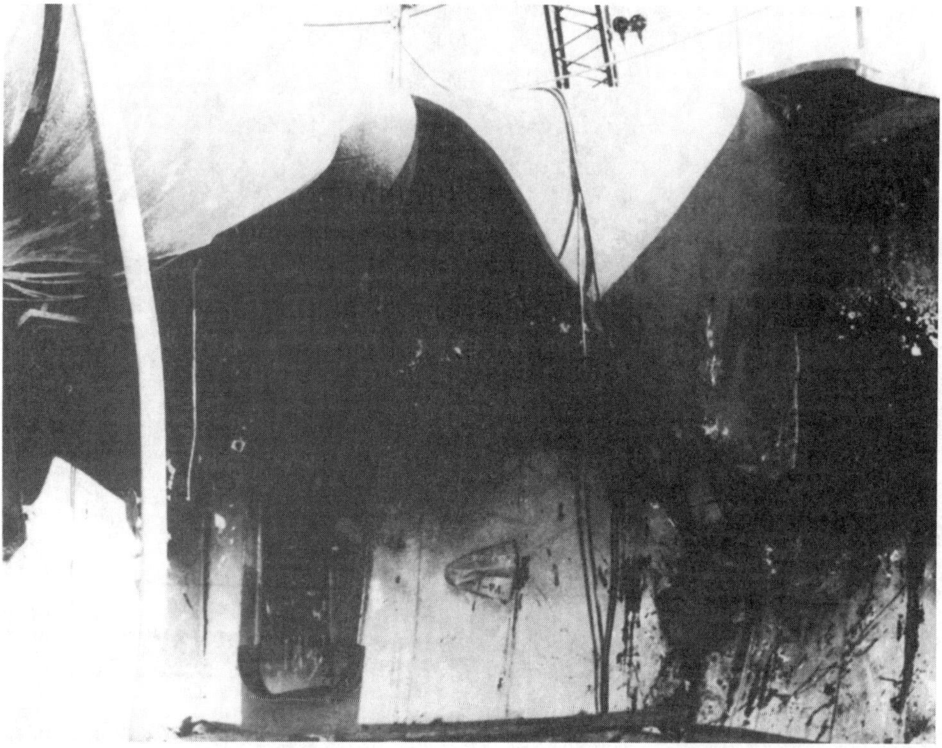

Underside of hole at frames 256 to 260 as seen from the 03 level compartment. U.S. Navy photo, Gates collection.

Fantail, Main deck under the explosion at frames 256 to 260. Oblong hole is from an unexploded bomb blown through the deck. U.S. Navy photo, Gates collection.

Shows stern of Enterprise in Pearl Harbor. Large hole near waterline is where unexploded bomb deflected from off a crushed stiffener and ripped through along with a piece of broken up flight deck plate higher up. Note burned out port point defense missile battery. U.S. Navy photo, Gates collection.

classical of what we would expect from a 500 pound bomb in the normal position. We get a good size dent in the order of 6 feet in diameter. It hit very close to a weld. That is the first strake inboard, and that split the STS in the normal fashion. One of the troubles with an STS weld is that in itself, it is very strong and tough material but in the heat effect, it will almost always fail at the weld. This is what it did, so that you do get a hole in the form primarily at the split with a fairly deep crater, and those are the holes.

Questions by Lieutenant Smith;

Q. I would like to ask him questions about this if I may. Mr. Lovell, could you explain to us your opinion of what caused the pockmarked area here near frame 245, and just inside the shell, port side?
A. Yes. That is a rather strange pattern, one that is not obvious. But from what it would look like, it would be a fairly small weapon, warhead, or series of them in order—In line, rather, that went off at the same time. The result is that they went off above the deck because you get pocking which is characteristic of a side spray, fragments from a warhead and this is the way weapons do cause damage. You get side spray. You get a bomb or weapon of any kind (at this point the witness sketched on a sheet of paper, attached as Exhibit 11), the pattern goes off this way, and there's the shatter. You get something off the ends. But it looks like something fairly close and about this long, so that you'd be in pocking like this, and this comes right on across, and the distance is about 18 inches wide, which indicates a very small weapon, small bomb or something like that, perhaps a 5 inch warhead (rocket).

Q. Could you tell enough from the indentations to indicate if it was, in fact, a warhead, whether or not it was high order?
A. To get that kind of fragmentation, it's high order. Otherwise, you do not get that kind of fragmentation.

Q. And what was indicated here physically is consistent with what you'd expect from say, a ZUNI going off, on the position of the mount . . . station?
A. Yes, sir.

Q. You are aware it's a shape-charged warhead.

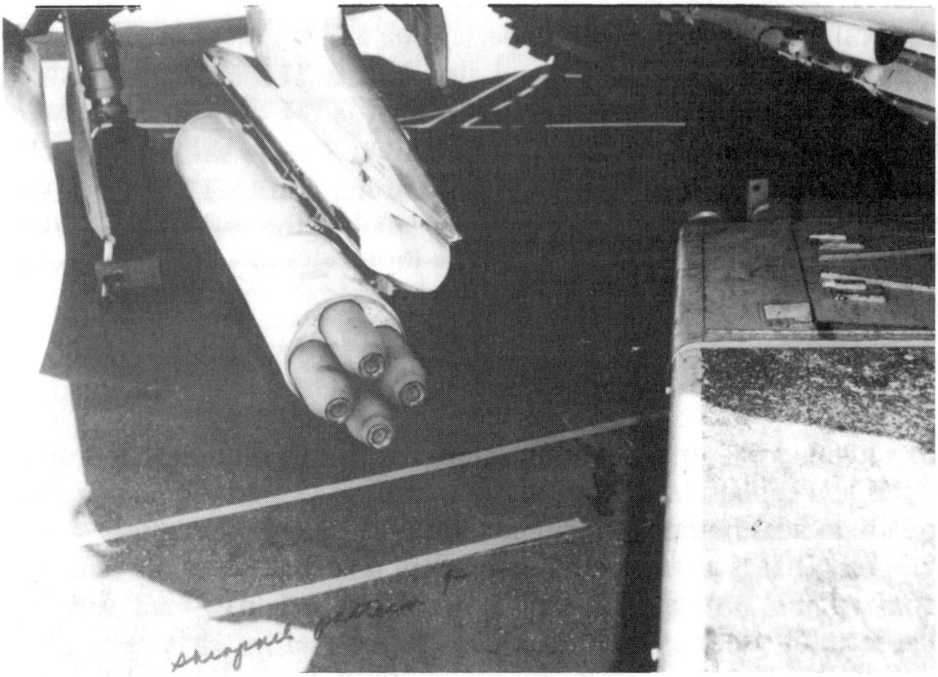

Mockup of the accident of 14 January for the official investigation shows an F-4 and tow tractor placed on deck where the originals were at the time. Shrapnel pattern is highlighted with tape. Zuni rockets are mounted without fuses. U.S. Navy photo, Gates collection.

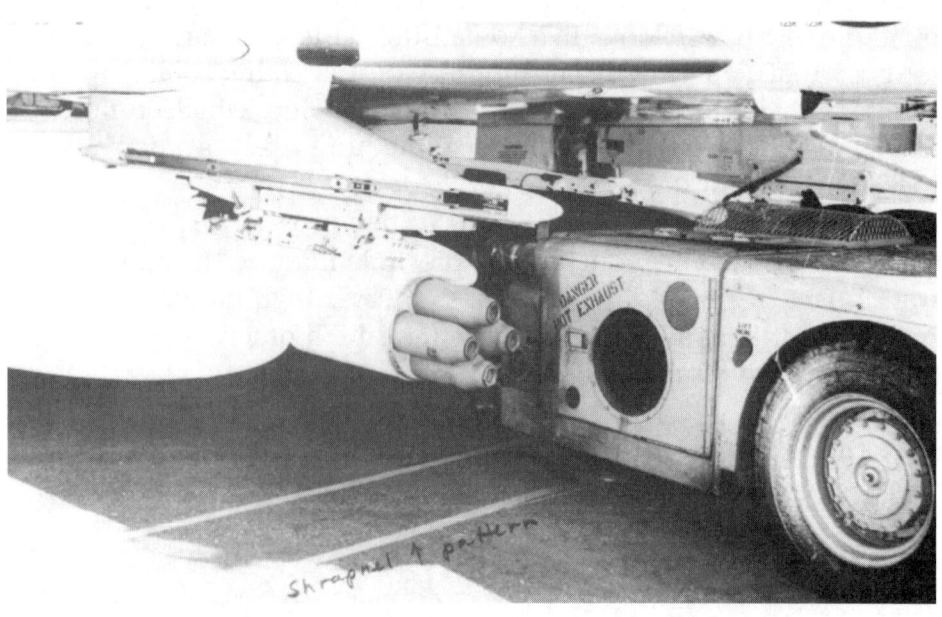

Another view of the mockup. U.S. Navy photo, Gates collection.

212

Armored flight deck heavily pocked from shrapnel pattern. U.S. Navy photo, Gates collection

Shows configuration of weapons and attitude of men working under 106 when initial rocket detonations went off on 105. All were wounded. U.S. Navy photo, Gates collection

Mockup of accident back at Pearl for the investigation places aircraft approximately where they were. Aircraft across deck represent from right to left, 106, 105 and 113. Holes in deck prevent exact spotting. Note hole in deck at bottom of picture. U.S. Navy photo, Gates collection.

Mockup shows position of 105 and holes punched through the flight deck by the shaped charge warheads of the port rocket pod going off in succession. Note frame number painted on deck. U.S. Navy photo, Gates collection.

A. Yes, sir. This would not really affect it too much, except that on one end, you would get everything concentrated in the linear jet, but it would not affect too much when it came off the side (indicating on Exhibit 10).

Q. Now, would you explain, in your own words, the smaller diameter hole just inside the outboard shell which is to the port and slightly forward of the big petaled holes in that area?
A. All we did was, look at that and say, "That's a hole." In trying to figure out exactly what it is, we were unable to do so.

Q. Do you have any observations for the larger holes which are slightly outboard the shell, located about frame 238, in that area?
A. There again, we looked at it, we observed it as a hole there, it does not lend itself to anything to say definitely just what caused it. I couldn't say.

Q. It is your observation that the two large holes in the immediate area, the pocked area, was definitely high order explosive?
A. Yes, sir.

Questions by Senior Member:

Q. Is there any ballistic evidence around there that you would suspect was caused by fuel tanks blowing?
A. This gets into another question. Fuel tanks, as I understand them, will go off at lesser detonation rates. It would be difficult to distinguish something like that from a low order detonation from a bomb, or even a rocket propellant case going up, and the effect would be essentially the same. How to distinguish it, I would not know.

Questions by Capt. Parks:

Q. Would you be able to estimate the high order, 500 pound types, that apparently went off?
A. In individual events? There would be one, two, three, four, five, (indicating on blueprint, Exhibit 10).

Q. Five events. But some of those consisted of more than one bomb?

Flight deck dished in and split from bomb lying on deck, starboard side, frame 246. U.S. Navy photo Gates collection.

Underside of dished in deck at frame 246. Longitudinal stiffener buckled and heavy bulkhead shorn. U.S. Navy photo, Gates collection.

A. Yes, sir.

Commander Hicks:

Q. I think it might be well to also establish on the starboard side frame 245, outboard of the shell, there's a deep depression. Would you, Mr. Lovell, care to tell us what caused that?
A. It is 7½ inches deep, there were no petaling's, and it was fairly short. It did not go down through the deck. It did not cause a hole, there was no pocking and it was fairly sharp. So we would say it was a contact explosion from the fact that it did not blow through this plating, which is light, and that it was either small or low order.

Lieutenant Smith:

Q. Could this possibly have been caused by Class C explosives going off in high order?
A. I don't follow your term. If you are talking high order, I'd say high order detonation that is by itself. If you are talking about something that is normally burnable or propulsive going into a detonation type, then yes. It would still be different from the effects of high order detonation.

Q. There are such things as a low Class or Class B going off in high order which has been shown in some of our rocket tests and especially if they are heated and go together. Could this have possibly been caused by . . . perhaps that type of explosion?
A. I think if we shake down the terminology we're using, we're in agreement.

Capt. O'Neill:

Q. Mr. Lovell, do you know if it is possible to take a mall and beat on the steel deck and make indentations in it? Can you beat on this deck and put marks on it?
A. Yes, but it's difficult. That's tough material. It would have to be something of very high force to do that. It's really tough material.

Q. You said before that this deck is designed to prevent the penetration of a 500 pound bomb. From what height would it have

to be dropped? Do you have any criteria on the dropping altitude?
A. Well, what we are talking about there, was from any height. In other words, if it hit above a certain height, it would, instead of going through, it would break up and disintegrate.
The witness was warned concerning his testimony and withdrew from the boardroom.

Lt. (j.g.) E.M. McCULLOCH, U.S. Navy, was called as a witness by the Board, was sworn and testified as follows:

Questions by Council for the Board:

Q. Would you state your name, your rank and your present duty station?
A. Edwin McCulloch, Lieutenant Junior Grade, *USS Enterprise*, TAD (temporary assigned duty) from EODGROUPPAC, (Explosive Ordnance Disposal Group Pacific).

Questions by Commander Hicks:

Q. Mr. McCulloch, would you please describe the action taken by your team in disposing of explosives during the course of the fire on the *USS Enterprise* on the 14th of January?
A. Yes, sir. There were several instances throughout the day, probably, I'd say during a 30 to 36 minute period in which explosives were jettisoned, both from flight decks, from the hangar decks, and from the fantail. To point out any specific instance would be extremely hard at this point. There were many bombs thrown over the side from the flight deck by my people and people assisting them. I think to point and make references to them would be very difficult.

Q. Well, would you describe the sequence of events as you saw them immediately following the fire during the first two hours on the flight deck?
A. Yes, sir. I was down below, in the EOD locker which is on the main deck, at the time when I heard the first explosion, the EOD team having observers aboard was waiting for a drill of some type, and knew they were going to have a conventional ordnance problem. So, at that time, there was no immediate sound that, "This is a drill!", or anything of that type. I called up flight deck control and talked

to A02 Downs. He told me they had a fire involving ordnance.

I immediately went to the flight deck, I couldn't really tell you which door I went out—I'm not sure, but I went out on the (flight) deck and proceeded to the port side of the ship aft. And during that time, there were two explosions. I saw one hose there. There were some people on it. They completely disappeared. I returned forward to the island, I met Chief Burgess, and by that time, they had pulled, I believe it was 312, to the center of the deck, Chief Burgess and I were going to proceed back to this plane, at that time this plane was engulfed in flames so we turned back. I believe the Chief went forward but I'm not sure. I went back to the side, to the flight deck, and we received calls from the fantail at that time. They had ordnance and I went down and checked that, and there was a hole, I believe, on the fantail. There was some rubble there, as far as ordnance, we had white phosphorus burning above where we were standing on the fantail. The firefighters trying to fight the fire were trying to keep water on the white phosphorus at the same time, and they were having a pretty hard time doing it.

Questions by the Senior Member:

Q. Where did the white phosphorus come from?
A. I believe there were lockers on the 02 level of the fantail. I'm not positive of that. Then, after checking the situation there, we jettisoned both marine markers and they were water actuated, and some other markers; they were also initiated, some pyrotechnics lockers from the 01 level on the starboard side. Then we proceeded back to the flight deck and I'd say for two or three hours we responded to calls. 20MM shells on the flight deck, LAU-68 rocket pods, both rocket pods were 2.75 rockets, they were crushed by airplane wings. We had calls on high pressure air bottles from the fantail which were actually burned out. And later in the day, we policed the flight deck for broken parts of ordnance. During that time, there was an enormous amount of 20 millimeter and other things that appeared to be ordnance.

Questions by Commander Hicks:

Q. In your opinion, how many high order explosions occurred on *USS Enterprise* during the fire?

A. I've thought about that quite often, and in my own opinion—I've heard several people say, "I heard seven", "I heard nine." I would probably have to agree with any one of those figures. I really don't know. I wasn't counting at the time.

Q. Is it fair to say that you heard a number of high order explosions?
A. Yes, sir.

Q. How is a high order distinguished from a low order?
A. A high order is a complete explosion of explosive material, of the weapon itself. Low order is usually caused by some break or discontinuation of a firing phase of the burn rate, or rupture of the packing, air bubble, something of that type will give you an incomplete explosion.

Questions by the Senior Member:

Q. Was any of the debris you saw up there later, explosive of a low order?
A. Yes, sir.

Q. So you conclude from the evidence that they were low order?
A. Yes, sir, I would. I would say two, possibly three bomb casings thrown over the side were low order.

The witness was duly warned concerning his testimony and withdrew from the boardroom.
    Billy C. Boatright, Lieutenant, U.S. Navy, VF-96, was called as a witness for the board, was sworn and testified as follows.

Senior Member:

As I indicated to you informally, we are concerned about all pertinent things relating to the incident on the 14th. So if you'll proceed and tell us precisely what you saw and experienced, we'll use that method of getting your information.

Counsel for the Board:

Q. Would you state your name, rank and duty station for the record?

A. Billy C. Boatright, Lieutenant, U.S. Navy, VF-96. I was assigned to alert bird 112, scheduled to man at 0800. The regular launch was not scheduled to spare anything or to launch but I did want to get a turn (start up), on the airplane because it hadn't been turned for awhile. I indicated to the plane captain I didn't want to turn until the other aircraft got started. My Radar Intercept Officer, Lt. (j.g.) Dave Schwabb and myself manned it shortly before 0800, relieving Lt. (j.g.) Ingle and I don't remember who his RIO was. While ascending the aircraft, I noticed that the external power was connected which was the first time I've noticed that this year. So we got in and strapped in, got our helmets on and turned the power on and I went through my preflight check.

Questions by the Senior Member:

Q. Do you mean you were getting deck edge power instead of power from a huffer?
A. Yes, sir, and I checked the Internal Communications System with all the things you have to check with electrical power and then turned the power off. And what seemed a short time later, here came the huffer to start us and this seemed strange that they should be starting me already since I was last priority to get started. This was probably 15 after, something like that. He was just backing in, we hadn't gotten power from him yet. We had canopies down so I really didn't hear the blast. It was more or less a loud whoosh. It sounded to me about like the same noise I'd get if I threw a lighted match into a bonfire, something that had been soaked with gasoline. No detonation like I heard later on but just a loud whoosh, a very loud whoosh and I don't remember feeling any heat.

 I turned to my right and from the area between 105 and 106, in that area, there was a large fireball rolling out from underneath the aircraft at that time. I observed it for only a second and saw that it was going to be pretty serious so I went through the procedures to get out of the airplane, the emergency harness release, detaching my parachute and seat pan, jumped out of the airplane and ran to the area of #4 wire, approximately about amid ship of the landing area or middle of the landing area. I turned and noticed that my RIO was still on the wing of 112. He'd gone back to get something.

Then I turned and looked down the deck; and, of course, the fireball had spread by then and one significant point that I believe I put in my statement was that I thought I saw a white trail of smoke going across the flight deck toward the A-7's and I thought that and remembered thinking in my mind that it was strange, what an ironic thing that this was the same way the *USS Forrestal* thing had started.

Then I ran from the area of #4 wire up to and shortly past #2 wire, if I remember right. And at this time I remember seeing a man in the fire and he was beyond help. We couldn't do anything for him and I was assisting the fire fighting crew in getting the hoses out, telling them where to go. They seemed to know better where to go than I could tell them though. And shortly after that the first explosion went off and we all went running back up deck, I don't remember how far, a short ways. It wasn't a violent explosion. I turned around and went back into the same general area. This time I remember seeing an ordnance man, he was 20 feet, 30 feet from the edge of the fire. We couldn't get any closer because of the heat. He had a broken leg and was up on his arms looking at us. I grabbed a man with a fire hose and asked him to squirt water on me and I would try to go in and get him. The fire hose was salt water and it wasn't putting out water more than six to eight feet so he went as far as he could with the heat, squirting water on me and I couldn't get in within 30 feet of the man because we just didn't have enough water pressure.

At this time one of the bombs went off, apparently, because there was a violent explosion. I ran all the way up to the . . . about the island. All the time I was running up there, there was debris coming down. I remember a piece of canopy floating over my head one time. I turned around and went to the . . . not quite so far back this time and I stood there. I remember seeing several of the gas tanks going off, fuel tanks and several white explosions and some that I couldn't explain, they were white fireballs; from what I heard later it was probably some magnesium parts exploding or going up. I didn't know what they were. I remember seeing some rockets, rockets detonating back in the starboard area of the fantail and they were going basically straight up.

And after I stood there a few seconds or minutes—time completely escapes me—I went back toward the area of the fire and remember seeing a man. It stuck in my mind, it was probably the same one I saw crawling but he had crawled out of the fire and was lying there a short ways from the edge of the fire but he was obviously beyond help. Standing there, about the area of 403, that's strictly speculation but that's where I'd say it was, the second and third explosions went off and this was apparently something large from the area of 214, in that general area, and as I turned I felt the concussion, turned to hit the deck and a piece of shrapnel—I remember it very vividly—hit a man standing next to me in the side of the head. It broke his head wide open and that's the only way I can phrase it, and this pretty well shook me up. I got up from there and my mind is a blank from there on.

The next thing I remember, my Warrant Officer, the maintenance control officer for VF-96, WO Champion, was grabbing me by my arm and told me to get off the flight deck, I was in shock and was in no condition to be up there. He led me to the ready room and that's all I remember seeing of it.

Q. The water pressure you observed on this hose when you were trying to get in to pull the man out was obviously low and unsatisfactory?
A. Yes, sir.

Q. Was this the result of damage to the hose, could you tell? Had it been this way all along?
A. I don't recall seeing any damage to the hose but I noticed three distinct instances up there where I was disturbed. This was one because we could have gotten that man out of there had we the water pressure, I believe. Maybe I couldn't have gotten any closer, but the next one, I was somewhere up forward of 112, up there in the area of #4 catapult, deck edge foam station. There were several people milling around trying to get this fog foam hose out and so I took command there and tried to tell them where to go with it and what to do. We started pulling the hose out and I said "Keep going" and they said "That's all the hose we've got, sir," and then they turned it on and it just kind of piddled out the end. The only thing it was good for was to spray down the flight deck over there in case the fire started up the flight deck. There was maybe four or five feet of water and foam coming out of it.

Q. In the initial fire fighting efforts that you participated in, was

there adequate pressure then on the hose?
A. Well, this one particular hose over in the area in front of 103 and 403, in that general area, that hose did not have sufficient . . . I can't speak for all those. I did see one man in an asbestos suit going in the fire with a gooseneck, I do not know the correct name for that but he was getting plenty of water. That was shortly after the fire started. So at least one was working right

Q. Now you reported later after observing what you thought were bombs and tanks going off, rockets going off. How did you arrive at that conclusion?
A. Well, there were two or three of them that ignited and I remember thinking that they were like the 4th of July rockets.

Q. They had a vertical path?
A. Yes, sir, they went up.

Q. They left a stream of smoke, a wake of smoke?
A. Yes; sir, white smoke. I remember also thinking at the time that those were ZUNI's but they didn't go high enough to be ZUNI's I could be wrong, they could be something else. I thought it was rockets at the time.

Q. All right. Now in your statement you referred to the first heavy explosion. Do you have an estimate of how long after the initial explosion that occurred?
A. Anything I say, any statement I'd make, Admiral, would be pure conjecture because I thought I was up on the flight deck only two or three minutes and later, watching the PLAT (film) I saw I was up there about ten minutes so I had absolutely no conception of time up there. If you want a guess, I'd say four to five minutes.

Q. During the course of the time that you were there, did you have a feel for how many hoses were actually fighting the fire back there?
A. No, sir, I didn't have. All I can say is there were an awful lot of them. After the first couple of minutes, there was at least, I'd say, four to five back in that area where the fire was itself. And people were busily taking them all further (towards it.)

Q. And before the first big explosion, did you feel that you were

making any progress in fighting the fire?
A. No, sir, we were not making any progress. I did notice that when the twin agent unit came in there, they really made some headway in a hurry over in the (port) corner; but over where I was at, more to the left there, it just kept getting bigger and bigger.

Questions by Capt. Parks:

Q. Have you viewed the PLAT film since the incident?
A. Yes, sir, I've walked into the ready room twice when it had been going about five minutes, people said. But while I was up there, you asked what kind of progress they were making. While I was up there I watched 112, which I was sitting in, on the port side catch on fire and all the while they were trying to fight the fire and it just kept coming right on up the flight deck. Of course the explosions weren't helping any. Every time those would go off everybody would just drop what they were doing and run for cover; but it was only for a few seconds and then they would be right back in there. It also spread up the starboard side. I remember the flight deck—the Air Boss saying, "Let's get somebody on 414, first of all I want to get 312 out of there", and it caught on fire so quick they had to abandon it. I remember seeing a man run in and attach a truck to 414, a tow tractor, I believe it was 414, and the Air Boss said, "Get out of there, 312's going to go," and shortly after that 312 did go.

Questions by Senior Member:

Q. You commented that the water pressure was low in at least one instance. Did it improve later? Did you observe any changes?
A. Yes, sir. I can only state for sure that the salt water hose over on the starboard side of the landing area aft and the fog foam hose from the catwalk along #4 catapult were both low pressure initially and another thing I noticed in connection with this was the goose neck salt water fog thing. I don't know how that thing attaches in there. I grabbed one and tried to put that goose neck into the fitting. Every time the water came on, it popped out. I noticed one of the enlisted troops up there had the same problem. So that was useless. I finally gave up on that. I couldn't get it to stay in.

Q. I think your observation is particularly useful. What was your general opinion of the effectiveness of the fire fighting from the standpoint of equipment, as opposed to people? We'll talk about people later.

A. Well, I'm really in no position to judge but from strictly a layman's point of view, I remember thinking there is no way to fight this fire until it dies down, you just can't get close enough to it to fight it. I could get within 100 feet, I'd estimate, at the most before the heat became too intense to go any further. Unless you've got a lot of water pressure, you can't fight a fire from that far away. I just got a feeling of complete futility because I could see no way to fight that fire until it died down.

Q. Did the fire itself give you that impression, exclusive of the bombs going off?

A. Well, the bombs going off certainly had something to do with it, but yes, sir, I would say exclusive of that. Of course, it's the biggest fire I've ever seen and that may have some bearing on my feelings. Maybe someone who had seen a lot of fires would realize that (this) fire could be put out, if the bombs hadn't been going off in that very short time. My feelings were it could not.

Q. Let's turn to the performance of the people. With the equipment that they had on hand, what was the general opinion there?

A. Well, quite frankly, Admiral, they had a lot more guts than I had, because after the third bomb went off I didn't want to go back in there. They picked up the hoses and there they went, they didn't hesitate at all. Of course, every time something like this happens you hear a lot of tales about bravery, but it's true, particularly the fire fighting teams. They just grabbed the hoses and went. A bomb would go off and they would scatter and hit the deck, pick up the hose and go at it again. The lad that hooked that yellow truck to 414, I realize he didn't save the airplane but he deserves some sort of medal because there was nobody around there. 312 was just a mass of flames. He went in there and put a truck on 414 and was out getting the (tie down chains off) himself with the plane next to him burning and when the Air Boss said . . . I don't know if he survived or not, but the Air Boss said, "Get away from there, 312 is going to go!" I didn't see 312 go so I don't know if he is still (alive) or not.

Q. This sort of direction from Primary, did you observe this in other instances also?

A.   Yes, sir. The Air Boss was doing a very fine job, I thought. He didn't lose his head. He was kind of rooting for the guys, so to speak. I heard him say "Let's get in there and fight the fire, let's don't lose the ship." That kind of brought me to my senses. That was what was at stake at the time.

There being no further questions, the witness was warned, was excused and withdrew from the room.

Lieutenant Commander Jack J. Parks, Jr., U.S. Navy, *USS Enterprise*, Flight Deck Officer, was called as a witness for the Board, was sworn and testified as follows:

Questions by Lieutenant Smith:

Q.   Mr. Parks, what did you do when you heard the explosion on the flight deck and the next couple of minutes?
A.   Well, at the time of the explosion I was standing behind the #3 and #4 catapults. I was looking forward, checking the spot on the catapults, because it was getting close to launch time. When the explosion went off the first indication I had that anything was wrong was a dull thud. I can't really explain exactly what it was. I turned around and saw a ball of flame, more or less rolling towards the center of the deck from the port side, aft, from the vicinity of those aircraft. I turned immediately and ran back towards that area and at the same time I called over my mouse (radio) to get the twin agent units moving. They passed me on the way aft. One was pointed to the fire. It made a U-turn and backed up a little bit. I started to run over to charge it but someone beat me to it. Someone, I don't know who they were, had the hose out, so I walked around in front of the twin agent unit on the port side, around #2 or #3 wire and was just standing there when the second explosion went off and knocked me down. I rolled probably 10, 15 feet up the deck. When I got up and turned to the twin agent unit, I saw that the man who had been on the nozzle was gone, the nozzle severed and the unit wrecked. At that time I noticed a man trying to roll someone out who was on fire. To the right another man was on fire with someone trying to, not rolling him, he was just patting him, more or less. I ran over and he and I both rolled the fellow out. When we had him out we saw that he was in no real need to be rolled out because his head was pretty well blown off. I turned and they had just turned on the foam, and

were shooting a direct spray, more or less, over the aircraft. I ran over to the head man on it and told him how to play the foam and from there on out, Admiral, I was moving about the flight deck directing hose teams.

Q. Can you comment on the adequacy of water pressure?
A. There were a few times that I remember, I don't know exactly when, but I remember being by the head of a hose, either helping or standing there, and we would lose pressure. Somebody would take off back down the line and it would come back on almost immediately. It wasn't like you would lay the hose down and forget it for three or four minutes. It was more or less off and on.

Q. Would it go off completely?
A. Yes, sir, it would. Well, the stream would start to die down. The people would—as the stream was dying down and they weren't hitting what they wanted to hit—they would be moving forward and they would just keep doing this until they realized that it was the pressure that was dropping. Then all of a sudden it was just nothing, I was trying to direct the salt water on the foam people as much as possible. We got to a point where the explosions were pretty well over and it was salt water that put the E2 out. The port side of the E2 was on #3 elevator and we dragged it out of that area to make a fire break. There was no foam available in that area that was not used on something else more important. Two fire hoses, salt water hoses were directed on that particular aircraft and within, I'd say, seconds, not more than a minute and a half, the fire was out on the wing of the E2.

Q. Can you comment on the relative intensity of the first explosion and the second one?
A. Well, the first explosion wasn't intense at all. It was the fire that was intense. In other words, it—I wouldn't really classify it as an explosion. It was just a big ball of fire.

Q. Would you describe the second one?
A. The second one was just one hell of an explosion. It threw pieces straight up and straight forward. That's the one that caught the twin agent unit, and broke the (pressure) ball. (LT. COMDR. PARKS WAS THEN ASKED BY THE BOARD TO COMMENT ON EQUIPMENT,

ORGANIZATION AND DESIGN IN REGARD TO FIRE FIGHTING CAPABILITY. THIS WAS A LONG ENCOMPASSING DISSERTATION THAT WILL NOT BE GONE INTO, IT IS THE INTENTION OF THE AUTHOR TO FOCUS PRIMARILY ON CREW PERFORMANCE.)

Questions by Senior Member:

Q. All right, thank you very much. Now if you could give us the same sort of comment, anything you wish to say in the area of organization and performance by individuals with the equipment that was on hand?
A. Yes, sir. The organization seemed to me at the time—and I remember thinking about it—seemed to be running too smoothly, actually, for the chaos that was going on. In other words, things seemed to be moving back in a very good pattern. I mean there was order, seemed to be order. This is the very first time I have been through any thing like this and I've always thought that when it did happen there would just be complete and mass confusion, but it just did not seem to be there. I was on the port side and Chief White and the Bosun, Chief Warrant Officer Helton, were on the starboard side. I really can't tell you where the order came from. I remember they were there. If I saw both of them on the port side, I would go to the starboard side. I mean, we seemed to be criss-crossing and I'm sure they were thinking about it too. Wherever we were and whatever we were doing, we really didn't want to be in the same area, and the first people to get the hoses out, whoever they might have been, as soon as the hose hit the deck there was just an unlimited amount of people to grab the hose and move it back. Everybody was just right there and seemed to be a fantastic amount of thinking going on by everyone involved considering what was going on.

Q. Was the effort interrupted by the heavy explosions?
A. Yes, sir.

Q. Could you comment on how rapidly it resumed?
A. Well, a couple of times when I got up off the deck I seemed to be almost, not the last one up but getting up with the last people, everybody else seemed to be up and moving. I noticed, or remember, but at the time not really thinking about it as far as people charging these idiotic explosions. You'd think at a time like that, as things

started fizzling, everybody would turn and either go down or be backing off from it. Not running but backing off from it.

Q. You were referring to a fizzling. What are you referring to?
A. Well, there were two or three times over on the port side there, rather than an explosion it was like you would take a fire-cracker and pinch the end and light it. You know, the end of it would make a kind of SSHHWHOOOM! I'm sure it was rocket propellant going off, just sitting there, kind of sparks. These would go off and the people would turn their backs and fade away from it but there was no mass exit a all that I could see. And I really think sometimes that the people who were close to the explosions, for some reason—and I really can't understand why I got as little as I did except for the fact that when an explosion went off it knocked me flat and everything went over me. That's all I could think of.

Q. Was there a precursor or a blast wave in front of the shrapnel?
A. I guess, I don't know. I have thought about this now and I just can't imagine being in that area with all this going off and only getting a couple of little pieces. It's the only thing I can think of because I know every time an explosion went off it knocked me down to the deck.

After further questioning, the witness was warned concerning his testimony and withdrew.

Commander Arthur L. Bureau, U.S. NAVY, was called as a witness for the Board, was sworn and testified as follows:
Counsel for the Board:

Q. Would you please state your name, rank, and your present duty station for the record, please?
A. My name is Arthur L. Bureau, Commander, United States Navy, Serial Number 108389. My present duty station is Weapons Officer of Comcardivone Staff (Commander, Carrier Division One). "At about 0820 (on the 14th of January) I was on the second deck and heard an explosion and headed for the flight deck and I believe I arrived on the flight deck following what I believe was the . . . the third major explosion. I came out of the island between the mobile crane and the island and looking aft, I saw a fire that was far bigger than I

had imagined it would be. I knew we would have a fire and I was sure that ordnance was involved by the sound of the detonations. I never expected to see a fire of this size but it was.

Looking aft, I saw Mr. Brackin with some firefighters and then I went aft. I started aft to offer him assistance and there was another detonation at which time everyone appeared to hit the deck and I followed suit. Not hearing any shrapnel, I stood up and went aft and spoke to Mr. Brackin. He told me he needed some hoses. His hoses were apparently leaking. I went forward and told a yellowshirt to get some hoses, hose lengths aft. By the time I came aft again, I was passing between the mobile crane and the island and I met Mr. Brackin and he was about to say something to me when there was a major detonation which to me was the most severe one of the day. We were both knocked down and there were high velocity fragments that we heard passing overhead, which we later found hit the bridge. I got up and Mr. Brackin was gone by the time I got up and he was rallying his crews. He had discovered some hot bombs near the RA-5C Vigilante parked aft of the island out on the #3 deck edge elevator. At the same time, he was calling for EOD assistance. A short time later, Chief Burgess, of the EOD team in *USS Enterprise* appeared on the scene. He decided that the bomb nearest the RA-5C was endangering the island and the RA-5C so he decided to jettison the weapon as soon as he could. He instructed the fire nozzleman to . . . a certain way to play the water on the bomb at which time Chief Burgess went to the bomb and knelt down in front of it and removed the fuse, they threw the fuse overboard and returned to the bomb and screwed a hernia bar into the fuse cavity and motioned for help. Two sailors came forward, colored shirts, I don't know what color, and they dragged the bomb over to #3 elevator and jettisoned it over the side. The bomb was smoking and burning by the base plate as the bomb went over the side of the elevator. Following this, the other bomb was jettisoned by whom, I don't know. The one that was on #3 elevator. It had been cooled by Brackin's other fire crew. Brackin and I decided that all the ordnance must have been detonated at this time and we could get on with fighting the fire and we proceeded to start aft on the starboard side and putting out fires in the A-7's, starting with the foremost one, I believe 415 and moving aft. By the time we got aft, the fires were essentially burned out in the after aircraft. That's about all.

Crater and split in deck from contact explosion, starboard side frames 206 to 208. U.S. Navy photo, Gates collection.

Number 4 aircraft elevator burned and melted through from magnesium fires of 614. U.S. Navy photo, Gates collection.

Hole ripped through island from 312 explosion. U.S. Navy photo, Gates collection.

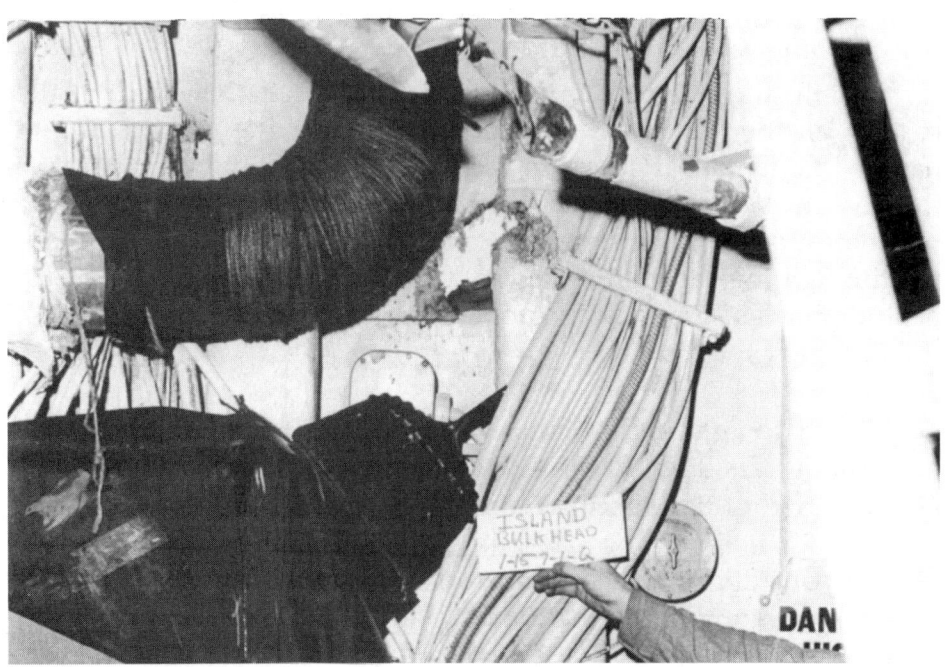

Inside island where shrapnel from 312 explosion blew apart the 8 inch firemain riser serving the entire island structure with fire fighting water. Riser has been patched and repaired. U.S. Navy photo, Gates collection.

Questions by Commander Hicks:

Q. Could you locate what you might categorize as the last big explosion?
A. Yes, I'm almost positive it was on an A-7, side number 312.

Q. How effective were the fire fighting systems employed?
A. I was amazed at how ineffective the fire fighting systems were. At no time did I feel that the fire fighting was influencing the outcome of the fire. We had no control over any of the A-7's. We had no effect on the fire as long as there was ordnance and fuel. By that time we began to get the upper hand. I recall at the height of the fire thinking that if someone were to move an F-4 out into the middle of the deck and ignite it with a bomb detonation, as the F-4's were ignited, that all the fire fighting equipment up there could not have extinguished that single airplane.

Q. Commander Bureau, In your long career, you have observed changes in capabilities of Naval aircraft in respect to weapons and fuel, would you care to comment on the hazards as opposed to World War II and Korea?
A. I think the hazards are far greater now than they were in the past. In all the fires I've seen, I never saw anything like the fire we had on the fantail. It seems to me that we probably have from five to ten times the fuel on the flight deck and probably in the neighborhood of three times the ordnance load and I don't believe the fire fighting capabilities has anywhere near kept pace. We are far behind and just based on this one experience, we are far behind in fire fighting capability.

Q. Could you give us an outline of your past experience?
A. Well, I started out in carriers in the old *USS Lexington* in 1936 and after a period of fire fighting training, I was assigned, two of us were assigned for maintaining safety in the landing area. We were there for two years during which time we were required to be the first ones on the scene for a number of landing area fires. Probably a dozen, at least. These were single plane fires and we were able to extinguish those fires with the help of other hoses that came out and were able to get . . . we never had anyone burned up in an airplane back there during that time. During the War, I was assigned to the carrier *USS*

Randolph and we were hit by a suicide plane which destroyed about thirty of our aircraft. There was no ordnance, very little ordnance involved. We did have . . . fire got into a 40 millimeter magazine but no major ordnance detonations aboard. We had a major fire when we were hit by a man flat-hatting (flying flat-out low to the water) in a P-38 which consumed 16 of our aircraft. We were alongside *USS Bunker Hill* when it had a major fire with ordnance and heavy detonations from a suicide attack. We were alongside *USS Enterprise*, (CV-6), when it was hit by a suicide plane. Those were the major fires that I have been close to.

Q. Based on your observations, are there any other changes in design of fire fighting equipment that you would recommend?
A. I think in the type of fire that we had, (14 January), that any system to be effective against it would have to have no personnel actually handling it above deck. I was sickened by how fragile the men appeared in handling the hoses. It seemed archaic and ineffective. I think if we are going to really fight the fire that we have to have something that's controlled, possibly manually from below decks. But men can't be any good in the midst of the fire and particularly if there is ordnance present.

Q. What is your opinion as to the state of training of fire fighting personnel on the *USS Enterprise*?
A. I thought the ship got a tremendous performance from the men. They did a tremendous job with the equipment that they had. I felt that they deserved a lot better equipment than they had. I did hear originally . . . It took awhile to get pressure on the line. I don't know whether that's in the system or what, but by the time I got there all the hoses were functioning and I was proud of the people.

Questions by Senior Member:

Q. Can you distinguish between the performance of the people per se and the damage control organization?
A. I don't believe I can, Admiral, I had a strong feeling that the people fighting the fire on the starboard side were, I don't know if they were regularly assigned to the hoses or what, they were willing, they seemed to know what they were doing and Mr. Brackin settled them down after each detonation beautifully and with that nozzle-

man leading them, they looked like seasoned firefighters.

Q. Would it be fair to say that there were failures of material rather than the people?
A. I think that's a very fair statement. I believe that the material was grossly inadequate.

Senior Member:

Commander Bureau, I want to thank you for the assistance which you have given this Board, not only in your testimony today but also in the past two weeks in helping us to gather information.

The witness was duly warned concerning his testimony and withdrew from the room.

Commander Harold W. Mount, USN, was called as a witness by the Board, was sworn and testified as follows:

Counsel for the Board:

Q. Would you state your name, rank, and present duty station?
A. Commander Harold W. Mount, Commander Fleet Air Hawaii Staff.
Questions by Senior Member:

Q. What is your job, Commander, on the Staff?
A. I'm presently filling the primary billet of Regional Air Space Officer, working as a liaison with the FAA (Federal Aviation Authority), I just left the current operations job a couple of months ago, Fleet Air Hawaii Staff.

Q. How many Operational Readiness Inspections have you participated in?
A. All ORI's in the Pacific since August of '65.

Q. What was your assigned job on this particular ORI?
A. I was senior observer for the Air Department.

Q. Where were you during the initial fire, initial explosion?

A. I was in Flag Bridge looking forward towards the bow at the time. I thought to myself that the scheduled hit that we had for 9:15 had been set earlier without my knowledge. I wasn't aware of the initiation of such an incident until I went to the window and saw what happened. Then I proceeded immediately to Primary.

Q. Would you describe briefly your observations from Primary, particularly in regard to the effect of damage control equipment and personnel?
A. By the time I reached Primary, the twin agent unit had arrived in the vicinity of the fire, which by this time had spread to, and encompassed three to four aircraft on the aft port quarter, and there were hoses being brought out from the deck edge in the aft end of FLY 2 and forward end of FLY 3 areas. Shortly thereafter, and I don't know the time frame. The second blast went off and it was a significant size blast, knocked several people off their feet on the flight deck. And this, of course, caused some retreat of the people with the hose lines. At the same time, the fire was spreading quite rapidly. I was amazed at the rapidity that the flight deck crews re-manned their hoses after temporary retreats, and then proceeded into the vicinity of the fire.

I don't have anything specific, I think there were several demonstrations of uncommon valor in the attitude that the deck crewmen had in manning their hoses and going back into it. When an explosion would cut half of them down, additional people would appear, re-man the hoses, go back into the area of the fire.

Q. Do you have any comment on the coordination, or leadership, the control of the fire fighting effort?
A. No, sir. It was difficult to determine from observation any specific organization except for spotty groups. Team leadership, the type of thing that comes out of the damage control textbook was, not overall as such, but was more or less as a group on each specific hose, and the coordination that was effected came apparently through PRIMARY FLY and the Air Boss who was on the 5MC at the time. He was directing the efforts of specific groups by the names of individuals that he recognized in the crew.

Q. Was it effective?
A. Yes, sir. It was particularly effective in getting the aircraft that

presented additional threats forward, off the fire area, getting them clear before the fire reached them. I would guess that there were as many as six, seven aircraft that were removed from the area that the fire would have spread to if they had not been moved forward on deck.

Q. This actually created a fire break effect?
A. Yes, sir, very much so.

Q. Concerning the effectiveness of the fire fighting systems that were activated, what comment do you have on these?
A. The twin agent vehicle at the time it arrived on the scene was confronted with a real significant fire flame pattern. I would estimate twenty, thirty feet in the air, and mushrooming laterally as fuel spillage fed the fire. It was ineffective for that type of fire at that time. The initial effort with salt water or fog foam was hampered by the lack of pressure. Some of the initial blasts penetrated, of course, the hoses that were on deck; very possibly some of the stations. The first several minutes the entire fire fighting effort was near totally ineffective because of the lack of pressure. It wasn't until several minutes after the (initial) fire that they got hoses from sufficiently forward and they got adequate pressure. But once you got adequate pressure in the foam and salt water hoses, it was extremely effective in containing the fire. I don't think they were actually making progress in controlling the fire until after the last ordnance exploded. That I believe was A-7 #312, which they made some valiant efforts to get out of the fire zone, but were unable to. Their tractor was disabled.

Q. Do you have anything further that you would care to say about this, Commander?
A. No, sir. Except that I did view the *USS Forrestal* films very carefully. We had a copy out here because it stopped off enroute to CONUS (Continental U.S.). We had the opportunity to take the films and run them and re-run them all afternoon, and at that time I gathered all the men who assist me in the ORI and we literally studied the film. What was so markedly different about that first (*USS Forrestal*) episode was that the *USS Enterprise* flight deck crewmen didn't quit. They went into the fire with what equipment they had at hand. Many of them were hoses that didn't have a stream of water

or foam coming out of the hose any more than 6 to 10 feet, totally ineffective. But they went ahead and they did what they could with it. When some of them were cut down they went back in without hesitation. And I think it was—I think the flight deck crews deserve a great deal of credit in containing and limiting the damage as much as possible.

Senior Member:

Thank you very much.

There being no further questions, the witness was warned and withdrew from the room.

Capt. Robert A. Hoolhorst, USN, was called as a witness by the Board, was sworn and testified as follows:

Questions by Counsel for the Board:

Q. Would you state your name, your rank, and your current duty station?
A. Robert A, Hoolhorst, Captain, U.S. Navy, Commander Fleet Training Group, Pearl Harbor.

Questions by the Senior Member:

Q. Captain, what we would like for you to tell us, in a narrative form, what you observed on the 14th.
A. On the 14th, approximately 10 minutes past 0800, I went to the bridge to consult with Capt. Lee about the previous days exercises and drills. I was up there to be on hand for the morning drills which were scheduled to go at 0900. I was walking toward the port side of the bridge when I felt and heard what I thought was a bomb exploding. This was immediately followed by a huge fireball and black smoke which billowed out the port side. I went to the aft end of the open bridge where I observed what was going on. I was rather cool, calm and collected because I had nothing else to do but observe what was going on. The fire was centered in the area of 105. I then looked all over the deck. I believe that planes 414, 312, 403 were armed. I could see bombs hanging from these planes. I was not able

to see the planes aft because of the intense smoke and flames. I saw four men, one man was adjacent to plane 403 who was on fire. There was a second man down, centered on the flight deck between 103 and 105 who was wounded and trying to crawl away. There was a third man coming aft with a very small hose and he was trying to get this man out. The fourth man was approximately here abreast of 312 and he was in a state of shock, After I observed this situation I went back into the bridge and the Captain was there then. I believe at that time I told him what I'd seen back there, I'm not sure about that. He was in command of the situation, everything was going on in a normal way. I then went down to the Flag level and talked to Capt. Daniels and gave him the same lay-out. I told him I thought there were going to be a lot of bombs going. All these planes were armed and I could see the fire jumping. While there, the fire jumped forward from 105 to 106. Immediately thereafter, there was a sudden larger, heavier blow but I did not observe whether it came from 106 or not. But it was in intensity 4 or 5 times that of the first bomb. At the instant it went, the whole port side again was covered with a rolling ball of fire. Smoke, yellow flames, orange ball. Capt. Daniels and I both hit the deck, it was a real lulu. After that, I went back up to the bridge and during the fire (acted) as an aide to Capt. Lee. I would like to add that the fire fighting was really chaotic in the beginning for several reasons. One, I observed that there was not enough pressure on the fire mains. The first hoses brought to the fire were virtually putting nothing out. It wasn't till the second time that I'd come back from the bridge and went aft with Capt. Lee that the hoses still weren't putting out. Actually this corrected itself, and they started getting pressure and then they kept leading hoses from the forward areas aft and very shortly thereafter, the pressure from the hoses were playing on the fire. I observed that the hoses were virtually doing nothing. They weren't effective for the type and amount of fire that was there. Obviously there was a very intense, hot fire and no matter how you were able to bring it to play on these planes, it wasn't enough to cool them down. In spite of the water being placed on the planes, the fire kept jumping forward on the port side and kept jumping to planes 214, 114, 103, 312, 414, 313 and 415 in order. Because the intensity of the fire was well aft and the heat was so much, you couldn't get across back there. This coupled with the bombs blowing made fire fighting ineffective and assinine. In my opinion, it was assinine trying to fight this fire until the bombs had blown themselves out. You couldn't possibly fight that fire. Many of the bombs and ordnance going and the men were knocked down. I don't know how many were killed or hurt because of the ordnance going but I did find out after the fire was all over that the aft end of the island was pretty well pocked up and scarred by shrapnel. When I was up in the forward end of the bridge, I observed a man way forward struck by shrapnel. He went down, he was way up forward, on the forward end of the flight deck. This was the first time I have seen a fire of such size before. I am firmly convinced that the fire fighting gear that we have presently on these ships is worthless when you try to put out a fire such as this. It isn't capable; there isn't enough water; there isn't enough hose; there isn't enough shielding and the men are exposed to anything that might go. Also, I'm of the opinion that we have been teaching in our fire fighting school that we go in and try to cool down the fire and cool down the ordnance in order to prevent it from blowing. I think this is wrong too because once this fire jumped from any of these planes to another plane which was armed, immediately the ordnance started to go. The other thing I observed was the foam fire fighting, I mean hoses were not doing the job. We have been using foam but we have been using it in confined spaces where there are some stops to it where the foam can build up a thick blanket. In an open fire like this where the stuff is just hitting the fire and rolling off, the foam is not effective. In fact it is less effective than a plain salt water hose. In merely cooling the fire down, when you fight a fire like this, what you are really trying to do is cool the fire down. Even after the fire got manageable after all this was blown out and the intensity dropped, then you had some effective firefighting. Then the men proceeded to work aft along both sides, plane after plane after plane. But this stuff all aft here was burning its merry way out. There was nothing that they could do.

Q. What comment do you have on the effectiveness of control that was exercised on the Bridge?
A. Excellent, very, very fine. Capt. Lee was in command of the situation throughout, the Bridge was a very quiet orderly place, it functioned the way it was supposed to function.

Q. Did you feel that the Commanding Officer was furnished with adequate information?
A. Precisely, Admiral, he was getting excellent dope. I was there

with him time and time again and the dope was coming up from Central, it was all plotted, where the fires were, the kind of fire, who was on it, what was being done. It was an outstanding actual demonstration of the way the thing should work.

Q. Are you aware of anything that could have been accomplished at that level to minimize the damage that was not done?
A. No, sir. Well, I want to get this straight. Everything was done that could possibly be done, Admiral.

Q. Had you an opportunity to form an opinion of the general damage control capabilities during this period?
A. Yes, sir. As the actual drills go, we had already conducted 3 hits, 3 drills, which made 4 hits really, one of these was a double hit. After each one, I received reports, that evening I sat down with those people and we talked it up, and saw what happened, how the actual grading was going and so forth and so on. Besides that, the day before, the 1st day, Capt. Lee and I had quite a little talk on the Bridge, talking about damage control, the need for the state of training and Capt. Lee, at that time, told me that he had been hitting it hard, and felt that this ship was going to show well in that damage control area. As you know, Admiral, most ships have a great deal of trouble qualifying in this damage control area. Capt. Lee told me that he had been working them hard and it actually showed. The first days drills usually start off slow because you don't make a good or an excellent on the first drill. As a rule, the first ones are kind of poor and then the second days drills actually start to pick up and if a ship is really on the ball they come out with a grade of "good" for the overall ORI. Capt. Lee's ship at the end of the first day was averaging "good" which I think is excellent.

Q. This is above the average you'd expect from the previous CVA's?
A. Yes, sir, it is. Of course, when the fire actually occurred, you could see that the men had been trained up and there had been work done because of the way that they went at it. You could readily see that this was not because someone told them to do it but because they knew what to do, from what I was able to see.

Q. Do you feel that the fire was limited to the degree that could be expected by the methods that were pursued?

A. I believe the ship did even better than that, Admiral. When I first looked aft, and I saw the kind of fire it was and the number of planes and bombs involved, I thought we were going to have a terrible, terrible disaster. I was jubilant to see the ship perform and to meet the situation as they met it to contain the fire, and I believe that if the ship hadn't done that and hadn't been trained up, this fire could have been costly, much, much more costly than it actually was.

There being no further questions, the witness was duly warned and withdrew from the room.

Commander R.A. Millington, USN, was called as a witness by the Board, was sworn and testified as follows:

Q. Counsel for the Board: Doctor, would you state your name, rank, and present duty station.
A. R.A, Millington, Commander, Medical Corps, USN. Duty station is *USS Enterprise*.

Questions by Commander Hicks:

Q. Commander Millington, will you describe the sequence of significant events which occurred in Main Battle Dressing Station aboard the *USS Enterprise* on 14 January, 1969?
A. Yes, sir. At the time of the explosion, the initial explosion, I was in my office with the senior medical observer, Capt. Kwiatkowski the Medical Officer from Barbers Point, and we were discussing imposing casualties during the up and coming drill. Of course, we were jarred by the concussion. I have in my office a 5MC so I could hear Commander Stollenwerck directing the fire fighting.

General Quarters went immediately, and I would say, within two minutes we had our first casualty, and from then on it was just casualties after casualties. We had aboard a Lieutenant Commander flight surgeon from Barbers Point, who was more of a rider than an observer, by the name of Dr. Carlson, and he pitched in and helped too. We had several things going for us: J-Dial was operative at all times, and this enabled us to prove the theory of Battle Dressing Stations. We were in contact with them at all times. They held the casualties for us so that we really wouldn't congest Main Sick Bay. Things proceeded in a very orderly fashion. The first casualties who came down came with battle dressing supplies that were brought by crewmen. We checked . . .

We had a very active first aid program aboard the *USS Enterprise* as everyone knows, and we'd been a little bit disappointed because during these drills and graded exercises the crew doesn't look like they have learned a thing. But after the first few casualties we could tell that the crew had really learned. The battle dressings were applied professionally. And there were few of them that we had to remove. From then on, we tried to begin resuscitating the patients who needed I.V. fluids, who were having difficulty with the airways, stabilizing the patients so that we could go ahead and evacuate them on the helicopters. I was extremely proud of the skill exhibited by not only the corpsmen, who really worked hard, but the medical officers, the dental technicians, and the dental officers. They did a marvelous job, way outside their training. The stretcher bearers were great. We had offers—we had to kick people out of sick bay. We had that many people who wanted to donate blood. Everybody was most helpful. I'm very proud of the crew. Without their efforts we couldn't have done as well as we did, I could say that honestly I don't think we lost a single casualty due to delay of treatment. Everything was just like the book said it ought to go. It was great.

Q. How were the casualties moved into the main battle dressing stations?
A. The procedure is, if a man is injured and he is still conscious he applies self aid. This is his white hat, baseball cap, anything on the wound to stop the bleeding. And the man near him goes to a first aid box, gets what he needs out of there to help the man. This is called "Buddy Aid". Then the man is taken to the nearest BDS by people who are around. They are supposed to know where the closest stretchers are. When in BDS they are examined there. If they can be deferred, that is, held, so that we can take care of the emergencies, well, then they're held there. If the man needs immediate attention, Central Control is called, the bearers that are attached to the BDS carries the man down to the main BDS and there he is given definitive care.

The stretchers were used effectively, they even used pipes. In fact, I don't know how they got patients down there so fast. It's just amazing. Of course, we utilized bomb elevators and the pilots elevator #1 was operating full time so that was a big help.

Q. Did you have any difficulty as far as gaining information as to the status of the ship fire fighting-wise and during the course of the fire?
A. I really didn't think much about it and we were busy, we were doing our job. I did hear them say over the 5MC, "Secure the water washdown system," and then the Captain came down . . . My time frame references are really compressed. It seems like it all happened in an hour.

Q. Is it fair to say that the information you needed externally was available to you?
A. Yes, sir. Unfortunately I wasn't handing out much information to the beach, though. They kept wanting to know how many casualties. Of course, we couldn't tell them.

Q. Based on the injuries that you observed, are there any changes in flight deck clothing which you would recommend?
A. Well, our injuries were basically in three categories. We had burns, we had missile wounds, shrapnel wounds, and we had group of miscellaneous fractures and lacerations and things, and there were combinations of all three of course. The greatest number of wounds, of course, were missile wounds. We had some severe burns. But the majority were missiles. And I don't think there is any flight deck clothing short of a vest that would stop things.

Q. How many physicians are assigned to the ship?
A. There are four, sir. Senior Medical Officer, the Flight Surgeon, the General Surgeon who is Board eligible . . .

Q. Do you have two additional people from Barbers Point?
A. Yes, sir, as ORI observers. And then when the beach got the word, well then we received 6 doctors and 16 corpsmen.

Questions by Senior Member:

Q. Could you handle the casualties with the same level of loss without external help?
A. I can think of two patients that we very well might have lost without that external help. When other medical officers reported aboard, they either had their own corpsman with them or we would

find them one, and they had more time to spend on one patient. And there were two that were resuscitated, one had cardiac arrest—this was picked up by one of our helpers and we brought him back alive. And there was a very bad wound of the chest which had been covered up. No one had noticed that. And we were able to put a tube in his chest to help expand his lung, so they were of value. However, I think we could have—it would have been a period of 72 hours where no one would have gotten any sleep. But I think we could have gotten along.

Q. Commander, what conclusions were you able to reach based on this experience that would relate to your ability to deal with casualties of this magnitude or larger, considering the facilities and people that you have assigned?
A. Without establishing an expectant category, which is the catesssgory in triage where you don't think you're going to be able to do anything for the man, that he is probably going to die, without establishing such a category, I think we handled just about the maximum without outside assistance. In order to enlarge on this, and I repeat to you, you may want this, what Tripler told me, it is the feeling of the Chief of Surgery, Colonel Layman, that we put just about as much on them as they could handle without starting to put two tables in each OR and calling in the civilian physicians. They think that we put about the maximum number of casualties without establishing the expectant category.

Counsel for the Board:

Q. Doctor, are you able to tell us the total number of injured personnel as a result of the fire?
A. My best estimate is around 345, (this figure was subsequently raised to 371)

AFFIDAVIT

Personally appeared before me, the undersigned officer authorized to administer oaths, ABHC Gerald M. Cordeau, who after being duly sworn, on oath does depose and say that:

The 0830 launch was called away by the Air Officer to start engines on certain aircraft at approximately 0810. At this time I left Flight deck Control to observe the start as I usually do on every launch. I proceeded aft to around #3 elevator and was checking around for a normal start when a burst occurred to my left from aircraft 105 on its starboard side and next what seemed like an explosion of a gas tank and fire swept around the surrounding aircraft. I was then blown down or fell down and ran forward of #3 elevator to pull hoses and rushed it towards the fire. At this time I could hear the Air Officer directing us on the Bullhorn or the Main Communications to attack the fire and keep fighting it, also notifying us of the danger of various aircraft or rockets ready to burst. The aircraft seemed to burst one after another with the blast moving us out temporarily and we would come back. I saw the light water unit enter the center of the fire and a small umbrella effect of foam came from it as another burst came and the hose man was blown away. Flames then engulfed us once more and the light water unit was then in flames. The foam at the fire would stop at times as hoses were blown apart or cut and after each blast the crew would grab what equipment was still functioning and go in again. I was blown down several times during this and at times I could hardly see from the foam in my goggles and the deck was a blanket of foam and I heard the Air Officer call to shut down the water washdown system aft as it was diluting the foam which was effective on fuel fire on the deck and holes in the deck. The sprinkler system was also hampering me as it would hit me in the face with a hard stream which made it harder to see. As I was blown down the deck and ran with every burst I could see hoses forward and people would drop off and come aft to help and it seemed at times that there were three or four waves of back up crews forward that just kept coming aft as people were injured and took up hoses that were loose. During this time I remember in helping getting an A-3 untied behind the island and the flight deck petty officer was driving the tractor and I was with another yellow shirt directing him out and we hit a helicopter next to the island. At this time also, a flood of foam from forward was blinding us, we then got the E2-A out with its port wing on fire and the blanket of foam seemed so heavy that by the time we got it to the angle the fire was out on it. About this time, I don't remember too much, I last remember helping on a foam hose with an ordnance Chief and my side and shoulder hurt. I was told I was crawling forward on my knees when members of my team (COMNAVAIRPAC Handling) picked me up and took me to flight deck control and laid me under the planning board. I have read the Russel Report and I solemnly believe high velocity foam system aft on the island structure would have been very, very effective. In my opinion the reason why the crew reacted so efficiently was the coordination of the Air Officer as he prompted us, directed us, and never did anyone quit on him. The Flight Deck Officer remained the strong arm on deck as he followed the Air Officer to the letter and not once did I see him fall back on any burst, except to pick himself up and send in another charge with himself at the head of everyone.

Gerald M. Cordeau
Sworn to and subscribed before me this 22nd day of January, 1969.
R. G. Tisinger Lt. JAGC USNR

EPILOGUE

Work to repair *USS Enterprise* began as soon as the ship tied up on the 14th of January. Materials and extra workers were flown in from west coast yards. For fifty days, under the supervision of Bull Bennett and Blacky Wong, shipyard gangs worked round the clock cutting out wreckage and rebuilding the ship.

On the 51st day, tugs pulled *USS Enterprise* clear. She sounded a blast on her ships whistle and was underway with her port point defense missile battery inoperative and #4 aircraft elevator restructured and welded in position to the flight deck. As she rounded the north side of Ford Island she ran aground on a sand bar injecting mud into the steam plant condensers and all operating reactors had to be shut down. Emergency diesel generators were put on line and *USS Enterprise* sat there for hours until the mud was cleared from the condensers and the reactors were running again. Finally, the ship cleared harbor and sailed for the western Pacific. On March 31st she took position off the coast of North Viet Nam known as Yankee Station.

M.J. Carlin
PO Box 98
West Grove, Pa., 19390

Dear Carlin,

    I read that you were interested in hearing from personnel who were aboard the *USS Enterprise* during the "69" cruise when we had that damned fire.

    I was the Chief Petty Officer in charge of Combat Air Traffic Control that morning, and had reached my duty station at about 7:15. I was all by myself until later when one of our young airmen talkers showed up. We were doing nothing other than routine launch preparation paperwork, and then felt the ship lurch quite noticeably, and a muffled sound . . . I looked up at the two television's overhead the entry hatch and since they were trained on the bow and "CAT" areas, nothing seemed amiss . . . Then, someone turned the cameras around toward the stern and it was such a sight I was speechless. I had already dialed our Watch Officer, Comdr. Cawley, as I knew SOMETHING was wrong right from the first movement of the ship, when he came on the phone, I described what was on the T.V. screen at the stern. I think he dropped the phone and said he was on the way. More explosions started about that time, probably only 3 to 5 minutes had elapsed, and the workspace started to fill up with sailors in all sorts of dress as they had all responded to General Quarters immediately. Comdr. Cawley immediately ordered us to set up communications with Pearl and get helicopter support for evacuation of wounded, and to notify Tripler. From that point on its really hard to remember the details as everything happened so quickly. But I remember the destroyer coming up alongside and strapping hoses to the guns so they could direct the water by aiming the guns and it enabled them to get much closer. Pushing the burning aircraft off the ship, the picture of the fire fighting crews on the T.V. monitor rushing in to extinguish the flames, explosions going off, blowing men and equipment all over the place, then, other sailors or maybe the same ones who could get up, picking up the hoses and running in again, only to face another explosion. This was repeated a couple of times. It was hard to believe the scenes on the monitor.

    When I was finally able to get up to the flight deck, the destruction was unbelievable, the smell, the sounds, wounded being helped all around, body bags here and there . . . but, the sight of those sailors getting up and going in again and again to fight the fires will stay with me forever, they were very brave.

After we docked at Pearl, I had the afterbrow watch and had to log the body bags as they were taken off the ship and put into large trucks that were waiting for us . . . one of the toughest things I had to do, as some of them were good friends of mine.

As I mentioned, some of the details are hard to bring back, partly because lots of things were happening quickly, and because I think I just don't want to remember, I don't know.
Hope this helps . . .
Sincerely,

Bill Schultz (ACC, USN Ret,)

APPENDIX

ENTERPRISE Airwing, 14 January, 1969

CVW-9	Carrier Air Wing Nine

SQUADRONS

VF-92	F-4J PHANTOM, all-weather fighter-interceptor
VF-96	F-4J PHANTOM, all-weather fighter-interceptor
VA-146	A-7B CORSAIR II, attack bomber
VA-215	A-7B CORSAIR II, attack bomber
VA-145	A-6A INTRUDER, all-weather attack bomber
RVAH-6	RA-5C VIGILANTE, multi-sensor reconnaissance
VAQ-132	A-3/KA-3 SKYWARRIOR, electronic coutermeasures and in-flight air refueling
VAW-112	E2-A HAWKEYE, electronic early warning
HC-1	UH-2C SEASPRITE helicopter detachment

GLOSSARY

ABH2	Aviation Boatswains Mate, Handler, 2nd Class
AE2	Avionics Technician, 2nd Class
Air Boss	Air Officer, in charge of all Air Operations
AMR	Auxiliary Machinery Room
AMS3	Aviation Mechanic, Structural, 3rd Class
AO3	Aviation Ordnanceman, 3rd Class
BDS	Battle Dressing Station
Cat	Aircraft launching catapults
Comdr.	Commander
Central	Engineering Central Control
CINCPACFLT	Commander-in-Chief, Pacific Fleet
CONFLAG	Conflagration control stations in the Hangar Bay
CVA	Aircraft Carrier, Attack
Flight Quarters	Carrier evolutions preparing for, and the actual launch and recovery sequences
Go-Bird	Aircraft scheduled for launch
GPM	Gallons per minute
GQ	General Quarters
Helo	Helicopter
Huffer	Tractor mounted aircraft starting unit
I.V.	Intravenous solutions
JBD	Jet Blast Deflectors
JOOD	Junior Officer of the Deck
JP-5	Jet fuel
Lt. Comdr.	Lieutenant Commander
LSO	Landing Signal Officer
1MC	Main Communications
MEDEVAC	Helicopter borne medical evacuation
OOD	Officer of the Deck
PLAT	Pilot Landing Attitude Tape
Primary	PRI-FLY, Primary Flight Control, where the Air Officer and Assistant Air Officer oversee and direct flight Operations
PSI	Pounds per square inch
OBA	Oxygen breathing apparatus
Trap	An arrested carrier landing
W.O.	Warrant Officer
V.I.P.	Very Important Persons

NAVY TABLE OF RANK

Adm.	Admiral
Vice Adm.	Vice Admiral
Rear Adm. (u.h.)	Rear Admiral, Upper Half
Rear Adm. (l.h.)	Rear Admiral, Lower Half
Capt.	Captain
Comdr.	Commander
Lt. Comdr.	Lieutenant Commander
Lt.	Lieutenant
Lt. (j.g.)	Lieutenant, Junior Grade
Ens.	Ensign
WO4	Warrant Officer, Grade 4
WO3	Warrant Officer, Grade 3
WO2	Warrant Officer, Grade 2
WO1	Warrant Officer, Grade 1

ENLISTED

MCPO E-9	Master Chief Petty Officer
SCPO E-8	Senior Chief Petty Officer
CPO E-7	Chief Petty Officer
PO1 E-6	Petty Officer, 1st Class
PO2 E-5	Petty Officer, 2nd Class
PO3 E-4	Petty Officer, 3rd Class
AN, FN, SN E-3	Airman, Fireman, Seaman
AA E-2	Airman Apprentice
SA E-2	Seaman Apprentice
E-1	Recruit

REFERENCES

All places and names in the 1st chapter, The Legend, are fictitious. Everything contained in the succeeding chapters, except for the Rider on the Pale Horse and the Legion of the Dead of the Sea are true.

USS Enterprise is faithfully depicted in this book as she was fitted out in January, 1969. My thanks to Bud Owens, Historian for the *USS Enterprise* Association for the information supplied.

The data on the sea battles of 1812 came from "The Naval War of 1812" by Theodore Roosevelt and the won/loss count can be found on pages 397-398 specifically.

The section on the Tomb of the Unknowns contain information taken from, "In Honored Glory, Arlington National Cemetery: The Final Post" by Philip Bigler and "Arlington National Cemetery, Shrine to America's Heroes" by James Edward Peters.

The section on Tripler hospital contained information taken from the Honolulu Advertiser of 15 January, 1969.

USS ENTERPRISE (CVA(N)65)

COMMENDATION

The Commanding Officer United States Ship ENTERPRISE (CVA(N)65)

takes pleasure in commending

Michael Joseph CARLIN
Airman, United States Navy

for service as set forth in the following:

CITATION

"For outstanding performance of duty while attached to and serving in USS ENTERPRISE (CVAN 65) as an Aviation Fuel Crew Leader from 18 March to 25 June 1969 during combat operations against the enemy. Airman CARLIN consistently performed his duties with outstanding ability and resourcefulness, enhancing combat readiness. Airman CARLIN, acting in the billet of a Third Class Petty Officer, supervised his crew with great skill, utilizing proper procedures and exercising safety precautions to the highest extent. His leadership was reflected in his crew constantly filling aircraft to the proper fuel loads, enabling the embarked air wing to meet their requirements. Airman CARLIN's skill and judgment contributed significantly and directly to the successful accomplishment of the ship's mission and to the United States' effort in Vietnam."

K. L. LEE
Captain
United States Navy

VOLUME II

(17 years later)

This was the USS Enterprise as designed and built and appeared in 1969. With her massive white, slab sided, square island she was easily the most distinctive aircraft carrier ever built. There was only one of her class and she remained distinct from all other carriers throughout her long career. The Author served on Enterprise for over three years as she looked in this picture and she was, to him and many others, the most beautiful Warship ever built by any Nation.

AFTERBURNERS

As I write this it is now April of 2010 and rather than go into a complete third edition of my book about the 1969 Enterprise Fire I have decided to ad a few pages and pictures to the original. This gives me the opportunity to bring several things to light relating to our "Day Of Days", event of 14 January, 1969.

First off let me ask the reader to consider what Admiral James L. Holloway, Former Chief Of Naval Operations, had to say in his review of my book. I was both humbled and overjoyed that Admiral Holloway even agreed to do it. I thought he might give it a shot since he was Commanding Officer of Enterprise for the ships first and second WESTPAC cruises before being relieved by Captain Kent L. Lee for the following tour during which we had our catastrophe. Well, Admiral Holloway gave me a review and I could not have asked for anything better. Among some of the pertinent things he said was that I should have identified myself where I appear in some of the pictures that are in the book. At the time I did not think that was important. He also said that I had achieved a level of objectivity that was made possible since I wrote my own account in the third person. I wrote my account in this way because I could not adequately convey my fears and emotions otherwise. I wanted to put the reader right where I was and in this way more accurately and more honestly tell the tale of our fight at sea. I was turned down by a major Publisher because of this but I felt it was necessary that the story be told the way I wrote it. So, I went and published this book myself and I think it is better that I did.

Now, I will identify myself in the pictures where I show up. On the cover picture, in the lower right hand corner, I am third in line on a new hose team forming on the port side just forward of the Angle. My jersey looks red in some shots but it is really purple. Jim Fitzgerald is two or three guys behind me. This was the team that put out the flaming E-2A Hawkeye as it was being towed past us. On this hose we had to continually ad in new lengths of hose to get us back to where A-7 #310 and F-4 #112 blazed away back behind the Waist Cats Jet Blast Deflector area. There were no operational fire hoses left aft of us on the port side.

On page 81 I am second to last on the fog Gooseneck hose team. Jim Fitzgerald is to my right and Terry Arrick is to my left. The rest of that team are V-1 Division guys and Crash/Salvage Officer Jim Helton is in that area somewhere although I cannot identify anyone except those of my crew. In the other picture on page 81, ASBURY is the guy going down under the wing of #310, slipping through the fingers of Twig Tordoff.

On page 86, I am the purpleshirt who has taken over the Gooseneck nozzle. This is after being blown to the flight deck with extreme violence and being completely out cold for I don't know how long. But some of us came to and tried to rejoin the fight only to be struck by what seemed to be the Hammer of Thor again and again. I have never experienced such violence and fear since that day and it was of a magnitude incomprehensible to anyone who has not lived through something like that.

Another issue I would like to clarify is that for over 30 years our 1969 Enterprise Fire History was obscured by the fact that our existing motion picture footage, both hand held 16MM and our PLAT deck edge monitor film, were used extensively in the making of the Navy Training Film, "Trial By Fire." This film was made in the early 70s and it was about the USS Forrestal Fire of 1967. What little actual Forrestal film used in this video was taken by their color motion picture TV camera mounted high up in their Island structure. This camera actually recorded the first minute or so of actual Forrestal Fire footage including John McCain climbing out of his burning A-4 SkyHawk, jumping down to the flight deck and running out of the picture as the Crash/Salvage Team deploys fire fighting gear right in front of the aircraft. In those opening scenes the scope of the camera recorded A-4 SkyHawks across the entire fantail and all of the way forward on the port side. Also recorded were two A-4s spotted for launch on both waist catapults. Then the 1000 lb. bomb under McCains aircraft went off taking out the Crash/Salvage Team and apparently the man running the camera high in the Island because in the next scenes of the explosions, which are spellbindingly spectacular and in black and white, the action is now being recorded by the PLAT deck edge monitor film of action on Enterprise which has the cross hairs in it because this is fixed to sight straight down the centerline of the landing area so pilots can review their traps after recoveries.

In this PLAT film we can clearly see – lo and behold—A-7 Corsairs and F-4 Phantoms where before there were only A-4 SkyHawks in actual Forrestal footage. And she clearly had no A-7 Corsairs on deck because they did not even come into the Fleet until a year later. In another sequence of hand held motion picture footage in the training film an F-4

Phantom is shown being towed clear of the waist cats as a terrific explosion goes off behind it. This is also Enterprise film because Forrestal had only SkyHawks on her waist cats. A comparison with the Forrestal is in order. Both events were similar with detonating bombs, rockets and ammunition. Forrestal aircraft mounted 1000 lb. bombs whereas ours were 500 pounders going off in multiples. Forrestal had 130 dead, almost five times our number of 28. Most of the dead of Forrestal were killed below decks being blasted by explosions from above or suffocating in their General Quarters stations from smoke and flames. We did not lose a single man to smoke inhalation, having learned lessons from Forrestal and only four of our dead were blasted from above while fighting in Repair Party Teams. All other personnel were evacuated from their spaces by pilots escaping their aircraft on the flight deck and Repair personnel sweeping the spaces clear in the aft spaces beneath bomb laden aircraft. Forrestal had 100 wounded while Enterprise had 343. This disparity is easily borne out in every video and still picture sequence which clearly shows men on deck fighting throughout the entire range of the fight through all of the exploding ordnance and ammunition. Forrestal had no place to evacuate her seriously wounded except to other Navy ships in the area which did not have as extensive medical facilities as Forrestal herself. While we, being only 70 miles from Pearl Harbor, benefitted from Coast Guard, Air Force, Marine and Navy helicopter Medevacs which flew our worst 46 cases to Tripler Army hospital while our ship still burned. These 46 might have all expired without that timely medical attention rather than just one who died enroute. It was quite a fight.

Regarding us who fought on the flight deck I tried to put the reader in as close as my hose team was but I know that I cannot adequately describe the searing heat and fear that gripped all of us. The reader would have to place himself at the very edge of a very large bonfire to appreciate the pain of it. You would have to get in so close that you could smell the hair burning off your hands, arms and face. So close that your exposed skin shrieked in pain. Then, when you reached that point, move in closer. Move in till your clothes began to smoke and steam vapor rose from the ground at your feet. I saw Jim Helton, I am pretty sure it was him, he came up and grabbed our fog nozzleman by the shoulder and the twin agent nozzle operator by his shoulder and he drove us all into the wall of flames. Both hoses blew a small hole through the flames and he pushed us through those gates of hell and he took us downtown. He drove us in to get the cooling water onto those bombs under the aircraft. For those of us in so close it was a blessing when the first bombs exploded under #105 even though some of us were killed. It was a blessing because we were all going to die from the heat of the flames and those bombs going off blew the flames down for a few seconds and gave those still alive relief.

It has been my personal crusade ever since I first saw that training film to get Enterprise and her crew proper credit for our own history and courage knowing full well how dearly we paid in blood, death and suffering to save our ship. All of this is so blatantly evident that even a casual viewing of that film would reveal it but it went on and on for all of those years. The entire video record of Enterprise was given to those producers of that Navy training film and in doing so they effectively erased from history the greatest fight for life of any Naval Warship since World War Two. The U.S. Navy should study and celebrate the fight of the Enterprise on 14 January, 1969. The U.S. Marine Corps -- God Love 'em – would surely ad this episode as another in their long and cherished tradition. The U.S. Navy, on the other hand appears unsure and even embarrassed with how to deal with this history and it is absolutely bewildering to me.

I have since learned that the flash temperatures of the exploding rockets and bombs on that day was 6000 degrees. Any exposed flesh caught in these flashes was instantly severely burned even if not touched by actual flames. It seemed that the flash burns from the rockets were worse than those of the exploding bombs. The only explanation I can see for this was that when the bombs detonated all hands were blown flat instantly and the flash of the burning explosive train likely went over us. With major caliber weapons such as 500 pound bombs going off in high order the detonation is so great and powerful that the expanding explosive train pushes a pressure wave of compressed air ahead of it that feels almost solid when you are in close. And remember, none of us on the flight deck had on any kind of fire fighting gear whatsoever except for the two Hot suitmen who were both wounded. We only had on thin cotton jerseys and, if we were lucky, work gloves.

In the case of the 5 inch Zuni rockets the blast effect was not as great and the shaped charge warheads projected a stream of 6000 degree flame. You will notice in the picture on page 81 those of us on that Gooseneck fog hose. Since I do not know the names of everyone on that hose I don't know if any were killed. I do know that Arrick, Fitzgerald and myself were blown completely flat and none of us were burned or wounded. This good fortune was not likely for the rest of our team. These were 500 pound bombs going off in multiples and the only explanation I can come up with as to why we survived is that the bomb rack on #105 had to have been blown loose and those bombs still connected to the rack had to be pointing directly at us when they went off with most of the blast and shrapnel blowing out from the sides of the bombs rather than from the ends. Either way, it is still a miracle to me to be within ten yards of those exploding bombs, twice, and live to tell about it.

George Norsworthy might have been with us on that hose but I did not see him there and never found out. He was hit in several places about his body and was in very bad shape. After we carried him back in the catwalk to our crews shelter and turned him over to Allen Theide we never saw him again. The same goes for many of our wounded from both Squadrons and ships company. A lot of them just simply never returned to us.

It took me about ten years from the time that I started gathering information about our fire until the finished product was in my hands in book form. I wrestled with how I could present all of the things that I had in mind in a story line for almost two years until I settled on the Horseman and the Legion of the Dead as the way to bridge those aspects of history, tradition and legacy. I had hoped to make our story something that would endure the times and lend itself to Naval lore. I was also keenly aware of the heavy responsibility I was taking on regarding my ship and shipmates.

I solicited for first hand accounts of the fire in various magazines and newspapers and conducted interviews on cassette tapes through the mail for three and a half years. I managed to get 40 guys altogether and went ahead with them. I have a box full of those interviews sitting in a corner of my den to this day. Those interviews were always interesting. Many were very sad and some were downright eerie. I would ask a series of questions on the tape to get general information so I would know what to ask about on the second round. I would listen to the voices coming out of the speakers for hours. These people were always alone and they would open up. They would speak of certain things and I would hear them halt or change the inflection of their voices. They were remembering things that many of them had locked away for sanity's sake and they had reached a difficult issue. On the next round these were the issues I asked them to clarify, those areas where the subject had difficulty answering.

In this way they were persuaded to go back and revisit the nightmares. Most would only go so far. They simply would not cross that line and open those doors. They would not go there again. There were others who would go, however reluctantly, and they would descend those dark dusty corridors in considerable discomfort. And then there was one who had visited those nightmares many times. I would listen to these tapes and hear those voices reveal far more than just what was said. Their voices coming from the tape recorder grew nervous and halting the closer they came to that door. The voice would falter and then stop. The tape became tomb silent. I knew that behind that door was madness and humiliation, vileness and desecration. To the subject there were heard rustlings and moaning of demons and a gnashing of teeth.

Then there was a twittering of embarrassed, painful, mirthless giddiness as he pushed open that door. He would gather himself with steeled determination and lead me through that door into those vaults of nightmare. And I knew that confronting these things that haunted the sufferers was, in the end, a good thing because they seemed to escape those demons they had been chained to for so long. And I myself knew of these demons also because I had borne witness and could never forget. I had witnessed the purest, most brilliant white light man is capable of in the form of courage in the face of hideous destruction and certain death. It was good against evil. White light against flame and smoke. And I felt a wave of love for those who stood up to it. Perhaps someone loved me too.

But then I saw the madness. It borders on blasphemy when such displayed virtue is utterly violated, defiled and smashed to nothing. Your beliefs are put to the severest test and you come away questioning. My God, My God, why hast Thou forsaken me? Whoever it was that said, "Death is no respecter" must have witnessed these very same things. It changes you. When I wrote my account as the crewleader of crew two of the purpleshirts, it was written in absolute Truth. Everything in my account is exactly the way it happened with me right down to the confrontation with the V-4 Division chief. When I wrote of being alone on that fog hose and being stunned by the voice which told me to get away, that is all pure Truth.

For some reason, I had been permitted to live. When I turned and ran those few steps a nameless, faceless V-1 Division blueshirt passed me. He was running up to join me on that fog hose and I at once felt a wave of love for him. Then that tremendous blast went off behind me with a solid chunk of metal hitting my hip pocket and destroying my wallet. Those several layers of leather, plastic and whatnot had absorbed the energy of that piece of shrapnel. Had I been facing the other way, I would have been disemboweled.

I never knew who that blueshirt was or what had happened to him but I had been permitted to live. There are no phony embellishments in my account, no self serving smugness or false bravado. I know my God is a just and jealous God and having been spared I dared not tell my story with anything but truth. Having been pressed through the Makers forge, all of those impurities had been burned away. If anyone claims to have been very close to their last drawn breath on earth and are not humbled by it, then they just have not been that close. My personal burden of humility is very great.

"I was standing in the jet shop at the rear of the Hangar Deck just about to leave the shop when the first explosion went off which we were directly under. Not knowing what had happened, a few seconds later there was another explosion. Then a voice came over the 1MC that said, "THIS IS NOT A DRILL". Then someone noticed the rear jet shop doors that lead to the fantail were hot. The crew where we were, all effort was to battle the fire that was being fed by the fuel washing down through the holes blown through the flight deck. That is where I

remained through most of the fire and explosions. My thoughts at the time were, we were under attack and we were going to go down. At some point later there were calls for blood, especially anyone having type O, which I had. I went down to Sick Bay and there were many donors and also a call for volunteers to fight on the flight deck. I will never forget the climb to the flight deck by way of the Admirals Passageway, normally in pristine condition, the bulkheads were covered in blood and smoke. When I reached the Island the corpsmen were working people and there was a hole through the door of the Captains elevator. The flight deck was a total mess. Two crew members were carrying another burnt from head to foot. I still remember that. I can remember more but right now it is starting to get to me".

"I was on the information desk in Sick Bay that morning. When the fire call came over the 1MC I went to the Mid Auxiliary Battle Dressing Station in the Chiefs Quarters. Our Medical Officer was Commander Wilkie, a Dentist and a good leader. At first the casualties came in pretty fast and the first was one of your guys with a broken wrist and several shrapnel wounds with a large piece of metal sticking out of his chest. Next there was a Yellow Shirt carried by a couple of guys stuck in the doorway trying to get him in. When I got to him I saw why they were having so much trouble with him. His leg had been nearly severed about mid thigh and split almost to the crotch. Fortunately for him, someone had put a tourniquet above the wound or I am sure he would have bled out before he could have reached the dressing station. Then the lights went out and the casualties came in so fast I can't remember the order or their wounds. One of the next was our first DOA so we set up a morgue in the next berthing compartment. As soon as we could after they were stable we transported the more serious cases to Sick Bay with the Ship Stewards we had assigned as stretcher bearers. I remember one guy who could walk and had a shirt tied around his waist because we had to cut his pants off to treat the wounds he had on his legs and upper body. When things calmed down and the casualties slowed we had to move the patients on the lower level racks up a level because the water level was getting them wet. Now, you have to remember that I was below decks and it was dark except for the battle lanterns. Then, we moved our dead to the Hangar Bay and began to identify them. Most were identified by dental charts. Some we could not even identify them that way. We did the best we could and let the final ID up to the FBI. It was a day that I will never forget".

When my book came out in '93 I immediately wrote a letter and sent it along with a copy of the book to then Commanding Officer, Captain Richard Naughton. Enterprise was then in the Yards in Newport News, Virginia. I believe at the time the Navy was deciding whether to go ahead with another nuclear refueling of Enterprise or have another carrier built in a number of years for just twice the cost of that refueling. The decision was made to keep Enterprise in the Fleet and go ahead with the refueling.

Captain Naughton then ordered 12 copies of my book to be placed in the ships library and that was when this long lost history of the most terrible day of Enterprise was revealed to the crew and the Navy in general. Since that day over 550 copies of TRIAL have been sent to the ship. One crewman aboard Enterprise who read the book, PhotoMate 2nd class, Alan Warner, wrote me a letter stating that he intended to paint a Mural about the 1969 fire and asked for some specific information regarding those who were killed that day. I gave him what he needed and asked if I could have a picture of the Mural when he finished it. It took over a year but I don't think anyone could have come up with anything better than what Alan Warner did. To me his Mural is the greatest compliment ever bestowed on our ship and crew for January 14, 1969. It is my greatest pleasure to include that picture in this third edition of TRIAL. I am also including some other pertinent pictures that I did not have when the book was first published.

I had been in communications with the Senior leadership aboard Enterprise ever since '94, principally through a succession of Command Master Chiefs. It was through these men that my books became available to the crew of the ship. I had initially entertained the hope that I could get these books sold through the ships store but ran hard aground on a bewildering mass of Navy regulations. The Command Master Chiefs came to the rescue, however, and case after case of books were sold to the crew through the Chiefs Mess. What follows is a review of the book by Chief Terry Hensley for the benefit of the crew and sent to me also.

TRIAL: ORDEAL OF THE ENTERPRISE   a book review by ABHCS (AW) Hensley for the benefit of the crew.

The time is 0819;26 and the flight deck is shaking off the lethargy from the previous nights slumber. The moving tow-tractors are rubbing the sleep from the flight decks eyes and it stretches and yawns with the powerful roar of starting jet engines. Suddenly, a flash and a bang,

then a huge fireball races upward and outward simultaneously. Immediately aircraft 105 is engulfed in flames. A seemingly voracious monster spreads from the stricken aircraft consuming men and machines, growing as if a living thing. You are shocked, stunned and surprised. You look aft and see Hell itself has cracked open to spew its fire demon. Scenes of horror, men stagger out of the demons grip, bodies totally ablaze, pieces of aircraft and men hurtle skyward assaulting your senses and your very sanity. What do you do?

Mirriam Websters Dictionary defines a trial as, "a test of faith or stamina through subjection to suffering". TRIAL; ORDEAL of the ENTERPRISE is a book about honorable, courageous and committed men who faced that test on January 14th, 1969, on this very ship. Eighteen detonations, fifteen aircraft destroyed, seventeen damaged, twenty eight dead and three hundred and forty three wounded are the statistics. Author Michael Joe Carlin writes not just about the number but of the personal trial of men when confronted with a holocaust on their ship. This is the true story of the Enterprise crew fighting to save their ship and their shipmates, written by a man who was there.

With his engaging prose, the author transports you back to that day in 1969 when Enterprise fought for her life. Woven together with legend, fact and personal accounts, this tale of horror, courage and eventual triumph, cannot fail to inspire the reader.. This is a story not just about the flight deck, but the whole crew mobilized by a threat to the very survival of the ship itself. The reader can almost feel the heat and the trembling as successive explosions rocked the ship. You will also get caught up in the heroic efforts to fight the holocaust and save the lives of her crewmen. The forty black and white and twelve color photographs superbly enhance the reading experience by giving the reader a sense of the conflagrations dimensions and how it spread to other parts of the ship.

This is a story that all men and women who go to sea in ships should read. It is this readers fervent hope that he would perform as well as those men. They truly embodied our Navy's core values, honor, courage and commitment. Read this book! You won't be able to put it down!

"I was Director of the Fire Protection Division of the Naval Sea Systems Command. In essence, I was the life cycle engineering manager for all shipboard fire protection systems, including the flight deck AFFF systems (flushdeck, deck-edge, hoselines, bomb farm, weapons elevators, etc.). I served on the NAVSEA technical lessons learned team that investigated the fire on Enterprise and provided on-site testimony to the formal Enterprise JAG Board. I had previously reviewed in depth the July 1967 flight deck fire on the Forrestal and at the time of the Enterprise disaster I was conducting a development program to upgrade fire protection on the flight deck by trying to incorporate AFFF into the washdown system. After the Enterprise I was assigned the responsibility to monitor and oversee the Navy's compliance with the recommendations of the Russel Panel, the Enterprise JAG, and the Carrier Aviation Support Study – all of which recommended major fire protection improvements covering everything from weapons cook-off to flight deck fire fighting vehicles. I later testified to Congress, the House Armed Services Committee, on survivability enhancements to aircraft carriers. I also investigated other fire-related incidents on carriers. Additionally, I ran all of the full scale flight deck tests at China Lake. You might not be aware that the Navy actually built a simulated flight deck in the middle of the Mojave desert to evaluate scenarios such as Forrestal and Enterprise and to develop appropriate fire fighting systems and equipment".

I have received a couple of hundred letters over the years, most of which are from shipmates who were aboard with me that day. They all write a little or a lot about their own experiences. I saved most of them and could easily put them all together for another publication. There are many other letters from people who read the book and were just compelled to write to me. Most of these lead to a few pleasurable exchanges between them and myself. There are others that are very serious. These come from relatives of our dead and they have questions that the Navy had no answers for. Some of these relatives are bitter. All have the same sadness for their loss. One woman, a widow, grieves her lost son to this day. She has written me many letters. It started when she wrote to then Chief of Naval Operations, Frank Kelso, and stated that she wanted to know what had happened to her son on that day because the Navy never told her anything except that he died as a result of fire and explosions aboard Enterprise. Frank Kelso wrote her back and told her about my book which was the most extensive history of the Enterprise fire. So I sent her a copy and told her what I could about her boy. Relatives of the dead want to know everything. They want to know exactly what happened right down to his last second of life and last breath. They have the right to know and they want me to tell them. They are all very brave about it but it is something that is very hard to do. I knew that this was likely to happen when I started writing the book. I did not know that I would be taken to such depths of anguish and sorrow. These good people tell me things that they probably do not tell anyone else. Never again can I ever see a single fallen soldier or someone badly wounded and not know with absolute certainty the lives left in ruins because of it. It is something that I carry around with me now. All of the things I have been told over these years are still with me today and always will be. I have been changed by it. Anymore I cannot bring myself to talk openly about our fire or even a lot of other things for that matter. Some trigger brings things rushing back from a far place in my memory and I just freeze.

There were many relatives of our Fallen Brothers in attendance at our Washington, DC, reunion where we placed a Commemoration plaque with the names of all of our dead on the Naval Memorial Wall. One woman with her family about her came up to me and bravely stated that she fully intended to read my book but has been unable to do so as yet because her family won't let her. She wanted to know everything about her lost son. She was smiling that brave smile at me but her eyes glittered with pain and sadness. I at once was overcome and had to leave the room. Triggers. I also was unable to answer a sister of the same family because she too had those sad eyes behind her smile. I hope they understood my sadness. Later in the evening I was at the bar and was able to take the brother aside. I told him why I could not respond to his mother and sister. Then I told him everything I knew about how his brother died. I told him it was a very hard death but much more merciful than the deaths of many others. I left it in his hands and he thanked me for it.

There have been many others. One woman looked up my website about the Enterprise fire because her brother was one of our dead. She sent me a short e-mail message and said she had been troubled by a feeling of guilt for years because she had been told that her dead brother was the cause of the whole thing. This made me very angry and I responded to her that no individual or group of individuals on our ship were responsible for what had happened. Her brother, just like all of the rest of us, were carrying out our responsibilities as best as we could. I could sense the sadness in this woman's message. There were several factors that went wrong. Taken individually, these factors likely would have been overcome. Taken collectively, they produced the event we had because Carrier Operations are inherently a very dangerous business. To make these operations work demands almost perfect timing and all supporting activities have to work smoothly. Once the timing is affected, the situation begins to break down and a train wreck is in the offing.

A certain letter I have received I will quote from but he shall remain anonymous. **"I was down in Air Ops observing the last recovery on the previous day and I was privy to the argument between the Air Officer and the Air Ops Officer. Commander Stollenwerk wanted to cancel the last event and complained to _____ about the senseless pace of operations just to prove that Enterprise could hack the program. I'll never forget Stolle's comment to the effect; "What are you going to tell the Board of Inquiry after a few people get knocked off because you're pushing them too hard."**

I guess you would have to consider that another factor. The simple fact that these air operations go on around the clock with no mishaps is amazing considering what has happened. Chalk that up to dedication by the crew and a testament to the reliability of the youth of our Country. The weapons in use back in those days were another factor. I was told by pilots that those Zuni rockets caused far more damage to our side than they ever did to the enemy. There must have been millions of them in warehouses left over from World War Two and Korea because every attack aircraft carried eight of them in addition to a store of bombs on all three WESTPAC cruises I was on from '66 to '69. The pilots had to dive on target and hold their course to aim those rockets and it was playing Russian Roulette flying into the teeth of radar directed AAA. Warheads and bombs of today are designed so that they cannot explode in a high order detonation from flame or heat. That was not the case in '69.

At this time I think it appropriate to insert this letter. **"I, too, was aboard Enterprise on 14 January, 1969. It was my third deployment to Yankee Station. I was a Lieutenant serving as Electronics Evaluations Officer in the Integrated Operations Intelligence Center (IOIC). We were located on the 03 level just aft of mid ship. I performed evaluations on the miles of tapes recovered from the Passive Electronics Counter measures cans in the back of the RA-5C Vigilantes.**

This information was used to locate active SAM sites and fire control AA batteries in order to give our guys a better chance.

I was in IOIC when the first explosion occurred. The overhead of our spaces was the flight deck. Underneath was the Hangar Bay. No one had to describe the aircraft loaded with JP-5 and ordnance parked on our roof, the aircraft in the Hangar Bay, or the locations and contents of the magazines. The sound of the first explosion made it clearly evident that this was not a drill.

Our Battle Station assignments were to take care of the classified materials as best we could and secure the spaces. At one time we had explosions on the flight deck above and fire in the Hangar Bay below. Everyone was busy performing their tasks in silence for nothing needed to be said. Some provided assistance to the medics by taking care of the wounded and later provided blood. Our Division was indeed fortunate. Our spaces just happened to be far enough forward that we did not receive direct hits. Others aft on the 03 level were not as fortunate.

Everyone on board had been pushed hard by the ORI team. It is my recollection that we recovered the last aircraft at approximately 0130 on the morning of the 14th with a scheduled 0600 launch. Personally, I got 45 minutes sleep after performing electronic analysis from the previous days flights and preparing for the 6AM launch. I mention this because I was not an exception. My 45 minutes nap was typical of everyone on the ship. Subsequent to the fire, we calculated that if the young huffer driver participated in the last recovery operations and performed his duties on his assigned aircraft, he could not have hit the rack until 0300. Therefore, if he did not shower, have a midnight meal or breakfast nor go to the head, the most sleep he could possibly receive was one hour.

Your book revived some old memories. After consciously repressing the fire, the three combat cruises to Viet Nam, and both the civil and political turmoil in the US, three key truths remain.

First, the landing camera located in the angle deck was activated immediately after the first explosion. The film demonstrated uncommon valor by the members of the flight deck crews. There were a few key men in different colored jerseys that led the charge. Rank nor rate did not seem to matter that day. Leadership and honor were the keys to saving the ship. You have captured that spirit in your book.

Second, it did not have to happen. I hold no animosity towards the young huffer driver. However, if you can remember the name of FLTRANGRU and find his address, I will be happy to personally send him a copy of your book so he can place it on his nightstand for the rest of his life. History teaches us that you can only push men, equipment and ordnance for so long before something blows.

Third, there is only one book that I have saved for my children to try to understand what we were doing there. The name is, "On Strategy", by Green. He was an artillery officer that took the twelve cannons of warfare and performed a detailed analysis of each indicating where "we" (the American people) went wrong. Succinctly stated, the war was lost in the newsrooms and in the halls of Congress – not on the battlefields or in the air. It is the only book I have found worth reading about the political side of the war.

Again, thanks for sending me the book and for a vivid and detailed account of a day that will live forever in the minds of the men who were there, and in United States Naval History.

Today we have a 1969 Enterprise Fire Group made up of over 400 shipmates and relatives. This Group owes its existence to Mike Neville, formerly a Plane Captain with VA-146. Mike was with us on the flight deck for our fire that day and he became the driving force that formed our Group. He put together our first reunion at Pearl Harbor and subsequent reunions in Washington, DC. , Norfolk, VA, and Seattle Washington. I will let Mike provide the details. Following this are some accounts that I think are necessary to give a larger picture to our story. It must be remembered that there were 5,600 of us on the ship that day but also hundreds of others who were involved ashore, in the air and afloat and each one has a story to tell.

As of this writing of TRIAL there have been three thousand copies in circulation of the first two editions. I did this myself having advertised in a few magazines the first few years. This was entirely too expensive for a one man band like me so I gave that up and put up a website on the internet at www.enterprisefire.com. I have sold all of these books out of my basement and hand carried each one to the Post Office to mail. I have sold these books in every NATO Country along with many other points of the globe. Since I get most of my orders through my website I also get very many messages from those who order after they have read the book. I don't think I have ever received anything negative about it. I do know that TRIAL has been used as a teaching tool for creative writing in two college literature classes because the teachers wrote and told me so. The long, hard road had some exhilarating moments.

There has been a lot of badmouthing of Vietnam Veterans over the years. Whenever Hollywood needed a bad guy or someone deranged he was usually portrayed as a misfit Vietnam Veteran. It is not so bad for us now because we have a couple of other wars under our belts and Hollywood has new targets to castigate. Now the focus has been shifted to Bosnia, Iraq and now Afghanistan Veterans as the new crazed bad guys. Always remember that those doing the portrayals and the bad mouthing have never placed themselves into harms way other than college protest marches, as if that took courage. Then my generation had to endure the proclamation that the All Volunteer Military of today is far superior to what we had in Vietnam. It is said to be superior in talent and dedication to those forces of yesteryear. Again, this is a slap at Vietnam Veterans but I have to take this opportunity to clarify certain things. To satisfy rising demand for half a million soldiers during the Vietnam war, draft notices were sent out to young men a month after graduating high school along with those who did not graduate. Any young man who was going to jail, court or showed up on the unemployment rosters was immediately drafted. The demand was so great that men were put into uniform who would have been turned away in later years. I think my shipmates on Enterprise and V-4 Division in particular, were a microcosm of the makeup of the entire Armed Forces of the day.

What an assemblage! We had roughnecks, rednecks and black militants. We had city wise guys and country boys along with dropouts and college grads. Some were hard to understand and some could hardly read and write. We had everything this country had to offer and it was quite an eye opener. But I will tell you what we did not have. We did not have many cowards. Most of those had found ways of avoiding military service and college deferments were the preferred way of getting out of it, like one of our former Presidents had. And then, a lot of them went on to be war protesters which caused a lot of grief for our own people in uniform along with a like measure of elation for our enemies. I believe it was Colonel Harry Summers, US Army Historian , who wrote of the Vietnam War and he said, "All throughout the entire course of the war no organized fighting unit down to a squad level ever surrendered, on either side." The statement is as profound as the fact. There was no surrender on Enterprise in 1969 just as there is no surrender for our forces that fight today. To submit to the enemy is to accept certain execution. I believe the days of chivalry died out a long time ago. With that I will end this chapter with an ode to those of my generation that it fits. We are beginning to die off ourselves so I wanted to include this ode that I wrote a long time ago.

We were the Battling Bastards of Vietnam.

We were rocketed, mortared and spit upon

We were ambushed, booby trapped and faced every hardship.

Then were scorned, maligned and handed bags of dog shit.

We sacrificed. We suffered. We fought hand to hand.

We flew. We sailed. We obeyed every command.

Abandoned, betrayed, we had no political aspirations.

We bled, we died, for the honor of our generation.

And we were the only ones who gave a Goddamn.

What I would like to do now is to include some of the more profound letters that have been sent to me. These people will have to remain anonymous because I do not want to compromise their privacy so I will just write out some of these letters and edit where necessary. This one is a favorite of mine written by a Sailor after he had read one of the books that were in the ships library.

"I am stationed aboard the USS Enterprise and I have just finished reading your book. The reason that I am writing is two fold. The first to tell you that I could not put that book down for a minute. I was riveted to each and every page. I know many of the spaces and areas of the flight deck that you described. The descriptions you gave were so graphic and real that I honestly did feel I was on deck at 0819 on 14 January 1969. It was truly a great book. I did not realize until after I had read the book that you were the crewleader. I believe that was your intent, right?

The second reason that I write this letter to you is a bit more extensive. I transferred to Enterprise in '92 from USS Iwo Jima LPH-2, Enterprise was in the yards and we all worked very hard. Some days it seemed the work would never end. Being a sea going Sailor I came to have a very bad attitude towards this ship. I would say things less than becoming of any person with half an upbringing. The more I read your book the more conscientious I became. Many times it is not the place where you work it is your attitude that determines how you perceive something. You and your fellow Sailors fought and died for this ship because you believed in it more than anything. I will never know how it felt to be on deck that day but I do know that each time I look at this ship now I look at it with a different set of eyes. The truth you spoke of is a terrible thing and I am glad that you saw and were able to tell others. Anyway, I transfer. I just wanted you to know that your book inspired a feeling I have not felt in a long time. Thank you for sharing your experience. This is truly a great ship."

That Sailor took the time to write to me and in doing so he gave to me a priceless gift, straight from his heart. That is one of the many rewards that I have had. Next we have one from a civilian whose father was a Navy man in the Pacific in World War Two. "**I do not normally sit and write letters but your book had such a profound effect on me that I had to send you this. I am a 40 year old US Airways pilot and have never been in the Military but I fly with men and women who were and many are Naval Aviators who have flown hundreds of missions over Southeast Asia. I am a History buff and was also aware of the Enterprise tragedy of 1969 so I had to buy your book. I was not prepared for the emotional roller coaster you were about to put me on!**

What an incredible story of unselfish duty, honor and courage! Men who had to know in their hearts that they were about to die for their Ship and Shipmates, stepped up to the plate without hesitation! Those men who stood with you, many of whom did die, are great Americans and true heroes. Without this sacrifice many more would surely have died and possibly the Enterprise lost forever.

Now, I can't even pretend to know, or even understand what an event like this would be like. But I would like to believe that I can at least appreciate the Honor,

courage and sacrifice. I will freely admit that I had tears rolling down my cheeks many times as I read TRIAL. I have the greatest respect for you and the men who stood with you that day"

And now here is one written to me in 1997 by a man who sat on the Board of Investigation and I will not include any rank or initials to keep him anonymous but he will know who he is if he reads this. **"It will have been almost 30 years since the experience of the horror of your excellent book, "TRIAL" occurred. I was moved to tears many times as you related the facts of the Enterprise ordeal in its pages. My duty assignment was to Naval Air Systems Command Representative Pacific. My specific task was to investigate and help solve the many weapons systems problems that then existed in Naval Air Weapons Systems.**

Previous to the Enterprise situation I had made a trip to Yankee Station to investigate problems with the Bullpup Missile System. While on Yankee Station I had visited all of the Carriers then operating in WESTPAC. The last Carrier I visited was Forrestal, in fact, I had departed Forrestal on the morning COD to Subic Bay. Upon arriving at Subic, we were told that the Forrestal ordeal had begun within the hour of my departure from her.

Upon my arrival back in the states I made a trip to Washington, DC, to report to NAVAIR my findings. The Bullpup Missile should be removed from the Carriers. The problem was its design features were outdated, and was not suited for the environment that it was being used in. I was then assigned to investigate a problem that the Marine Corps was having with the 2.75 rockets. As a result of that investigation, I recommended pulling both the 2.75 and the 5 inch HVAR rockets from Naval service.

You must understand that change comes hard to the Military establishment. The Navy especially since money was tight and replacing complete systems was very costly. The Bullpup was removed from service but I had not been completely successful with the rockets. The Bullpup had an operational problem when over the

target. The rockets were another problem. They were designed when the use of electrical power on aircraft was at a premium. Therefore, the amperage requirements for fuse ignition had to be very low. Also, there were no high powered RADARS on Carriers at the time of these designs. The Forrestal ordeal was caused by that design flaw in rocket motor ignition. Increasing the amperage requirements for rocket motor ignition would have prevented the Forrestal fire.

In any event, I was assigned to the Enterprise Board of Investigation and arrived on the ship the morning after the fire. I was charged to fix blame for the fire and there were no restraints placed on my part in the Investigation. We already knew from the Squadron load list and testimony from crew members that the culprit was a 5 inch HVAR war head and I reported that I believed the absolute cause of the fire was equipment design. Cause was discussed and voted on by the Board and it was agreed. And that it would be recommended that Naval Air Systems Command re-design the huffer exhaust to preclude a reoccurrence of this problem on other Carriers.

It was my belief then and it is my belief now, that time was the critical element in any action that could have been taken to stop the circumstances that led to the initial explosion. Once a fuse or warhead is hot enough to change the metal color, there will be an explosion. There can be no action taken by man to prevent it. Even if there had been time to put water on it, the water would only concentrate and drive the heat onto the explosive content of the warhead or fuse. I was aware that there was only honor among the brave hero's of Enterprise. Thank you for your excellent book and the proud reminders of the men of character that serve in the US Navy."

Now I am going to take the reader into a deeper emotional plane. This next letter was from a young widow who was only married for a short time before her young man died in our fight that day. I am including this because she is representative of all of the relatives of our dead and this letter is as profound to me now as it was when I received it. I know this book will be read by a lot of our survivors from the Enterprise fight and I wanted all readers to consider the words of this fine Lady.

"After seeing the Discovery Channel special about the fires and explosions on the USS Enterprise in May, I was disappointed to learn that I could not get a copy of the book, "TRAIL, Ordeal of the USS Enterprise". My husband, Joe W. Oates, V-1 Division, died in that ordeal and I wanted to know what it was like for him that morning. However, by the grace of God, Commander Gary Lawn, who served with him from basic training to the Big E (and flew in to be a pall bearer for his military funeral), visited Joe's mother and had a copy of the book. She told him that I wanted one and today I received in the mail an autographed copy of TRIAL by Michael Joe Carlin, "In Memory of Little Joe." I have just finished reading it. I want to thank you for remembering and honoring all those who served and fought so valiantly the fires and explosions of that devastating Tuesday morning, January 14, 1969. It is a healing balm for me.

I wrote the Navy in 1969 requesting specifics of how Joe died and all I received was a terse response stating that he died of injuries sustained in the fire aboard USS Enterprise. As if I didn't know that. I only wanted to know what he had experienced, what he saw, what he did. I wanted to know if anyone knew and cared that he died. I wanted to see his name written with care by someone who was his friend. I wanted him remembered. This book is a strange comfort to me. I love him deeply. The love never died.

I want to assure you that you not only did justice to the memory of all of our loved ones, you wrote an

EXCELLENT NOVEL. THE FACTS MIXED WITH THE LEGEND AND THE LEGION WERE A PERFECT COMBINATION TO HANDLE A DIFFICULT, HAUNTING AND TRAGIC EXPERIENCE. I WAS NOT AT ALL REPULSED BY YOUR DELICATE AND CREATIVE HANDLING OF THE HORRIFIC DETAILS. YOU WROTE WITH AN EXPOSED HEART AND A MODEST ACCOUNT OF YOUR OWN ACTIONS. THANK YOU AGAIN FOR WRITING THIS BOOK. I KNOW THAT IT IS IMPOSSIBLE FOR ME TO EVEN IMAGINE WHAT IT MUST HAVE COST YOU EMOTIONALLY, MENTALLY AND PHYSICALLY TO PUT ALL OF THIS INTO WORDS. BUT THROUGH YOUR EFFORTS YOU HAVE BROUGHT HEALING. PARTS OF THE BOOK SUCH AS THE BEAUTY OF THE NIGHT SKY ON JANUARY 13TH LINGER IN MY MIND AND I AM THANKFUL THAT THEIR LAST NIGHT WAS A BEAUTIFUL DISPLAY OF GOD'S CREATION. I KNOW THAT YOU CARE FOR ALL OF THOSE THAT YOU WROTE ABOUT. YOU DO THEM ALL HONOR WITH YOUR WORDS."

I had been in contact with the family of Joe Wheeler Oates of V-1 Division for a number of years. This was chiefly because of Joe's older sister, O'Clair. She had written to me and told me the story of how Joe had married his childhood sweetheart when he came home on Boot Camp leave. He had joined the Navy with his friend, Gary Lawn, and they went to Boot Camp together and both had gotten orders to Enterprise together. After the fire Gary Lawn escorted Joe's body back home to his family for burial. Lawn then went on to make a career out of the Navy and retired as a Commander. He wanted to have his retirement ceremony aboard Enterprise, which was in Norfolk, VA. , at the time. In arranging the details of the ceremony he was talking with his counterpart, Commander Rick Gile, Weapons Officer and third in Command on Enterprise. During the conversation in the Weapons Officers office it was disclosed that Commander Lawn was aboard Enterprise during the '69 Fire. At that Commander Gile produced from his desk a copy of TRIAL and Lawn asked if he could borrow it. Afterwards he contacted me and also showed the book to the family of Joe Wheeler Oates. Commander Lawn told me he wanted to get a posthumous award to present to the family and asked me for a qualifying statement. I did this and also contacted Henry Mendoza who was Joe Oates ' superior in V-1 Division and asked him to do the same. Henry wrote a statement to the effect that Oates was a Fly One director and was struck down in the Fly Three area proving that he was in the fight. My statement, supported by documents, was that by the very nature of his wounds it was clear that Joe Wheeler Oates was struck down facing the fight.

Commander Lawn took these statements and walked the issue through the various Navy offices to get the results he set out to do. Sometime later I received a VHS tape in the mail. I viewed it and it was a recording of the ceremony in which Commander Lawn read an official statement from the Navy recognizing the courage of Joe Wheeler Oates during fire and explosions aboard USS Enterprise on 14 January, 1969. Joe's parents were standing there along with his sisters and at the end of reading the statement Commander Lawn presented the Navy/Marine Corps Medal, the highest award given for a non-combat situation, to the mother of Joe Oates. Upon accepting the medal she was immediately overcome. So was I. It was a heart rending scene. She had been given a little something of her long lost son. This is one of the rewards that have come from writing the book about our Enterprise fire.

"I had been standing at the entrance to Sick Bay with the surgeon and another corpsman. I helped a casualty into the surgery room and onto the operating table while the surgeon got ready. This man lost his leg. I then ran for additional surgical supplies for the surgeon and was fortunate to locate a corpsman who knew exactly what I needed. Only the day before, the 13th, the surgeon and I were talking and comparing casualty treatment sea stories. I remember telling him that I had trained at one of the largest trauma centers in the United States and had worked in the emergency room and on the streets of Atlanta for two years. He knew about the trauma center and said he was concerned about his loss of skills due to the lack of cases. The next day he asked me to get him some suture gut for the casualties. Fortunately, the ship had the same material we used at Grady Memorial Hospital. I started to set up the surgical tray for him while he got ready. Once he was into surgery, I only had time to go back into the surgery room twice more. I was overloaded on the ward and in the passageways.

As crewmen were brought into Sick Bay, I would examine each patient and initially I tried to start fluids myself but was missing the veins due to my own lack of recent experience. The patients needed fluids. I asked for the lab technician who became immediately available. I then asked the lab technician to start fluids on all of those soaked in blood. He appeared especially happy to get to work. Fluids were also started on others who were losing their blood pressure. Many had to remain in the passageway as there was no room in Sick Bay. The crew were treated as they sat. Moving one from the deck of the passageway to Sick Bay only meant moving them to the deck inside. I spent a lot of time removing battle dressings, a redo patch job to control the bleeders and set any broken bones. I asked for the sick call corpsman who had some experience with seeing real blood. He stayed with me for a short lesson and then went out on his own to do likewise.

Medical was overloaded. Many of the crew had unknown's regarding their internal wounds. Shrapnel could be anywhere, internal bleeding was an unknown. Each patient needed advanced medical attention. Time was critical. At Grady Memorial Hospital our average response time was about 15 minutes. Six critical care rooms operated around the clock as needed. The ship needed more than this and it did not exist. The application of battle dressings was superb. We were working hard to control and stop all bleeding and other wounds. Calming the treatment teams was another task. Many crewmen had penetration wounds from shrapnel. It was unknown what the degree of damage was internally. Some burned patients were expected to have shrapnel wounds under their now cauterized skin. Armando Limon had third degree burns everywhere and was nearing death. He and many others were in painful agony. Extensive burns are probably the most severe form of injury to which the crew were exposed. One pilot was struggling just to breath. His nylon torso harness was melted over his flight suit and had hardened. The death or survival of these men was going to depend on the severity of the burn and the incidence of complications such as severe infection or respiratory tract injury during the days or weeks after. We needed the seriously wounded flown ashore. Time was critical.

I was ordered to come up to the bridge by a Captain from FLTRANGRU to give him a status report. Although just an LT. at the time I actually had an argument with him about the need to push aircraft over the side to make way for helicopters. There was a little shouting and he remarked about the risk of landing helo's on a crowded flight deck. He asked questions and then more discussion. I think we both were more than excited. Indeed, there was some risk in conducting MEDEVACs. I did not know that at that very moment USAF pilots were in a pattern and expressed reservations about coming aboard. The main point is that the patients needed surgical attention. There was a risk of movement but the risk of letting them bleed to death internally was unconscionable. I was fortunate to have had an avid listener. Many patients were evacuated. However, I never knew the extent until I read your book."

At this point I am going to include letters I received from two F-4 Pilots. One was from VF-96 and the other from VF-92. I did not have much to represent the pilots when writing the book so I wanted to include these at this time. I really wish I could identify these guys but since these letters were written several years ago and I have no permission I cannot reveal their names. Some of you out there will probably know who these gentlemen are.

"Understandably, most of your narrative concerns the port side of the flight deck. This was where most of the firefighting effort was concentrated and was the area which received the largest holes in the armor plated deck. Maybe I can offer additional information and insight into what went on in the area to starboard.

On page 212 there are a couple of photographs showing the position of the huffer relative to the LAU-10 pod on Showtime 105. The parallel lines labeled shrapnel pattern show the reflection angle of the blast. If you examine this in connection with the diagram on page 70, you can see that this shrapnel pattern was directed at the 300 gallon external fuel tank on the port wing of my bird. This is further supported by your text where on page 45 you wrote that Captain Lee took a quick look at the holocaust developing on the fantail: "...Aircraft 105 was completely engulfed and fire was under 103 on the starboard side."

This is how it looked from my perspective. Since I was flight leader, my aircraft was the first to be started. At the time 105s rockets cooked off, I had completed all of the cockpit checks and was looking across the deck in the direction of the waist catapults. I heard a loud pop, like a large dropped light bulb would sound, and a loud thump against the drop tank. Instantly, my canopy was covered with a translucent frosting. Something was wrong, but since this live ordnance flight was a major event in the ORI, I hesitated for a few seconds to verify that there was a legitimate reason to cancel the flight. Engine instruments showed everything to be operating and there were no abnormal warning lights. My RIO was not talking to me because he was busy bugging out. Nonetheless, I made the decision to shut down. To Hell with the ORI grade!. I deliberately brought each throttle back around the horn and switched off the radios and engine master. In my peripheral vision, I saw the white frosted canopy suddenly turn to chocolate brown and then to a liquid pumpkin orange. The canopy was melting because Showtime 103 was on fire!

My immediate reaction was to use the Martin-Baker ejection seat. I sat erect and reached for the face curtain with both hands. But just before pulling the curtain handles, I saw that the starboard side of the canopy was transparent and there was no visible fire upwind. I felt I might have over-reacted and decided to climb out of the aircraft normally. I undid the rocket jet fittings and released the leg restraints to detach myself from the ejection seat.

I actuated the pneumatic control to open the canopy and for the first time, realized that this was no drill. An intense wall of flames surrounded the airplane and it looked like the only escape route would be over the side into the water.

As I stood up, my oxygen hose was still attached and I had to sit back down again to undo the safety lock release. Standing up again, I climbed out onto the starboard canopy rail and dropped forward to the flight deck ten feet below landing on all fours.

I looked up and saw my plane captain, Airman Bill Skinner, standing in front of the plane with his hands covering his face. His fuel soaked jersey was on fire and he was completely stunned. I pulled him by his arm and said, "Come on, Skinner, we are going swimming!"

As we moved to the edge of the deck, it was obvious that he was bleeding and the thought of sharks changed my plans of jumping over the side. At the deck edge I wrapped my arms around him in a bear hug to smother the flames. My Nomex suit and gloves were fire resistant and fortunately the flames went out in just a few seconds. I took off my gloves and swatted the burning remnants of his brown flight deck jersey.

About five steps down the catwalk ladder was a door leading to the 03 level at approximately frame 245. A Sailor wearing dungarees whose name I never knew, opened the door and asked, "What's going on?" I told him to grab Skinners legs and I reached around his chest to support him from behind. Together, we carried him down the ladder and into the small athwartships passageway on the 03 level.

Inside, we laid Skinner down and assessed the situation. He kept protesting that there were others on the flight deck who were worse off than he was. I assured him that we would take care of them and not to worry. Three or four other Sailors appeared and I sent them to find a stretcher.

Suddenly, the passageway filled with thick, greasy black smoke. Burning JP-5 was pouring over the deck edge scupper and dripping through the open door. My companions and I closed and sealed the door. Shortly thereafter, the smoke cleared and the Sailors returned with a stokes litter. I don't know where they found it but it was filled with a hundred feet or so of half inch line and I cut the line away with my survival knife.

It was just about this time that the ordnance from my burning aircraft began a series of explosions directly over our heads. Each time we were lifted about three feet into the air and slammed back down onto the steel deck again. Shrapnel ricocheted around the steel bulkheads and as the metal fragments spent their energy, another, then another, and yet another weapon exploded perhaps three or four seconds apart.

Obviously, the relative sanctity of our passageway compartment was compromised and it was time to move on. The Sailors each grabbed a corner of the stretcher and moved forward in the main passageway on the starboard side of the 03 level. As we moved forward, Sailors in the arresting gear spaces were hunkering down beneath the arresting engines. I told them to forget General Quarters stations and evacuate the area. This seemed like good sense to them and they joined our little party.

Continuing forward our progress was blocked by Sailors wanting to move aft to help fight the fire. This was a futile endeavor because there was no way that they could get to the flight deck. We were able to reverse the flow and soon we had a parade of troops moving forward with the stretcher bearers leading the way.

One last thought. Everyone aboard Enterprise was a survivor of the fire and the courageous connotation of this became a career enhancing ticket. For political purposes, the Navy had to prove that Enterprise could not be put out of action because of the fire. The accident had to be quickly forgotten and it was important that the ship continue westward to put in an appearance in the combat zone even though her capability was severely limited.

Allowing you and your shipmates to fight this holocaust barehanded was unconscionable. Enterprise Sailors manning the hoses were every bit as courageous as the soldier who covers a grenade with his body to save his buddies. In combat, the Army usually recognizes this self-sacrificing act with the Medal of Honor. The leadership should have recognized the effort made by the flight deck crew with a plaque or mural listing the names of the individuals that fought the fire. It is senseless to honor just the dead, for they were only the victims. The crew that saved the ship survived.

Bill Skinner was a lucky guy. He was hospitalized with 3rd degree burns over 40% and shrapnel wounds over his entire body. He healed rapidly and rejoined VF-96 when we made our last port call at Cubi Point.

And lastly, this letter from another F-4 pilot who was with us that day. This one was from VF-92. "I JUST FINISHED READING TRIAL; ORDEAL OF THE USS ENTERPRISE LAST WEEK AND FROM ONE OF THOSE WHO WAS ON THE SHIP AT THE TIME OF THE FIRE, I WAS MOST IMPRESSED AND MOVED BY YOUR WRITING.

AS A MEMBER OF THE AIR WING WHO COULD JUST AS EASILY AS NOT BE AIRBORNE DURING ANY SHIPBOARD EMERGENCY, WE DID NOT HAVE SPECIFIC GENERAL QUARTERS DUTIES.

Our station was the Squadron Ready Room -- to keep out of the way. I happened to be in Ready Room Two as I recall, which was located on the 03 level at approximately frames 200 - 210, when the fire broke out. We were just beginning our briefing for the third event. The second event was preparing to launch and the first event was arriving overhead awaiting the conclusion of the launch. It became apparent quickly that we needed to evacuate the Ready Room when we saw the rapid progress of the fire on the PLAT monitor. We all went to the VF-96 Ready Room on the 03 level just aft of the "Dirty Shirt" wardroom.

I think that most of us who had no specific duties, while doing our best to stay out of the way of those who did, tried to contribute in some way. The wardroom near the bow was being utilized by medical personnel to treat some of the wounded and prepare some of those for airlift to Tripler. I tried to help by running for supplies (sheets, blankets, pillows, wraps, etc.) needed by the medics and doctors on the 03 level.

Until I read your book I never knew the "Big Picture" of what actually went on on the flight deck and hangar decks. Nor did I really understand the contribution and heroism of those on the USS Rogers. What was evident then, though, and has stayed with me since that day was the debt we all owed to those who responded to "The force of a simple Virtue...a common bond shared by all those who answered their Country's call to war and accepted the hardship and sacrifice as their duty." Very strong words, Sir, and SO well said.

Despite two subsequent cruises to Vietnam -- Enterprise '69 and America '70 with 120 combat

MISSIONS, 300 TRAPS, NEARLY 100 OF WHICH WERE AT NIGHT ETC, ETC, IT IS THE EVENT OF 14 JANUARY, 1969, ABOARD THE USS Enterprise THAT STAND OUT IN MY MIND AS A TESTAMENT TO THOSE IN UNIFORM.

THANK YOU FOR YOUR OUTSTANDING CHRONICLE OF THAT DAY.

Back in 2006 I read a short article in the Enterprise Association newsletter about the changes being made at Great Lakes Recruit Training Center. All of the Barracks were being rebuilt and now, each one was named for a famous Navy ship. Naturally, one of these Barracks - Ship 10 - was named USS Enterprise, honoring both CV-6 and CVN-65 along with the other six ships named Enterprise. Since there was an address in the article I started sending letters to the Training Center asking if I could donate some books of TRIAL. I received a reply from LT. Michael Essig, Group Commander, USS Enterprise -Ship 10 - Recruit Training Command. I sent him six books and told him I would get any pictures from the book blown up to size for his Quarterdeck and also a picture of the Virtue Mural if they had room for it. I received a few e-mail messages back and here is what LT. Mike Essig had to say.

Thank you again for your continued efforts in improving the quality of our training environment here at the USS ENTERPRISE-SHIP TEN. Your photographs are hanging on our Quarterdeck and Petty Officer Jefferies is doing a fine job creating a shrine to the 28 brave men who gave their lives that day. I can assure you that we will be sending you some pictures once the finishing touches are completed here very shortly. I also read a few passages from your book during our division commissioning's to hit home the importance of teamwork and the life-or-death conditions that these recruits could see in the fleet. I think your words went a long way to say what I could not.

For the Virtue Mural we were thinking about two pictures, one 24 inches wide by ?? high to maintain the proportions of the picture. This size was selected due to our limited wall space on the quarterdeck, and to pick a spot that would compliment the Enterprise fire pictures already hanging. If possible, we would also like a much larger picture five feet wide by ?? high of the Virtue Mural to hang on the back wall of the LCPO's office. This is the main counseling office in which recruits are individually trained and mentored by the ships Officer and LCPO. We think that this Mural would be a very powerful training tool to motivate our recruits that need assistance returning to the path of success. If this is possible we would really appreciate it.

Done as requested, and proudly so. Now our day of fire and steel is taught, learned and held high as a measure to live up to.

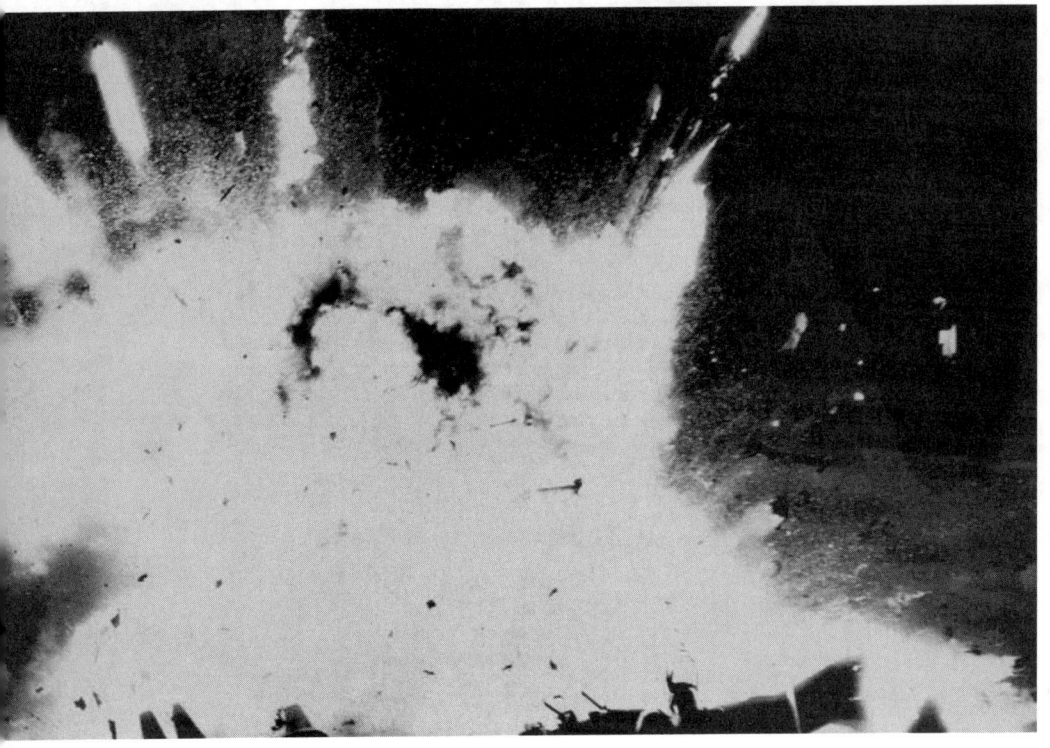

DEPARTMENT OF THE NAVY
RECRUIT TRAINING COMMAND
3301 INDIANA STREET
GREAT LAKES IL 60088-3127

22 December 2005

Michael J. Carlin
Tuscarora Press
P.O. Box 98
West Grove, PA 19390-0098

Dear Mr. Carlin,

Thank you very much for your generous donation of the three large photographs capturing the horrific images of the fire on board the USS ENTERPRISE. Your book Trial: Ordeal Of The USS ENTERPRISE 14 January, 1969 is a graphic and heroic account of this shipboard tragedy, and a testimony of the bravery and sacrifice of you and your shipmates.

Our mission here at Recruit Training Command is to transform civilians into Sailors, basically trained and ready to support the mission of the US Navy around the world. An integral part of that training is the "Battle Stations" phase, which teaches the combat of realistic casualty scenarios to test not only the recruits' knowledge but also their core values of Honor, Courage, and Commitment. Your story, and these photographs are an invaluable tool for teaching our recruits of the inherent dangers at sea.

Recruit Training Command is the quarterdeck of the NAVY. Our appearance and our facilities have a direct impact on the careers of our newest Sailors. The quarterdeck of SHIP TEN – USS ENTERPRISE is a showpiece decorated with the generous gifts of the Sailors and friends of CV-6 and CVN-65. Your donated photographs will bring the ordeal onboard the USS ENTERPRISE to life and honor the memory of those who gave the ultimate sacrifice for their nation, and their shipmates.

Respectfully yours,

Michael L. Moran
Captain, USN
Commanding Officer
Recruit Training Command

DEPARTMENT OF THE NAVY
OFFICE OF INFORMATION
1200 NAVY PENTAGON
WASHINGTON DC 20350-1200

IN REPLY REFER TO

1551
Ser MC00/329
6 Dec 99

The Honorable Joseph R. Pitts
Member, United States House of
  Representatives
P.O. Box 837
Unionville, PA 19375

Dear Mr. Pitts,

    Thank you for your inquiry of October 29, 1999, on behalf of your constituent, Mr. M. J. Carlin, regarding the training film, "*Trial by Fire: A Carrier Fights for Life.*"

    The film, "*Trial by Fire: A Carrier Fights for Life,*" produced in 1973, is a training film designed to ensure Sailors take shipboard fire fighting training seriously. The producer and scriptwriter of the film never intended for it to be used as a chronological documentary of the July 1967 fire aboard USS FORRESTAL (CVA 59). Consequently, the producer and scriptwriter, wishing to emphasize the horrors of fighting a fire at sea, used film and video footage from several shipboard files.

    Other scenes include those of fires aboard USS FRANKLIN (CV 13) in 1945 and USS ORISKANY (CVA 34) in 1966. USS ORISKANY can be identified by the wooden decking and by the modification to the starboard side elevator. And, of course, there are several scenes of the fire aboard USS ENTERPRISE (CVAN 65) in January 1969. These scenes were identified by your constituent, Mr. Carlin.

    Selected scenes from all four tragedies were combined to create dynamic sequences, which were needed to drive home the film's message to the target audience. This compositing method was, and still is today, a common practice when producing motivational and training films or videotapes. The narration, which accompanies the composited sequences, clearly identifies the mistakes made by USS FORRESTAL's crew. At no time does it defile the men of USS ENTERPRISE, USS ORISKANY or USS FRANKLIN. But, neither does it give proper credit to the courage and sacrifice of those brave crews.

    Despite its age of nearly 27 years, "*Trial by Fire: A Carrier Fights for Life,*" is probably the most widely viewed training film in the history of the United States Navy. Because the film's message is still valid today, requests for videotape copies of the film are still being filled. But, because of its age, the film has, likewise, been declared to be in the public domain and has been cleared for public exhibition and sale.

Unfortunately, there is nothing that Naval Media Center can do to change the thousands of motion picture prints and video tape copies which have already been distributed or sold. Naval Media Center can, however, make a corrected videotape master from which all future copies can be made. A graphical message will be edited onto the close of the video master stating that the fire fighting scenes used in this training film are comprised of footage from four separate carrier fires: USS FRANKLIN in 1945; USS ORISKANY in 1966; USS FORRESTAL in 1967; and USS ENTERPRISE in 1969. The Navy wishes to recognize the heroism and sacrifices made by those crews as they faced their *Trial by Fire*." Master duplication tapes will then be made from the primary master tape and sent to the Navy Library in Norfolk, VA, the Department of Defense Joint Visual Information Agency in Tobyhanna, PA, and the National Archives in College Park, MD.

Again, I appreciate your taking the time to share Mr. Carlin's concerns on this issue. If I can be further assistance, please let me know.

Sincerely,

THOMAS J. JURKOWSKY
Rear Admiral, U.S. Navy
Chief of Information

This is the Quarterdeck display of ship Number 10, USS Enterprise, In Recruit Training Center, Great Lakes, Illinois. These pictures are held as inspirations to the new reruits

Magnificent "VIRTUE MURAL" painted by PhotoMate 2nd Class, Alan Warner, aboard the USS Enterprise

ISSUE IN DOUBT. High Tide of the Fury. It was at this point that our Captain Lee phoned down to Damage Control and asked Engineering Officer, Commander Bill Neel, if he was going to lose his ship. Neel responded, "Not on my watch!"

USS ROGERS crosses our wake as Enterprise continues its turn to port and is already coming into the wind.

Tense moments for the ROGERS crew as their ship closes on the burning Carrier.

ROGERS draws abreast as a major detonation shakes the Destroyer with a wave of concussion. Hang on Sailor! You're going where they are going.

Photos Courtesy of Dan Reick

Explosion on the starboard side carries burning fuel and metals high aloft.

At this point all fireighting stations and gear aft of this new team forming on the angle has been destroyed and overtaken by the advancing tide of burning fuel.

In this picture crew two of the purpleshirts are just forward of the starboard wing of #310 putting their mate, Asbury, into the Stokes hard wire stretcher.

Blast sweeps the flight deck with a storm of flame and steel. Those standing exposed, as you see here, were added to the steadily rising numbers of casualties as the fight went on and on.

This is the Crewleader of crew two of the purpleshirts during the 1968 WestPac cuise to Yankee Station.

ECHOES OF THE CATACLYSM

Mike Neville VA-146

When I was eleven years old, living in the high desert of rural northern Nevada, I read about the commissioning of the first nuclear powered aircraft carrier, the USS Enterprise. It was at that moment that I thought that I would join the Navy when I grow up and serve aboard that ship, as only an eleven-year-old can dream. I did in fact join the Navy after high school graduation and, while my interest in aviation drove me to strike for ratings that would likely place me on a carrier, I had no reason to believe that I would actually serve aboard the Enterprise. But as fate would have it, my first duty station out of boot camp was VA-146, an A-7 squadron of Carrier Air Wing 9, deployed aboard the USS Enterprise.

As an air wing sailor rather than part of ship's company, I only made one cruise on Enterprise, a West Pac deployment in 1969. Our primary area of operation was the Tonkin Gulf off the coast of Vietnam, although in April of that year we steamed to the Sea of Japan as the flagship of Task Force 71, responding to the North Korean downing of an American EC-121 electronic surveillance aircraft. Prior to deploying to the combat area, our carrier group underwent an Operational Readiness Inspection (ORI) off the Hawaiian Islands. On the second day of this exercise, 14 January, 1969, Enterprise suffered a catastrophic series of flight deck explosions and fire that reached to the waterline, resulting in twenty-eight deaths and over 350 wounded.

I would defer to Mike Carlin for a thorough account of the events leading up to the fire, the courageous struggle to save the ship and our shipmates, and the subsequent investigation into the causes. Mike was a member of V-4 Division (responsible for fueling the aircraft) at the time of the fire and like so many of us who were on the flight deck at the time, was seriously involved in this struggle. Mike has done extensive research on the fire and in 1993 published a riveting book on the subject, Trial: Ordeal Of The USS Enterprise. That having been said, here is what I personally experienced:

At the time of the fire, I was an eighteen-year-old airman apprentice in VA-146, assigned to the ordnance shop. We were responsible for the loading of bombs, missiles, rockets, and guns on A-7 light attack aircraft and maintenance of their weapons delivery systems. That morning I was specifically assigned to an arming crew. Our job was to install arming fuses in the bombs once they had been loaded onto the aircraft. We were working on an aircraft on the starboard side aft of the island and were just finishing up when the first explosion hit, across the deck probably thirty yards away. The concussion drove me to the deck with unbelievable force. While regaining my feet and still not comprehending what had happened, a second explosion put me flat on the deck again.

The fire and explosions having begun on the aft port area of the flight deck, everyone's natural reaction was to run forward, which I did. By the time I arrived roughly abreast of the island, the entire aft section of the flight deck was engulfed. At this point many of us began downloading thousands of pounds of live ordnance from the aircraft on the flight deck while firefighting teams deployed. The process of removing the ordnance from aircraft and throwing it overboard was a true testament to the power of adrenaline. Normally, loading (or unloading) a 500-pound bomb required four crewmen. In many cases half that many were stripping the bombs from their wing stations and tossing them in the ocean. After all of the unexploded ordnance had been disposed of, I joined a fire hose team until we secured from general quarters.

Over the years as I have looked back on that day I continue to be amazed by the randomness of the shrapnel. There were six of us arming the plane when the explosions began, congregated in an area of probably 100 square feet. Three were hit with shrapnel, one, Larry Goble, very seriously, and the other three of us came out of it virtually unscathed. After viewing PLAT camera footage of the explosions I am amazed that anyone escaped injury.

Prior to 2002 I was unaware that Mike Carlin had written his book or that in 2000 the Discovery Channel had produced a documentary on the fire based upon Mike's book and incorporating many of fire veterans referred to in his book. One day in early 2002 a co-worker came to me and told me about the Discovery Channel documentary he had seen the night before. In an effort to obtain a video copy of the documentary on the Internet I came across Carlin's website on which I discovered and ordered his book.

After reading Mike's book I began to communicate with him via e-mail. We decided that it would be a good idea to have a reunion of all who were aboard Enterprise that day. I jumped right in and coordinated a three-day reunion at Pearl Harbor surrounding January 14, 2004, the 35th anniversary of the fire. This reunion included a memorial service on the fantail of the USS Missouri. It was an emotional but extremely rewarding event for all hands.

In attendance at the 2004 reunion were the widows and other family members of three of those lost in the fire. Each of these ladies, and other widows and family members who have been contacted since that time have expressed their disappointment in the absence of their loved ones' names on the Vietnam Wall. This issue, a circumstance that I have referred to as an accident of geography, prompted me to pursue an alternative venue to memorialize our lost shipmates. I found the US Navy Memorial's Commemorative Plaque Wall in Washington, DC to be an ideal choice. I put it to our shipmates to raise the necessary funds for two plaques memorializing the fire and honoring the twenty-eight who died. We secured the funds and commissioned the plaques. We planned our next reunion to coincide with the plaque dedication ceremony in Washington, DC.

While I was working on the fire plaque project, U.S. Navy Memorial Director of Planned Giving, Paul T. Haley pointed out that there was not a plaque commemorating the USS Enterprise CVA(N)-65 and that if one could be commissioned in a timely fashion, it could be appropriately placed adjacent to the fire plaques. I immediately contacted USS Enterprise Association Chairman Chas Folcik who charged ahead securing the commission of the ship's plaque in time to join the fire plaques on the Commemorative Wall. By this point, the dedication of the fire plaques had already been set for October 6, 2006 and it was agreed that the dedication of the ship's plaque would be incorporated into that ceremony. While this was done essentially for convenience sake, it turned out to have significantly enhanced the impact of the dedication ceremony. The combined dedication was a prime example of the whole being greater than the sum of its parts. Because Enterprise was at sea at the time of the dedication, her representation was limited but impressive. Speaking on behalf of the ship was CTOC Karl Parsons. Also in attendance were Jan Rice and Terrie DeClercq, the wives of Enterprise CO Larry Rice and CMC Paul DeClercq. In addition to his comments, Chief Parsons presented a short video produced by the Enterprise crew. This video not only highlighted the Enterprise's forty-five years of honorable service, it honored the 1969 crew and surviving family members by speaking of the lessons learned, thanking them for saving the ship, and remembering their dead.

Representing the 1969 crew were over fifty shipmates and their families, two sailors from the USS Rogers, whose aid to Enterprise during the fire was crucial, and roughly forty family members of five of the twenty-eight. Speaking on behalf of the 1969 crew was retired VADM Kent Lee, Enterprise CO at the time of the fire, and speaking on behalf of the surviving families was Robert Pyeatt, father of LTJG Buddy Pyeatt who died in the fire. Clearly coming from the heart, their comments spoke personally and sincerely to those in attendance.

Rounding out the ceremony were the reading of the names and tolling of the ship's bell, beautiful renditions of the National Anthem and Navy Hymn by a barbershop quartet, and reading of Senate Resolution 569 honoring the ship and the losses from the fire. These segments were each conducted entirely or in part by fire veterans. The unexpected attendance of VCNO ADM Robert Willard added significantly to an already memorable experience and was appreciated by all hands.

In August 2009 we held our third reunion in Seattle, WA. While the previous reunions had been scheduled and located to accommodate the significant dates and/or locations, the third reunion was not so restrained. We wanted to choose a location on the West Coast so as to accommodate those shipmates who were unable to make the long trips necessary for the first two reunions. Ultimately I settled on Seattle because of the amount of help I would receive from shipmates living in the area.

The Seattle reunion was a simpler affair than the past reunions but we still included a memorial service in honor of our lost shipmates. This memorial service was conducted at the Seattle Museum of Flight at Boeing Field. In the furtherance of their educational goal the museum staff asked us to participate in a question and answer forum with the general public on the topic of the USS Enterprise fire. We agreed and staffed a discussion panel for this event following the memorial service. The event was coordinated with the selling of Mike Carlin's book and a book signing. This event proved to be a great success not only for the general public but for many of our shipmates and family members who still had questions or unresolved issues about the fire.

When I set out to organize that first reunion I had never done such a thing before. Using a variety of Internet sources I began locating and contacting shipmates who had been aboard Enterprise during the fire. By the time of the 2004 reunion I had located approximately 100 shipmates, half of whom were able to attend. The locating and contacting of new members is an ongoing process and to date we have 375 members in our group.

Early on, Len Cochran, who was the navigator on the bridge during the fire, volunteered to assist with the reunion preparation. He designed a reunion logo and set up a line of reunion apparel that he has made available for each reunion and other gatherings. He also spearheaded the commissioning of reunion mugs for the 2006 reunion. Len has attended all three reunions. He has been active in all of the memorial services and was one of the discussion panel members at the Seattle reunion.

Having organized the Pearl Harbor reunion on my own and entirely by long distance, I was inclined not to do another reunion unless I would be able to get assistance from shipmates living in or near the venue city. This proved to be no problem. In preparation for the 2006 reunion in Washington, DC I was ably assisted by Kathy Merendino, wife of shipmate King Merendino; Bill Neel, engineering officer during the fire; John Reisinger (now deceased), weapons officer during the fire; and Don Stoneman, VA-145. For the 2009 reunion in Seattle, WA I had the able assistance of Roy Duncan, Litton tech rep with VA-145; Rich Hawley, VF-96; and Russ Hendricks, Navigation.

When I set out to organize the first reunion I had no way of knowing if it would be successful and certainly was not thinking of it becoming a regular occurrence. But it has become something very special for me and for all of our shipmates. I only wish that I had begun this many years before I did and hope that I will be able to continue to do them for many years to come.

Address by VADM Kent L. Lee, USN (Ret)

USS Enterprise Fire Memorial Plaque Dedication

US Navy Memorial

Washington, DC

October 6, 2006

Thank you thank you. Thank you thank you. Admiral Willard, shipmates of Enterprise, families of shipmates, and friends of Enterprise. I'm delighted to be here today and to see you all again. And as Mike said earlier, these are hard acts to follow. But I would like to give you a little, a picture as I saw it from the bridge on January 14, 1969. But before I do that I would like to honor three men that played a key role on that day.

Number one was the Executive Officer, John Alvis, whose widow is here today and also whose son is here, Scott. He played a key role that day and in the days to follow when we were trying to put the pieces back together. Number two was Bill Neel, Rear Admiral William Neel, who is here today with his lovely wife, Colleen. And he managed Damage Control on that day and as you can imagine, it was a very key element in our winning the day in the end. Number three was Commander Stollenwerck, who was the Air Boss, and he ran the flight deck crews and fought the fire on the flight deck. And we lost that day twenty-eight of our wonderful shipmates but we also lost three hundred and forty-three injured, and most of them on the flight deck. When Commander Stollenwerck was organizing crew after crew to go in and fight this fire.

Now we knew almost immediately, when that first Zuni rocket went off, and I was in the sea cabin, which is just behind the bridge, at the time, and I immediately went out to the navigation bridge and looked aft and saw all that black smoke and fire, and I knew we were in trouble. So of course we went to General Quarters and turned the ship into the wind to blow the smoke and fire aft. But the shrapnel from that Zuni rocket punctured dozens and dozens of fuel tanks. We had about fifteen aircraft on the after part of the flight deck loaded with 500-pound bombs, ammunition, Zuni rockets, and the like. And the fire was so intense in a very short order that those 500-pound bombs cooked off, one after another, and blew big holes in that two-inch steel flight deck, into the 03 level, a berthing area. And the issue was in doubt for perhaps an hour, an hour and a half. Our goal was to keep the fire to the flight deck. In the meantime, streams of burning jet fuel were going over the side, carrying flames with them. But we believed that we could keep the fire to the flight deck, we could save the ship. And you might remember that we had about five thousand people on board. We flooded the hangar deck and sprayed water on all the hot bulkheads. And after about an hour, an hour and a half, we believed that we could save the ship and contain the fire to the flight deck. And in another hour or two why the fire had about burned itself out and had gotten so hot that magnesium and aluminum burned on the flight deck. But it was a day that all of us who were a part of it and witnessed it won't forget. We think of it almost every day. Thank you.

The Lone Sailor Article

On October 6, 2006, veterans of the 14 January 1969 fire aboard the USS Enterprise CVA(N) 65, family members of many of those lost in the fire, and a contingent of the current ship's company dedicated three plaques commemorating the ship, the fire and the twenty-eight lost sailors in an emotion-packed ceremony at the US Navy Memorial. Far from spontaneous, this event evolved out of the dedication of many people to the memory of the fire, their lost shipmates, and the legacy of one of the finest and most recognized ships in the Navy.

In 1993, fire veteran Michael Joe Carlin published Trial; Ordeal Of The USS Enterprise, a riveting account of the fire and a moving tribute to the brave crew who fought to save the ship, twenty-eight of whom died in the effort and 343 wounded. Several years later another fire veteran, Mike Neville, inspired by Carlin's book, sought to reunite his shipmates, resulting in a reunion and memorial service at Pearl Harbor on January 14, 2004, the 35th anniversary of the fire.

In attendance at the 2004 reunion were the widows and other family members of three of those lost in the fire. Each of these ladies, and other widows and family members who have been contacted since the reunion have expressed their disappointment in the absence of their loved ones' names on the Vietnam Wall. This issue, a circumstance that Neville refers to as "an accident of geography," prompted him to pursue an alternative venue to memorialize his lost shipmates. He found the US Navy Memorial's Commemoration Wall to be an ideal choice and he and his shipmates raised the necessary funds for two plaques memorializing the fire and honoring the twenty-eight who died.

While Neville was working on the fire plaque project, Navy Memorial Director of Planned Giving, Paul T. Haley pointed out to him that there was not a plaque commemorating the USS Enterprise CVA(N) 65 and that if one could be commissioned in a timely fashion, it could be appropriately placed adjacent to the fire plaques. Neville immediately contacted USS Enterprise Association Chairman Chas Folcik who charged ahead securing the commission of the ship's plaque in time to join the fire plaques on the Commemoration Wall. By this point, the dedication of the fire plaques had already been set for October 6, 2006 and it was agreed that the dedication of the ship's plaque would be incorporated into that ceremony. While this was done essentially for convenience sake, it turned out to have significantly enhanced the impact of the dedication ceremony. As Neville has put it, "The combined dedication was a prime example of the whole being greater than the sum of its parts."

Because Enterprise was at sea at the time of the dedication, her representation was limited but impressive. Speaking on behalf of the ship was CTOC Karl Parsons. Also in attendance were Jan Rice and Terrie DeClercq, the wives of Enterprise CO Larry Rice and CMC Paul DeClercq. In addition to his comments, Chief Parsons presented a short video produced by the Enterprise crew. This video not only highlighted the Enterprise's forty-five years of honorable service, it honored the 1969 crew and surviving family members by speaking of the lessons learned, thanking them for saving the ship, and remembering their dead.

Representing the 1969 crew were over fifty shipmates and their families, two sailors from the USS Rogers, whose aid to Enterprise during the fire was crucial, and roughly forty family members of five of the twenty-eight. Speaking on behalf of the 1969 crew was retired VADM Kent Lee, Enterprise CO at the time of the fire, and speaking on behalf of the surviving families was Robert Pyeatt, father of LTJG Buddy Pyeatt who died in the fire. Clearly coming from the heart, their comments spoke personally and sincerely to those in attendance.

Rounding out the ceremony were the reading of the names and tolling of the ship's bell, beautiful renditions of the National Anthem and Navy Hymn by a barbershop quartet, and reading of Senate Resolution 569 honoring the ship and the losses from the fire. These segments were each conducted entirely or in part by fire veterans. The unexpected attendance of VCNO ADM Robert Willard added significantly to an already memorable experience and was appreciated by all hands.

STATEMENT FROM REAR ADMIRAL WILLIAM NEEL

On January 14, 1969, I was the Engineer Officer aboard USS Enterprise CVA(N)-65, having reported aboard the previous June 1968. I was supported in this role by three Major assistants, the Damage Control Assistant, the Main Propulsion Assistant and the Electrical Officer, all of whom were exceptionally capable nuclear trained Officers. With respect to the fire, all of these men, their assisting Officers, Chief Petty Officers and men played important roles. LCDR Larry Gifford was the Damage Control Assistant and a vital key to the successful fire fighting efforts. Larry had assisted me previously when I was Engineer Officer at the D1G prototype reactor plant in upstate New York so I was familiar with his outstanding capabilities.

Captain Lee, our Skipper, supported a high tempo of Damage Control/Fire fighting training among many conflicting priorities. Repair "Parties" and "Lockers" are terms composed of men assisting from all Departments of the ship and can train as a team only when all personnel are at their General Quarters Battle Stations and a high degree of water-tight integrity is set. A competition was set up among the Repair Units with a special team of experts selected to test and grade the units competitively. Additionally, competition among the ships Divisions was established to improve setting of water-tight integrity conditions. Captain Lee supported this by announcing the winners over the ships public address system, the 1MC. The competition was keen and served to hone the crews capabilities in Damage Control. Captain Lee established a ships policy that every crew member will attend Navy Fire fighting training, either the flight deck or ship board version, according to individual assignments. A most important part of the fire fighting training is the oxygen breathing apparatus (OBA) training, a device worn by fire fighters by which the OBA generates oxygen by activating a chemical reaction by breathing. A chemical canister is inserted into the device, activated by the wearer, providing an oxygen supply for a maximum of 45 minutes. This enables the fire fighting teams wearing OBA's to enter smoke filled shipboard compartments to directly engage fighting interior fires.

The Navy operated FF schools in various locations on the West Coast but demand for school slots was very high and in the last half of '68 the ship arranged to activate a former World War Two FF school in Manchester, Washington, not far from Puget Sound Naval Shipyard (PSNSY), where the Big "E" would undergo a restricted availability for avionics modifications and repairs. The duration was to last about two months. Instructors came from R Division augmented by a few others from the Navy FF schools. Throughput in this FF school was such that Enterprise was able to train virtually every crew member. During At-Sea periods after the ship had left PSNSY, Damage Control/FF drills were conducted every day which was most beneficial to increasing proficiency. At the time we departed Alameda in January for Hawaii and Deployment LCDR Gifford and I were much encouraged in DC/FF team proficiency.

Another interesting event occurred in our preparations for deployment. Since the ship would round Cape Horn and enter Newport News Shipyard shortly after our return from South West Asia, a Navy inspection and survey team (INSURV) came aboard in

November before we Deployed for a pre-shipyard inspection. This inspection was to assist the ship in assuring that all deficiencies would be recognized for correction during the shipyard over haul. Installed in Enterprise were 17 high capacity fog-foam generating stations strategically dispersed on the second deck, just below the Hangar Deck. Their purpose was generating a solution of 3.5 – 6% protein foam in sea water and pump this solution through piping to outlets on the flight deck and hangar decks to supply foam for class "B" fires (burning hydrocarbons). The protein foam is delivered to the ship in 5 gallon cans and they are then emptied into a large tank, then joined with sea water in a positive displacement lobe-type pump which discharges the proportioned solution into the aforementioned vertical pipes. To test the operation of these pumps we followed precise written directions supplied by Navy Planned Maintenance System (NPMS) cards. In this case, a calibrated beaker was held at the appropriate hose nozzle to receive the foam sample, the unit was started at the hose station by a push button and soon the foam would emerge from the nozzle and the beaker filled. Then we Timed the collapsing of the foam bubbles against a specified standard. We always tested the 17 stations both at the flight deck and hangar deck levels the specified times and they were always satisfactory. As it turned out, the INSURV team observed our test, then told us to allow the foam to exit the nozzle for at least 30 seconds before testing. It was found that 16 of the 17 generating stations failed to generate foam properly because when the generator was first started there was little resistance in the dry pipes, but when the pipes filled with solution and nozzle back pressure was established, the pump would slow somewhat and allow leakage between the lobes and the pump casing caused by lobe erosion from the gritty solids found in the foam. We were in a real jam. Deployment was just two weeks away.

We pulled two pumps and sent them across the Bay to Hunters Point Naval Shipyard where they rebuilt the pumps back to the proper specifications. We put them back in and tested them and they immediately wore down again! So, as a very worried Chief Engineer, I called the factory, the Hale Company, in Conshohocken, PA, and talked to the Manager who turned out to be a retired Chief who was one of my instructors at Destroyer Engineering school in 1955! After hearing my plea he obtained authority to start shipping new units to me as quickly as they could be assembled since it would take too long to repair our existing units. We arranged for Navy aircraft pick up the new units at Willow Grove Naval Air Station, PA, and fly to Alameda as they came off the production line. The last four units were installed just 4 days before we left Alameda! As events turned out, these pumps were absolutely critical in contributing to the successful fire fighting on January 14th.

The morning of January 14th, 1969, after breakfast in the Wardroom, I went to my 2nd deck office to attend to the steady stream of paperwork that is a necessary part of the Navy, "Forces Afloat". I was anticipating the call to General Quarters (Battle Stations) that would mark the resumption of our Operational Readiness Inspection (ORI). Todays drills would largely determine our final grade. I knew that our extensive training efforts had reflected well in the previous days drills. Success today should demonstrate to Pacific Fleet Command that Enterprise was their top Carrier.

An unanticipated, "Now Man All Fog Foam Injection Stations", was surprisingly heard over the 1MC which usually meant a fuel spill on the Hangar or flight deck. Suddenly, I felt the tile deck lift under my feet and a muffled but loud sound of an explosion. Then, "This Is No Drill. All Hands Man Your Battle Stations!" I hustled down to my Battle Station in Main Control and quickly verified communication circuits with Bridge and Primary Flight Control were established. Among others in Central Control were CDR Kellogg, the Reactor Officer, LCDR Gifford, the Damage Control Assistant, LCDR Tsantes, Main Propulsion Assistant and LT John Gallamore, Electrical Officer. LCDR Tsantes, a brilliant and outstanding Naval Officer, an Usher in my wedding in Idaho Falls in 1959, was tragically assassinated in November, 1983, in Athens, Greece, where then Captain Tsantes was heading up the US Navy Assistance Group.

LCDR Gifford immediately checked communications with the Damage Control Repair Parties and Repair Units and received manned and ready reports from all but the unit on the port side, aft, 03 level, where the unit Locker there had been blown away by the first bomb detonations. Orders were issued for all Parties to check their assigned areas for smoke or damage. As more missile and bomb explosions and JP5 fires took place all of the Repair Parties Midships and Aft proceeded to do their jobs well, augmented as necessary with men from the Forward Parties. These were pressed into service as needed to augment the OBA canister supplies for the more engaged fire fighters.

One very immediate attention item for me upon arrival in Central Control was that one of our largest high capacity steam driven fire pumps was on the binnacle list because of a faulty governor, awaiting parts not available aboard. I told LCDR Tsantes to do everything possible, including governing the pump by human manipulation, but get it on line since we were already receiving reports of periodic low fire main pressure due to ruptured hoses, pipes, and heavy use of the Hangar deck sprinkling system and the flight deck water washdown systems.

Indeed, one example of this was that the 8-inch diameter fire main serving the entire Island was ruptured by flying shrapnel that destroyed a 90 degree elbow at the flight deck level inside the Island. Although this breach was quickly isolated, gallons of salt water poured into the area where Triage of the wounded and burned was taking place.

All Manner of reports were flowing into Central from Repair Parties and units. As the below-deck fires were being isolated and extinguished, heavy smoke became a very serious problem in the Aft section of the ship. OBA canister supplies were running low and the danger of running out received my attention. Knowing that we were operating helo's to transport the injured to Tripler Army Hospital, I called the Captain and requested that he initiate action for a back up supply from Pearl Harbor. As I understand it, a call went out to all ships present in Pearl to provide canisters to Tripler Helo Pad ASAP. Fortunately, and very soon, significant numbers of canisters were being delivered to the flight deck and directed to where they were needed most. In more recent years that is called a "Just In Time" supply model.

I must say that I was extremely proud of our 960 man Damage Control Organization that morning. LCDR Gifford, cool throughout, judiciously applied his talented and well trained people to tasks at hand, reinforcing where necessary, borrowing from less engaged units as required. The all important fire main pressure was maintained superbly in light of ruptures and extraordinary, simultaneous fire fighting usage. At one point in the most seriously challenging period of the fighting Captain Lee called me in Central asking, "Bill, am I going to lose the ship?" I answered, "No Sir. Not on my watch, Captain!" And I sincerely believed what I told Captain Lee.

With the fires out, except for a pesky grease fire in Number 4 aircraft elevator cable trunk, I began to survey the damage to get a handle on the extent of it for the meeting I knew would convene soon after arrival in Pearl. That evening, soon after we had moored, I attended a meeting at Pearl Harbor Naval Shipyard with the shipyard Commander and other reps from Pacific Fleet HQ. With a special phone hook up we had interested Navy parties in Washington, "On The Line."

The Major decisions from that conference were;
1. The ship would be repaired in PHNSY.
2. The PHNSY Trades roster would be augmented by special welders and others so that other ship overhauls/repairs taking place in PHNSY would not be seriously affected.
3. DCNO Air to visit US Steel Corp. to negotiate production of necessary flight deck steel in sheets that could be accommodated by USAF C-141 Starlifter aircraft and delivered to Hickam Air Force Base which is adjacent to Pearl Harbor Navy Base.
4. Navy Supply Systems Command would set up high priority system with one senior civilian and senior Supply Officer at every supply demand control point answering to Enterprise requirements. This brilliant action produced a miraculous effect! Parts which had been on order for months before the fire, came out of the woodwork at warp speed and arrived on board, much to my surprise. One example was the Deck-edge flight deck announcing system (5MC) speakers which, ruggedly built as they were, suffered life ending tailhook strikes now and again. Having the parts and materials needed the get the BIG "E" back on line was an absolute necessity and the Supply people made it work beautifully!
5. Newport News Shipbuilding and Drydock Co. to supply the latest drawings and specs along with personnel to advise.
6. A three shift day, 7 days a week work routine was initiated.
7. Ships Force would provide electrician manpower for lighting circuit repairs and other areas as required
8. Elevator #4 would be structurally repaired and welded in place in the "UP" position until permanent repairs could be affected at the post deployment overhaul and reactor refueling at Newport News Naval Shipyard.

Enterprise was successfully repaired and resumed her transit to the Tonkin Gulf in just seven weeks.

Account Of Captain Henry J. C. Schwartz

I was assigned to the Submarine Base Clinic in Pearl at the time of the Enterprise fire. At the time SUBASE was under the Submarine Base Commander and had five doctors, all Submarine Medical Officers. I had arrived at the Clinic early, and only one or two other medical officers had arrived when word came that they needed medical help on a ship. Since the Senior Medical Officer was not there yet and I was next senior, it was natural that I would go. I think I was the only doctor to go from SUBASE, along with two Corpsmen. There were also three other doctors and six Corpsmen from the shipyard medical clinic. We were told to wait at the helo landing pad at the Ford Island Ferry. Two helicopters landed and picked us up. They were Marine 34s and very noisy so I rode with my fingers in my ears to save my hearing for the stethoscope after landing.

I did not give much thought to the pros and cons of flying out to a burning ship. Medics and Submariners go where they are told and I was both having made three patrols on the USS DANIEL BOONE and one Polaris patrol on the USS JAMES MONROE. We could hear nothing on board the helo other than engine noise. We circled over ENTERPRISE once before landing on the forward flight deck and I will never forget the brief view of the entire aft end of the flight deck with flames, smoke and wrecked plane hulks. After landing we were led below. We all went to exam and treatment rooms and started working on patients. The ships medical team was extremely competent and probably would have done well without us. Our contribution was to get people seen and treated much faster. Ships complement medical department was sending patients our way and the flow was smooth from my perspective. Burned patients were given the briefest treatment and sent by helo to Tripler Army Hospital.

There was a remarkable person I saw during a break. Sometime during the afternoon things in sick bay were under control and I took a five minute break and went up to the flight deck. I probably spent no more than 30 seconds scanning the damage and was heading back to the Island to return to sick bay. At that moment an officer came up to me. I think he was a warrant. He asked how things were going in sick bay and I told him things were quieting down. He said that maybe he would stop down there and have them take a look. Then he turned around and his entire back was pocked with shrapnel. He had been on the Damage Control Team and was too busy saving the ship to worry about a few scratches

Account of CDR Jack Greear

On the morning of 14 January, 1969, aboard ENTERPRISE as an Operational Readiness Inspector for Commander, Fleet Air Hawaii, I am preparing for three events with the ships medical department; (1) Mass Casualty Drill; (2) Debrief the evaluation and (3) Flight ashore.

At approximately 0805 I call the Air Transfer Officer (ATO) to ask for flight launch fro ENTERPRISE back to NAS Barbers Point. He is not in so I call back at 0818 and he answers and goes to check his schedule of anticipated launches. Then I hear the sound of an explosion. The ATO comes back on line for only a moment and says that Zuni rockets are exploding and he has to go. This is immediately followed by the Main Communications system (1MC) announcement, "GENERAL QUARTERS, GENERAL QUARTERS, THIS IS NOT A DRILL. THIS IS NOT A DRILL. ACTIVATE THE WATER WASHDOWN SYSTEM. CONDITION ZEBRA WILL BE SET IN FIVE MINUTES."

As minutes pass there are more detonations. Since, as an Inspector, I did not have an assigned Battle Station, I decided to stay right there in sick bay. Much appears to be happening on the flight deck. One hears it, feels it, and pays close attention to the 1MC announcements. Expressions on the faces of everyone are of serious concern and anticipation. Then, in what seems to be about four minutes, the first patients arrive. The island had held patients on the flight deck until conditions had become overcrowded. Leading the group was a man with massive trauma of his leg. He is immediately carried into the sick bay surgical room while the surgeon begins scrubbing up. A corpsman arrives and sets up a surgical tray. By this time more blast victims are already arriving on the ward, about ten of them. I am told men are coming down by elevator. I am doing what I can to get things prepared. There are now others with incredible burns while yet many more are bleeding profusely through their rapidly applied Battle Dressings. Some still need dressings. Their flight deck clothing is burnt and bloody. Some have their clothing completely burnt off and only flight deck boots remain. More blasts are continuously heard even as trauma victims arrive. These very young men are paying a terrible price for saving the ship. I help the man to a bunk that has a compound broken leg. The burned young men have severe burns over their bodies yet are still walking. Some have shrapnel wounds too – cauterized by the heat and blast.

I ask a corpsman for morphine but there is a problem in getting it released from a secure lockdown. I run back to the man with the broken leg who is in incredible pain and somewhat vocal about it. His leg needs to be set and the bleeding stopped. I use a belt tourniquet and tell him I have to straighten it now before it gets worse through swelling. He acknowledges and I rapidly straiten it without morphine. He wrenches in pain and then sighs in some relief. The burnt men are moaning as well. We still have no morphine for them. Seriously wounded men are continuously brought into sick bay and it is now quite crowded. To my relief and delight, the supply corpsman and one of his assistants soon came up with armfuls of supplies and continued his task of keeping everyone on the ward and in the passageways fully supplied. This prompt action saved many men from bleeding to death. The many corpsmen were able to focus on emergency treatment and supplies were continuously long after the explosions subsided. To this day I am thankful for the efforts on the part of the medical administrative officer, and I was very fortunate to have served with him and his supply petty officer that came over and kept the supplies flowing. Then, we heard over the 1MC, "ALL RIGHT! THAT'S THE LAST OF IT! THAT'S ALL THE ORDNANCE! LET'S GET IN THERE AND GET THOSE FIRES OUT!"

I asked for a team of inexperienced corpsmen who were anxious to pitch in and do all they could. They were given the task of cleaning up patients by removing burned and dirty clothing even cutting it off if they had to and wash everyone up so they were easier to monitor. They became experienced real fast. Some of the ships crew were cleaning away debris, helped cut off working uniforms and flight deck clothing, change sheets etc. This allowed the regular medical people to more easily recheck and identify those with fresh blood. It also helped us prepare the stable ones for the MEDEVACS.

As crewmen were brought down to sick bay, they needed fluids. I asked the lab technician to start fluids on all of those soaked in blood. Fluids were also started on all of those who were losing blood pressure. Many had to remain in the passageway as there was no room in sick bay. The crew were treated where they sat. I spent a lot of time removing battle dressings, a redo patch job to control the bleeders and set any broken bones. I asked for the sick call corpsman who had some experience with seeing real blood. He stayed with me for a short lesson and then went out on his own to do likewise.

At one point I was called to the bridge for a short and intensive brief with a Captain from Commander, Fleet Air Hawaii. He had ordered me up from sick bay for a status report. I told him that Medical was overloaded. Many of the crew had unknowns regarding internal wounds. Shrapnel could be anywhere and each patient needed advanced medical attention. Time was critical and the ship needed more than this and it did not exist. We were working hard to stop the bleeding and other wounds. Calming the treatment teams and crew was yet another task. Burned patients were expected to have shrapnel wounds under their now cauterized skin. Extensive burns are probably the most severe form of injury and many were in painful agony. We needed to get the seriously wounded flown ashore. Although I was just an LT. at the time I actually had an argument with the Captain who commented about the risk of landing helicopters on a crowded flight deck. There were questions, some shouting, then more discussion. I wanted to have aircraft pushed overboard. I did not know that at that very moment the USAF pilots were in a pattern and expressed reservations about coming aboard. There were risks in conducting MEDEVACs. There were risks even of movement of the wounded but the risk of allowing them to bleed to death internally was unconscionable.

Then I was dismissed and departed the Bridge. Once I was outside of the island, I saw the flight deck and the helicopter landing. At that point I was starting to realize the magnitude of what had happened, was still in process and of the ongoing struggle. By that point, 1030 hours, the battle to save lives was short but very intensive and would go ward and in the passageways fully supplied. This prompt action saved many men from bleeding to death. The many corpsmen were able to focus on emergency treatment and supplies were continuously long after the explosions subsided. To this day I am thankful for the efforts on the part of the medical administrative officer, and I was very fortunate to have served with him and his supply petty officer that came over and kept the supplies flowing. Then, we heard over the 1MC, "ALL RIGHT! THAT'S THE LAST OF IT! THAT'S ALL THE ORDNANCE! LET'S GET IN THERE AND GET THOSE FIRES OUT!"

I asked for a team of inexperienced corpsmen who were anxious to pitch in and do all they could. They were given the task of cleaning up patients by removing burned and dirty clothing even cutting it off if they had to and wash everyone up so they were easier to monitor. They became experienced real fast. Some of the ships crew were cleaning away debris, helped cut off working uniforms and flight deck clothing, change sheets etc. This allowed the regular medical people to more easily recheck and identify those with fresh blood. It also helped us prepare the stable ones for the MEDEVACS.

From the memory of a Allman F. Brandon aboard the USS Enterprise Jan. 14TH 1969..............
...

We were 70 miles off the coast of Hawaii on carrier ORI drills, before going on to the Tonkin Gulf for what was my third trip. I was at that time an Aviation Bosun Mate, 2nd Class, working on the flight deck in V-4 Division Repair 7 and contamination control. I also was in charge of the AVGAS Pump room way down below if AVGAS was needed for napalm or any non-JP-5 aircraft. It seemed there were not enough V-4 Division Petty Officers so many of us had several responsibilities.

My General Quarters Station was the AVGAS Pump room on the 6th deck. Part of our ORI drills involved going to General Quarters Stations but on 14 January, just after 0800 hours, I heard for the first and only time, "GENERAL QUARTERS! THIS IS NO DRILL".

I also had two Airmen with me in the Pump room, Tyrone Nesbit and Richie Lane. They had reached the hatch to the Pump room within seconds after I did. They both wanted to know what was going on. I told them I did not know either but to get into the Pump room and get on the sound powered phones and call in to Gas Control and tell them that all is secure here and that all hatches are closed and secured. After we were down there for what seemed like hours but was only 5 or 10 minutes,, we had smoke pouring in the ventilation ducts. And with each and every explosion the entire AVGAS Pump room felt like it was coming apart.

The smoke kept pouring in and the more that came in the more we wanted out. At one point I thought that Tyrone was going to leave but I was on the sound powered phones and was told by Gas Control that we would be okay. But we knew we would not last much longer because the smoke was very heavy and it was choking. We thought we were being forced to die to save the ship. This was every below deckers worst nightmare.

The smoke was very heavy and after about 45 minutes we were told to secure the Pump room and all hatches and get up to the flight deck. YES SIR! We were very glad to finally come up from below to the top hatch on the Mess Decks. The hatch to AVGAS Pump room was just a few feet from the rear opening to Sick Bay. I remember looking in and seeing many bodies, one was a friend wearing a purple jersey, David Asbury, from the flight deck fuels crews. At that time I could see that we were in big trouble and that there was a job to be done on the flight deck.

After making our way to the flight deck, we could see the mess and fuel, planes blown all over, not to mention body parts. Choppers were coming and going to take wounded off the ship which was still on fire. That was a bad day in my life and will never go away. I had blanked many things out but they all have come back. Thanks to friends like Mike Carlin and Allen Theide and others, I now have someone to talk to about that day.

Some people say that the ones up front fighting the fires were heroes. Well, in that moment they were but all any of us were doing was our jobs. It is what we were trained to do in fire school and aboard ship. Our job was to be the best that you could be. If you fell down, get up and go in again.

After getting back to Pearl Harbor and being able to see the ship from the pier, you had to onder how we go back into port at all. This was the worst looking ship I had ever seen and the hole in the fantail just above the waterline made me thank God that many of us made it back. It also made me wonder why I was okay and so many were not. It was two or three days before I was able to get a call home to let my folks know I was okay. They said they did not see my name on any casualty list so they just hoped I was alright.

In the days to follow we worked hard on the ship every day, unless we had liberty. There were 7 of us who bought a '57 Chevy convertible. We used it to go back and forth from a beach we would camp out at or a couple of days at a time. We had a chief in V-4 who was sent to S2M Division on the Mess Decks while we were in port. Chief Boggs would send word up to us every couple of days to sned someone down to pick boxes of steaks, burgers and hot dogs. That is what we lived on. All we had to do was buy gas and beer and we would swim and party. We loved it. Then it was time and we had a '57 Chevy to do something with. We left the keys and title on the dash board and parked it close to the pier with a note saying,'If you want this car you can have it. It served us well. V-4 Division USS Enterprise"

Account of Lt Scott Finkboner VF-92 Pilot January 14,1969 aboard the USS Enterprise CVAN-65

It was a typical Hawaiian weather day on January 14, 1969 -bright sunshine and scattered cumulus clouds against a clear blue sky. My RIO LTjg Eugene Williamson and I did the usual briefing for a fighter escort flight for an attack training mission both F-4 squadrons were part of. We were scheduled for the second launch of the day-0830. The first launch had occurred earlier at 0700.

At approximately 0800 the ready room briefing was complete and we gathered our gear for our 0830 launch. The aircraft preflight was normal and the plane captain assisted us into our cockpits. Our aircraft # 210 was adjacent to the island and was facing aft.

At 0815 hrs I started the starboard engine and it was idling satisfactorily. At 0819 hrs I was just about to start the port engine when a large "Bang" sounded and I looked up to see a huge fireball coming from an F-4 on the port side aft. We were literally showered with flaming debris and shrapnel. I saw many of our shipmates literally blown into the air. We had a birds eye view looking nearly directly at the inferno.

I felt it too dangerous to exit the aircraft immediately as numerous 500 lb detonations and resulting shrapnel kept showering our F-4. I immediately shutdown both engines. My canopy kept me protected initially deflecting many pieces of shrapnel and debris. The canopy literally saved our lives.

It seemed like an eternity but after a few minutes during a lull between explosions we exited the aircraft. I stayed near and behind my F-4 as other explosions of aircraft and 500 lb ordinance kept cooking off. It was literally suicide to go into the inferno at this point. Part of my flight gear I was wearing included flares and many rounds from my 9mm and .45 side arms.

I lost track of the time as more detonations kept cooking off. Then I noticed the automatic deck water sprinkler system fail. I knew we were in trouble so decided to stay on deck. There I could try and assist wherever I could help. If we had to abandon ship, I was in position there rather than being below deck where the fire and explosions were spreading. I lost contact with my RIO and believed he went below and forward.

It seemed like an eternity but water pressure was finally restored. I assisted in manning a few fire hoses. Several of us were near an A-3 Sky Warrior tanker full of jet fuel parked on the port side of No 4 elevator. Spilled fuel from other aircraft as well from ruptured tanker tanks began to burn against the bottom of the A-3's fuselage and its undercarriage.

The A-3 began to burn more as the firefighting efforts were loosing ground. Then I heard the announcement from the Air Boss
"Looks like it is going to blow, get the hell away from there". I immediately started to turn and run when the A-3 blew up in the largest fireball imaginable-3500 gallons of JP-5. I

and others next to me were blown almost half way across the flight deck, skinning my elbows and knees right through my flight gear. A sailor who had been standing next near the A-3 landed next to me. I tried to assist him as much as possible but he appeared deceased. Everyone had to retreat further from the burning A-3 to avoid further injury or death.

Aircraft and ordinance kept cooking off aft and now began to head up the starboard side of the flight deck. The island was now in jeopardy. I was trying to lay low in case the 20mm rounds in the A-7 Corsairs started to go off over our heads. Firefighting crews kept at the fires all over the flight deck. I did not know what if anything was happening below but it did not look good. I kept assisting on the hoses until all fires on the flight deck were out.

At about 1200 all fires were extinguished. I then assisted others in locating the injured and deceased and my squadron's Line Division personnel. Ships crews were clearing the flight deck of the wrecked planes and equipment. At approximately 1330 I went below and found all my squadrons flight crews in VF-96's ready room forward and advised them I where I had been.

At approximately 1500 we docked at the carrier pier at Pearl Harbor. There was crowd of approximately 5000-10,000 people there. From the starboard side of the flight deck I was able to spot my father standing in the crowd. He was employed at Pearl with the Naval Investigative Service(NIS). I was born and raised in Honolulu so it was a sort of homecoming but not the one I had imagined. I signaled to him I was ok and to call my mother the same. Luckily I had received no serious injuries. It was a day I will never forget.

THE WORST DAY OF MY LIFE

All I could see was yellow and Orange, my plastic goggles melting down over my glasses. Then, through a window in the fire, I could see the bridge and I heard someone scream!

Chief Ron Hay was my boss on both the 1968 and 1969 cruises. He was a great guy. Before we got into Pearl Harbor, I had asked for over night liberty and the Chief had said OK. In Pearl, Captain Lee, Commanding Enterprise, wanting to make sure everyone was ready for the ORI (operational readiness inspection), said no general overnight liberty! I asked the chief, about it and he said; "I said you get liberty and you get liberty! That's the kind of boss he was, if he said something, he meant it. There was no B.S., if you did your job well, He was 100% behind you, if not, you could not be a troubleshooter for him, and you went back to your shop. Early in the cruise in 1968, we needed a new squadron insignia for our F4's. I remember on the flight deck, Chief Hay came up to me and opened a matchbook. In ink there was a sketch of an angular shaped black falcon diving in attack with its claws open. He asked me, what do you think of this for the tails of our planes? I said; I think that's great Chief! I guess everybody liked it because shortly thereafter, it was painted on the tail of all VF 96 F4's.

The flight deck was no place for anyone who did not do their job well. It was a place where, if one did not do their job well or pay attention, someone would die. It happened, all too frequently, people got injured and killed. It was a very loud place with a lot of big machines in a small place, moving very fast, loaded with ordinance and fuel. Next to being shot at in combat, it may well be the most dangerous place to be.

My third cruise on Enterprise in VF 96, World famous fighting Falcons. We had all the missile shoot records. We had shot down 2 migs and with Enterprise and her Air wing, a Naval Unit Commendation in 1968 for delivering more ordinance than any ship in history. I was proud to be a trouble shooter, an elite crew of 8 to 'make them fly". Enterprise CVAN65 was the only nuclear carrier, the flagship of; the Battle Group, the Pacific Fleet, the Navy, and of her nation! Enterprise was the biggest, fastest, mightiest warship in the world. I was on the best crew, in the best fighter squadron, on the greatest ship; world class!

Lt Jim Berry, 25, was my new division officer; He was Chief Hay's Boss. He was great, an F4 phantom pilot, new to our squadron this cruise. He would come into our shop on the starboard bow and spend time talking with us. Some officers seemed like they thought they were better than enlisted men, but not Lt. Berry, He treated everyone well and with respect. We liked him a lot and looked forward to working for him. The pilots and Rio's (radar Intercept Officers) were mostly nice to me anyway; I was an AME, the guy who fixed their ejection seats.

Lt. Buddy Pyeatt was another officer who treated everyone nice and with respect, he was from a farming family, just a ways north of Denver Colorado. In 1968, I asked him if he would take my camera with him over North Vietnam and take some pictures for me. He just smiled and said sure! He took my camera several times and got a lot of pictures of our Phantoms flying CAP (combat air patrol) refueling and of bombing runs over the North. He was only 25 and religious, he was deeply concerned that our bombs may be killing innocent civilians including women and children, but he never wavered in his duty. He was just that kind of Man.

Henry Yates, AMS2, a heck of a worker, always neat and clean in the morning, but by midshift, dirty like 'pigpen' on Peanuts. He would just get right into the Phantoms and fix them. Henry was also funny, with a heck of a sense of humor, always smiling and happy. He was great to work with; with Henry around we always got a lot done.

I always thought Lt Carl Berghult was a special kind of officer. He was an ordinance officer. He was different, He led by example. When it was time to hoist a bomb up into the racks, he'd holler, let's go, and grab the bomb with his men and hoist it into place. It has been a long time, but I remember going with other guys including Ordinanceman Rich Hawley to help him move and having beer and barbequed hamburgers for a reward.

Everybody Liked Armando, Armando Limon. He was Hispanic, a third class, ADJ plane captain, 26, and young at heart. He was a great guy, a great friend to all and funny. It was January 13, 1969. We had been issued a new type of cloth helmet. It had pockets for insertion of fiberglass sponges for head protection. It seemed everybody had one but me. In the plane captain shop next to the trouble shooters, was a cardboard box with pieces of these helmets in it. I had hit my head on enough on airplane wings to know a good idea and besides I was always interested in safety. I remember digging through the box with Armando to find a white or green helmet to match a trouble shooter or maintenance jersey color. We couldn't find white or green, or even pieces of either color. Finally Armando came up with a brown (Plane captain) piece and a red (Ordinance) piece to make a complete helmet. We put it together and I put it on. Armando was pointing at me and laughing, saying I looked like a clown in a circus. I laughed too, saying; "if they don't like it, I'll tell them to send me to sea or get me one the right color". I wore that helmet when I was on the flight deck until the next day, when it saved my life and turned black.

Akers, Paul	Marks, Dennis
Asbury, David	Martineau, James
Berghult, Carl	Mason, Joseph
Berry, James	Milburn, Dennis
Bovaire, Richard	Oats, Joseph
Bullington, Richard	Pyeatt, Buddy
Floyd, James	Quintas, Jacob
Froster, Ernest	Snipes, James
Girty, Delbert	Tyler, Russell
Hay, Ronald	Vonfeklt, Lavern
Holbrook, Roger	Ward, Robert
Hunt, Dale	Webster, John
Lacy, Donald	Yates, Henry
Limon, Armando	Yoakum, Jerome

Just a list of names, JUST, A LIST! Each of them, only one man, each, one of 28. All of them, with mothers and fathers, brothers and sisters, wives and children, waiting, waiting, waiting, for their return from the sea. All of them brave, proud, my friends, my shipmates, dead.

Some of them died in an instant, others within minutes, all but one within hours. Lt. Berry, no, he wouldn't die. I lay there beside him as He fought death for weeks, suffered horribly, but then he also lost.

January 14, 1969, started as a beautiful day. We were steaming west of Hawaii, conducting Operational Readiness Inspections (ORI). Everything just like on the line off North Vietnam. It was my third cruise to Vietnam on board the Enterprise. It seemed like I knew almost everyone, I was a "salt", an experienced troubleshooter, working mostly with guys from the last cruise. A few guys were missing, getting out of the Navy and there were new guys to help train. This would be my last cruise, as I planned on getting out and returning to college. I would make 2nd Class Petty officer in 2 days. More money, things were good, and it was good to be at sea again.

We had already sent out our first strike, all of the planes loaded to the max for their live bombing runs. We were getting ready for our second launch, scheduled for 08:30. It was almost 08:20. The planes were all loaded, full of fuel, wing tanks, bombs and rockets. The carrier Air group commander (CAG) had noticed, his parachute was not tied exactly right and Chief Hay had asked me to fix it. The CAG was upset that the Parachute riggers had not rigged it right. It wasn't my job, but I knew how it was supposed to be, so as the CAG watched closely, I fixed it properly. The CAG smiled and thanked me, saying good job Nimsic. I was feeling pretty good, everything was going great and the CAG had thanked me for a good job. I left "Showtime" (a phantom painted special for the CAG) and walked to port. I was standing by the VF 96 phantom with Lt. Berry and Lt. Pyeatt in it, with my hand on its Radome. They were hooking up the Huffer to start it; I was looking around for Chief Hay to tell him I had fixed the CAG's F4. I saw him walking toward me from the starboard side. I walked over toward him and as I got to him, gave him the hand signals that I had fixed the CAG's plane and that it was up. Chief Hay was a real serious guy, nice but seldom smiled, but he gave me a smile, his last, and a thumbs up. We walked past each others and I heard a horrendous blam behind me!

What was that? Too early for the marines to throw hand grenade over the side to start the battle stations drill due at 08:30, I started to turn around to see what it was. Before I could turn to see, I was hit by an incredible force, blasted through the air and slammed face first into the flight deck. I was stunned or maybe unconscious for a moment. I tried to pick myself up, but only rolled sideways a little, so that I could see back. I saw that my pant legs were on fire and then beyond that; I could see a huge fireball coming from our plane that I had just walked away from. It was the Phantom with Lt. Berry and Lt. Pyeatt in it. Where was Chief Hay? I could see debris flying and men down. The fireball was roaring towards me. I was able to struggle to my feet and try to run, but when I stepped with my right leg, I would go down, roll and come up again, over and over.

The fire kept coming as I tried to get away, but I couldn't, It seems as if it were slow motion, evil tongues of fire were wrapping around me, trying to embrace me, embrace me, hold me, they kept coming, I thought, I have to hold my breath and keep going. All I could see was yellow and orange, with my plastic goggles melting down over my glasses.

Time nearly stood still, it seemed like an eternity. Then I saw a window in the yellow and orange, I could see the Island, the Bridge, I heard someone scream, and then I realized it was me screaming! I thought to myself, "what are you screaming for you dumb shit", I reached out and fought to get out of the fire and then suddenly I was out.

My shoulders felt hot, I looked and my Flight deck Jersey was on fire. I tried to put it out but my left arm wouldn't work, but I was able to kind of **pat out the fire on my shoulders with my right hand. I went a little farther to** starboard, stumbling and falling as I went.

Suddenly there were 3 or 4 guys around me, trying to hold me up and help me. I was so thankful, but then a huge blast and shrapnel hit us. A big piece of shrapnel buried itself into my left side just below my ribs and spun me like a top. Somehow I didn't go down, but all the guys trying to help me were down, on the deck, rolling around screaming and holding their guts. I saw them, but I could not help them! I could barely stand on my feet. I was burnt, full of holes, my left arm had a compound fracture, a big chunk of metal sticking out of my side 6 inches, and my Achilles tendon was sliced completely in two. They had tried to help me, but I couldn't, I wanted to, but I couldn't help them. It was all I could do to keep going. I had to leave my…..Shipmates behind. They were Heroes; they had tried to save me.

I went forward along the A7's parked on the starboard side. It seemed very strange, surreal, there was no one else around, no one to help me. I felt very lonely. I could see the fire, it was huge, all around and getting bigger, fast. I had to keep going forward. I went under a wing, and then another huge blast, shrapnel was making a strange rattling noise between the wing and the deck and fuel was pouring out of the wings. It was hitting me again, wouldn't it ever stop? I wondered; is this hell, going on forever and ever, being hit over and over and over? Maybe I was already dead, No, I thought, I am not dead, I have to keep going. I got to the edge of the flight deck and was preparing to try to ease myself down into the catwalk. I knew I was hurt bad and had to be careful. NO! Another blast, more shrapnel, it hurt, I dove headfirst down into the catwalk.

I found myself setting up in the catwalk, my back against the bulkhead. Trying to understand what was happening. My head felt hot! I reached up and pulled my special brown and red helmet off, it was on fire and….black.

There were many big blasts and Enterprise shook, I could hear the fire, roaring with a loud crackling sound, but in the catwalk I was below the level of the deck and not being hit by shrapnel anymore. I could see the blast debris and fire being blown over my head and I knew I had to keep going, but keep my head down. In High school and college, I had played fullback. I always had to keep going, no matter how many times I was hit, I had to keep going. I have always thought that If I had not played football, I would not have been able too keep going, I would not have survived.

I picked myself up again and went forward to a ladder, I was carefully going down the ladder, and I looked at my left arm because it would not work and then I saw my hand. It was burnt and the skin was hanging from it like strings of spaghetti, I thought, "oh well, they'll fix me up again".

Still no one to help me, where was everybody? I reached the bottom of the ladder and entered the hatch. There were a lot of sailors, trying to get out of the back of the ship. The bombs going off were ripping holes in the flight deck, blowing holes into our berthing compartments, killing everyone in the way.

A chief saw me and screamed, we have a casualty here, get that litter off the bulkhead, some sailors started for the litter but then KABLAM, KABLAM, KABLAM, three huge explosions, blowing fire extinguishers and everything else off the bulkheads and deck. I said, "We haven't got time for that thing Chief, we have to get out of here! He said, you're right sailor, let's get out of here.

A shipmate put his hands under my arms to help me and we went to the passageway. It was full of sailors streaming out of the aft compartments. A big guy saw me and put his arms out bracing against the bulkhead to stop the flow of men and let us enter the flow forward.

We were moving as fast as I could with help and we soon got to a battle dressing station. When some guys helped me in, there were already some guys hurt on the deck and one on the table. They took the guy off the table and put me on it. The corpsmen started cutting my clothes off and injecting me with morphine. They wrapped my wounds and burns. More and more bombs kept going off and stuff would fly around, the lights would swing. I said, every time one of those goes off, more guys are getting killed. They said we know; lets hope for the best. I told them, I couldn't run and my leg hurts. The corpsmen picked up my right leg and said, oh yeah, we see the problem. I was there for what seemed like a long time. They watched me close while taking care of a lot of casualties. Some guys they patched up headed back out to fight the fire, others could not go anymore and stayed there. The explosions became less frequent. I knew my shipmates were winning the battle to save our ship.

Eventually, the Corpsmen put me on a litter and some other sailors packed me down to sickbay. They almost couldn't get me in, it was packed. The corpsmen and Docs were really working hard. It was bloody, but under control, men setting up against bulkheads and lying on the deck. They packed me in and took a guy off a table to the floor and put me on the table. A Doc came by and asked me how I was doing? I said, well probably not too good, but I think I'll be OK. He said you'll be ok, but his eyes didn't seem too sure. I told him, something was bothering me, scraping my tooth; He looked and said, oh, just a second. He got some tools and cut a big piece of shrapnel out of under my lip that had been bothering me.

The Doc's were really busy with a hispanic guy on the next table. Somehow I knew they were cutting off his leg. He was tough and brave. I felt really bad for him, I started talking to him. I asked him if he had a wife, he said yes. I asked her name, he told me, I asked him if he had any kids, I think he said yes, two. I thought I was doing a good job keeping his mind off what was happening and then he said; haven't you got the damn thing off yet Doc? Toughest guy I ever talked to.

They came with a litter, slid me onto it. They carried me forward, I remember my shipmates looking at me, I said, looks like I am going to beat you guys back ashore, they looked at me, They didn't say anything, they just looked at me. I was taken up a bomb elevator in the bow. The air was fresh, Enterprise was moving fast. She had made it and headed back to Pearl.

They put me in a big chopper, probably a Huey. I don't know how many of us, but as I remember there were several of us in litters and 1 Corpsman. I think I was on the first chopper off. God, this is really hard to write. Gotta keep going! I had a plastic sleeve around my left arm, an inflated splint. My IV was swinging around, hitting the side of the chopper. The Corpsman was really busy, He was working really hard on the other guy, giving him mouth to mouth and pushing on his chest. I reached up with my right hand and held the IV bottle the rest of the way in.

The way in was to Tripler Army Hospital in Hawaii. I could see out the open door, we landed on a big lawn with the hospital above it. There was a bus with a big cross on the side. Some guys come running up to the chopper and they screamed at the Corpsman, which one first. The Corpsman said; it doesn't matter, any of them, except this one, I lost him on the way in. He was mad and half yelling and crying as he said it. I found out later, it was everyone's friend Armando who had died on the way in.

They took me off the chopper and took me to the bus which was rigged with racks to hold litters. As we started to move, the Chopper was up and headed back to the ship. They took me off the bus and put me on rolling litter carrier. They wheeled me toward some big glass doors and there were dozens of doctors and Nurses waiting for me. They looked at me, eyes big and mouths open, in shock. I thought; I must really look bad.

I was in Tripler for a few days, I received the last rights and the priest spent time with all of us. They asked my parents phone number and I told them. They called but no one answered. I didn't remember that my Mom and Dad had my new Camaro, and had gone south to visit my Uncle after they saw us off at Alameda a week earlier.

At Tripler, I was in a strange bed with big wheels and I was suspended on a flat bed section in it. They would sandwich me between bed slabs and then spin the bed and turn me over, kind of like a barbeque, Appropriate I guess. The first time they applied a medicine called Sulfa Mylon Acetate to the burns on my back, the pain was incredible, worse than being burned. I was screaming and using all the words in a Sailors vocabulary, cursing at them. I remember they ran away and I thought because of my screaming at them, but they came back with morphine. Twice a day, to a tub with water, where they used wet gauze to scrub my burns, incredible pain, and then the Sulfa Mylon Acetate. Burn patients called it white lightning. The pain is indescribable, but it saved most of our lives. At Tripler, in the next couple days, there were a number of operations, I remember some but I don't know how many. They would scrape dead skin off the burns, called debridement. They removed all my fingernails as the tissue underneath was burned.

Some new people came, Doctors, Nurses and Medics from Brooke General Army Hospital in San Antonio Texas, a burn Hospital, the best in the world. They were going through and checking all who were burnt. They took one look at me and said that I couldn't go with them, that I would not survive the flight. What were they talking about? I was going to be ok, they had to fix me up again, I knew I would be ok. After further checking on how I was doing, my vital signs and records, they said, Ok I just really looked bad, they would take me with them to Texas along with 7 other guys.

I had ridden in one of these before, in 1967, A Lockheed C141. I had gone from Travis air force base in one to Clark Air force base in the Philippines. I caught a chopper to Subic Bay and there saw the Enterprise pull into port. This time I was in a stretcher, hooked to the bulkhead. I had seen this before, on my flight to the Philippines, there were South Vietnamese in stretchers, going back to Vietnam after medical treatment in the U.S.

I talked to the Army Medic a lot on the way. I remember, being incredibly thirsty and wanting water. He wouldn't let me have any. I got really mad, He called the Doctor. The Doctor explained to me that if they gave me water by mouth, the fluid might make my neck swell up, close my airway causing me to die. Later the Medic, who became a friend, told me that all the other guys were out from the morphine, but that I was awake and talked to him much of the trip.

We landed at Travis AFB, in California. We were there to refuel, but the weather was really bad and the pilots decided we should spend the night there. When they were packing us off the plane, it was dark out. The wind was blowing hard with torrents of rain. There were bright lights and television cameras filming for national news. Then we were inside, everyone was rushing around, the Lt. Nurses were calling the Corporal medics Sir. Anything and everything the burn team asked for was done, fast.

The next morning, we were taken back to the plane and continue on to Texas, and again television cameras for National news.

My poor parents, they were at my Uncle's house in Palm Springs. They had heard about the fire on the news. My Uncle had no television, but got one so they could watch the news. He had no phone and my Mom and Dad spent hours at a pay phone trying to find out about me. When they saw the coverage, the devastation on the flight deck, Dad told Mom, that's where Tom told us he worked; I doubt that he had a chance of surviving. He is probably gone. They kept trying. After 3 days, they found out I was alive, badly injured and headed for Texas.

I lay there in Intensive Care beside Lt. Berry. Lt. Andermann a very special person and nurse came in and said, Tom, your parents are here. What, My Parents are here I thought, it can't be, I am in Texas, it so far, it would be so hard for them, I know I am going to be Ok. They must know I'll be ok. Am I the only person who knows I'll be Ok? Mom and Dad walked in, Mom came to me and gently hugged me, Dad reached out and touched me, tears poured from my eyes and theirs. (Just like now writing this). I asked Mom: how do I look, Dad looked pale, She said you look fine Son; you are going to be just fine. Only later did I find out that walking down the hall, they had seen me through an open door, Mom had looked at Dad and said: "thank god that isn't Tom" only to have them bring them to me. I guess when you own Mother doesn't recognize you, you must look pretty bad.

For a couple months, I improved. My parents stayed there in barracks set up for visiting family. Lt. Berry's Parents were also there. His parents and mine became good friends.

Gradually, I improved; Lt. Berry did also, but not much. He was very badly burned, and receiving skin grafts, but there wasn't anywhere to get the grafts. They kept me in intensive care to keep Lt. Berry company. We talked, for weeks we talked. I told him how if he had only rolled the canopy off his plane, he could probably have ejected to safety as the seat would not fire with the canopy on. There was a cable from the Canopy to keep it from firing if the canopy was on.

After about 3 months, I was able to leave with my parents on sick leave. A full arm cast on my left arm. A walking cast on my right leg. They gave me medicines and bandages to take care of some unhealed burns and wounds. Lt. Berry tried to smile for me when I said goodbye to him. I told him I would be back in a month. There was sadness in his eyes, I was leaving and I was the only one still there from our squadron.

A few days later when we got to my Brothers house in Alameda, It was on the news; Lt. Berry had died.

(To be continued)

And The Sea Shall Give Up It's Dead

This last chapter is composed entirely of our rescue helo efforts that day. When I received the investigation documents I was curious that there was nothing in them at all about that part of events. The only thing I had was what had been written in the Honolulu newspaper the day after our fire in which a few quotes from those involved appeared. I also had no first hand account from anyone who was involved. I knew that there were sections of the Investigation that were omitted or erased by a censor so as not to disclose the names of certain of our dead and wounded and the nature of their wounds.

It was not until years later, after the book was written, That Jim Zils, our rescue swimmer from that day, read TRIAL and sent me the following letter. He also included the entire testimonial section of the investigation which was removed regarding, "Angels 004", which pulled several people from the sea. I doubt if I would have included all of this back when I originally wrote the book but now, with the passage of years, I am including all of it. I know our Fallen Brothers would want our entire story to be told truthfully and in that interest I am including the entire testament of the "Angels 004" saga here as it was recorded.

I would not have undertaken this 3rd edition without the backing of Mike Neville and our '69 Enterprise Fire Group. Mike has done the lions share of forming our Group to almost 400 strong in a few short years. With this writing I think my job has now been completed regarding our day of fury. I have often wondered why I was spared when so many others were not on that day. I really believe a Divine Hand was at work and also compelled me to undertake this endeavor later. With such a terrific catastrophe involving the life and death struggle of the mightiest and most famous Warship in the world, why had no one else written the story? I have a tremendous pride, a humble pride, in being the one to do the job. What has been achieved is that our story has taken its rightful place in Naval History. We have lost many of our shipmates since that day and those of us left know we are nearing our last sunsets, just as our great ship is nearing its own end. As Jim Zils said, "God care for those it is really written for". Yes, keep them in patience because we are all coming. On that day when the sea shall give up its Dead, we will all be together. Again.

March 5, 1998

Mr. Michael J. Carlin
c/o Tuscarora Press
PO Box 98
West Grove, Pennsylvania 19390

Dear Mr. Carlin,

I recently ordered and received your book, Trial. Reading your extensively researched and documented account of the events and activities related to January 14, 1969 onboard Enterprise brought back some very vivid memories and some still overwhelming emotions, even after 29 years.

I was onboard Enterprise on that day and on the flight deck at the time of the initial explosions. I was part of Helicopter Combat Support Squadron One; detachment 65 assigned search and rescue duties in support of Carrier Nine Wing operations. I was the rescue swimmer on Angel 004, the ready helo awaiting launch when the initial explosions occurred aft of our position on the angle deck. My first reaction was to exit the starboard side cargo door of the helo thinking that our port engine had exploded due to the intense heat and blast I felt on my back, which was facing the aft direction of the ship through the open port cargo door. After jumping out to the flight deck, my attention was immediately drawn to the horrific spectacle that was just beginning to take place on the after section of the ship. There was a tremendous fire with multiple ordinance and fuel explosions taking place in its midst. I saw several flight deck and flight crew personnel running toward the island away from the fire and explosions, several completely engulfed in flames. I saw one body being hurled out of the flames, high into the air, as a result of an explosion. There was ordinance and shrapnel flying through the air in all directions. Without being told, the helo crew instinctively knew we had to launch the helo because there surely was going to be victims overboard needing assistance. We did immediately and successfully launch under difficult and dangerous conditions (what wasn't that day?) and began a search for survivors in the water.

I have attached a copy of the official rescue report for Angel 004 for that day which explains what we were able to do to help four survivors, one who was badly injured. In addition, we located the body of the sailor you identify as Girty, which was subsequently picked up by the Stoddart. We decided to not recover the body to conserve space and weight capacity for other survivors who we still anticipated finding.

AOAN Mason of VF92 (page 202) is referred to in the Angel 004 rescue report. After attaching LTJG Schneider of VF92 to the hoist cable and providing AN Helco of VF92 with my UDT floatation vest to keep him afloat, I turned and started swimming towards where Mason was last seen and tried to locate him. When I originally saw him from the helo, before jumping into the water to help Schneider and Helco, he appeared to either be struggling to stay afloat or was in a state of panic. Helco mentioned to me in the water that he thought Mason's legs were badly injured. When I turned towards him in the water I caught a brief glimpse of him and he was at that point quiet, possibly unconscious or already dead. I lost sight of him due to the high sea state, and because of how low he was in the water, and so I dove under several times fearing that he had sunk below the surface and was drowning. I didn't see him in the 60'+ visibility water but did see a large shark swimming away from where I thought he should be. I searched the surface again and couldn't locate him. At that point Schneider had been lifted into the helo and the hoist cable was being lowered again for Helco. I swam back to Helco and came up with him on the hoist. We searched the immediate area for Mason without success. I believe I was the last person to see him just before he disappeared. Not being able to get to him quickly enough and possibly help him bothered me deeply for years.

It was a day of uncommon valor, exceptional professionalism, strong leadership and highly effective teamwork. Without all of those factors to the extent they were present, the Enterprise would surely have been lost along with a much higher loss of life.

If anyone wants to study a lesson in what individuals with unselfish courage and total commitment can accomplish under extremely difficult and trying conditions, your book should be read. It is also a tribute to an unbelievable ship, which was able to withstand more damage than most of us probably thought possible. She certainly lived up to her legacy, which you so interestingly establish in your book.

Congratulations on an excellent book. I learned many details of that day that I didn't know. Best of luck to you in the future. God care for those that it is really written for.

Sincerely,

James A. Zils

SPECIAL HANDLING REQUIRED IN ACCORDANCE WITH OPNAVINST 3750.6F

STATEMENT OF H.A. ECKARDT, AA, USN, FIRST CREWMAN OF HC-1 DET 65,
HELICOPTER 004

THE HELO WAS MANNED AND TURNING ON THE BOW OF THE USS ENTERPRISE WHEN
WE HEARD THE FIRST EXPLOSION. AT FIRST I THOUGHT THE EXPLOSION WAS
OUR NUMBER ONE ENGINE, BUT AFTER LEAVING THE AIRCRAFT I SAW A JET AFIRE
IN THE AREA OF THE NUMBER FOUR ELEVATOR. IMMEDIATELY I GOT BACK IN THE
HELO AND WE WERE TOLD OVER THE I.C.S. THAT THERE WAS A PILOT IN THE WATER,
PLUS PROBABLY OTHERS. MY SWIMMER STRIPPED AND WAS READY TO ENTER THE WATER
BY THE TIME WE TOOK OFF. AS WE HEADED TOWARD THE RESCUE VICINITY MANY
MORE EXPLOSIONS OCCURRED AND FOR A FEW MINUTES THE HELO WAS IN DANGER OF
BEING HIT BY FLYING DEBRIS. AFTER SPOTTING TWO MEN IN THE WATER WE MADE
OUR APPROACH AND I THEN PUT THE SWIMMER IN THE WATER PLUS A SMOKE BOMB.
I WAS GOING TO PICK UP THE PILOT WITH THE SWIMMER FIRST AND THEN PICK
UP THE PLANE CAPTAIN. WHEN THE HOOK REACHED THE SWIMMER THE PILOT STARTED
POINTING TO THE AFT OF THE HELO. I SAW ANOTHER MAN STRUGGLING AND IT
APPEARED HE WAS DROWNING. HE WAS ABOUT 150 FEET DIRECTLY BEHIND US.
THE SWIMMER MOTIONED TO PICK UP THE PILOT. HE GAVE HIS UDT VEST TO THE
PLANE CAPTAIN AND HEADED TOWARD THE STRUGGLING MAN WHILE I BROUGHT THE
PILOT UP. NEXT, I SENT THE RESCUE SLING DOWN TO THE RETURNED SWIMMER
AND PLANE CAPTAIN, AND BROUGHT THEM UP THE WIRE. BOTH THE PILOT AND PLANE
CAPTAIN WERE IN GOOD PHYSICAL CONDITION. THE STRUGGLING MAN COULD NOT
BE FOUND BY THE SWIMMER WHILE THE PILOT WAS BEING BROUGHT UP THE WIRE.
THE PILOT TOLD US LATER THE MAN WAS LEGLESS.

THE THIRD SURVIVOR WAS SPOTTED ON AN UNINFLATED RAFT. WE MADE OUR
APPROACH AND AGAIN THE SWIMMER ENTERED THE WATER. THE SECOND CREWMAN'S
UDT VEST WAS INFLATED, SO HE ENTERED THE WATER WITH A MAE WEST. ON
THIS PICKUP WE HAD SOME TROUBLE KEEPING A STEADY HOVER DUE TO HIGH WINDS
AND HEAVY SWELLS. WHILE THE SWIMMER WAS PUTTING THE HORSE COLLAR ON THE
MAN WE STARTED TO DRIFT. BEFORE I COULD DIRECT THE PILOT BACK TO THE RAFT
AND LET OUT MORE CABLE I REALIZED WE WERE DRAGGING THE MAN BY HIS ARM
WHICH HE HAD AROUND THE SLING. WHILE CORRECTING OUR DRIFT THE SWIMMER
SWAM TO THE MAN AND WAS ABLE TO HOOK HIS OWN "D" RING TO THE RESCUE HOOK.
I AM GLAD THAT I HAD A VERY STRONG SWIMMER BECAUSE THE MAN WAS IN SHOCK
AND STRUGGLED WITH THE SWIMMER FIERCELY. AFTER GETTING THE MAN INTO THE
CABIN WE PLACED THE INJURED MAN ON THE PASSENGERS SEAT. WE COVERED HIM
WITH OUR BLANKET AND CHECKED FOR INJURIES. THE MAN SEEMED TO BE IN
COMPLETE SHOCK AND HAD FIRST DEGREE BURNS ON HIS FACE, HANDS, AND FEET.
HIS RIGHT ARM WAS FRACTURED, PLUS THE SKIN ON IT WAS RIPPED OFF FROM THE
ELBOW DOWN TO HIS FINGERS. I REPORTED TO THE PILOT THE CONDITION OF THE
THREE MEN AS WE HEADED BACK TO THE SHIP. WHEN WE REACHED THE SHIP WE
PLACED THE INJURED MAN IN A STRETCHER BEFORE HE WAS TAKEN OUT OF THE HELO.
AFTER THE THREE SURVIVORS WERE OUT OF THE AIRCRAFT WE IMMEDIATELY TOOK
OFF AGAIN. OUR NEXT SURVIVOR WAS SPOTTED ON A RAFT, AND SEEMED TO BE IN
GOOD CONDITION. IN THIS PICK UP WE HAD NO PROBLEMS AND EVERYTHING WENT
SMOOTHLY. THE MAN HAD NO INJURIES. MY SECOND CREWMAN WAS PRETTY TIRED
AND CHILLED SO I SWITCHED POSITIONS WITH HIM.

SPECIAL HANDLING REQUIRED IN ACCORDANCE WITH OPNAVINST 3750.6F

SEARCHING THE AREA MORE WE SPOTTED A BODY, SO WE PLACED A SMOKE BY HIM AND SIGNALED A NEARBY DESTROYER TO PICK UP THE BODY. BY THIS TIME WE WERE RUNNING LOW ON FUEL SO WE HOT REFUELED FROM THE OTHER DESTROYER. WE CONTINUED OUR SEARCH FOR SOME TIME AND THEN RETURNED TO THE ENTERPRISE AFTER FINDING NO FURTHER SURVIVORS. WE WERE THEN RELIEVED BY ANOTHER CREW.

                              HERBERT A. ECKARDT
                              B51 86 33, AN

SPECIAL HANDLING REQUIRED IN ACCORDANCE WITH OPNAVINST 3750.6F

STATEMENT OF R.G. HELCO, AN, USN, PLANE CAPTAIN VF-92

AFTER I JUMPED OFF THE SHIP ALONG WITH MASON (AN ORDNANCEMAN) AND MR. SCHNEIDER (VF-92 R.I.O.) I STARTED TAKING OFF MY PLANE CAPTAIN HELMET. I ALSO TOOK OFF ONE OF MY PLANE CAPTAIN JERSEYS. I TRIED TO TAKE MY SHOES OFF BUT COULDN'T GET THEM UNTIED. THEN I NOTICED MR. SCHNEIDER SWIMMING WITH HIS LIFE VEST NOT TO FAR AWAY. I YELLED AND STARTED SWIMMING TO HIM. I REACHED HIM AND HUNG ON TO HIM TILL THE HELO CAME AND RESCUED US. DURING THAT TIME OF WAITING, WHICH WAS NOT TO LONG, I SAW MASON FLOATING IN THE WATER. AT FIRST GLANCE WITH HIS EYES OPEN AND SECOND GLANCE WITH HIS EYES CLOSED. THE HELO CAME PICKED MR. SCHNEIDER UP FIRST AND THEN PICKED UP ME AND THE FROGMAN UP NEXT. I NEVER SAW MASON AGAIN.

                                           ROSS G. HELCO

SPECIAL HANDLING IN ACCORDANCE WITH OPNAVINST 3750.6F

STATEMENT OF LTJG RONALD D. SCHNEIDER, RESCUEE

18 January 1969

I, Ronald D. Schneider, do hereby make the following statement concerning the helicopter rescue on 14 January 1969;

Once Helco and I got together in the water and were being supported by my MK-3C Life Preserver, I immediately saw the helicopter making its approach to pick us up. I pointed toward a wounded man in the water but they continued their approach to us and by that time I had lost sight of him and was somewhat disoriented in my direction. I waved both arms at the helicopter to make sure he saw us which they obviously did being quite close to us.

Once they were overhead, one man jumped in the water and swam to us. In a very calm manner, he quickly got Helco off of me and put a life preserver on him while at the same time hooking me up to the hoist. I was hoisted up to the helicopter and pulled in. I was soon followed by Helco and the swimmer. After picking up another man we were brought back to the ship.

I cannot overemphasize the quick and efficient work of the entire helicopter crew, but especially the swimmer. His actions in the water showed the results of good training and the ability to cope with emergency situations in a cool efficient and knowledge manner. It is my recommendation that this man be recognized for a job well done.

Ronald D. Schneider
LTJG   USNR

SPECIAL HANDLING REQUIRED IN ACCORDANCE WITH OPNAVINST 3750.6 SERIES

Statement of LTJG R. J. HELTEN, Co-pilot of Angel 004

    The first helo launch on the morning of January 14th was at 0640 when approximately fourteen aircraft were launched from the ship. The hop lasted a half hour and the helo was back on deck at 0710. The following launch was to be at 0830 and the pilots had preflighted and were strapped in shortly after 0800. At ten minutes past the hour the helo was instructed to start. At 0819 the helo had engaged and only a couple of items remained on the check list. The helo was spotted forward on the angle on the number two spot. The ship's heading was passing throught the quadrant 090° - 000° in a port turn. Surface winds were approximately 280°.

    The first explosion occurred at 0819. I don't recall feeling any concussion from this one. I looked aft, leaning out the port door. The entire fantail was engulfed in flames and black smoke. I told the pilot it was definitely a fire. He called the tower and informed them we were ready to lift. The tower cleared us to lift, then added that we had less than optimum winds. The pilot replied that under the circumstances we would overlook that.

    We cleared ourselves of chokes and tiedowns, lifted off and started a port turn wide of the ship as the second explosion went off sending shrapnel and flames a couple hundred feet or more into the air. We circled wide to port, and intersected the ships wake about a quarter mile aft. There were numerous ship's life rafts and debris in the water. The wake was splattered with green dye marker, and the clouds of black smoke pouring off the fantail created a dark shadow over the

SPECIAL HANDLING REQUIRED IN ACCORDANCE WITH OPNAVINST 3750.6 SERIES

water for one half mile behind the ship, but the visibility was good.

We made a left turn in toward the ship and continued the turn around When our starboard side was coming around to face the ship astern the third explosion ripped loose. We felt the concussion, saw flying shrapnel and the pilot increased our bank to the left.

Coming out of our turn over the wake, we let down to about 60 feet and I spotted a red shirted man in the water about 500 yards ahead. Then I saw two more people in the water about fifty yards south of the first man. We passed between them, turned left, and made an approach to the two men who were together, dropping a smoke when we were slightly to the left of them. We dropped down and the swimmer entered the water. The swells were extremely high and the winds very gusty. I switched off the pilots UHF and tried to watch the guages and keep the man in the red shirt in sight at the same time. While picking up the first two men I lost sight of the man in the red shirt. The hook was lowered and the crewman told us the RIO was coming up first because the other man would need the sling. I could see the smoke in the water off to our left. I gave the pilot an extimate of winds at 300°. The RIO in the water came aboard easily, then the sling was lowered for the other man and the swimmer. After picking them up we broke hover slowly, looking for the third survivor, but could not locate him. We circled left and coming around to a northerly heading again we spotted another survivor about 200 yards north of where we had picked up the first two. This man looked to be badly burned as his face was completely blackened. Making our approach, the pilot dropped down to 10 feet, close to the

SPECIAL HANDLING REQUIRED IN ACCORDANCE WITH OPNAVINST 3750.6 SERIES

survivor. The swimmer jumped from the helo. During the previous pickup the ship's tower had contacted us and we had informed them of our activities. They called again and I told them we were picking up a third man. We had difficulty holding a stable hover but I didn't realize at the time the difficulty the swimmer was having trying to help this man into the sling.

We had lifted from the flight deck at 0820. At 0825 the first two survivors were aboard. The third man was aboard the helo at 0830, and noting that he was in critical condition it seemed advisable to return to the ship immediately. I was sure I had spotted another survivor a couple hundred yards straight ahead of us while we were picking up the third man. We searched the area ahead enroute to the ship but could not see the man again. The ship cleared us to land, and at 0835 we were on the deck. Two of the rescuees walked away from the helo, the third was put in a stretcher in the helo before being taken out.

Immediately after the survivors were delivered from the helo, we were cleared to lift again. At 0840, in the same area where I earlier thought I had spotted a survivor, we saw a man sitting in a large red raft. We made our approach, dropped the swimmer, and the sling was dropped and both men were hoisted aboard.

We conducted a long search following the fourth pickup. The survivor seemed in good condition and he helped look for other survivors. With about 1100 pounds of fuel remaining we were told that one of the destroyers was prepared to refuel us. Enroute to the destroyer one of the crewmen spotted a body floating face down in the water and completely limp. We notified the other destroyer close by and marked the spot with a smoke.

SPECIAL HANDLING REQUIRED IN ACCORDANCE WITH OPNAVINST 3750.6 SERIES

We then proceeded to the destroyer and took on fuel. We had requested from the destroyer a couple of blankets for the rescuee and our swimmer. They prepared a bundle of blankets and we hoisted them aboard before departing.

Our search continued for more than an hour longer, during which time we were turned over to the control of a P-3 in the area. The ship called us back at 1030 and we were relieved by another crew.

Beginning shortly after the first explosion the ships tacan was inoperative, however we had no need for it. The searching area was well defined by the ship's wake, undeployed as well as deployed rafts, debris, and particularly green dye marker.

Both crewmen in these rescues performed exceptionally well. The high swells and gusty winds made there jobs particulary difficult, and the swimmer had expecially exhausting demands put upon him in handling the third man who was badly injured.

R. J. HELTEN

SPECIAL HANDLING REQUIRED IN ACCORDANCE WITH OPNAVINST 3750.6F

STATEMENT OF J.A. ZILS, AMH2, USN, SECOND CREWMAN OF HC-1 DET 65 HELICOPTER 004

AT THE TIME OF THE ACCIDENT ABOARD SHIP, I WAS SECOND CREWMAN-SWIMMER IN THE READY HELO, AWAITING LAUNCH TO ASSUME THE PLANE GUARD POSITION FOR THE 0830 LAUNCH. THE HELO WAS SHAKEN BY AN EXPLOSION WHICH AT THE TIME SEEMED IN THE IMMEDIATE VICINITY. I RELEASED MY SEAT BELT, EVACUATED THE HELO AND OBSERVED A LARGE FIRE BREAKING OUT IN THE AREA OF NUMBER FOUR ELEVATOR. MINOR SECONDARY EXPLOSIONS WERE OCCURRING AT THIS TIME. KNOWING THAT THE HELO WOULD BE IMMEDIATELY NEEDED, I GOT BACK IN, STRIPPED DOWN TO MY SWIM TRUNKS AND T-SHIRT AND DONNED MY FINS AND MASK IN PREPARATION FOR PICKING UP ANYONE WHO MIGHT HAVE JUMPED, OR WAS BLOWN OVER THE SIDE. WE LIFTED, TURNED TO STERN TO SEARCH THE WAKE OF THE SHIP, WHEN A MAJOR EXPLOSION OCCURRED. OUR FIRST SPOTTING WAS SOON AFTERWARD. A PILOT FLOATING IN HIS MK-3C AND A PLANE CAPTAIN WITHOUT FLOTATION, HOLDING ONTO THE PILOT'S BACK TO STAY AFLOAT. I LEAPED INTO THE WATER, INSPECTED BOTH SURVIVORS FOR INJURIES AND ENTANGLEMENT WITH DEBRIS OR GEAR. THEY INFORMED ME OF A THIRD SURVIVOR SOME FIFTY YARDS OFF WHO WAS HAVING TROUBLE STAYING AFLOAT. I SIGNALED FOR THE SLING TO BE SENT DOWN SO THAT I COULD HOOK BOTH SURVIVORS UP AT ONCE AND SWIM TO THE AID OF THE THIRD, BUT THE FIRST CREWMAN HAD ALREADY LOWERED THE HOOK ALONE, SO I ATTACHED THE PILOT BY HIS "D" RING AND GAVE MY UDT VEST TO THE PLANE CAPTAIN TO KEEP HIM AFLOAT. I THEN TURNED TO SWIM TO THE THIRD SURVIVOR, BUT COULD NOT LOCATE HIM AGAIN, SO I STAYED WITH THE PLANE CAPTAIN, HELPED HIM INTO THE SLING, ATTACHED MY "D" RING AND WAS HOISTED ABOARD THE HELO. WE THEN SEARCHED THE AREA AGAIN FOR THE THIRD SURVIVOR, WITH NO LUCK. AFTER APPROXIMATELY FIVE MINUTES OF FURTHER SEARCH A FOURTH SURVIVOR WAS SPOTTED FLOATING ON AN UNINFLATED RAFT. I AGAIN LEAPED INTO THE WATER, THIS TIME WEARING A MAE WEST AFTER HAVING TO GIVE UP MY UDT VEST TO THE SECOND SURVIVOR. THIS SURVIVOR WAS IN A COMPLETE STATE OF SHOCK, SEVERLY BURNED ON THE FACE, HANDS, AND FEET, AND WITH A FRACTURED RIGHT ARM. THE SLING WAS LOWERED AND I ATTEMPTED TO PLACE IT AROUND HIS BODY, BUT AT THE SAME TIME THE CABLE WENT TAUT, DUE TO HEAVY SWELLS AND GUSTING WINDS, AND I LET GO OF IT WANTING TO STAY WITH THE SURVIVOR AND NOT RISK PULLING HIM OFF THE RAFT UNTIL I HAD HIM FIRMLY ATTACHED. IN DESPARATION HE CRABBED HOLD OF THE SLING WITH HIS LEFT ARM AS I LET GO OF IT, AND WAS PULLED FROM THE RAFT. AT THE SAME TIME THE MAE WEST (WHICH I CONSIDER INADEQUATE FOR THIS KIND OF WORK) WASHED UP OVER MY FACE SO I COULDN'T SEE WHAT HAD HAPPENED. WHEN I NEXT REALIZED THE SURVIVOR WAS NO LONGER ON THE RAFT, OR NEXT TO IT, I DOVE UNDER TWICE TRYING TO LOCATE HIM IN THE EVENT HE WAS SINKING. NOT SEEING HIM I TURNED TOWARDS THE HELO AND AT THAT TIME SAW HIM BEING DRAGGED BY THE SLING. I SWAM TO HIM, PLACED HIM CORRECTLY IN THE SLING, HOOKED UP THE "D" RING AND HELD HIM AFLOAT UNTIL WE COULD BE LIFTED OUT OF THE WATER. HE WAS LAIN ON THE CABIN SEAT AND COVERED WITH A BLANKET FOR THE TRIP BACK TO THE CARRIER TO DROP OFF THE THREE SURVIVORS. WE IMMEDIATELY TOOK OFF AGAIN TO RESUME A SEARCH. OUR NEXT SPOTTING WAS A SURVIVOR IN A RAFT. I LEAPED AGAIN INTO THE WATER, SWAM TO THE RAFT AND BOARDED IT TO CHECK THE SURVIVOR WHO HAD NO APPARENT INJURIES.

SPECIAL HANDLING REQUIRED IN ACCORDANCE WITH OPNAVINST 3750.6F

IN A BIT OF EXCELLENT FLYING BY THE PILOT AND FIRST CREWMAN THE SLING WAS QUICKLY PLACED INTO THE RAFT WHERE WE HOOKED UP WITH NO TROUBLE AND WERE HOISTED ABOARD TOGETHER. AT THIS TIME, DUE TO BECOMING QUITE CHILLED, I SWITCHED POSITIONS WITH THE FIRST CREWMAN. WE CONTINUED OUR SEARCH FINDING A DEAD BODY WHICH I MARKED WITH A SMOKE MARKER FOR THE DESTROYER TO PICK UP. WE THEN WENT TO ANOTHER DESTROYER FOR INFLIGHT REFUELING AND TO PICK UP A LOAD OF BLANKETS TO CARRY BACK TO THE CARRIER. AFTER CONTINUING OUR SEARCH FOR SOME TIME MORE, WITH NO ADDITIONAL SPOTTINGS, WE RETURNED TO THE CARRIER WHERE ANOTHER CREW RELIEVED US AND THE SURVIVOR WAS OFF-LOADED.

                                          JAMES A. ZILS
                                        998 22 05, AMH2